T0293625

Wealth of Wisdom

Wealth of Wisdom

TOP PRACTICES FOR WEALTHY FAMILIES AND THEIR ADVISORS

Tom McCullough
Keith Whitaker

WILEY

Copyright © 2022 by Tom McCullough and Keith Whitaker. All rights reserved.

Published by John Wiley & Sons, Inc., Hoboken, New Jersey.
Published simultaneously in Canada.

No part of this publication may be reproduced, stored in a retrieval system, or transmitted in any form or by any means, electronic, mechanical, photocopying, recording, scanning, or otherwise, except as permitted under Section 107 or 108 of the 1976 United States Copyright Act, without either the prior written permission of the Publisher, or authorization through payment of the appropriate per-copy fee to the Copyright Clearance Center, Inc., 222 Rosewood Drive, Danvers, MA 01923, (978) 750-8400, fax (978) 750-4470, or on the web at www.copyright.com. Requests to the Publisher for permission should be addressed to the Permissions Department, John Wiley & Sons, Inc., 111 River Street, Hoboken, NJ 07030, (201) 748-6011, fax (201) 748-6008, or online at http://www.wiley.com/go/permission.

Limit of Liability/Disclaimer of Warranty: While the publisher and author have used their best efforts in preparing this book, they make no representations or warranties with respect to the accuracy or completeness of the contents of this book and specifically disclaim any implied warranties of merchantability or fitness for a particular purpose. No warranty may be created or extended by sales representatives or written sales materials. The advice and strategies contained herein may not be suitable for your situation. You should consult with a professional where appropriate. Further, readers should be aware that websites listed in this work may have changed or disappeared between when this work was written and when it is read. Neither the publisher nor authors shall be liable for any loss of profit or any other commercial damages, including but not limited to special, incidental, consequential, or other damages.

For general information on our other products and services or for technical support, please contact our Customer Care Department within the United States at (800) 762-2974, outside the United States at (317) 572-3993 or fax (317) 572-4002.

Wiley also publishes its books in a variety of electronic formats. Some content that appears in print may not be available in electronic formats. For more information about Wiley products, visit our web site at www.wiley.com.

Library of Congress Cataloging-in-Publication Data

Names: McCullough, Tom (Financial planner), editor. | Whitaker, Keith, editor.
Title: Wealth of Wisdom: top practices for wealthy families and their advisors / [edited by] Tom McCullough, Keith Whitaker.
Description: Hoboken, New Jersey : John Wiley & Sons, Inc., [2022] | Includes bibliographical references and index.
Identifiers: LCCN 2022013207 (print) | LCCN 2022013208 (ebook) | ISBN 9781119827702 (cloth) | ISBN 9781119827726 (adobe pdf) | ISBN 9781119827719 (epub)
Subjects: LCSH: Estate planning. | Finance, Personal. | Families—Economic aspects. | Family trusts. | Wealth.
Classification: LCC HG179 .T589 2022 (print) | LCC HG179 (ebook) | DDC 332.024/01—dc23/eng/20220317
LC record available at https://lccn.loc.gov/2022013207
LC ebook record available at https://lccn.loc.gov/2022013208

Cover Design: Wiley
Cover Images: © varuna/Shutterstock

SKY10062727_121423

This book is dedicated to our granddaughter Sunny, who brings us all so much joy, reminds us of how we are connected to each other as family, and helps us imagine the future.

— Tom McCullough

To Jay Hughes, founder of the field of family wealth, consummate professional and personne de confiance, *mentor and dear friend.*

— Keith Whitaker

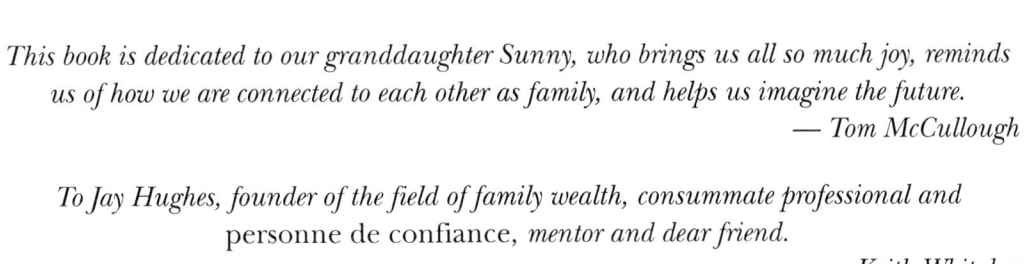

Contents

Foreword

James E. Hughes, Jr.

"On Entering the Room"

When Tom and Keith invited me to contribute to this new book, they posed to me (and to the other wonderful contributors) a challenging question: What is the one practice that you have found most powerful in helping families?

Through reflecting on this question, I could not decide on just one practice, and so I offered two, the Family Bank and Grandchild-Grandparent Philanthropy. The editors generously included both chapters in the pages that follow.

But in approaching this completed volume, and thinking about you, the reader, one more practice came to my mind, which I want to share with you here, as you embark on this learning journey.

Many years ago, I found myself outside a conference-room in a large resort. I was about to enter a room where 25 or 30 family members of a family I'd gotten to know fairly well had gathered.

They had asked me to come and talk with them. As I approached the room, I was full of the "curriculum" that the family leaders and I had spent weeks assembling. We had really worked hard to prepare for this meeting.

But suddenly I found myself standing outside the door and experiencing a feeling I had had sometimes in the theater. I thought, "I have to stop for a minute here." And so, I found a quiet place, and I thought, "Well, if I'm five minutes late, I'm sure it will be alright."

I sat down, and in that moment, I received a gift. The gift was that I began to think, somewhat randomly at first and then much more conscientiously, about each person whom I was about to touch. As I thought about each person, the question came to me, "How can I help?"

I began to find myself smiling about each of those people. I began to think, "Gosh, she's 35. I imagine her questions might be so-and-so. And then, oh my, he's about 70. He's at different stage of life than she is. I wonder what his questions are?" As I went through those 25 or so people rather quickly, each of them came into my consciousness. I could see each one of them, at the stage of life he or she was in. I could imagine what kinds of questions each of them might have. And I began to feel calm.

Then I began to think of them as a community. What stage of life was their community at? What were the likely questions of that community, at that stage of life?

I began to smile. I thought, “I know why I’m doing this. I knew that the curriculum would be okay. And the materials will be okay. But really my task is to gently help the good ideas in the curriculums move into connection with, into awareness of, the lives of each of those people, at each of their stages of life, and in response to the questions of that person, in that stage of life.

I have now done this same exercise hundreds of times. I do not enter a room without thinking about each of the people inside. I think about the kinds of questions each person will have, the questions proper to his or her stage of life.

By the way, one of the things that happens when you enter the room this way is that you leave your expertise at the door. It just vanishes. You go into that room with a beginner’s mind, no matter how well you prepare, no matter how much material there is. You greet your colleagues with a hug, and you greet the family with a hug. Because you’ve met them already.

Now one more thing: Turn this exercise upon yourself. You are the person in the room of your life. These many contributors, these many chapters, wait outside the door, ready to greet you. Who are you? What stage of life are you in? What are the questions you face? How about the people dearest to you—where are they in their lives and what are their questions? Take a few minutes to sit and think through these questions. Then give yourself a hug and open the door.

Acknowledgments

From Tom and Keith

Welcome to *Wealth of Wisdom: Top Practices for Wealthy Families and Their Advisors.* We are excited to introduce it to you.

We are particularly enthused because of the book's practical nature and the fact that the exercises and tools you will find inside have been used successfully in the real world. No family or advisor has all the answers, and we can all learn from each other, so this work pulls together rich, hands-on content from diverse sources and shares it with all families.

They say you should create the book you want to read. So that's what we did!

In putting together a book like this, there are many people to recognize and thank for their contributions—including inspiration, encouragement, writing, and editing. Just like our first book, *Wealth of Wisdom: The Top 50 Questions Wealthy Families Ask*, this volume draws on multiple voices and countless practical experiences to answer the questions and address the issues that so many families of wealth face. We are grateful for the many hands that have brought this volume to life. For us it has been a labor of love and a community project and has built a literal "wealth of wisdom" for families around the world.

We would like to particularly thank our contributing authors. They are the best in the world in their fields and have a wealth of experience, which they have enthusiastically shared with us in this book. They are family members, family advisors, educators, business leaders, authors, speakers, thinkers, practitioners, and mentors, and a literal "Who's Who" of the global experts in issues that are important to families of wealth.

We gratefully acknowledge and express our appreciation to Stacy Allred, Patricia Annino, Josh Baron, Doug Baumoel, Linda Bourn, Jean Brunel, Greg Burrows, Joe Calabrese, the late Charles Collier, Joan DiFuria, Andrew Doust, Zahra Ebrahim, Etienne Eichenberger, Jamie Forbes, Dean Fowler, Richard Franklin, Jim Garland, Joline Godfrey, Stephen Goldbart, Sharna Goldseker, Katherine Grady, Jim Grubman, Stephanie Hardwick, Barbara Hauser, Lee Hausner, Scott Hayman, Kofi Hope, Jay Hughes, Bo Huhn, Suzanne Huhn, Susan Hyatt, Dennis Jaffe, Kim Kamin, Josh Kanter, Kristin Keffeler, Voyt Krzychylkiewicz, Małgorzata Smulowitz, Rob Lachenauer, Kathy Lintz, Eugene Lipitz, Susan Massenzio, Greg McCann, Kathryn McCarthy, Ian McDermott, Scotty McLennan, Keith Michaelson, Arden O'Connor, Don Opatrny, Danielle Oristian York, Michelle Osry, Bart Parrott, Natasha Pearl, Scott Peppet, Ellen Perry, Leslie Pine, Mark Pletts, Courtney Pullen,

Mimi Ramsey, Ned Rollhaus, Kirby Rosplock, Guillermo Salazar, Jill Shipley, Ruth Steverlynck, Christian Stewart, Claudia Tordini, Jamie Traeger-Muney, Blair Trippe, Wendy Ulaszek, Peter Vogel, John A. Warnick, Matthew Wesley, and Susan Winer.

From Tom

I would like to thank the partners and staff at Northwood Family Office who serve and support our client families and help them with all the strategic and practical activities required to manage wealth and develop successful thriving families. I would also like to thank the families who have entrusted their wealth and their lives to Northwood's care.

I would also like to express my appreciation to a very experienced author and friend, Mark Daniell, who got me started on this journey of writing books when he invited me to co-author *Family Wealth Management: 7 Imperatives for Successful Investing in the New World Order.* I will always be grateful.

And I would like to thank Keith Whitaker, my co-author in *Wealth of Wisdom: The Top 50 Questions Wealthy Families Ask,* as well as this book—*Wealth of Wisdom 2.0.* Keith is an experienced family advisor, a wise thinker, and a superb writer. He has been a pleasure to work with on both projects, and we too have become friends.

Finally, I would like to thank my family—Karen, Kate, Ben, Miranda, and Sunny—for their support, encouragement, and belief in me and the importance of projects like this.

From Keith

Wealth of Wisdom was my co-editor Tom's vision, and I am deeply grateful to him for inviting me upon the journey with him.

Many thanks go to my associates at Wise Counsel Research and to our client families, from whom I have learned so much, as well as to my partner, Susan, who has always been ready to recall me from the clouds to life's practicalities.

Introduction

Welcome to *Wealth of Wisdom: Top Practices for Wealthy Families and Their Advisors*, or, as we call it, *Wealth of Wisdom 2.0.*

Why "2.0"? Because it follows our first book, *Wealth of Wisdom: The Top 50 Questions That Wealthy Families Ask.* In that volume, we collected essays from leading practitioners in the field of family wealth, each of whom wrote about a question that client families face in managing significant financial wealth or a family business together. Those essays aimed to deepen readers' thinking and their understanding of the complexity of the task of mixing money and family.

This volume now turns that thinking into practice. As in *Wealth of Wisdom 1.0,* we have gathered insights from leading practitioners from around the world—more than 60 of them. But this time, we asked our authors to share with you, our readers, the tools, practices, or exercises that they had found most useful to families in their many years of advising.

The result is a book that complements *Wealth of Wisdom 1.0.* A thoughtful plan begins with recognizing the problems or questions to be addressed. But it then moves from that recognition into well-grounded action.

While readers would benefit from exploring *Wealth of Wisdom 1.0* first, it's not required in order to use the exercises and practices contained here in this book. In the rest of this Introduction, we will share with you how we created this book and how you can get the most out of it.

To help you orient yourself to the many tools and exercises in this book, after the Introduction we have added a brief section, "Assessing Your Family's True Needs," which contains an exercise to guide you in your reading. This exercise is based upon Wise Counsel Research's Family Balance Sheet™, an assessment that has been used by more than 200 global families to identify areas to grow their "qualitative," that is, nonfinancial capital over generations.

Who Are Our Contributors?

Family wealth is as old as families. But the field of professional advice to families with significant financial assets is relatively young. It has grown out of the related fields of law, investments, and psychology. The combination of these different practices reflects the complex and many-sided nature of the work of managing financial wealth over generations of a family.

Even though the field itself is young, there are professionals who have been practicing in it or its predecessor fields for many years. Those are the people to whom we turned to provide contributions to this book. Each of our authors has decades of experience working with wealthy families. They are leading consultants, lawyers, psychologists, investment advisors, teachers, and speakers. We selected contributors who are prominent in the field not only through practice but also through publishing articles, essays, or books of their own. Some are themselves members of families with significant financial wealth.

As mentioned previously, we asked each contributor to write about the one practice, tool, or exercise that he or she found most useful to families. We worked with our authors to make these practices as accessible as possible to readers who may choose to apply them on their own. We also shared our potential list of practices with colleagues to identify gaps in our lineup. The result is, we believe, the first truly comprehensive set of tools offered to general readers and the field.

What Are the Practices?

To organize this book, we have divided the 62 different exercises into nine separate sections. These section divisions are not hard and fast. Since family wealth is an inherently interdisciplinary topic, an exercise that may primarily be about, say, "Planning" may also have great relevance to "What Matters Most" and "Family Dynamics."

Here is a brief overview of these sections:

1. Thinking through What Matters Most: Chapters in this section help to clarify family members' values and their beliefs about what matters most and fosters well-being. These chapters also draw attention to the different needs of family members at different stages of life, such as managing cognitive decline in family leaders.
2. Becoming a Learning Family: A key strength of families who succeed over time is to become a shared learning organization. Chapters in this section offer ways for families to organize their shared learning (such as creating engaging curriculums) and be sure to benefit, as a whole, from individuals' self-directed learning.
3. Planning Thoughtfully: Planning takes the insights from shared learning and values and turns them into thoughtful action. The chapters in this section offer specific avenues of action from creating a family bank to identifying the family's "infrastructure" needs and much more.
4. Investing Wisely: Wisely investing financial wealth in the context of family takes more than experience with finance. As chapters in this section show, families also need to practice understanding risk, spending, and portfolio construction.
5. Seeking Sound Advice: Since the field of family wealth is so complex, families face a host of advisors to choose from to help them manage their affairs. The chapters in this section offer ways for you to assess the choice of advisors, such as trustees, coaches, or a family office, as well as insights into understanding how much advisors are paid.
6. Raising the Rising Generation: The "rising generation" is the future of the family, whether they are rising in their teens or in their 40s or 50s. Families

who succeed over time create rituals to instill a sense of responsibility in their rising generation members; they also, as these chapters show, take specific steps to invite younger members to join the family "enterprise," to develop effective leadership succession, and to ensure that rising generation voices are heard in the management of the family's affairs.

7. Navigating Family Dynamics: The lifeblood of family is communication, which in turn builds trust and lays the foundation for effective collaboration. The chapters in this section offer means for better understanding the particular dynamics of your family and then enhancing relationships, across generations or within a generation (such as among siblings).
8. Making Shared Decisions: A family that is going to manage significant assets or a business enterprise together must learn to make decisions together. This takes time and practice. The chapters in this section give readers specific practices for becoming more aware of how you are making decisions now and how to provide structure and clarity to your desired decision-making structure, such as in well-designed family meetings with agreed-upon ground rules.
9. Giving Together: Another strength of families that succeed over generations is fostering connections to communities beyond the family itself, often through shared giving. The chapters in this section give you a roadmap for thinking about your philanthropy in a strategic way, as well as for encouraging philanthropy among different generations of the family.

How to Use This Book

As with *Wealth of Wisdom: The Top 50 Questions Wealthy Families Ask*, this book is a collection of resources. It is not meant to be read straight through, from cover to cover (although that is an option).

To help you orient yourself to the book as a whole, after this Introduction we have provided a section entitled, "Assessing Your Family's True Needs." This section will guide you through a brief self-assessment of your family to identify your family's needs in a variety of areas. As mentioned, this self-assessment is based on the Family Balance Sheet™, a diagnostic tool developed by Wise Counsel Research that has been used by families around the world who manage significant wealth or operating companies together. This self-assessment can identify areas of opportunity for growth and learning that you may not even have considered. Your results on the self-assessment will then guide you to specific sections of the book to consider more closely.

At the beginning of each of the nine sections of this book, we have provided a brief description of the section and of each of the chapters in it. Let these chapter descriptions guide you to an appropriate starting point.

You can also simply review the table of contents and pick out chapters whose titles sound relevant to the task and challenges that your family is facing at present. As you begin to read, each chapter will also likely raise questions that may direct you to other chapters in turn.

Almost all the chapters also follow a similar format: Each summarizes the recommended practice, tool, or exercise; describes the process for using it with your family; highlights the results or outcomes you can expect from using it; offers a case example of its use; and then suggests additional readings for you to explore the topic further if you wish.

Many of the chapters contain charts or checklists that embody the specific tool or practice whose use they describe. These checklists are designed so that you can use them yourself or with your family members. When in doubt, it's always wise to seek professional consultation or a professional facilitator to help you and your family make the best use of a specific tool or exercise. But with that caveat in mind, these exercises are offered with the hope that you "*do* try this at home"!

Families are dynamic organizations. They change over time, as members pass away, new members join the family or are born or grow up, and as family members learn and develop throughout their lives. Given the reality of change, our hope is that your use of this book changes over time too. Try the self-assessment each year to see what new needs and what new possibilities have arisen, and what practices or exercises might speak to you with new relevance.

Summary

The task of managing financial wealth together as a family has often been described as a journey. As with any journey, it is crucial to think through where you are trying to get to, based on your desires, values, and needs. It is also crucial to prepare for the journey with the needed supplies. This book aims to equip your family with tools that have passed the test of time. We hope that these practices and exercises contribute to your family's success, as they have for so many other families around the world.

Assessing Your Family's True Needs

Keith Whitaker

When you review the table of contents of this book, a particular chapter or exercise might stand out to you, as addressing your family's true needs.

You may wonder, however, "What are my family's true needs?" So often there are possibilities for growth and learning that we are not even aware of.

This section offers you a way to assess your family's needs when it comes to living well with significant wealth. It does so by adapting the Family Balance Sheet, an assessment tool designed by Wise Counsel Research, a consultancy that works with some of the most enterprising families around the world.

Wise Counsel's Family Balance Sheet was developed based on research into what leads families to succeed when they are engaged over multiple generations in managing significant financial wealth or a family business. This research includes Wise Counsel Research's *100-Year Family Study*, which studied more than 100 families around the world who have transitioned a family enterprise through at least three generations of family leadership.[1] From this research and practice, Wise Counsel identified five factors of long-term family success, each of which aligns with one of five forms of nonfinancial or, as we call it, "Qualitative Capital":

	Success Factors	Qualitative Capital
1	Long-term resiliency, growth, and development	Human Capital
2	Shared values and core purpose	Legacy Capital
3	Cross-generational engagement and support	Family Relationship Capital
4	Governance policies and structures that guide development and decisions	Structural Capital
5	Commitment to community beyond family	Social Capital

[1]See Dennis T. Jaffe, *Borrowed from Your Grandchildren: The Evolution of 100-Year Family Enterprises* (New York: Wiley, 2020).

The five forms of Qualitative Capital can be represented this way:

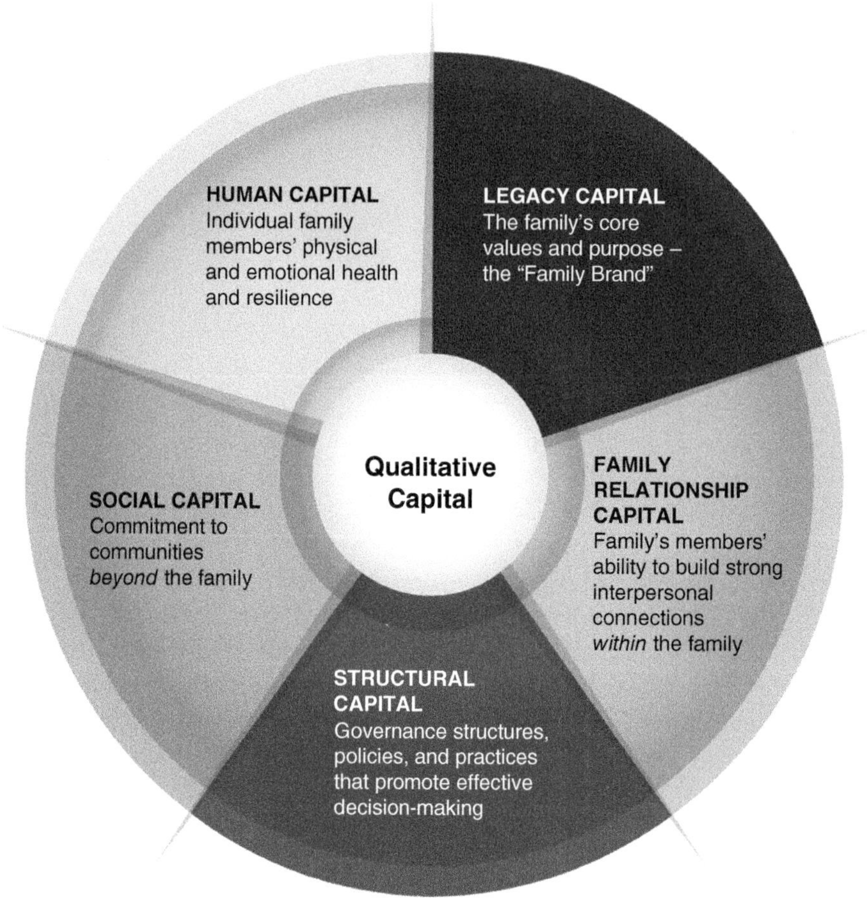

Since the five forms of Qualitative Capital are grounded in these five success factors, by measuring and then intentionally growing each form of Qualitative Capital, a family ensures a legacy of true wealth to its descendants.

Who is Your Family?

Following I offer an abbreviated version of Wise Counsel's Family Balance Sheet. (It represents about one-quarter of the original assessment.) This exercise will allow you to begin to assess your family regarding the five forms of Qualitative Capital. From this self-assessment then flows possible directions for your reading.

As you review the assessment, you'll notice that it asks you about "my family." Think about who you consider family for this purpose. Who are you managing money or a business with or for? How about their spouses? Where do you draw the line around "my family"? There are no right answers to these questions. One of the points of the exercise is to prompt these thoughts.

If you are an advisor filling out the assessment regarding a client family, think through those same questions based on your knowledge and experience of how the family speaks and acts.

As you complete the assessment, you may want to consider how other members of your family (or how members of your client family) would respond. Would their responses be significantly different from yours? Do you have enough information to be able to guess accurately at their responses? Perhaps not, which itself points to a key area of opportunity: to learn how your family members view themselves.

Again, the main reason for offering you this abbreviated form of the Family Balance Sheet here is to help you orient yourself to promising lines of inquiry in reading this book. Following the assessment, I offer recommendations for sections and chapters to consider based on your results.

It may also help to know how Wise Counsel uses the fuller version of this assessment. Every year we ask every adult in our client families to fill out the Family Balance Sheet. We aggregate those results to create a report that details the family's Qualitative Capital. It benchmarks the family's results against the over 200 global families in our database. And this annual report highlights for the family its areas of strength and areas of opportunity for growth and learning.

Based on those results and benchmarks, we present the family with recommendations for actions and education that are based on a sound diagnosis of the family's current conditions. We convene family members in at least two family meetings each year, at which they discuss these recommendations, prioritize the actions they want to take, and evaluate their progress in pursuing these plans. As a result, families who engage in this annual, iterative process of "Family Qualitative Capital Management" measure, manage, and grow their *nonfinancial* wealth with the same intentionality and results as with their financial assets. You can learn more about Family Qualitative Capital Management at Wise Counsel's website, www.wisecounselresearch.com.

Let's turn now to the assessment.

On the following pages, you'll find a definition of each of the five forms of Qualitative Capital. You'll be asked to respond to each statement on a scale of 1 to 5, from "Strongly Disagree" to "Strongly Agree." At the bottom of each form, you'll see a space where you can add up the numerical total of your responses. Following the assessment are recommendations for sections of the book to consider reading.

Assessing Your Family's True Needs—Abbreviated Family Balance Sheet

As you read the following statements, think about your family and mark down your initial responses. Respond to the statements as honestly as possible; don't overthink the statements or your answers.

Human Capital: Family members' physical and emotional health and ability to grow, learn, and adapt.

1 = Strongly Disagree, 2 = Disagree, 3 = Neutral, 4 = Agree, 5 = Strongly Agree

1. Most of my family members have good physical health.

1 2 3 4 5

2. Most of my family members have good psychological health.

1 2 3 4 5

3. Most of my family members are engaged in meaningful work.

1 2 3 4 5

4. Most of my family members feel emotionally connected with people they care about.

1 2 3 4 5

Total for Human Capital: __________

Legacy Capital: The family's core values and purpose.
1 = Strongly Disagree, 2 = Disagree, 3 = Neutral, 4 = Agree, 5 = Strongly Agree

1. My family members share stories about the family's history.

1 2 3 4 5

2. My family members work to maintain shared traditions.

1 2 3 4 5

3. My family has clarified its guiding values.

1 2 3 4 5

4. My family has a shared vision for its future.

1 2 3 4 5

Total for Legacy Capital: __________

Family Relationship Capital: Family members' ability to build strong interpersonal connections with each other.
1 = Strongly Disagree, 2 = Disagree, 3 = Neutral, 4 = Agree, 5 = Strongly Agree

1. My family members communicate effectively about difficult topics.

1 2 3 4 5

2. Most of my family members work well with each other.

1 2 3 4 5

3. Most of my family members trust each other.

1 2 3 4 5

4. The family includes members' spouses in important discussions.

1 2 3 4 5

Total for Family Relationship Capital: __________

Structural Capital: Structures, policies, and practices for effective decision-making.

1 = Strongly Disagree, 2 = Disagree, 3 = Neutral, 4 = Agree, 5 = Strongly Agree

1. My family members have a good understanding of their personal finances.

   1 2 3 4 5

2. My family has clearly communicated policies regarding the management of shared financial assets.

   1 2 3 4 5

3. My family has effective family meetings.

   1 2 3 4 5

4. My family has a clear plan for transition to the next generation of family leadership.

   1 2 3 4 5

Total for Structural Capital: ________

Social Capital: Commitment to communities beyond the family.

1 = Strongly Disagree, 2 = Disagree, 3 = Neutral, 4 = Agree, 5 = Strongly Agree

1. My family cultivates in its members a spirit of giving to others.

   1 2 3 4 5

2. Most of my family members are using their financial assets to make a positive difference in the world.

   1 2 3 4 5

3. My family's philanthropy reflects individual family members' values.

   1 2 3 4 5

4. My family allocates funds for individual family members to pursue their own philanthropic interests.

   1 2 3 4 5

Total for Social Capital: ________

Interpreting the Results

First, look at the sum you added up for each capital. Each sum should be a number between 4 and 20.

- If the sum for a particular capital is **18** or higher, that result indicates that your family likely enjoys a *significant strength* in that capital. Only 10% of families in Wise Counsel's survey population enjoy such high results in any one capital.

- If the sum for a capital is between **14 and 17**, that result indicates that your family has a *developing strength* in that capital. Nearly 40% of families have results in this range in each of the five forms of Qualitative Capital.
- If the sum in a capital is less than **14**, then that capital needs attention. But don't despair. At least 50% of families have results in this range when they begin the intentional work of growing their Qualitative Capital.

Once you have surveyed your overall results, look more closely at each capital. Where in that capital did you rate your family most highly? Where lowest? Again, ask yourself if your responses would likely be shared by other family members. If not, what would explain the possible differences?

Directions in Reading

All the sections and chapters of this book touch upon at least one, and often several, of the five forms of Qualitative Capital. Here are suggestions for further reading, keyed to each form of Qualitative Capital. If you or your family members scored your family on the lower range regarding a particular capital, review these sections' introductions and see which chapters in those sections could be particularly promising places for you to begin:

Human Capital

Section 1: Thinking Through What Matters Most

Section 2: Becoming a Learning Family

Legacy Capital

Section 1: Thinking Through What Matters Most

Section 3: Planning Thoughtfully

Family Relationship Capital

Section 6: Raising the Rising Generation

Section 7: Navigating Family Dynamics

Structural Capital

Section 3: Planning Thoughtfully

Section 4: Investing Wisely

Section 5: Seeking Sound Advice

Section 8: Making Shared Decisions

Social Capital

Section 8: Making Shared Decisions

Section 9: Giving Together

Additional Resources

For more on the Family Balance Sheet and the Family Qualitative Capital Management Program, see www.wisecounselresearch.com.

In addition, you can learn more about Family Qualitative Capital from:

James E. Hughes, Jr., Susan E. Massenzio, and Keith Whitaker, *Complete Family Wealth*, 2nd ed. (New York: Wiley, 2022).

James E. Hughes, Jr., Susan E. Massenzio, and Keith Whitaker, *The Cycle of the Gift* (New York: Wiley, 2012).

James E. Hughes, Jr., Susan E. Massenzio, and Keith Whitaker, *The Voice of the Rising Generation* (New York: Wiley, 2013).

Biography

Dr. Keith Whitaker is an educator who consults with leaders and rising generation members of enterprising families. Family Wealth Report named Keith the 2015 "outstanding contributor to wealth management thought-leadership." Keith's writings and commentary have appeared in the *Wall Street Journal*, *New York Times*, and *Financial Times*. He is the co-author of *Wealth and the Will of God*, *The Cycle of the Gift*, *The Voice of the Rising Generation*, *Family Trusts*, *Complete Family Wealth*, and *Wealth of Wisdom: The Top 50 Questions Wealthy Families Ask*. Keith has served as a managing director at Wells Fargo Family Wealth, an adjunct professor of management at Vanderbilt University, and an adjunct assistant professor of philosophy at Boston College. Keith holds a Ph.D. in social thought from the University of Chicago and a BA and MA in classics and philosophy from Boston University.

SECTION 1

THINKING THROUGH WHAT MATTERS MOST

We begin this book of tools and exercises at the beginning: with what truly matters to you. Of course, the aim of these chapters is not to tell you what matters or what should matter to you, but rather to help you and your family members discern and clarify what matters to yourselves.

The first *Wealth of Wisdom* volume (*The Top 50 Questions Wealthy Families Ask*) offered its readers questions to explore. This volume focuses on exercises or tools, but sometimes questions can be tools too. In the first chapter in this section, Ellen Perry offers four questions to discuss as a family:

1. What can I do more of that makes you feel close to me?
2. What can I do less of that makes you lean out emotionally?
3. What do you wish I understood more about who you are or what you value?
4. What are your favorite stories from childhood and why?

Sometimes the simplest questions are the hardest to answer and the most rewarding to discuss.

Many people express what matters most in the form of "values." As a result, many families seek to clarify their shared values, as a guide to action. In the next chapter in this section, Doug Baumoel and Blair Trippe help readers discern their "actionable values," that is, values that, in one's experience, have led to specific outcomes or results. By focusing on actionable values rather than individuals' beliefs (political, moral, or otherwise), families can mitigate conflict and identify powerful shared direction.

Sharna Goldseker and Danielle Oristian York also take up the subject of values, by offering readers a simple but powerful tool in the form of lists of values-words on cards that readers can sort for themselves and then use as a group to distinguish individual and shared values. This simple process can offer insights to families in fields such as philanthropy and enterprise governance and, most importantly, in simply understanding and appreciating each other.

In the next chapter, Richard Franklin and Claudia Tordini broaden the lens on what matters by taking up the subject of well-being. (The root of the word "wealth" itself points to "well-being.") Franklin and Tordini offer readers ways to assess their own sense of well-being and to talk, as a family, about what well-being means to them, using different domains of physical, social, career, community, and financial well-being. Through these discussions, families can more clearly decide how to allocate their financial wealth to foster their true well-being.

Kofi Hope and Zahra Ebrahim focus readers on the topic of identity, which for many is an important element of their personal "wealth." Using a wheel listing various forms of identity, and a process of first clarifying how you see yourself and then how the world sees you, they set up the basis for a family conversation about what identities members bring to shared work such as philanthropy or business.

Human beings have long recognized that character is absolutely essential to our happiness; as the distillation of our choices and habits, it becomes our destiny. Kristin Keffeler uses contemporary psychological tools to help readers identify their own signature character strengths, which then allows family members to see how their strengths may complement or conflict with one another, and to concentrate their efforts on developing desired strengths.

Another element of what matters most is a sense of purpose and meaning in life. In this chapter, Don Opatrny and Keith Michaelson share the Japanese concept of "Ikigai" ("a reason for being") as a tool to allow readers to clarify the intersection of what they love, what the world needs, what they can be paid for, and what they are good at.

Financial wealth is no doubt something that matters—but, beyond paying for basic necessities, why does it matter? That's a question that each of us would likely answer in different ways, and the answers matter to our sense of who we are and how we should use our wealth. To explore one's relationship with money, Courtney Pullen offers a framework of stages in wealth integration. It is meant to be used by families in a half-day setting, in which family members can explore both the positive and negative aspects of their beliefs about financial wealth.

Another way to approach our relationship to money is through reflecting on the stories that we tell ourselves about it, stories that are often rooted in long-ago events or even in stories that we heard from our parents or grandparents. In the next chapter, Jill Shipley gives readers a process for identifying the beliefs they hold about money, locating the root of those beliefs in stories they tell themselves about financial wealth. She then shows how readers might reconsider their desired relationship to money and come up with new stories that foster that desired way of living.

In the last chapter of this section, Jamie Traeger-Muney brings together many of the threads of the other contributions into an exercise focused forward: the work of "Designing Your Future, Now." This exercise is rooted in visualization, to move from past and present beliefs to imagining what you would like the future to look like, as it relates to your family, friends, work, leisure, contribution to the community, and other areas. This exercise allows "what matters most" not only to meet reality but to shape it.

CHAPTER 1

Four Profound Questions for Families

Ellen Miley Perry

During my 30 years advising families, I have come to believe that there are a few important questions that, if handled thoughtfully, with care, can be a pathway to deep connection, emotional intimacy, and greater familial well-being.

For many of us, it is not always natural or easy to identify what we truly need to know or appreciate or understand more deeply about ourselves or our family members in order to learn, evolve, and grow as human beings and loving, caring family members, spouses, parents, and siblings.

Too frequently we fall into the old predictable patterns when we are with our family of origin (siblings and parents). We forget to come to family relationships with curiosity, reverence, and a willingness to change our minds. Rather, we often come with certainty, decades-old stories, narratives about the others, and hurts long ago borne.

So often families call advisors like me with a problem, a transition, or a worry. They rarely call when they think that tomorrow will look just like today and that things are going pretty well. Families often look for help or advice with concerns about individual family members who seem lost or stuck or when the family as a whole is facing important changes, such as illness or death, a transaction, or an important transition ahead. Stated another way, it's usually when the skills and strategies that got them to ***here*** don't seem like they will get them to ***there.***

Strategies and practices that support a family's ability to engage with one another in deep and meaningful conversations can help them move ahead with more confidence and clarity. That usually involves listening to one another better, empathizing more, learning new things, and evolving personally and as a family. Sounds pretty basic! But deeper understanding, empathy, and connection require forethought, skills, good facilitation, and dollops of patience and good intentions to human improvement and family well-being.

Optimally, the family would engage in these questions and conversations thoughtfully and intentionally, not over a chaotic meal, a casual moment, or attached to another event. The hope is for a rich conversation and open exploration. I wouldn't advise trying this when family tensions are high and trust is too low. It's important to hold the tender moments that might happen.

You can engage in such conversations as a pair—with just one other family member—or in a small group.

And to be clear, if you are the one asking these questions to another family member—a parent, sibling, or adult child—when they answer you with something that hurts or surprises you or simply seems downright incorrect, the best response from you is, "Thank you so much for sharing this with me. Let me give this more thought." It is not the time to help them understand why they are wrong, how they misunderstood you, why their memory is faulty, or to help them see that they are too sensitive. Ideally you might ask neutral follow-up questions aimed at understanding more about their feelings.

These questions are meant to be approached with thoughtfulness, curiosity, and an authentic intention to become closer to the other family member(s).

1. **What can I do more of that makes you feel close to me?**
   This question is an acknowledgment that while we may do much right, there is likely much more we can do to deepen our family relationships. There are actions, conversations, and ways of connecting that deepen the relationships with some family members and make that person feel close to us. And we want to know what those are. Clearly. And it is also a declaration that we want to make the other feel loved and valued. Try to recall when the other people in your family each brought you joy. That can only happen if you are grateful for that person.
2. **What can I do less of that makes you lean out emotionally?**
   Let's be honest, we all make mistakes in family relationships. We miss cues, we get busy, we make assumptions, we sound critical, judgmental, disinterested, etc. This question gives permission but is also an invitation to our family members to be honest with us. And importantly, it gives us the opportunity to understand how we are perceived by others. Please understand that for many of us, there is fear involved with being honest with others. We worry that the relationship cannot withstand the honest feedback or criticism. We hold back and bite our tongues because we fear that the other will end the relationship if we say our truth. Often in families, we would rather be polite and safe than honest and risky.
3. **What do you wish I understood more about who you are or what you value?**
   It is hard to change our narratives, stories, and assumptions about the other members of our family. It's equally hard for them to update those assumptions and stories about us. Wouldn't it be great if we asked others what they would like us to see in them? This question is an acknowledgment that we don't understand all there is to understand about them, we don't "see" all of them, and we don't know the many parts of them that they may dearly wish us to know. For most of us, we have insights into others that are limited by geography and time frames. Perhaps we are siblings who haven't lived near one another in decades, or maybe our children are now adults with whole

lives and people we don't know well. This question is a beautiful opportunity to allow others to update our assumptions for us and help us see them more fully. And you too can offer those parts of yourself to others.

4. **What are your favorite stories from your childhood, and why?**
   We can learn so much from the stories that we tell each other. We learn what moves, scares, delights, hurts, and inspires someone through the stories they choose to tell. So too we learn what and who has had an impact on our family members through the stories. This question is a wonderful one for family gatherings and one that can be repeated over and over throughout the years.

As a rule, I think that approaching these questions over time is better than pouncing on them all at once. Families can benefit most by savoring the conversations that spring out of these questions rather than looking at this as a checklist of Q&A to be accomplished. The possibility of deeper connection and an updated understanding of family relationships is an extraordinary opportunity. Best wishes!

Additional Resources

Edgar H. Schein, *Humble Inquiry* (Oakland, CA: Berrett-Koehler, 2018).
Rosemond Zander and Ben Zander, *The Art of Possibility* (New York, NY: Penguin Books, 2002).
Warren Berger, *The Book of Beautiful Questions* (New York, NY: Bloomsbury, 2018).

Biography

Ellen Miley Perry is the founder of Wealthbridge Partners, LLC. She has 30 years of experience serving as a strategic advisor for family enterprises and family-led organizations. Her work has focused on governance, succession planning, leadership development, and conflict resolution.

Ellen, author of *A Wealth of Possibilities—Navigating Family, Money and Legacy,* is a frequent speaker, author, and advisor on the practices and strategies that create and sustain thriving families over multiple generations. She is a director of both for-profit and nonprofit organizations. She has a particular interest in the neuroscience of trauma and the psychology of well-being. Ellen lives with her family in Washington, DC.

CHAPTER 2

Identifying Actionable Values for Family and Enterprise

Doug Baumoel and Blair Trippe

Values statements, whether for corporate, family or individual purposes, are too often aspirational rather than actionable. A common fate is for these well-intentioned statements to simply hang on a wall, get included in a governance document of some sort, and gather dust. This exercise is designed to uncover values that are specific to individuals and families that serve to **actively** guide desired behaviors and help avoid undesirable behaviors, both in the family and in their enterprise. The exercise is based on identifying important events in the evolution of a family and its enterprise, and connecting those events to the underlying values which drove those outcomes.

By focusing on events that impacted the family and its enterprise and teasing out the underlying values that drove those events, we can shift the focus from individual values to group values. Exercises that begin with identifying individual values, hoping to generate consensus around group values, rely on the implicit conclusion that those values are indeed relevant to the group and/or its enterprise. Instead, we have found that investigating values that have impacted the group or enterprise in the past is a more direct and relevant way to uncover a set of values that can be actionable for the group.

This exercise also posits that articulating the values families would like to **avoid** is as important and useful as articulating the values families would like to **reinforce**. It begins with identifying specific, important past events in the lives of the individual, family, or enterprise that resulted in **desirable outcomes** and, separately, in **regrettable outcomes**. Once these events have been identified, and a list of those important events has been created in timeline form, a discussion can be facilitated about the behaviors of individuals and groups that led to those outcomes. Because behavior is driven by values, the underlying values that led to those desirable and regrettable behaviors can be teased-out through discussion. These are actionable values. They are actionable because they were part of the story of the family and its enterprise and are connected to specific behaviors and outcomes.

Some steps in this process are designed to be private and confidential. Family members often have very different experiences and interpretations of family history and hold competing truths about what happened in the past. Digging into events from the past can be fraught, and this exercise is not intended to resolve old disputes or search for objective truths. While family members may not be able to agree on some of the facts in each of their tellings of a family story, they can more easily agree on the lessons learned from their experience together and frame even a difficult history in terms of shared values without the need to blame or to even agree on many of the details of the past.

This exercise is not a substitute for proactive conflict management, though it might be a part of such a larger, intentional process. This exercise is intended for families that are generally aligned and not engaged in active conflict.

	Enterprise				Family			
	Behaviors to Avoid	Anti-Values	Behaviors to Promote	Pro-Values	Behaviors to Avoid	Anti-Values	Behaviors to Promote	Pro-Values
Events								
Future (aspirational)								

Step 1:

Define the group. Will this exercise be initiated by a subset of the family—perhaps a committee of a family council? Will this exercise be open to anyone in the family or will it be a two-step process that will involve a larger group of family members after a smaller group has begun the process and achieved some result?

Step 2:

Have each individual stakeholder identify the key events in the family and the enterprise that led to desirable outcomes and those that led to regrettable outcomes. Give those events names or short descriptions. Each stakeholder should generate their own list, privately.

Step 3:

Identify the behaviors that led to those outcomes—both desirable and regrettable outcomes. (Privately—do not share)

Step 4:

Consider the values that drove those behaviors. In some cases, the values identified will be synonymous with the behavior; in other cases, you might identify a "value" that is broader or narrower than the behavior but is more representative of a value you either want to avoid or reinforce in your business or your family. Those values associated with desirable outcomes will be "Pro-Values" and those associated with regrettable outcomes are "Anti-Values."

Step 5:

Aspirational Values: These could be values that are important for the future but haven't been articulated yet in this process. Think about events that might arise in the future and the kinds of behaviors that would be hoped for. Try to distill underlying values that are desirable and those that need to be avoided. List these as "Aspirational Values."

Step 6:

Group Discussion: Once each stakeholder in the group has generated their map of Events, Behaviors, and Values, they should each review the values that they have articulated and select the five most important for the Enterprise and the five most important for the Family. These are the values that will be shared for discussion. Be careful not to assign blame and be sensitive to others' perceptions of events and behaviors in the past. A skilled facilitator can be used to help reframe difficult past events to uncover lessons learned so that actionable values can be identified.

Once a list of approximately four to eight of the most compelling values has been agreed upon, the group should craft language that describes each value in the context of behaviors. For example: "We will promote education and engagement of family members by being proactive in family governance, transparent in our enterprise, and generous in our funding of educational initiatives." Such a statement combines several values but is crafted to serve the core values of Education, Engagement, Generosity, and Transparency. Or to cite an anti-value of exclusion: "We will embrace our differences and not let them polarize us through gossip and exclusion."

A list of values is included next as prompts. Alternatively, a variety of Values Card Decks are available that can be used as prompts.

Step 7:

Review the generated list of Actionable Values regularly—perhaps yearly. Try to determine how family and individual behaviors were, or were not, in-line with the agreed upon values. Have the family's values changed? Are they no longer commonly held? What values need to be updated in order to continue to be relevant? Is there a divergence in values among constituencies that needs to be addressed?

Sample Values List

Value	Description
Achievement	need to create real value for society, advancing the state of art, sense of accomplishment
Acknowledgment	giving and receiving recognition
Adventure	exploring the unknown, testing limits
Appearance	need to present yourself impeccably, in grooming, dress and manner
Belonging	feeling connected to and liked by others
Community	feeling a meaningful connection to a group of people
Compassion	feeling sympathy, care or concern for others
Competence	amassing and applying specific skillsets and experience, being able to speak confidently on a topic
Conflict Avoidance	seeking harmony or reduced stress above perfection
Courage	standing up for your beliefs
Equality	respecting everyone's right to parity
Faith	religious identification, spirituality
Family	providing for and spending time with loved ones
Freedom	ability to exercise choice and free will
Friendship	experiencing close ongoing relationships
Fun	seeking personal enjoyment
Generosity	feeling of abundance, willingness to share
Health & Fitness	need to build in a health regimen to all aspects of your work and family lifestyle
Helping	meeting the needs of others
Industry	the importance of working hard, doing good work
Initiative	craving the challenge of new beginnings
Innovation	finding new and creative ways of doing things
Integrity	adhering to a moral or ethical code
Justice	Pursuing what is fair and morally right
Leadership	guiding people and projects, setting the pace
Learning	pursuing new skills and self-awareness, personal growth
Legacy	knowing how you will be remembered
Mortality	urgency borne of an awareness of an ultimate time limit to your endeavors
Obligation	committing to fulfill a duty or promise
Passion for work	need for pride and meaning in your work
Power	having the ability to influence others
Problem Solving	enjoying the challenge of solving problems
Questioning Authority	suspicion of power, status quo
Recognition	need to be acknowledged and appreciated for your talents, accomplishments, skills, beliefs
Responsibility	voluntarily doing what is expected of you
Safety	minimizing risk, securing what you have
Scarcity	need to ration, preserve assets

Value	Description
Spiritual Growth	seeking connection to a higher purpose
Success	advancing personal wealth and reputation
Tolerance	being open to different ideas
Tradition	respecting an established way of how things have been done
Transparency	need for access to information not within your control and willingness to provide
Trust	willingness to allow others to impact your interests

Value	Description
Vigilance	need to work hard, complete projects, attend to detail
Vision	knowing where you are headed at all times
Other	
Other	
Other	
Other	
Other	

Case Study

Falcon Enterprises is a family enterprise owned equally by two siblings, Jim and Mark. The founder, their father Dennis, created a great business in his lifetime. At his passing 15 years ago, the business had net sales of more than $100 million. Business leadership was taken over by Jim and his sister-in-law Ellen. Both had worked in the business for many years and were extremely competent. Jim served as president and chief executive officer, and Ellen was chief operating officer, focusing on production and distribution. Business has prospered under their leadership, with sales rising to $500 million, most recently. Jim and Ellen are supported by an excellent executive team and an independent board of directors. But the last 5 years has been difficult as the formerly close relationship between Jim and Ellen has begun to unravel.

Ellen and Jim's wife, Tracy, never had a close relationship. They were very different—politically, socially, and spiritually. Tracy and Jim raised their kids very differently than Mark and Ellen had raised theirs. Tracy had very strong ideas about politics, workplace culture and many other issues. Jim grew to adopt many of those same beliefs. The two families began to grow apart and their different values began to interfere in decision-making at the company. Social media posts drove them further apart as the posts offered clear examples of their incompatible values.

We were brought in to help realign the stakeholders and help develop corporate and family strategy to overcome these very apparent, and escalating, differences.

We suggested that we begin with a shared values exercise and were met with great skepticism. "All we have are diametrically opposed values—it would be an exercise in futility," was the uniform response.

We met with each of the four separately and asked them to trace the series of key events that led to their current business success—beginning with Dennis and the entrepreneurial beginnings of the company. We asked them to talk about how Jim and Ellen were hired and how they were eventually chosen to co-lead the business. We asked their spouses, Mark and Tracy, to do the same, from their perspectives.

What we found was that the process of going back to the founding history of the company provided a sense of perspective that transcended the urgencies of the current disagreements that invaded all conversations. By examining those key formative events in the company history and distilling the values that led to both good and bad outcomes, the family began to remember that they did indeed have many shared values: entrepreneurism, compromise, patience, risk taking, and vigilance, to name a few.

Conversations got heated when more recent events began to surface. Each side identified values that drove behaviors that were problematic for the other. However, when we dug into those more deeply, we were able to distinguish between beliefs and values. Once we were able to separate beliefs (e.g., being politically and socially liberal versus being politically and socially conservative) from underlying values (e.g., being concerned for the economy, the business, each other), we were able to discuss different ways of achieving outcomes that shared common values.

Another insight that came out of this work was the importance of accommodating different values and beliefs. In fact, many of those differences were eventually seen as a strength. Once the stakeholders realized that they had many shared values in common, but different beliefs and approaches to adopting those values, they could have a productive conversation with greater empathy. They were able to see different beliefs and approaches as a strength to leverage in decision-making, providing them with a broader palette from which to make decisions.

Biography

Doug Baumoel is the founding partner of Continuity Family Business Consulting. As an executive in his own family business for many years, he brings a unique understanding of the stakeholder experience to his work with enterprising families. He is co-author, with Blair Trippe, of *Deconstructing Conflict—Understanding Family Business, Shared Wealth and Power* and has authored several articles on family business governance, conflict management, and planning. He is a practitioner scholar and mentor for Cornell University's Smith Family Business initiative and is a fellow of the Family Firm Institute and National Association of Corporate Directors.

Doug earned his MBA from the Wharton School and a BS in engineering from Cornell University. He also earned his certificate in mediation from MCLE and director professionalism from NACD. He serves on the board of One Family in Massachusetts, a nonprofit providing support for families facing homelessness, as well as private company boards.

Blair Trippe is a managing partner of Continuity Family Business Consulting where she works with families who own and manage operating companies and/or share assets together on issues related to succession planning, next-generation education, corporate and family governance development, and conflict management. She brings a highly specialized approach to the understanding of family systems and the relationship challenges encountered when families work and own together. In addition to her consulting work, Blair serves on the faculty of Family Enterprise Canada (formerly FEX) and is a nationally recognized speaker.

Blair earned an MBA from the Kellogg School of Management, a BA in psychology from Connecticut College, and certificates from the Program on Negotiation at Harvard Law School. She is a fellow at the Family Firm Institute and on the board of the Boston Symphony Orchestra.

CHAPTER 3

Values That Matter

Sharna Goldseker and Danielle Oristian York

No matter how much wealth we have, no matter how many years of experience in the family enterprise, each of us has values. And when we come together to run a family business, govern a family office, or give together to catalyze change in the world, we have to align our values in order to make collective decisions. The challenge, however, is that we often are not conscious of the values that motivate our decision-making, and even if we are, our motivating values don't always line up with those of our family members.

For the past 20 years, 21/64, our nonprofit practice, has built tools to enable family members of all ages and stages to clarify their identities in order to thrive individually and to come to the family table prepared for group dialogue and decision-making. Our most effective (and popular) tool over the years has been our Motivational Values Cards.© This tool offers families and practitioners a key building block to help individuals and families to act strategically and in alignment with their deeply held values.

Motivational Values Cards

The crises of 2020 and 2021 and related falling away of many of the structures we relied upon for connection, revealed an opportunity for people at every stage and age of life to become clearer about what mattered most to them. Amid a global pandemic, where choices we made had potentially tremendous, and even life-changing impact, we were reminded that our intentions and decisions matter more than ever. This simple deck of cards (and the corresponding online version) allows for intimate self-reflection about what moves each of us, catalyzes conversations that matter, and provokes intentional actions.

The cards identify 30 values, each with an accompanying definition. While this is not a comprehensive deck, this set of values has been honed with input from action

Figure 3.1

research, surveys, focus groups, and field tested with high-net-worth individuals and families as well as 21/64 Certified Advisors.

Here are some examples:

Integrity: Acting in alignment with your deeply held values
Innovation: Finding new and creative ways of doing things
Self-Reliance: Acting independently using your own ability and resources
Equity: Distributing resources based on the needs of the recipients to reach an equal outcome
Responsibility: Voluntarily doing what is needed
Relationships: Caring for and spending time with family and friends

Of course, it's inevitable that someone's value is not represented in the cards. As such, we encourage people who don't see one of their values in the deck to add their own when doing the exercise. Similarly, some definitions may be different than what people expect. This tool, like any useful tool, invites people who are working together to lean in and discuss how they define their values rather than assume what they and others think about a given value and how it would be implemented.

How to Use Them

The instructions for the exercise are remarkably simple. Each individual, whether alone or in a group, should have access to their own deck of in-hand cards or the online version. Everyone is invited to sort through the deck and choose the values (three to five cards) that *most* motivate their decision-making and the values (three to five cards) that *least* motivate their decision-making. Individuals should sort their cards individually, experiencing an internal monologue, to notice which of their deeply held values rises to the top, and where they hesitate or negotiate with themselves.

There are no wrong values. The difficulty is in prioritizing the values that most motivate us, our decision-making, and therefore our behaviors. While sorting, people often notice competing motivations in their heads (i.e., the voices of their parents, religion, zeitgeist that would suggest prioritizing certain values over others).

We counsel clients to try to listen to their own voices and to quiet the noise, as this exercise is like holding up a mirror to their own consciousness.

The value cards are accessible and flexible; they can be used in myriad ways. We recommend using the tool either at regular intervals or in moments of transition. For example, families and groups might sort their cards at holiday gatherings, family assemblies, or board meetings to take stock of what is motivating individual family members (e.g., owners, board members) and what they value collectively to align the stakeholders each year. Or families might use them in moments of transition, such as when they're bringing next-generation family members onto a board. A new couple might use them to evaluate the values that will inform their choices around saving, spending, or giving; new parents might turn to them to clarify what they want to convey to their children. New donors might use them to inform their giving. Each time values are selected and articulated, we have an opportunity to bring them to life in our actions.

The Experience

What we know for sure after 20 years with this tool is that the sensory-based sorting experience is much more effective than an assessment or a list of values posted online. With their own decks in hand, or by sorting digitally through handheld devices, people take ownership of their values and articulate the ways they want to define their values for themselves and their families, which can be very empowering to people who may feel overwhelmed by the opportunities they have in life.

Armed with language that reflects their internal identities, they turn the words into values statements that guide their decisions and activities. Living in alignment with one's deeply held values can be a personally fulfilling way of being and an effective way of operating in a family organization. One client recently told us that posting her family's values on their foundation website attracted the type of professional staff whose values were in alignment with their own.

Research about adult learning styles teaches us that there are seven types of learning styles: verbal, visual, auditory, logical, solitary, social, and kinetic.[1] The values cards can address five of the seven styles. Many verbal thinkers like the words, clear and concise, to organize their thinking individually, and as families they end up with a well-crafted values statement to guide their decision-making. Some people like the visual nature of the tool, how they can see the words in front of them and organize them as their brain takes in the visual cues of the image and definition. Others appreciate the kinesthetic nature of being able to sort cards, making piles and stacks and lines as they integrate their ideas. And of course, the tool can be sorted solitarily as well as socially with others.

Putting It into Practice

Life cycle and life events can cause priorities to change slightly, so sorting the cards more than once has become a regular practice for many users. For example, those

[1]See Neil Fleming and Charles Bonwell, *How Do I Learn Best?* (Springfield, MI: Authors, 2019) and Howard Gardner, *Multiple Intelligences* (New York: Basic Books, 2006).

who sort them annually recognize that "relationships" might drop down in the priority order when they are differentiating from their parents versus when they are solidly in their generative stage of adulthood. Elders have noticed that "pleasure" has risen to the top as they advance to late adulthood and prioritize legacy and grandchildren over other pursuits. From our experience, people's core values often stay consistent, while some less-central values may evolve at different life stages.

Because the cards can be easily accessed, individuals have become comfortable pulling them out in moments of transition for self-reflection, clarity in their own decision-making, and to align their values with their next set of actions. For example, we worked with a 39-year-old next-gen client who was from a successful family in New York City. She was stepping into leadership and was being asked to join many boards. By sorting the values cards, she quickly clarified that "effectiveness" was her top value and then compared each organization to evaluate whether its executive team and practices aligned with her top value. She was then able to choose to join the board of an organization that was measuring and demonstrating its effectiveness as well as another that aligned with her second value of "equality" for women.

While this tool can be self-facilitated, we also have a team at 21/64 and a group of Certified Advisors who can help families navigate this process.

As families come together to form a governance structure, they are forming a new group and their values become an integral component of that group's identity. For example, in 2020, four individual family members approached us to ask for help setting up a family foundation where the individual family members would form a joint giving structure. We sent each family member their own deck of Motivational Values Cards and asked them to choose the values that most motivated their own decision-making. During a virtual family meeting, we asked them to share their top choices; after each family member had shared, we had 24 values on the Zoom screen.

We then asked the four family members to imagine serving as board members of the philanthropic fund they wanted to create and to sort their cards as if they were making decisions for the collective entity. Without much effort, they each identified their top two motivating values for the family's giving and arrived at a total of six values for their new structure. The elder sighed with relief at the winnowed-down list. He admitted he'd been worried they would never be able to make decisions together if they started with 24 distinct values among them. But when we encouraged them to shift from their individual values and sort for the values they would prioritize for the group, the family members understood that they would elevate the few values that were most important to the family system, while their individual values could be expressed when making individual decisions in other aspects of their lives.

While this is only one example, it is illustrative of the kinds of experiences families have had with the values cards. Individuals sort the cards—integrating their emotional and rational thought process as they sort—and come up with a list of the values that most motivate them. Then, with a second sort, families or groups prioritize a set of values that guide their collective decision-making. This simple yet powerful tool has been an essential component of the transformation of many individuals and the evolution of many families with whom we have worked over the past 20 years.

Additional Resources

Email info@2164.net for more information on the Motivational Values Cards. To explore these and other 21/64 tools such as Money Messages, Picture Your Legacy, or our Exploring Series, visit www.2164.net. And to discover the role that values play in the lives of next-gen donors, check out www.GenerationImpactBook.org.

Annie Murphy Paul: https://ideas.time.com/2013/05/08/how-to-perform-in-a-clutch/.

Aiko Bethea interviewed by Brene Brown in this podcast, https://brenebrown.com/podcast/brene-with-aiko-bethea-on-inclusivity-at-work-the-heart-of-hard-conversations/.

Biography

Sharna Goldseker is today's leading expert on multigenerational and next-generation philanthropy and—as a next-gen donor herself—offers a trusted insider's perspective. As founder of 21/64, a nonprofit practice serving next-gen and multigenerational philanthropic families, Sharna has mastered and developed the industry's gold-standard tools for transforming how families who give will define their values, collaborate, and govern in the decades ahead. Sharna is co-author of the award-winning best-seller, *Generation Impact: How Next Gen Donors Are Revolutionizing Giving*, published by Wiley. She is married with two children and lives in Baltimore.

Danielle Oristian York is a spirited, creative, systems thinker and fan of embracing complexity. Danielle has spent 15 years helping families, leaders, and communities have the complicated conversations about change, identity, and the future during moments of transition. Professionally, in her role as executive director and president of 21/64, a nonprofit practice serving next-gen and multigenerational families, she is a speaker, consultant, and trainer working with those who seek to change the future while embracing their humanity as a key component of strategy. She lives in Boston and is married with two terrific kids.

CHAPTER 4

A Framework for Family Wealth and Well-Being

Richard Franklin and Claudia Tordini

Family business transition and wealth and inheritance planning are frequently implemented with a heavy focus on risk management. Sophisticated mechanisms are crafted to preserve the financial performance of the family's assets. Detailed family governance structures are fashioned. Trusts with clear constraints for beneficiaries to access money are executed, and many other instruments are used to mitigate the risks associated with wealth depletion.

The underlying principle is that preservation of financial wealth is the purpose of inheritance planning. This singular focus on protection of financial wealth may be common, but it can also be detrimental to the family members' well-being. There is a more positive and transformative approach for families to consider like the one we propose here.

A well-being framework provides families with a positive platform to incrementally and over time improve family members' lives. The framework is built at the intersection of well-being theory (supported by a growing body of data) and the family's characteristics and goals. Wealth takes a supporting role and is best viewed as a necessary resource to support well-being.

A well-being framework enables an integrated approach to family wealth and inheritance. Rather than focusing individually on family governance, dynamics, legacy, mission statements, charity, estate planning, and so on, a well-being framework realigns those elements within the family's primary intention of supporting members' well-being and flourishing. In well-being theory, the core goals are increasing flourishing and the stuff that makes life worth living, i.e., better relationships, and more meaning, purpose and accomplishments.[1]

Parents are frequently very involved and engaged with their children's well-being while they are at home and during college. After college, however, some children experience a sudden decrease in their material means that may diminish their well-being, such as living in areas that are not environmentally safe or have higher crime and corruption, or poorer health insurance coverage coupled with higher

[1]Martin E. P. Seligman, *Flourish: A Visionary New Understanding of Happiness and Well-Being* (New York: Atria, 2011), 26.

stress.[2] There are no good data to support this approach; rather, the data points to providing sufficient resources to support good well-being throughout life. This can be seen in the experience of the Nordic countries that have strong social safety nets and robust resources available to support citizens' well-being.

What Is a Family Well-Being Framework?

A family well-being framework is a compass that orients family intentions and actions, including spending, toward a long-term goal of increasing well-being and flourishing. Well-being is a construct of various domains that reflect the different dimensions of life. For example, according to Gallup,[3] there are five essential elements of well-being: career, social, financial, physical, and community (Figure 4.1). Positive psychology founder, Dr. Martin Seligman, Ph.D., created the PERMA™[4] model, which includes Positive emotion, Engagement, positive Relationships, Meaning, and Achievement. Far from the simple pursuit of happiness, it is essential to grow in all the domains to increase well-being. This means that flourishing is a multidimensional task and not just excelling in only one.

The framework is crafted by the family based on the priorities of its members in the various domains of well-being. For each domain, families will decide on their short- and long-term goals and budget to accomplish those goals. For example, in the physical well-being domain, start by defining a baseline of well-being, such as ensuring that all family members have (i) quality healthcare coverage coupled with actual access to providers, (ii) access to high-quality food (i.e., are able to shop for

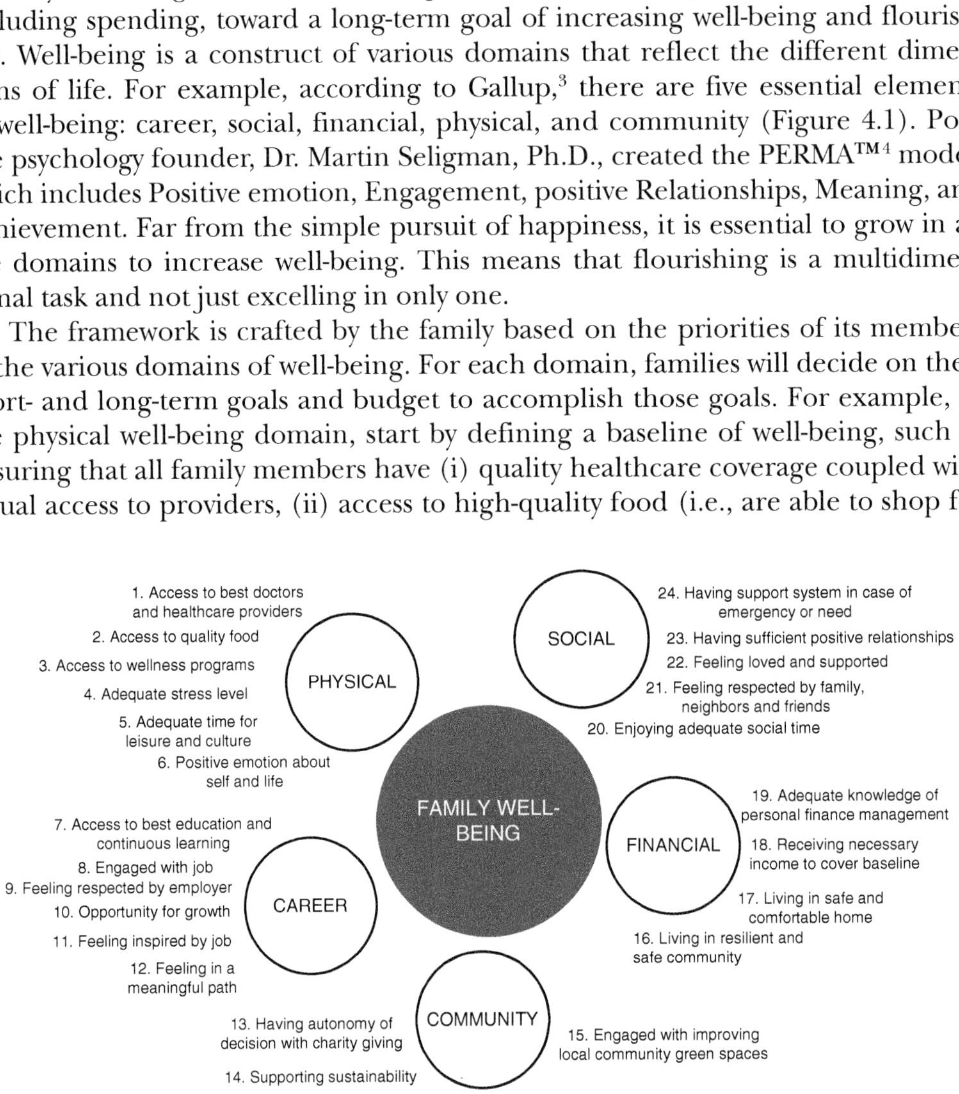

Figure 4.1 Example of Family Wealth & Well-Being Framework. 5 Well-Being Domeains based on Gallu's Well-Being Model and 24 Priorities of Well-Being for Family Members.

---

[2]See suggestions for supporting family members achieve baseline well-being: Richard Franklin, and Claudia Tordini, "Well-Being Supported by Family Wealth—A Foundation to Flourish," *Estates, Gifts and Trusts Journal* 45, no. 3 (May 7, 2020).
[3]Tom Rath and Jim Harter, *Wellbeing: The Five Essential Elements* (New York: Gallup Press, 2010).
[4]Flourish, *supra* note 1, at p. 26. PERMA™ is a Trademark of Martin Seligman, Ph.D.

organic food without feeling stressed), (iii) housing in a resilient and safe community that provides peace of mind, and (iv) access to health clubs and exercise equipment.[5] Fundamentally, a well-being framework should be designed to inspire growth.

At a more sophisticated level, a family who cares about sustainability could set ambitious goals—for example, deciding that everybody in the family will switch their energy consumption to renewable energy and reduce their emissions footprint by driving electric cars, living in sustainable housing, and flying airlines that are zero-emissions carriers. A plan like this can take several years to fully implement but would allow the family to build and strengthen its collective identity in one domain. Sustainability not only touches on each individual family member's sense of meaning, engagement, and achievement but it also creates a healthier environment that improves each individual's well-being.

The priorities should also be in line with the signature strengths and passions of each family member. This means, for example, that when deciding on community outreach, the activities and areas targeted should allow family members to tap into their capacities and not just check the "giving back" bucket.[6] In implementing this, parents can create individual charities (e.g., donor-advised funds or private foundations) for each of their children, giving them each the autonomy to decide how they want to give back to society based on their interests and strengths. "[P]eople are more likely to derive joy from helping others when: (1) they feel free to choose whether or how to help, (2) they feel connected to the people they are helping, and (3) when they can see how their help is making a difference."[7]

How to Implement

An initial assessment of the family well-being is a great place to start. There are plenty of available surveys and assessment tools that can help.[8] Asking simple questions such as *"Do you feel safe walking alone in your neighborhood?"* or *"Do you feel your boss appreciates and respects you?"* can be eye openers. These assessments will provide a good sense of where the family needs to set priorities. Use this to make a list of initial targets to achieve a baseline well-being level for everybody in the relative short-term. Think in terms of achieving the targets incrementally and over time. Once that baseline is achieved, the family can target a wider array of goals toward flourishing.

Families can set a yearly budget for resources available to any member focused on making progress in one of the well-being domains. For example, a certain amount of money could be available for evidence-based coaching, whether it is career, wellness, sports, or otherwise.

---

[5]Richard Franklin and Claudia Tordini, "Well-Being Supported by Family Wealth—A Foundation to Flourish," *Estates, Gifts and Trusts Journal* 45, no. 3 (May 7, 2020): 5.

[6]*Ibid.*, 14–19.

[7]Lara B. Aknin, Ashley V. Whillans, Michael I. Norton, and Elizabeth W. Dunn, "Chapter 4: Happiness and Prosocial Behavior: An Evaluation of Evidence," in *World Happiness Report 2019* (United Nations Sustainable Development Solutions Network, 2019).

[8]*See e.g.*, Ackerman, *Flourishing in Positive Psychology: Definition + 8 Practical Tips*, Positive Psychology .com (June 27, 2019); PERMA Profiler at www.authentichappiness.com; Flourishing Scale at https://ggsc.berkeley.edu/images/uploads/The_Flourishing_Scale.pdf.

Measuring progress, objectively and subjectively, over time is important to track and assure actual progress in improving people's happiness and life satisfaction. Subjective assessments are especially critical, as it matters most how individuals perceive their own life. Using a model that yields granular information regarding the well-being domains would inform next steps for improvement. Ideally, the family can measure each of the priorities they set and have a compounded measure of the family well-being. This would allow them to assess progress in the overall well-being and not just by domain or priority.

This is a step-by-step, item-by-item approach to improving key elements that data shows as critical to well-being. This methodical element is critical to the family well-being framework. There is plenty of room here for positive family member collaboration, each uniquely adding to the contours, depth, and texture of the family's well-being approach through time. This approach demonstrates why resources are needed and why they should be used prudently.

What's Next?

If reading this chapter sparks your curiosity and imagination, we suggest getting more acquainted with well-being theory and start assessing family's well-being. This will open a space of reflection and discussion with your family that can take the shape of a commitment to family wealth and well-being. If you want to take a step further, the following exercise offers a guided example to build your own well-being framework for your family. Reading through it will give more light about your family, your family's well-being, and the benefits of building a framework.

DIY Wealth and Well-Being Framework for Families

1. Take a well-being assessment to gain a sense of where every family member (adult) is in their path to flourishing.
    - A simple first step is the life satisfaction survey. You can use The Cantril Ladder of Life Scale[9] as adopted by Gallup.[10]
    - A more informative alternative is to create your own assessment, including a measurement of each of the priorities you set for your family. You can start with the example provided and built based on the 24 priorities shown in Figure 4.1 of this chapter.
2. Start a conversation with your family members to learn about the opportunities to improve their life satisfaction level. This is a conversation to approach from a space of curiosity and empathy rather than a judgmental attitude.
3. Set-up your family's baseline well-being threshold:
    - What is needed to raise everybody above unhealthy conditions or unmet basic needs level (if anybody is there) or a general sense of unhappiness in multiple domains?

[9]Hadley Cantril, *The Pattern of Human Concerns* (New Brunswick, NJ: Rutgers University Press, 1965).
[10]OECD Guidelines on Measuring Subjective Well-being (https://www.ncbi.nlm.nih.gov/books/NBK189562/).

- A minimum baseline well-being threshold might include the following for every member of the family:[11]
  - quality healthcare coverage coupled with actual access to providers,
  - access to high-quality food (e.g., are able to shop for organic food without feeling stressed),
  - housing in a resilient and safe community to feel peace of mind, and
  - access to health clubs and exercise equipment.

4. Set up your family well-being framework.
   - Select the DOMAINS: you can start with the five domains illustrated in the family well-being framework example:
     - Physical (and Mental) Positive Emotions
     - Social/Positive Relationships
     - Financial
     - Career/Achievement
     - Community/Meaning and Purpose
   - Determine the PRIORITIES: you can start with the baseline well-being priorities set above and the ones suggested in Figure 4.1.
     - For example, in the case of the access to good health care, the priority might be that everybody in the family will be upgraded to the highest level of coverage available in their health insurance network.
     - Set priorities that speak to your family in terms of what they need to move from struggling to thriving.
       - Continuing with the physical domain, ensure that your family members have adequate leisure opportunities and time to pursue them. This may translate to getting season tickets to the local theater, a membership to a local museum, family outdoors picnics, babysitting support for date nights, and outsourcing household chores, among other options that fit to your family's structure and dynamic.
   - Set a TIMELINE to implement and achieve the priorities: If there are baseline well-being priorities unmet, those should be the ones to focus on in the next 12 to 18 months. Other priorities can be set in a long-term horizon of 5 to 10 years.
     - For example: giving autonomy for each family member to determine his or her own charity giving can be a goal for the mid-term. You will need time to set up the legal mechanisms (i.e., donor-advised fund, private foundation) that facilitate the approach as well as support your children in deciding a meaningful "giving back" alternative in-line with their strengths and passions.
   - MEASURE well-being every 12 to 18 months to track and re-prioritize as needed. An expanded well-being assessment would include a Cantril's ladder-type questionnaire for the various priorities of your framework (see the following example).

---

[11]Richard Franklin and Claudia Tordini, "Well-Being Supported by Family Wealth—A Foundation to Flourish," *Estates, Gifts and Trusts Journal* 45, no. 3 (May 7, 2020): 3.

Example of well-being assessment using the 24 priorities of our example in this chapter. On a scale of 1 to 10 (1 being nothing and 10 being the most), answer the following.

1	How happy are you about your life today?	○○○○○○○○○○ 1 5 10
2	How happy do you expect to be about your life in 5 years?	○○○○○○○○○○ 1 5 10
3	Do you have access to the best doctors and healthcare providers?	○○○○○○○○○○ 1 5 10
4	Do you have access to quality food?	○○○○○○○○○○ 1 5 10
5	Do you have access to wellness programs?	○○○○○○○○○○ 1 5 10
6	What is your stress level?	○○○○○○○○○○ 1 5 10
7	Do you have adequate time for leisure, culture and other activities of your interests?	○○○○○○○○○○ 1 5 10
8	How satisfied are you with who you are today?	○○○○○○○○○○ 1 5 10
9	Do you have access to the best education and continuous learning?	○○○○○○○○○○ 1 5 10
10	How engaged are you in your job?	○○○○○○○○○○ 1 5 10
11	Do you feel your employer respects you?	○○○○○○○○○○ 1 5 10
12	At your current job, do you have opportunities for growth?	○○○○○○○○○○ 1 5 10
13	Do you feel inspired at work?	○○○○○○○○○○ 1 5 10
14	Do you feel your job is meaningful?	○○○○○○○○○○ 1 5 10
15	Do you have autonomy of decision with your charity giving?	○○○○○○○○○○ 1 5 10
16	Do you support sustainability in your community?	○○○○○○○○○○ 1 5 10
17	Are you engaged in improving local community green spaces?	○○○○○○○○○○ 1 5 10
18	Do you live in a resilient and safe community?	○○○○○○○○○○ 1 5 10
19	Is your house safe and comfortable enough for your family?	○○○○○○○○○○ 1 5 10
20	Does your household income meet your baseline needs?	○○○○○○○○○○ 1 5 10
21	Do you have a clear picture of your finance management?	○○○○○○○○○○ 1 5 10

22	Do you enjoy a positive and meaningful social life?	○○○○○○○○○○ 1 5 10
23	Do you feel respected by your family, neighbors and friends?	○○○○○○○○○○ 1 5 10
24	Do you feel loved and supported?	○○○○○○○○○○ 1 5 10
25	Do you have sufficient time to dedicate to your positive relationships?	○○○○○○○○○○ 1 5 10
26	Do you have a dependable support system in case of emergency or need?	○○○○○○○○○○ 1 5 10

Using a table-type display of everybody's assessment can help visualize areas that need attention. A weighted average by category can help compare categories over time and assess progress (only for comparison over time) but highlighting minimums might set the immediate priorities of focus of the family.

Well-Being Priority	Dad	Mom	Child 1	Child 2	Average
How happy are you about your life today?	9	10	7	⑥	8
How happy do you expect to be about your life in 5 years?	10	10	9	⑥	8.75
Do you have access to the best doctors and healthcare providers?					
Do you have access to quality food?					

Additional Resources

Claudia E. Tordini and Richard S. Franklin, "Wealth and Well-Being—What Wealthy Families Can Learn from Sovereign Government Policies and Measuring Human Progress," *Estates, Gifts and Trusts Journal*, 46, no. 3 (May 13, 2021).

Barbara Fredrickson, *Positivity* (New York, NY: Harmony Books, 2009).

Tom Rath and Jim Harter, *Wellbeing: The Five Essential Elements* (New York: Gallup Press, 2010).

Biography

Claudia Tordini provides coaching and consulting through Appanage LLC. She consults with families on wealth and inheritance planning, helping to design a family framework to support well-being and flourishing. She brings together her background in business, humanistic psychology studies, and art to offer an integrated positive approach to wealth and well-being.

Claudia teaches emotional intelligence and relational skills using an experiential learning through art model for graduate students at the University of Pennsylvania's School of Arts and Sciences. She has pioneered a powerful model for using art and art experiences to facilitate learning and development for individuals and families.

Claudia holds a Master of Philosophy in Organizational Dynamics at the University of Pennsylvania with a concentration in Organizational Consulting and Executive Coaching. She holds an MBA from the University of Pennsylvania's Wharton

School with a concentration in Human Resources and Strategy. She was awarded her BS in Industrial Engineering from the University of Buenos Aires, Argentina.

Richard Franklin is a member of Franklin Karibjanian & Law PLLC. His law practice focuses on estate planning, trusts and estate administration, and beneficiary and fiduciary representation. He is a member of the District of Columbia and Florida Bars, a Fellow of the American College of Trust and Estate Counsel and serves on its Tax Policy Study Committee.

Richard has a keen interest in the intersection of well-being theory and inheritance planning. He developed the Well-Being Trust—a reimagined trust and inheritance approach that uses well-being theory and empirical research, and well as other data, to increase beneficiary well-being.

Claudia and Richard's recent publications include "Wealth and Well-Being—What Wealthy Families Can Learn from Sovereign Government Policies and Measuring Human Progress," *Estates, Gifts and Trusts Journal,* Vol. 46, Number 3 (May 13, 2021); "Well-Being Supported by Family Wealth—A Foundation to Flourish," *Estates, Gifts and Trusts Journal,* Vol. 45, Number 3 (May 7, 2020).

Claudia and Richard have given numerous workshops and presentations to various groups and at educational programs on family wealth and well-being, the *Well-Being Trust,* and related topics.

CHAPTER 5

Understanding Identity and Social Power

Kofi Hope and Zahra Ebrahim

The identity wheel is a tool commonly used to help people understand the elements of identity that shape us, our experience of the world, and the power connected to aspects of our identity. Because it starts with self, and our own experiences, it's a much more accessible way to start engaging with this complex topic.

The activity is best done in small groups of two to six people. The first part is done individually and should take 10–15 minutes.

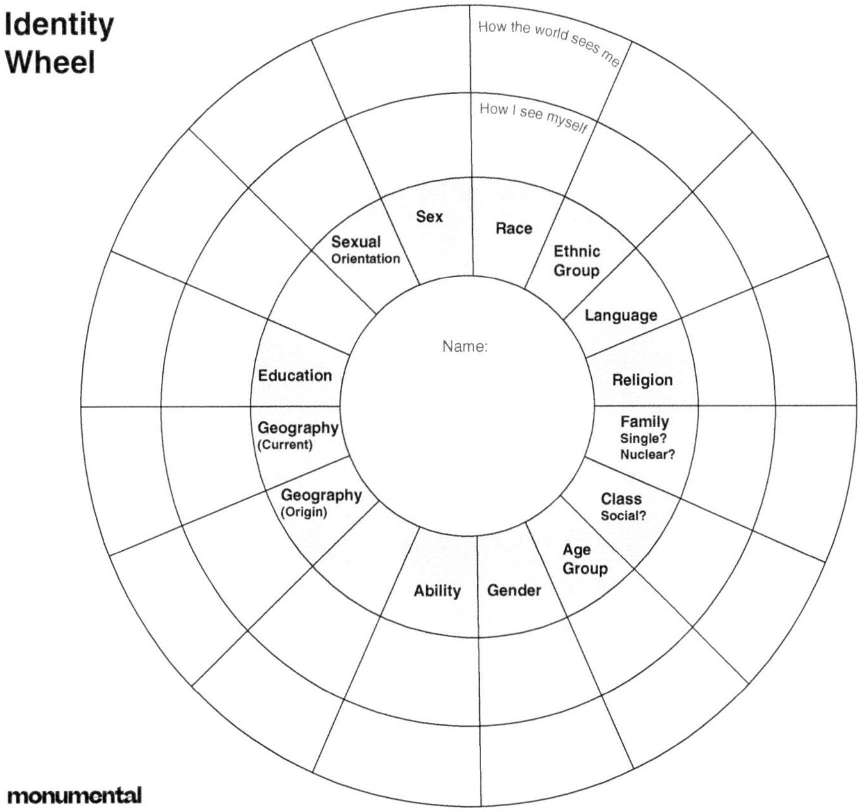

Step 1

Print the Identity Wheel worksheet (or draw it out on a piece of paper). Start by writing your name in the center, recognizing and acknowledging that our names are a core part of our identity.

Step 2

You'll notice on the wheel there are different sections or panels. Each is a possible part of your identity. You'll see that there are two parts to each section.

First, think about **how you identify yourself**. For example, what is your gender or your ethnic group? Write these in the "How I see myself" inner ring. The goal is not to have a precise answer, but more to think about what parts of your identity are clear to you and what parts require more reflection. If you can't fill in every section, that's okay; it's part of the learning! There is no right answer, and we encourage you to refrain from going online to search for definitions if terms are unclear. A key part of learning is understanding what parts of your identity you think about all the time, and what parts you seldom think about.

Step 2

The second (outer) ring of the panel is a bit trickier. It's asking you to write about **how you believe the world sees you**. The "world" can be defined as folks you pass by on the street, colleagues, neighbors, and other acquaintances. For example, you may see yourself as one social class. Let's say you were raised blue collar, and you still identify as working class. But due to where you work, how you dress, where you socialize, perhaps people in the world tend to see you as an upper-middle-class person. For some cases, how you identify and how the world sees you will be the same, and for some cases it may be different. Another example, someone may be of Hispanic background (for example their background is from Chile), but based on their facial features and skin, tone, when they walk around in a city like Toronto or Chicago, people assume their "race" is white. But that individual may identify their "race" differently.

Some people will find this really easy; some people will find it really hard. We've done workshops, and people who would be perceived as white have said, "I don't believe in race. I can't fill this in unless it's to say human." Define the first sections however you want, but for the "How the world sees me" ring, be honest and take this opportunity for reflection on how you truly believe the world sees you. It's worth taking some time for introspection.

Step 3

Once complete, find a partner and discuss the following questions for 15–20 minutes:

- How critical are each of these dimensions in your life?
- Which ones do you never think about?

- Which ones were really hard to fill-in?
- Which ones do you consciously leverage in the workplace (where/when)?
- Which ones create barriers for you or do you try to downplay in the workplace?

Don't feel pressure to share anything specific you've written, but more focus on what the experience of completing the Identity Wheel was like.

Step 4

Come back together as a larger group. Discuss what you spoke about and consider the following questions:

- If you completed this wheel for the people who are in your inner circle of friends and confidants, how similar would those people's answers be to your own?
- What parts of this wheel would you like to learn more about, what concepts are still difficult for you to understand?
- How do some parts of your wheel come together to shape your experience. For example, someone may say the intersection of their race and gender, like being an Asian woman, creates very specific experiences that are different from being an Asian man or a woman of another racial group.
- In what ways does identity impact your investment/philanthropy decisions?
- If there is a strong match between how you perceive yourself and how the world perceives you, how do you think this leads to a different experience in life than for those who see themselves very differently than how the world perceives them?

This exercise should help you understand the complexity of human identity and to see the ways that identity can connect to social power and privilege. So often we externalize and get very theoretical about concepts like race, power, privilege, and discrimination. Starting with ourselves allows us to move from theory to lived experience.

When this activity is done with diverse groups, the conversation becomes even richer as we can discuss in a safe space the different ways our identities impact our experience in society. The next step from this work would be a deeper exploration of how identity connects to social power and a better understanding of how in our families, our work, and our philanthropy we can be leaders who think about identity and difference and how it shapes our blind spots and decisions. It is one of the most effective ways to develop our cultural competence.

We have done this exercise many times with families and individuals who are looking to start charitable foundations. Philanthropists, by definition, tend to have a high degree of social power and usually use their investments to support those with less power. We talk about how the key to effective and impactful philanthropy is to ensure we are increasingly aware of the role our identity plays in our giving—how identity impacts our perspectives, whom we invest our money in, who is able to access our programs, who is at the table deciding our giving priorities. We ask people to begin to start reflecting on the identity of others in their work, asking themselves: Whom do I listen to in a meeting? Whom do I always feel comfortable asking for advice? Who is benefiting from my giving?

When we pay attention to identity in our work, we can start to see where conscious or unconscious bias may be impacting our decisions. We find many people come to these conversations quite nervous, thinking that talking about topics like ethnicity, gender, and race must be uncomfortable and intimidating. But this exercise helps open the door for further reflection on our place in society and others' places in a way that is invitational and starts with our own experience.

Activities like this are not meant to be done in isolation from other learning. It's the beginning of a practice that honors that our individual identities play a role in our personal and professional lives and to understanding where they may shape blind spots. We encourage you to use this activity to identify areas where you want to go deeper in your learning, in dialogue with the significant people in your life, family, and community. It can also be helpful to pay attention to the way our identities shift across contexts and eras of our lives. For some, engaging in further training or education around issues of discrimination, bias, and social power will be a natural next step. For others, an increased sense of self-awareness will open up new and unexpected avenues of discovery.

Additional Resources

Kimberlé Crenshaw, "The Urgency of Intersectionality," October 2016. TED video. https://www.ted.com/talks/kimberle_crenshaw_the_urgency_of_intersectionality?language=en.

Hadiya Roderique, "Black on Bay Street," *The Globe and Mail* (November 4, 2017). https://www.theglobeandmail.com/news/toronto/hadiya-roderique-black-on-bay-street/article36823806/.

Biography

Kofi Hope is a Rhodes Scholar, doctor of philosophy in politics, community activist and youth advocate. He has over 15 years of experience in managing community-based programs. Kofi was the 2017 winner of the Jane Jacobs Prize for his work improving the City of Toronto. In 2005 he founded the Black Youth Coalition Against Violence, a group that advocated for real solutions to the issue of gun violence. This advocacy work included a presentation for then–Prime Minister Paul Martin and led to him being named one of the Top Ten People to Watch in Toronto in 2006 by the *Toronto Star*. Previously he was the executive director of the CEE Centre for Young Black Professionals (CEE), a nonprofit that creates economic opportunities for Black youth in Toronto. He is a member of the board of directors for the Atkinson Foundation and Toronto Environmental Alliance. A global traveler, he has visited 22 countries around the world and calls Toronto, Ontario, home.

Zahra Ebrahim is the co-founder of Monumental. She is a public interest designer and strategist, and her work has focused on community-led approaches to policy, infrastructure, and service design. She is an established bridge builder across grassroots and institutional spaces and is a leading practitioner in surfacing key stories and narratives that build trust and connect communities. Prior to this role, she built and led Doblin Canada, focusing on engaging diverse sets of stakeholders to use design-led approaches to address complex organizational and industry challenges. In her early career, Zahra led one of Canada's first social design studios, working with communities to co-design toward better social outcomes, leading some of Canada's most ambitious participatory infrastructure and policy programs. Zahra has taught at OCADU, MoMA, and is currently an adjunct professor at the University of Toronto. She is the vice chair of the Canadian Urban Institute and the board chair for Park People. She was recently named Next City's Vanguard "40 under 40 Civic Leader," Ascend Canada's Mentor of the Year, one of "Tomorrow's Titans" in *Toronto Life*, and one of WXN's Top 100 Women in Canadian Business.

CHAPTER 6

Tapping Character Strengths to Move Families Forward

Kristin Keffeler

The Byron family was sitting around the handmade walnut conference table at their enterprise headquarters. Mother, father, and three grown children. They were fidgeting and making jokes, trying to dispel their discomfort. They had never had a business meeting as a family before, and today's topic felt like a charged one: Were they ready to make the changes necessary to move from a single decision-maker—their father—to a collective of family decision-makers for their enterprise? Would their hard-driving father accept what it meant to share his power with his adult children?

Recognizing the need to help the family members move from fear and tension to curiosity and possibility, the presiding advisor asked each family member to consider a time when they felt they'd been at their very best in a family interaction. Each of the five family members became contemplative. Some took notes. Others got the far-away look of being lost in a memory.

The advisor asked each person to share their chosen moment. The family went around the walnut table, and each in turn described their experience. The resulting laughter rooted in their joint memories broke the tension. Every family member was engaged. When it was the patriarch's turn to share, he paused, looked down at the blank sheet of paper in front of him and said, "Honestly, I don't think I've ever been at my best with my family. I don't think they get the best of me." There was silence as the weight of that statement fell on everyone in the room.

This moment of vulnerability provided a powerful opening, and the advisor capitalized on that opportunity by naming the strength that the patriarch had just exhibited: "John, you are known for your bravery in business deals. What you just acknowledged to yourself and your family was also brave. Would you be open to hearing when your wife and kids feel they have experienced you at your best?" He nodded. The others around the table each shared a story of a time they felt that the patriarch had truly shone in their family. He took notes on what each person said, and it was clear that everyone in the room was feeling the power of possibility and connection. The fear and tension subsided as the family members were all able to recognize and acknowledge the strengths of themselves and each other.

Character Strengths: A Tool to Enhance Individual Growth and Family Capacity

As the Byron family came to recognize, character strengths are an invaluable tool for helping individuals and families thrive. Research shows that increasing awareness and use of character strengths in human development and interpersonal relationships is associated with a heightened experience of flourishing,[1] increased life engagement,[2] higher relationship satisfaction,[3] and elevated work engagement, work satisfaction, and the experience of "work as a calling."[4] In short, the increased use of one's character strengths is a well-researched and well-vetted pathway for cultivating more of the vitality and engagement that makes life worth living.

But what exactly are character strengths? In general, *character strengths* are positive aspects of your personality that impact how you think, feel, and behave.[5] Social scientists have identified and categorized 24 culturally agnostic strengths that, when practiced and grown within individuals, form the backbone of human thriving. Like any character trait, the presence of any single character strength in an individual is partly due to genetics and partly due to environment. So, while some people may be born more curious, more grateful, or braver than others, with intention and focused action we all have the ability to further develop the strengths we've decided matter to us. The empirical framework underpinning these 24-character strengths is relatively new; the *Character Strengths and Virtues Classification and Handbook*[6] was published in 2004. However, the cultivation of character strengths is based on two ancient ideas: (1) that we can improve character through mindful striving and (2) that this mindful cultivation of character strengths can result in happiness.

---

[1]Lucy C. Hone, Aaron Jarden, Grant M. Schofield, and Scott Duncan, "Measuring Flourishing: The Impact of Operational Definitions on the Prevalence of High Levels of Wellbeing" *International Journal of Wellbeing* 4, no. 1 (2014): 62–90.

[2]Christopher Peterson, Willibald Ruch, Ursula Beermann, Nansook Park, and Martin E. P. Seligman, "Strengths of Character, Orientations to Happiness, and Life Satisfaction," *The Journal of Positive Psychology* 2, no. 3 (2007): 149–56.

[3]T. Kashdan, Dan V. Blalock, Kevin C. Young, Kayla A. Machell, Samuel S. Monfort, Patrick E. McKnight, and Patty Ferssizidis, "Personality Strengths in Romantic Relationships: Measuring Perceptions of Benefits and Costs and Their Impact on Personal and Relational Well-Being," *Psychological Assessment* 30 no. 2 (2017).

[4]Claudia Harzer and Willibald Ruch, "The Relationships of Character Strengths with Coping, Work-Related Stress, and Job Satisfaction," *Frontiers in Psychology* 6, no. 165 (2015).

[5]Institute on Character, "Bring Your Strengths to Live & Live More Fully," www.viacharacter.org.

[6]Christopher Peterson and Martin E. P. Seligman, *Character Strengths and Virtues: A Handbook and Classification* (New York: Oxford University Press, 2004).

How to Measure Character Strengths

An easy, validated, and free way to assess an individual's top character strengths is to use the VIA Character Strengths Survey (www.viacharacter.org). This open-access assessment is based on the rigorously researched and empirical 24-strength framework. The assessment produces a free report that rank orders an individual's character strengths. This tool is particularly useful for individuals and families because there are validated versions of the assessment for both adults and youths (ages 8–17).

The 96-question assessment takes 15–25 minutes to complete, and responses to all questions are on an easy-to-use five-point Likert scale. Following is a sampling of the types of questions in the assessment:

	Very much like me	Like me	Neutral	Unlike me	Very much unlike me
I experience deep emotions when I see beautiful things.					
I am an extremely grateful person.					
I always speak up in protest when I hear someone say mean things.					

Another advantage of the VIA Character Strengths Survey is that advisors don't have to take an expensive training course to use it (though it is useful to become familiar with the character strengths framework and its many practical applications—see the following Resources section). Also, families can immediately start experiencing the impact of focusing on their individual and collective strengths.

Tip for Advisors: On the VIA Character Strengths website, for no charge, you can set up a professional account that displays your organization's brand and ensures that client reports will be sent to your email address for analysis and easy integration into client work.

Practical Applications

The VIA Character Strengths Assessment is an open-access tool that is intended to be used by both researchers and practitioners. As a result, it has now been cited in literally thousands of research papers and, therefore, has many empirically vetted applications that researchers and practitioners have developed. While there are dozens of ways to use the VIA data with individuals and families, following are three simple applications—known as positive interventions—to engage individuals and families with the power of character strengths.

1. ***Signature Strengths***

   What is it? Signature strengths are typically the top five strengths in one's profile. These strengths are viewed as most essential to the person and are qualities that are especially energizing and natural for them to use.

How to apply this positive intervention: There are many ways to engage with signature strengths. Two practical ways for individuals and families to do this are the following:

- Individual: Create a daily practice of identifying when and how you are using or have used your signature strengths. Share what you are learning with a loved one.
- Families: Share a list of each family member's signature strengths at a family meeting. Pair family members and have each person talk about one of their top strengths for two minutes uninterrupted. They can share how the strength shows up for them daily, what life might be like without this strength, etc. After two minutes, the other person shares. Back in the large group, ask each person to share a story of when they saw their partner using one of their top strengths in a meaningful way.

2. ***Strength-spotting***

   What is it? Strength-spotting is the act of intentionally seeking to notice what people are doing when they are at their best.

   How to apply this positive intervention: This is the character strength intervention that was highlighted in the opening story of this chapter. It is one of the easiest of all the character strength interventions because an advisor (or family member) simply needs to be aware of when someone is doing something they are naturally good at, and then name it out loud. The key to successful strength-spotting is its outward verbalization and that the comment has to be *authentic* and *specific:* "Jim, I want to strength-spot your Love of Learning strength. The new decision-making framework you introduced to us today is a result of all the reading you enjoy doing—Thank you."

3. ***Family Character Strengths Genogram***

   What is it? A genogram is a formal way of mapping family relationships and patterns over generations.

   How to apply this positive intervention: After creating a standard genogram of a family, write down two or three signature strengths for each individual noted in the genogram. Look for patterns of strengths. Note the strengths that are commonly acknowledged by family members ("Mom has always had *perseverance!*") and those that may not be as apparent or celebrated within the family system ("Suzie has always been *creative,* but we haven't done a good job of celebrating that strength of hers").

Advisors and family members interested in learning more about the application of character strengths can explore these listed positive interventions, as well as many more, in the following resources.

Conclusion

The field of wealth and family enterprise consulting continues to evolve and adopt more science-based and strengths-focused approaches to support affluent families. Rather than the traditional approach of identifying and "solving" the problems present within a family system, positive interventions, like those listed previously, provide a structure that supports individuals and families to identify where they are strong and capable. From that place of strength, they increase their capacity to overcome the inevitable obstacles and see new solutions. The VIA Character Strengths Survey, backed by empirical data and with its many practical applications, can provide a powerful scaffolding of support for families and practitioners wishing to tap the many strengths embedded in every family system.

Additional Resources

VIA Character Strengths Assessment: www.viacharacter.org.

Christopher Peterson and Martin E. P. Seligman, *Character Strengths and Virtues: A Handbook and Classification* (New York, NY: Oxford University Press, 2004).

Ryan Niemiec, *Character Strengths Interventions: A Field Guide for Practitioners* (Boston, MA: Hogrefe Publishing, 2018).

Matthijs Steeneveld and Anuk van den Berg, *Character Strength Intervention Cards* (Boston, MA: Hogrefe Publishing, 2020).

Ryan Niemiec and Robert E. McGrath, *The Power of Character Strengths: Appreciate and Ignite Your Positive Personality* (VIA Institute on Character, 2019).

Lea Waters, *The Strength Switch: How the New Science of Strength-Based Parenting Can Help Your Child and Your Teen to Flourish* (New York, NY: Avery, 2017).

Biography

Kristin Keffeler is the founder and owner of Illumination360. She is an advisor and certified professional coach working with enterprising families, families of wealth, and rising generation family members. She has specializations in business design, human motivation and behavioral change, family dynamics, family governance, intergenerational collaboration, leadership development, and the "inner work" of money.

Kristin's undergraduate focus was in human biology and chemistry, with an emphasis on human peak performance. She also has a master of science in management with a concentration in public health from the University of Denver and a master of applied positive psychology from the University of Pennsylvania.

Kristin's top character strengths are Love, Spirituality, Gratitude, Perseverance, Perspective, and Love of Learning, which she feels gratified to use every day in her work. She started her firm in 2005, and it has become her "living laboratory" for uncovering her own Big Idea and living into a life of bigger impact.

CHAPTER 7

Using the Ikigai Model to Foster a Legacy of Meaningful Engagement

Don Opatrny and Keith Michaelson

All of us, regardless of circumstance, face the question of how we can live a meaningful life and actualize our full potential. Living a life of meaning and purpose for most people is entwined with finding a job or career in which they can provide for their families and make a contribution to the world.

Successful entrepreneurs, like many others, find a sense of purpose in creating financial security for their families. After establishing a sustainable business, they often focus on preserving wealth for future generations. But those who have achieved a level of prosperity at which their children and grandchildren essentially have no economic requirement to work, often develop new concerns, such as:

- What will be the effects of family wealth on the motivation of those loved ones they hope to empower?
- Will they be setting the conditions for following generations to feel entitled to wealth without being productive?
- Will inheritors tie their self-esteem to external status symbols without creating value that benefits others?

These concerns are often warranted because inheritors face very different challenges in finding purpose than the generation of wealth creators. Without the necessity to provide financially for themselves and their families, inheritors can question the reasons for working hard, building a business, or mastering a profession.

Despite high-profile examples of the negative consequences of wealth, the risks can be minimized. Intergenerational wealth can create the conditions for genuine individual flourishing and contributions to societal well-being.

Decoupling the Importance of Working from Earning Money

For most people the process of earning a living and providing financial prosperity requires the ongoing development of marketable skills. The marketplace provides crucial feedback and acts as a catalyst for maturation and conveys status to those who succeed in creating value. While it might seem like heresy to some, experience suggests that a key to actualizing potential in the context of significant wealth requires a decoupling of the significance of working from earning money.

In guiding their children, parents of inheritors do well to reinforce the idea that doing meaningful work is an essential part of human development and satisfaction. They can help their children recognize the importance of engaging in "any activity that challenges you and tests your abilities, that requires your dedication, and that also meets the true needs of others." In our practice, we have adopted the concept of Ikigai to help our clients find meaningful engagement in purposeful activities.

Exploring Meaning and Purpose with the Ikigai Diagram

Ikigai, pronounced "ee-key-guy," is a Japanese concept that is a combination of the terms *iki*, meaning *alive* or *life*, and *gai*, meaning *worth* or *benefit*. Together these terms mean "that which gives your life purpose." Ikigai is woven into Japanese culture, most notably on the island of Okinawa, which boasts the highest concentration of people over the age of 100 in the world. And Okinawans don't just live longer; they remain healthy and vibrant. The concept of "retirement" doesn't exist there the way it does in Western countries.

How might we take the journey to our particular ikigai, our unique intersection of heartfelt interest, talent, and contribution? And how might the journey be different in wealthy families? Family members, supported by professionals who occupy advisory roles, including grantors, trustees and family council leaders may more readily engage in this exploration if they have an effective tool for doing so.

Exploring Ikigai's personal and social dimensions using the Ikigai model includes four overlapping areas:

- What do you love?
- What are you good at?
- What does the world need?
- What can you get paid for?

Seeing an Ikigai diagram for the first time often has a powerful effect. It makes intuitive sense that activities at the overlap of the four circles offer meaning and purpose. We ask our clients to put a dot on the diagram to represent where they currently spend most of their time or energy, which is often illuminating by itself.

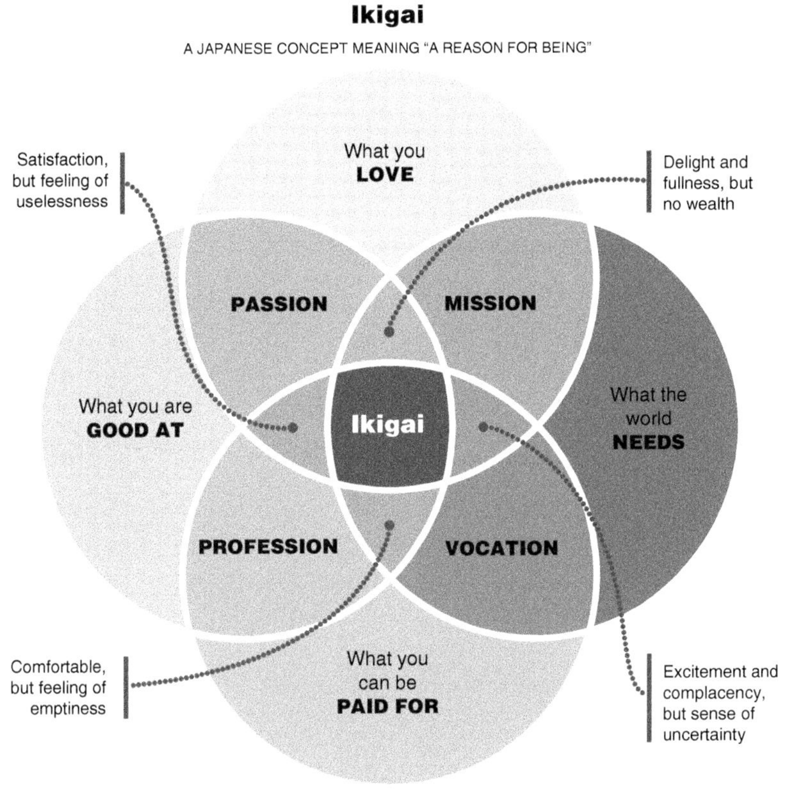

Figure 7.1

Source: Kishore B / Shutterstock

Because the bottom circle, earning money, is not a primary need for some inheritors, we explore personal Ikigai by first inquiring about the top three circles, collecting comments based on our clients' self-awareness and understanding of the world. Then we move to the financial arena in a way that acknowledges their special circumstances. Focusing on one circle at a time, we create separate lists gathering answers to the following:

What you love

What naturally captures your attention, brings you true joy or makes you feel most alive and fulfilled? This might be found in hobbies, intellectual interests, spiritual pursuits, or ways you experience relationships.

What you are good at

What are your unique skills? This could be an area where you have shown natural talent or been motivated to hone your capabilities. Items on this list can be found in unique interests, travels, or professional endeavors.

What you think the world needs/ways you want to contribute

The size of the "world" you are imagining doesn't matter. It might be the entire human family, a small community, or your own family. Whatever the sphere, the focus is on what you believe the world needs and the ways you truly want to contribute.

What you can get paid for/what money flow can enhance

This discussion is fundamentally different in wealthy families, who can change the economic equation by investing family resources in the Ikigai journey. This offers the possibility to support individual development or provide the capital necessary for entrepreneurial initiatives. However, the ability to create an "alternate economy" supported by trust distributions can also enable delusional thinking about what an inheritor is actually good at.

We encourage trustees to focus first on the top three circles and then examine how a calculated flow of family resources could enhance the discovery of untapped potential, while careful discussions of milestones of progress in the top three circles can be tied to resources flowing to the pursuit of any Ikigai-inspired journey.

Our Process

In the **first** of four sessions, we use a brainstorming process to identify unfiltered thoughts and feelings, and we commit to nonjudgmental witnessing of the Ikigai inquiry in a confidential environment. In the first session, we focus on one circle at a time (setting a timer for 10–15 minutes for each circle) and repeat the same question after each response. For example:

Advisor:	"Tell me something you're good at. . ."
Client:	"Learning new things to apply in my life."
Advisor:	Records response and says, "Thank you."
Advisor:	"Tell me something you're good at. . ."
Client:	"Listening to my friends when they are upset."
Advisor:	Records response and says, "Thank you."
Advisor:	"Tell me something you're good at. . ."
Client:	"Explaining complex ideas to my friends."
Advisor:	Records response and says, "Thank you."

When the timer sounds, we ask how the process felt, and whether anything surprising emerged. Then we move to the next circle. For example:

Advisor:	"Tell me something you love doing or that makes you feel alive. . ."
Client:	"Attending live sporting events."
Advisor:	Records response and says, "Thank you."
Advisor:	"Tell me something that you love doing or that makes you feel alive. . ."
Client:	"Service trips."

Advisor: Records response and says, "Thank you."
Advisor: "Tell me something you love doing or that makes you feel alive. . ."
Client: "Listening to podcasts about innovative technology."
Advisor: Records response and says, "Thank you."

We continue to the next question for 10-15 minutes, saying: "Tell me something you think the world needs or a way you want to contribute," and then pause the process. We encourage clients to continue expanding their lists, by talking with trusted friends or family members who can offer honest feedback about their talents and passions.

When we get back together in our **second** session, we explore areas of overlap, two circles at a time. In the example above, a client might say, "I see an overlap between my love for technology podcasts and my ability to explain complicated concepts." Finally, we explore areas where all three circles overlap. We encourage our clients to imagine engaging robustly in these activities and to explain what they see themselves doing. We keep going until they feel a vibrant desire to continue their explorations.

At a **third** session we fine-tune the vision with future-oriented questions such as: "Where do you see yourself in three years, and what needs to be happening for you to feel good about your progress?" "If we have a conversation in 20 years and you are delighted by your journey, how do you imagine your professional and personal life?"

The **fourth** session consists of making specific plans for the journey. This could include an education plan, a business plan, or preparation for a conversation with a trustee to share a vision and explore distributions to support progress. The aim is to engage the client's initiative to keep the process moving forward.

Applying Family Resources

Applying family resources to a vibrant Ikigai exploration offers an opportunity to support inheritors to courageously pursue their Ikigai journeys. Leaders of family enterprises and trust grantors can envision inheritance as a propellant for the development of character, competence, and contribution—three essential elements that contribute to self-actualization.

Now, put your own finger on the Ikigai chart where you spend most of your time. Imagine taking one concrete step that will move you closer to the center. How do you feel?

Additional Resources

For more on the importance of inheritors engaging in meaningful work see the following:

James E. Hughes, Jr., Susan E. Massenzio, and Keith Whitaker, "Facing the Waves," *The Voice of the Rising Generation: Family Wealth and Wisdom* (Hoboken, NJ: John Wiley and Sons, 2014): 61–84.

For more on Ikigai see the following:

Héctor García and Francesc Miralles, *Ikigai: The Japanese Secret to a Long and Happy Life* (New York: Penguin Books, 2016).

Tim Tamashiro, *How to Ikigai: Lessons for Finding Happiness and Living Your Life's Purpose* (Mango, 2019).

Biography

Don Opatrny is a founder and principal of the Lovins Group, LLC in Guilford, Connecticut. Don is a family business consultant and legacy wealth advisor who works with a wide spectrum of families, from the top of the Forbes 400 list to beloved local establishments.

Don is a husband, father, and veteran of his own multigenerational family business. He is a licensed marriage and family therapist, a member of the American Association of Marriage and Family Therapists (AAMFT), Attorneys for Family Held Enterprises (AFHE), Family Firm Institute (FFI), and the Leaders Council of the Ultra High Net Worth (UHNW) Institute.

As a principal and family business advisor with the Lovins Group, **Keith Michaelson** helps families navigate the challenges of major transitions in business ownership and leadership. Keith has 25 years of experience working with leaders and leadership teams in major corporations and nonprofit organizations, including the World Bank, the American Institute of Physics, Con Edison, General Electric, and *USA Today*.

Keith earned an MBA from Yale School of Management, an MA in executive coaching from Middlesex University in London, and an MA in marriage and family therapy from Fairfield University. He is a licensed marriage and family therapist.

CHAPTER 8

Stages of Wealth Integration

Courtney Pullen

The Stages of Wealth Integration is a half-day to full-day workshop for families or couples that is designed to help participants explore their relationship with wealth. It helps families explore the money relationship continuum, which on one side includes denial, worry, and guilt and on the other side deals with entitlement, shame, arrogance, and dissatisfaction. Interestingly, this continuum is not static as it can show up differently in one area of life versus another, like being in denial about money with friends but entitled in how you shop.

The goal of the session is to help you move to a sense of empowerment, where money is not simply a day-to-day headache, but the foundation from which you are able to support your life's unique purpose. Through this process you will begin to understand where you are avoiding the truth about your finances and recognize the patterns of equating net worth with self-worth. In order to have balance, it is important to explore your identity beyond your wealth.

The primary goals of the Wealth Integration tool are (1) to explore and increase self-awareness regarding your relationship with money so you can make more conscious choices around your behavior with wealth and (2) to develop more alignment with your values.

The power in the model is the conversations that ensue after people have a chance to absorb the content. Upon reflection, family members will describe times when they have been on both sides of the continuum. I invite you to reflect on the following questions and consider using them for your family.

1. Describe or reflect on times in your life when you have been on the denial side of the continuum.
2. Describe or reflect on times when you have been on the entitlement side of the continuum.
3. What circumstances create an imbalance?
4. During periods of stress do you trend toward denial or entitlement?
5. What money message do you recall having an influence in your life, for example, "Money doesn't grow on trees"?

6. Does that money message still have an influence on you today and if so, how?
7. What money messages do you/did you intend to give to your children?
8. Where would you like to be on the continuum and what will it take to achieve that goal?
9. How can you support each other in having a healthier relationship with wealth?
10. Review the Needleman quote offered in Figure 8.1. Rate yourself on a 1–7 scale with 7 being in complete balance. Is there a higher number that you would like to achieve? What would it take to reach that goal?

Ultimately the purpose of these questions and exercises is to facilitate an understanding of what it means to have an empowered relationship with money. Following are some examples of what that really means:

- Knowing who you are and what matters to you, then using money to support your passions
- Living life as a responsible adult instead of allowing wealth to keep you dependent
- Enjoying wealth and appreciating the advantages it brings into your life
- Not being ashamed of having wealth, but not being proud of it for its own sake, either
- Achieving a sense of balance based on understanding that money doesn't make you better or worse than those who don't have it
- Understanding that net worth is not the same as self-worth
- Accepting the responsibility of managing wealth with conscious attention instead of using it carelessly or destructively

This can be a lot to digest, so take your time to reflect, journal, be in conversation with your spouse or family members, and really listen to each other without giving advice. Practice the gift of generous listening in this process, including listening to yourself think and process.

How do families support their members to build healthy and empowered relationships with wealth?

- They are intentional. They neither use wealth with destructive carelessness nor pretend it doesn't exist.
- They choose to accept both the advantages and the responsibility of wealth and to create a plan for the family money.
- There is a focus on the rising generation and helping them to live a rich and fulfilling life.
- The family makes a deliberate choice to train family members in stewardship.
- Open communication. In my experience, families who openly talk about problems are the most likely to be able to solve those problems, and therefore, family members who communicate well and often have closer and healthier relationships. It is important for wealth creators to be open about their desired legacy and the expectations of the wealth, and to be an advocate for the voice of the rising generation.

Pullen Consulting Group
Effective change from the inside out

Stages of Wealth Integration

Stage 1 — Money Relationship Continuum:

Denial	Empowerment	Entitlement
Worry Fear Guilt Ignorance Dissatisfaction Pretending money doesn't matter	Balance Responsibility Satisfaction Intentionality Gratitude Using money to support life purpose	Emptiness Arrogance Carelessness Dissatisfaction Dysfunction Equating net worth and self-worth

Stage 2 — Balance:

"Balance occurs when one simply has money without emotional conflict. One uses it to pursue one's values, life goals and meaning."

—Jacob Needleman

Stage 3 — Identity beyond wealth:

"Your time is limited, so don't waste it living someone else's life. Don't be trapped by dogma – which is living with the results of other people's thinking. Don't let the noise of others' opinions drown out your own inner voice. And most important, have the courage to follow your heart and intuition."

—Steve Jobs

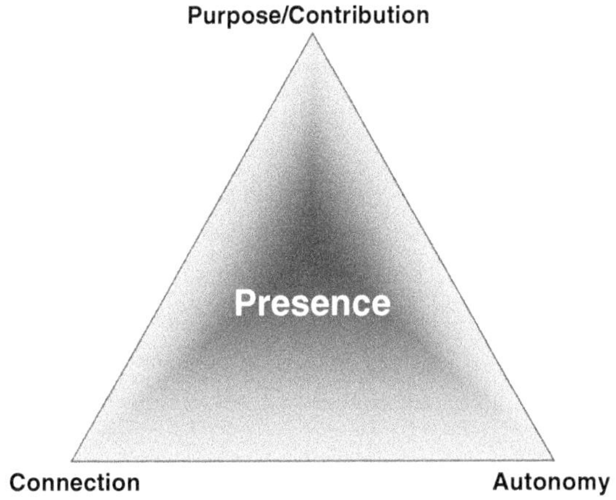

©2021 Pullen Consulting

Figure 8.1

The final step in using the Stages of Wealth tool is to better understand your identity beyond the wealth, as seen in Stage Three in Figure 8.1. So often in families of wealth, the members' primary identity is connected to money and how you are viewed in that limiting context.

We all have three primary drives in life: a drive to be in connection with people, a drive for autonomy to be our own person, and a drive to have a purposeful life. Ultimately the tension among these three is held together by being fully present in your life.

All of this is hard to navigate! If you have children, reflect for a moment on your child's journey through the terrible twos. They were trying to strive for autonomy when they were saying no to everything. The tension between connection and autonomy is classic and rears its head again in the teenage years. If we are honest, this tension is present throughout our lives. It is exacerbated in wealthy families because they are "required" to share trusts, family properties, attend family meetings, etc. This can feel like a forced fit for the family and can intensify the tension between connection and autonomy.

With all of this in mind, what can you do to educate yourself and your family? I suggest using the model as a tool for conversations. Families tend to understand the diagram very quickly after they are given a couple of examples. Then start by opening a conversation and asking questions like the following:

- How do you think our family is doing in balancing the need for connection and autonomy?
- What could we do to improve?
- Are you finding a purposeful life? Describe that journey.
- Read the Steve Jobs quote, and ask yourself: Are you finding the courage to follow your heart and intuition?
- How can we support each other in doing so?
- Please share the ultimate dream you envision for your life.

There is a lot that you can do with this tool, and it opens the door for many unexpected and delightful conversations. Let me offer a few examples of how families have used this exercise.

Several years ago, I was working with a large multigenerational family, and I used this tool in a breakout session for a group of 25 cousins. I asked them a similar set of questions to the ones above. They all shared stories of their struggles with money, what it was like growing up with significant wealth, and how they felt like they were "just members of the lucky sperm club." We talked about what it was like to forge a professional identity beyond the family. They all shared surprise at the realization that others in the family felt the same way as they did, which was an enormous relief, and they all asked for the opportunity to continue the conversation beyond our allotted time.

Using the exercise mentioned earlier, I worked with another family whose young adults spoke about their specific struggle, because the name of the family business was their highly visible last name. They expressed what it was like to try and hide their last name or downplay who they were; at some level they hoped for a more "normal life." This conversation provided them the first opportunity to openly discuss these issues. They didn't need to be "fixed" but needed a supportive space in which to discuss their struggles and figure out a way to normalize them.

Lastly, during a workshop with a different family, the members of the rising generation were asked by their parents, "How are we doing in investing in your dreams and ambitions?" The rising generation gave very constructive feedback to the parents about what they could be doing to better support the young adults in the family.

Talking about money often seems taboo and difficult, particularly if you come from a wealthy family, but I want to leave you with hope. When you facilitate conversations using a tool like the Stages of Wealth roadmap, many doors will open for you and your family. A commitment to healthy, ongoing communication is key and the primary catalyst for positive change in your family. It will create a legacy for generations to come.

Additional Resources

Courtney Pullen, *Intentional Wealth: How Families Build Legacies of Stewardship and Financial Health* (Wheatridge, CO: Pullen Consulting Group, 2013).

Brad Klontz and Rick Kahler, *Facilitating Financial Health: Tools for Financial Planners, Coaches, and Therapist* (National Underwriter Company, 2008).

Ed Coambs, *The Healthy Love and Money Way* (Charlotte, NC: Author, 2021).

Biography

Courtney Pullen is the president of the Pullen Consulting Group. He has more than 20 years of experience as an innovative leader in family wealth consulting. Courtney specializes in working with affluent families by tackling the complexity of wealth. He helps the family and its individual members thrive through values retreats, family meetings, leadership and succession trainings, as well as individual coaching.

He brings forth his training as a psychotherapist, business and organizational consultant, and pioneer of wealth psychology and blends these modalities into a powerful model to support the family business or the family enterprise.

He recently published *Intentional Wealth: How Families Build Legacies of Stewardship and Financial Health.*

CHAPTER 9

Learning from Your Money History and Writing a New Story

Jill Shipley

Although money itself is neutral, the experiences and messages we heard growing up have an impact on our relationship with money as adults. Societal stereotypes and stigma surrounding the concepts of wealth, being an inheritor, marrying into financial wealth, and being "rich" also play a role in defining our attitudes, biases, associations, emotions, and behaviors related to money.

Often, we are unconscious of these drivers that impact our actions and attitudes. We may continue living as we were instructed by our parents or modeled by those around us as we were growing up, without pausing to reflect and shape our own relationship with money. We may be carrying around feelings of jealousy, guilt, fear, or shame tied to money without exploring the origin. Sadly, we can leak or project these negative feelings outward, which can impact the relationships with those we care about.

Personal reflection tools and guided conversations like the ones highlighted in this chapter can help you and those you care about unpack your money history, break down associations and biases around wealth, enhance communication about money, and ultimately write a new story fostering a positive relationship with money and wealth.

Considerations before You Begin

Achieving the benefits of this self-exploration and enhanced awareness requires us to be open and honest with ourselves. Looking deep inside, especially about our past, can be overwhelming, emotional, challenging, and, for some, traumatic. Self-reflection, coaching, mentoring, or therapy can be helpful in this journey. Investigating and codifying your core and aspirational values and exploring how you apply them to your decision-making is another activity that can be helpful as a precursor to the following activities.

If possible, consider having a family wealth professional, a therapist, or even a good friend help facilitate the process and act as a guide and support. This is not critical but can be very beneficial.

Avoiding Blame and Judgment

This exercise will remind us of lessons we learned, messages we received, or experiences we had growing up that are not helpful to us as adults. It is important to avoid placing blame on parents or others who raised us. Remember we all do the best we can with what we have. Strive to learn from your past, keeping what is positive and throwing away anything that does not align with who we want to be and what we want our relationship with money to be like.

A Four-Part Exercise:

1. **Explore Your Attitudes and Biases about Wealth**
   Consider the words that come to mind when you think of wealth or people who are wealthy. Write down words that arise or circle the words from the following list.

Snob		Security	Lucky	Opulent
Treasure		Successful	Abundance	Love
Accumulate		Luxury	Spoiled	Utility
Greed		Giver	Fun	Happy
Protect		Guilt	Fear	Shame
Privileged		Survival	Independence	Power
Freedom		Pleasure	Savvy	Choice
Worthy		Dependance	Control	Wise
Safety		Unequal	Spender	Waste
Burden		Opportunity	Pride	Unfair
Embarrassed		Hard Working	Generous	Inequality
Example: Flaunt	N			

   For each word you wrote or circled, note if the word has a positive (P), negative (N), or neutral (–) connotation or emotion in the space next to the word.

2. **Look Back to Be Able to Move Forward**
   Write down your answers to the following questions. Feel free to use bullets instead of writing sentences or paragraphs. Try to be as honest as you can.

   You do not need to share your answers with anyone, but it can be interesting to talk about these exercises with siblings or your significant other to better understand each other. You may have very different answers than your family members with contradictory memories of the same experience. Each person's truth or perception of a past event is their reality, and it is important to respect how we recall the experiences in our lives and the impact they have on us.

While you were growing up. . .

- What were the messages you heard about money? What do you remember your parents or influential people in your life saying about money?

- What experiences with money stand out? What experiences were rewarding? What experiences were difficult or challenging?
- Did your parents talk about money? Fight over their finances? What emotions do you recall related to spending money and paying bills?
- What were the roles your parents played related to money? How were decisions made by your parents? Who earned more? How did that impact how decisions were made?
- In what ways were your parents' (or influential family members') behaviors and/or messages about money aligned? In what ways did they differ?
- What were the financial circumstances of your parents' own childhoods? How could that have shaped their money stories? For example, Depression-era children might have a money story about scarcity.
- Did your family of origin experience a significant financial event? A job loss, divorce, substantial debt, windfall, etc.?
- Did you feel like you had more, less, or the same money as your friends? Did you make comparisons?
- How did you learn about the value of a dollar? When did you first have your own money? Did you have an allowance? Part-time job? What were your habits when you received money (save, spend, hoard, give)?
- How was money used? Was it used as a reward? Punishment? To control? To protect? To demonstrate love? To exert power? To apologize? To show appreciation? To help others?

3. **Reflect on Your Relationship with Money Today**
   Now, consider how the lessons you learned affect you today. Answer the following questions focusing on how you view past experiences and how your money history affects your current behaviors and perspectives.
   - What is your reaction to the money messages you heard or role modeling you witnessed? Circle the response that is most closely aligned with your reaction

Very Positive	Somewhat Positive	Neutral	Somewhat Negative	Very Negative

   - Was anything surprising? If yes, please describe:
   - How does your money history impact how you behave with and feel about money today? Put an X next to the statement that most closely answers the question.

________	My actions with money today are exactly aligned with the messages I learned growing up.
________	The lessons I learned inform how I behave with money today with a little variation.
________	My actions with money today are very different from what I learned growing up.
________	Today I behave the exact opposite way related to money compared to what I was taught growing up.
________	Other (please describe)

   - In what ways are your behaviors aligned with your money history? List examples:
   - In what ways do your behaviors differ from the messages or modeling you learned growing up? List examples:

- Consider the words you associated with wealth or wealthy in Activity 1. Consider why these were your initial associations. Are they based on your experiences with family, friends, peers, or neighbors growing up? Are they based on stereotypes you see in the media?
- Do you have a net positive, negative or neutral attitude about wealth and being wealthy? Circle one of the following choices:

Net Positive	Net Negative	Net Neutral

4. **Writing a New Story**

   Now, think about the relationship you **want** to have with money. It is likely there are aspects of your money history that you have continued that are aligned with your values. You may also determine that some messages, attitudes, or behaviors may not be serving you well today.

   With this enhanced self-awareness about your relationship with money, you can reorient your behaviors and attitudes to be intentionally aligned with your values. Begin to identify the ideal relationship you want to have with money. You can use the following questions to help you write your new story. Feel free to write free-form stream of consciousness, use bullets, draw pictures, or find images that represent your ideal money beliefs, attitude, and mindset.

   - What are the lessons or money messages you **want** to pass on to your children and/or future generations?

Consider using a collage of images to reflect your ideal relationship with money created using a collage tool like https://photo-collage.net/.

Figure 9.1

Source: driftwood / Adobe Stock; Issochor / Shutterstock; Sasint/Adobe Stock; cnOra / Adobe Stock; relif / Adobe Stock; Lucas / Adobe Stock; Lucas / Adobe Stock

- How do you **want** to feel about wealth and being wealthy? What words from the first Activity would you **want** to select?

Consider using a word cloud tool such as https://www.wordclouds.com/.

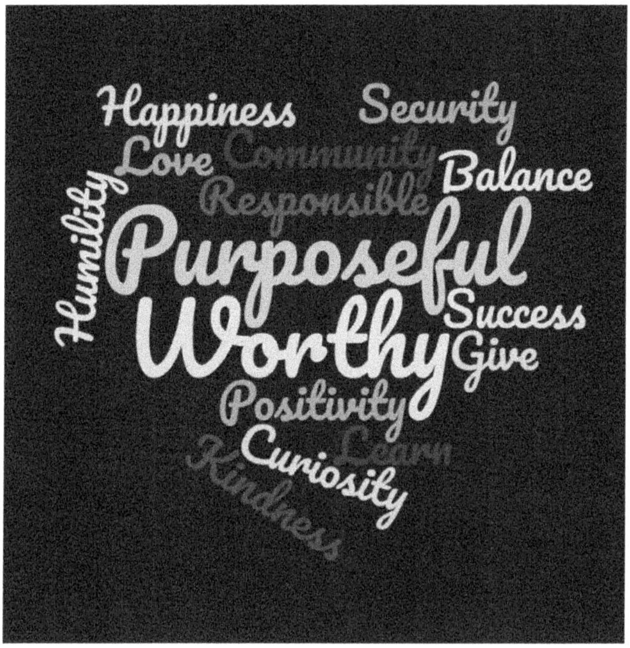

Figure 9.2

- How do you **want** to answer each of the 10 questions in the second Activity? It is helpful to change to present tense thinking about the messages you want to pass on, the relationship between you and your partner (if applicable), and the experiences your kids are having (if applicable).
- Are your current practices helping or hindering you from achieving your ideal relationship with money? What will you do more of, do better, do differently, or do less of to achieve this new story?

Consider using a sticky note maker like https://note.ly/.

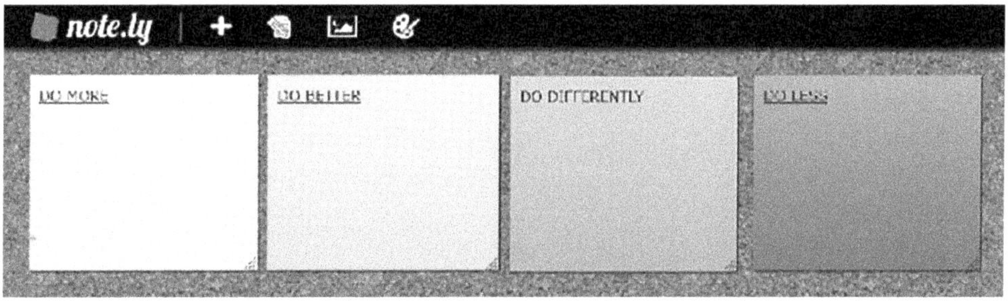

Figure 9.3

Real-Life Application

A couple in their 60s invented and sold a medical device business two years ago, resulting in a nine-figure liquidity event. They became clients of our family office following the sale and seemed paralyzed to make decisions about their new financial wealth. We asked them about the impact they want the money to have on their own lives and those of their families. They looked at each other, and John said, "I do not think we have even thought about these questions, but all I know is I do not like the impact it is having now."

We sent them each home with these exercises and encouraged them to reflect on their relationship with money—to define their attitudes, biases, and behaviors related to money and explore where these messages came from. We asked that they come prepared to the next meeting ready to share with each other their individual money histories, to discuss what they want their relationship with money to be, and how to intentionally and consciously pass these messages on to their children and future grandchildren.

The reflection was extremely powerful for John and Jane. They acknowledged they were proud that they achieved the "American dream" but were holding on to unconscious biases based on their money history and stereotypes about being wealthy. They recognized they had unnecessary fear they would run out of money and be back living paycheck to paycheck (a scarcity mentality which drove many fights about purchases and lifestyle spending).

They overcompensated for the guilt and shame they felt about having more than their siblings, friends, and neighbors by always paying bills, giving lavish gifts, and always saying yes when people asked for money (to the point of feeling taken advantage of and wondering about the genuineness of their relationships). They realized their identity had been wrapped up in their work and raising the kids and now needed to explore purpose and meaning in this new chapter.

They began to learn about how they could invest their time, talents, and resources in doing good through philanthropy and impact investing. They began reading about curating an abundance mentality and wanted to engage their children in this vulnerable, deep, and transparent exploration. With the help of a facilitator, they began having family meetings exploring this exercise and others as a family. It was a little uncomfortable and awkward at first, but these discussions changed the way John, Jane, and their children defined the meaning and purpose of the money and adjusted their behaviors putting money to work as a tool for good.

Additional Resources

Values Edge https://hrdqstore.com/products/values-edge-system.
Money Personality Quiz https://www.moneyharmony.com/moneyharmony-quiz.
Soul of Money book and course https://soulofmoney.org/som_courses/soul-money-workshop/.

Biography

As managing director and head of Tiedemann Advisor's Family Governance and Education Practice, **Jill Shipley** helps families, family offices, foundations, and family enterprises manage the impact of multigenerational wealth. She brings more than 20 years of experience and expertise in family systems, preparing rising generations for their rights, roles, and responsibilities, facilitating effective communication about wealth, navigating family enterprise transitions, defining family and business governance, and enabling strategic and positive activation of capital. She lives in Denver, Colorado, with her husband and son.

CHAPTER 10

Envisioning the Future

Jamie Traeger-Muney

The most reliable way to predict the future is to create it.

—*Abraham Lincoln*

Arriving at your desired destination is nearly impossible if you don't know where you are going. The same holds true for creating a fulfilling legacy. It is hard to get *there* if you don't know where *there* even is. I often ask clients who have created a successful family enterprise, "What is the purpose and vision of your business?" This is a question that they can easily answer, but when I ask them, "What is the purpose of your wealth and your vision for the future?," they almost always look at me blankly.

To help families answer these questions, I work with them to co-create their RichLife Portfolio.™ This is a unique process that explores your relationship with money and wealth. It consists of four parts:

- **Past:** Discover personal, familial, and historical stories related to money and wealth, and how these have played out in family dynamics.
- **Future:** Values-based processes focus on creating your vision, and the legacy stories you would like to live into.
- **Present:** Discover your wealth philosophy by tying in how the stories of the past and the hopes for the future play out in present-day decision-making and actions.
- **Plan:** Develop a plan to maximize your current actions in order to bring your created future to fruition.

This approach is positively focused, concentrating on what works, and building on strengths. Much as a startup company uses a business plan to implement a successful business strategy, this process provides:

- an aspirational set of values,
- a vision for who you could be, as individuals and as a family, and
- a mission for the family's wealth so there is clarity around what it is and isn't there to provide.

This chapter will focus on one aspect of The RichLife Portfolio, called Designing Your Future, Now. This exercise helps you envision the future you want to create and how your wealth can support these goals. If you're just creating goals without a larger destination in mind, it is aimless labor. Creating a vision puts meaning behind your goals.

Thinking about what you want your future to be can be overwhelming, though. It can activate your brain's "fight, flight, or freeze" response and make it very difficult to come up with an answer. As a psychologist, I learned a great trick to get around this problem. Instead of *thinking* about what you want, if you ask your brain to *visualize* it as if it has already happened, to really engage all of your senses in *seeing* this, you have a far greater ability to envision your future.

Visualizing and articulating what you want your future to be makes creating it easier. "It locates your destination, or as one of my clients dubbed it, your personal Oz." Once your Oz has been found, it is infinitely easier for your wealth planning team (financial advisors, estate planners, family wealth and philanthropic advisors) to effectively design your "yellow brick road," mapping the path and coordinating the journey that enables you to get from where you are currently to this desired future.

The exercise is simple, but it can have a tremendous impact on your life and that of your family. In order to get the most out of it, I recommend the following:

- Give yourself plenty of quiet time to do the exercise.
  - Set aside at least 90 minutes of uninterrupted time.
- Start by reading through the directions, including the various domains of life, and then close your eyes and really *visualize* yourself in this future.
  - What does it look like?
  - How do you feel?
  - What do you hear? What do you smell?
  - Who is there with you and what are you doing?
- Open your eyes and write down what you envisioned.
- Make it bold and creative. Make sure what you see inspires you.
- Really stretch yourself to make what you see as good as it possibly can be.
  - In order to do this, ask yourself, "Could I make it better?"
  - If yes, keep growing your vision and then ask yourself again, "Could I make it even better?"
  - Repeat until what you see is the best possible life you can envision.
- The more detailed you can describe how life feels and what it is like, the better.
- Once you have completed the exercise, put it away for a couple of days without looking at it.
  - Allow your brain to percolate on this future as it will.
  - After a couple of days, reread the life you have created for yourself and edit it to make it even that much better.
- Enjoy the process.

Following is a worksheet you can use to capture your reflections; it also includes further directions.

+++++

Designing Your Future, Now

Designing your future now begins with stepping back into the future. Imagine what your life will look like in 10 years if you have lived your vision and accomplished what you have set out to do.

Use all of your senses to *see* the best possible future for yourself in the various domains of your life. The point is to express your vision in each domain as if it has already happened and you have unlimited resources to create this new reality. What is your life like in 10 years after everything has gone as well as it possibly could? You have worked hard and succeeded at accomplishing your life goals.

See this as the realization and actualization of your dreams and true potential. The more detailed you can describe how life feels and what it is like, the better. Enjoy this process. If there are other, more relevant domains that are not listed, please add them so you see your life fully represented in the future.

Using the present tense as you write, answer as though your statements are true as of this very moment, beginning with the following:

In 10 years, this is who I am. . .

Family

____

____

____

____

____

____

____

____

Significant Other

____

____

____

____

____

____

____

____

Friends

Passions, Callings, and Career

Enjoyment, Travel, and Leisure Time

Contribution (Think about this in the broadest context: What do you have to give? Who do you want to positively influence?)

Community Involvement

Lifestyle

Financial (What role does money play in your life? How does your wealth serve as a tool toward fulfillment in this life?)

I recommend each family member does this exercise separately first, giving each person time and space to reflect on their own vision. Next, you and your partner can share your visions with one another and facilitate a discussion of where your visions are aligned and where you might see your futures differently. Then you re-do the exercise, co-designing the future you will work toward. From there, you share your visions as a family, listening to the futures each person hopes to create. Finally, you can do this exercise as a family unit to design a future that you are all aligned with and inspired by.

+++++

Sharing provides family members the following opportunities:

- to listen to what would be ideal for each person
- to support each other in attaining this desired future
- to build alignment and commitment among family members
- to create a shared future you want to live into together
- to point out where work may need to be done to get from the messages of the past, to the desired messages of the future

This exercise is never fully complete, and it works best when used iteratively, a work in progress to continue building upon. Doing it every three to five years allows you to reflect on what has shifted for you as individuals and as a family and to continue to examine how you can leverage your various capitals to bridge the gap between where you are and where you want to be.

This exercise is incredibly powerful and has been the impetus for significant pivots in the lives of individuals, couples, and families, and for some it has been life changing. Some clients switch professions or move. I even had one family that decided to sail around the world for a year as a result of doing this exercise.

Go ahead, I dare you to do this exercise and allow yourself to really see, with all of your senses, the best future you can possibly imagine! I'd love to hear what you create.

Additional Resources

Dennis Jaffe, *Borrowed from Your Grandchildren: The Evolution of 100-Year Family Enterprises* (New York: Wiley, 2020).

Jacob Needleman, *Money and the Meaning of Life* (New York: Doubleday, 1994).

Georg Simmel, *The Philosophy of Money*, trans. David Frisby (New York: Routledge, 2011).

Biography

Jamie Traeger-Muney, Ph.D., is the founder of the Wealth Legacy Group, a team of coaches specializing in the emotional impact of money, wealth, and privilege. She works with individuals, couples, and multigenerational families, helping them to concretize their values, develop a vision for their future, and create sound governance.

Jamie co-authored *Social Impact in 100-Year Family Businesses: How Family Values Drive Sustainability through Philanthropy, Impact Investing, and CSR* as well as part of *Borrowed from Your Grandchildren.*

Jamie's experience as a second-generation stakeholder and family foundation board member, combined with her expertise in wealth psychology, has given her a unique sensitivity to issues surrounding the intergenerational family dynamics of affluence.

SECTION 2

BECOMING A LEARNING FAMILY

Many people think of learning as something that happens only in class (or, maybe, by Zoom) in the context of formal educational programs. One of the most important developments in the field of family wealth in the last decade is the realization that families who succeed over time do not limit their understanding of learning; instead, they make conscious choices to become learning organizations.

Dennis Jaffe starts off this section with a chapter devoted to helping you learn about yourselves as a family, through comparison with global families who have succeeded over time. Jaffe's assessment—which focuses on three areas: Nurturing the Family, Stewarding the Family Enterprise, and Cultivating Human Capital for the Next Generation—reflects his extensive research into family enterprise success factors. It is a simple way to benchmark your family against these global success stories and identify areas where you want to grow and learn.

The next chapter, Jim Grubman's contribution on "Understanding What Wealth Preparation Really Means," moves us from the macro-level to very specific skills needed to manage financial wealth wisely in a family context. Grubman observes that family members often think they have the requisite skills, without knowing what they don't know. His process connects the roles needed for wealth management with the skills needed to succeed in those roles; it validates the knowledge family members already have while pointing out areas for additional skill development.

Stacy Allred, Joan DiFuria, and Stephen Goldbart then position this work of learning across the developmental stages of an individual life. With their "10x10 Roadmap," family members can pinpoint which of 10 competencies they want to work on, depending on where they are in a 10-part framework of life stages. This is a tool that provides individuals with direction while also allowing a family to map its members' progress together.

Learning can be a path for connecting what is with what can be. That is the path Bart Parrott leads readers on in the next chapter, in which he lays out a simple but powerful set of questions for families to discuss when facing important choices: What's true now? What's possible? What's our plan? This process of questioning and discovery can apply to choices all the way from the selection of an advisor to momentous decisions about selling a business.

The next two chapters bring the subject of learning back to a more familiar, curricular framework. First, Ruth Steverlynck and Greg Burrows give readers a structure through which to understand how your family could learn best, all the way from identifying the goal of the learning to determining what sorts of platforms or styles best suit family members' learning needs. In the next chapter, Kirby Rosplock offers readers direction in creating their own wealth education plans, to help family members gain specific money skills.

Finally, in a chapter reprinted from the first *Wealth of Wisdom* volume, Christian Stewart gives readers a plethora of tools to help their families become learning organizations. These tools range from reflective exercises for each individual family member to exercises that allow the family as a whole to chart its future path and understand better the stories that have defined its journey thus far. Stewart also summarizes exercises families can use to promote a "thinking environment" and to manage difficult conversations.

CHAPTER 11

Benchmarking Your Family Against Successful Global Families

Dennis Jaffe

This assessment tool offers your family a "snapshot" to discover how much you engage in practices identified as important to sustaining your family enterprise across generations and using your family wealth to make a difference in people's lives. It focuses on best practices in three areas—the family, the family enterprise, and the human capital of the next generation.

These practices were developed in several research projects over the past decade.[1] By using this assessment with members of your family, and comparing your responses and perceptions, you can organize a productive family conversation for how to develop your family governance to respond to emerging challenges, inside the family and in the business environment.

This assessment explores and compares family members' perceptions of governance practices that span the interconnected worlds of family, business/finance, and personal development. A successful family enterprise experiences a degree of balance in all of these areas; it would not be seen as fully successful if any one of these areas were troubled. For example, if the business produces wealth but the family fragments, or young people grow up collectively unhappy, unproductive, and unfulfilled, then the family is not likely to view itself as successful. Successful families rely on best practices from each of these areas or pathways—family, business, and personal development.[2]

The assessment looks at differences in perception among family members. While one would think it would be clear whether or not a family used a particular

[1]A summary can be viewed in the paper *Three Pathways to Evolutionary Survival: Best Practices for Multi-Generational Enterprise*, published by Wise Counsel Research in 2012.

[2]Our definition of best practice owes a debt of gratitude to a 2003/2004 study, *Eight Proactive Practices of Successful Families* by Amy Braden and JP Morgan Chase. This study covered many themes and practices but ultimately identified eight critical success factors that were diffusing globally and considered important for the future.

practice, in fact there are different perceptions about whether something is done by the family and how important it is. This tool asks each family member whether or not a practice is used regularly by their extended family and how important it is. The purpose is more than just noting the practices used by the family; it also is the basis for a discussion of the usefulness and importance of each practice for the future.

Evolving Practices for Family Enterprise Resiliency

Over generations, the small number of surviving enterprising families grows from a single family and business to several. The skills and practices that enabled them to succeed in the first generation must give way to new practices that align the interests of multiple family owners and multiple business and financial entities. The story of family enterprise evolution over generations is of increasing complexity, continual evolution, and change. Dealing with this expansion and change means that they need to evolve internal governance practices that enable the family to manage the emerging realities.

Most families do not adopt these practices and do not survive the generational transition. Participants in this study represent the exception to the rule and go against the tide of dissipation and fragmentation.

The search for excellence and the desire to achieve this in all aspects of living have created a hunger for reports of best practices that can lead there. There are best practices for individuals, for leaders, for businesses, and for families, and they take many forms. Often, they are not actually practices but states of mind or values that are well intended and clearly important but are not explicit in relation to practice and hard to define in terms of impact.

The concept of best practice is also somewhat exclusive—we want to see a relatively small and manageable number of practices, not a long list, in order to define the essence of family enterprise success. The practices in this study are all anchored in shared family behavior, so a family can understand and clearly report whether or not they use each practice. While each practice appears to be specific and clear, in fact, within a family, different family members may have different perceptions about the presence and use of each practice.

Three Pathways to Success

Beginning with the assumption that success for a multigenerational family enterprise is more than financial, we look at the common models in the field. These models begin with the principle that a family enterprise is concerned not just with financial returns, but with harmony in personal and family relationships and in the success and development of their children who inherit responsibility for and ownership of the family enterprise.

A successful family must balance three sometimes competing pathways:

- Harmony and connection to each other as a family
- Financial and business prosperity
- Personal growth and development of their next generation

In conversation with consultants and families around the world and from the literature and reviewing the materials shared at industry conferences, six critical practices emerged that are found within each of the pathways to success (for a list of the six practices within each of the three pathways, see the end of this chapter).

Pathway I: Nurture the Family

The first-generation business founder accumulates substantial wealth that is passed on within the family. While the second-generation heirs grow up together, each second-generation sibling begins his or her own family, and the third-generation cousins live separately and may not share the family heritage as clearly. For a family to remain together as a family enterprise, the members of several families in several generations must believe that there is a reason for them to remain as partners. They must have a common vision as an extended family that makes them want to work together. In addition, as partners and shared owners, they need to develop trust in each other, spend time together, develop personal relationships across families, and develop a common set of values. The first pathway is about how the family actively builds connection and shared purpose over generations, fighting the natural tendency for family members to move into separate worlds and greater disconnection.

Pathway II: Steward the Family Enterprises

The extended family has not just a family legacy, but a shared family business and/or several family financial enterprises that they own together. The business may be large and public and have a high profile in the community. As owners, family members are identified with the business and have personal expectations of what the business will provide and their role and relationship to it.

As there are more and more family members who are, or expect to become, owners, there must be clear rules for how to make decisions and work together to operate their financial and business entities. The family needs a plan for how they will grow and diversify and how the rewards and resources of their family enterprises will be distributed. The roles, responsibilities, and authority of each person need to be clear so that each family member feels that he or she is treated fairly. The family must organize itself for the business of the family and develop strategies to manage conflict. The practices in this pathway help the family make decisions that preserve both family harmony and financial returns.

Pathway III: Cultivate Human Capital for the Next Generation

The most unique element of a multigenerational family enterprise is that a new generation of young people grows up in the family, feeling a connection and an expectation to share in its legacy. The young people are the future. They need to be prepared for their role within the family and the business and to learn how to work with each other. The successful multigenerational family enterprise must actively develop the next generation. The practices in Pathway III represent a set of governance and family activities that encourage the personal development and preparation of each and every next-generation family member.

Do These Practices Actually Make a Difference for a Family?

Given so many unique and individual factors facing a family, where a single misstep can lead to a family-wide wealth collapse, it is hard to imagine how one would evaluate the differential effects of things like a family council, an independent board, shareholders or employment agreement, a next-generation education program, or other family activity. We might reasonably imagine that different specific practices will have differential impacts on different types of families and family situations. One practice may not be the universal "best" for all. But reflecting on where your own family stands in relation to these practices is a good first step in benchmarking where you are and where you want to go.

Using the Assessment with Your Family

You can complete it yourself, with your own view of your family, or several family members can complete it and compare responses. Different family members—having different places in the family—view the family differently. You may not agree on the presence of a practice in your family or on its need for the future. That can lead to a productive discussion, not argument.

Your responses represent your **perceptions** of the degree to which your family has adopted, or needs to adopt, each practice.

This sets the stage for a **Family Conversation** about how your family can grow, develop, and prepare for the succession and stewardship of the next generation. If you are a family advisor, you can use this tool to assess areas of strength and those that need development in the future.

If several members of your family complete this inventory independently, they can compare responses in a Family Conversation to explore areas of agreement, and where scores or perceptions do not agree. Then, as a family, you can proceed to develop a **Strategic Family Roadmap**, to design and implement the practices that enable your family to succeed across generations.

Best Practices for Multigenerational Family Enterprise

For each practice, indicate in the ***Current*** *column, on a scale of 0–3 (0 = our family does not do that; 1 = we have talked about this, 2 = we are beginning to do this, and 3 = we utilize this practice in our family), the degree you see your family using that practice at this time.*

In the ***Future*** *column indicate how important you believe this practice will be for your family to develop that practice in the next three to five years (from 0 = very low to 3 = very high).*

Practice	Current	Future
Pathway I: Nurture the Family		
1.1 Clear, compelling family purpose and direction		
1.2 Opportunities for extended family to get to know each other		
1.3 Climate of family openness, trust, and communication		
1.4 Regular family meetings as a family council		
1.5 Sharing and respect for family history and legacy		
1.6 Shared family philanthropic and social engagement		

Practice	Current	Future
Pathway II: Steward the Family Enterprises		
2.1 Strategic plan for family wealth and enterprise development		
2.2 Active, diverse, empowered board guiding each enterprise		
2.3 Transparency about financial information and business decisions		
2.4 Explicit and shared shareholder agreements about family assets		
2.5 Policies that support diversification and entrepreneurial ventures		
2.6 Exit and distribution policies for individual shareholder liquidity		
Pathway III: Cultivate Human Capital for the Next Generation		
3.1 Employment policies about working in family enterprises		
3.2 Agreement on values about family money and wealth		
3.3 Support and encourage to develop next-generation leadership		
3.4 Empower individuals to seek personal fulfillment and life purpose		
3.5 Opportunities to become involved in family governance activities		
3.6 Teach age-appropriate financial skills to young family members		

Additional Resources

Dennis Jaffe, *Borrowed from Your Grandchildren: The Evolution of 100-Year Family Enterprises* (New York: Wiley, 2020).

Dennis Jaffe, *Three Pathways to Evolutionary Survival: Best Practices for Multi-Generational Enterprise* (Milton, MA: Wise Counsel Research, 2012).

Biography

Dr. Dennis Jaffe, a San Francisco–based advisor to families about family business, governance, wealth and philanthropy, is senior research fellow at BanyanGlobal Family Business Advisors. He is author of *Borrowed from Your Grandchildren: The Evolution of 100-Year Family Enterprises; Cross Cultures: How Global Families Negotiate Change across Generations; Stewardship in Your Family Enterprise: Developing Responsible Family Leadership across Generations;* and *Working with the Ones You Love.* His global insights have led to teaching or consulting engagements in Asia, Europe, the Middle East, and Latin America. The Family Firm Institute awarded him the 2017 International Award for service, and in 2005 he received the Beckhard Award for service to the field. In 2020 he was awarded a special commendation as an individual thought leader in the field of wealth management by the Family Wealth Report. He has a BA degree in philosophy, MA in management, and Ph.D. in sociology, all from Yale University, and professor emeritus of organizational systems and psychology at Saybrook University in San Francisco.

CHAPTER 12

Understanding the True Goals of Wealth Preparation

James Grubman

It was the family's first family meeting, and naturally, everyone was a bit nervous. They were trying to grasp the implications of how Mom and Dad's chain of 13 "friendly local" home improvement stores across three states was bought several months ago for a staggering sum by a national conglomerate. The parents, in their late 60s, and their three adult children knew there was a lot to learn, but they all admitted to some confusion about the big picture: What was coming ahead? What did they need to know, and why? What will the young grandchildren need to be prepared for? It all felt very overwhelming. That was when I, as the facilitator, went to the front of the meeting room, set up a flipchart, and pulled out a marker. I asked one question and then, ready to write down their answers, I waited.

Families with new wealth often know they will need education about finances, estate planning, trusts, working with advisors, and a bewildering array of other tasks. Unfortunately, it usually just feels like a constant barrage of things to do in their new affluent life. Helping families think through a strategic plan, a big-picture framework, calms the process by integrating all the component tasks. The following exercise often dramatically puts things in perspective, unifies everything, and commonly reveals what these "immigrants to wealth" do not yet understand about preparing for wealth. It is, to say the least, eye-opening.

The Setup

Ready with a flipchart and with at least two generations of the family present—usually Generation 1 (G1) and G2—I ask the family to consider the following question: "**What are the roles and responsibilities that people have in adult life?**" I put no constraints on the task and don't go into much detail, since the question seems relatively straightforward. I might clarify a little bit if someone asks for further explanation, but I don't want to say anything too leading. It seems like an easy exercise, so people don't usually ask a lot.

Family members then begin to list obvious roles and relationships. I write them down in a vertical column on the left side of the flipchart, perhaps in two columns if the list gets long:

husband/wife/spouse
parent
brother/sister/sibling
adult child
employee
employer
coworker
member of community
member of a congregation
friend

And so on. A fairly complete list usually develops as people chime in, then they start to slow down as they run out of ideas. I might push them a bit about things omitted but only in standard areas. At some point when they seem satisfied with the list—usually with about 10 or 12 roles and responsibilities in it—I ask, "Is that all?" They say, yes.

The Hook

I then draw a vertical line down the middle of the flipchart. At the top of the right-hand column, I write down some role related to what I know about the family, the wealth, or perhaps the family business, for example:

Owner

I then start to add others, gradually, with the family's help:

Shareholder
Trust creator
Trust beneficiary
Creator of estate planning affecting others
Client of advisory firm/family office
Overseer of advisors in their activities
Member of foundation or contributor to charitable fund
Director on one or more boards
Member of family council
Family leader

We go through and add all the *extra* roles and responsibilities family members have when one is wealthy. This stimulates new discussion and brainstorming where people think up things like "Educator of Next Gens." Sometimes, someone will think of a role or responsibility and another family member will say, "I didn't know that," or "What is that?" We either explain it quickly or we park that for later discussion.

The Light Bulb Goes On

By the end of this second part, there is usually another column equal to or longer than the first set. I have the family sit and ponder the full list for a moment. I then lead a discussion on the following points:

- Coming from general society, it's easy to forget or not know the extra roles you have with wealth. It's not just about having money; it's all the extra things you have to know and do and teach that distinguish life with wealth. Many younger family members don't know about some of the roles, so it is especially instructive for them.
- Once cued by me, the family usually recognizes the second list. Yet, a crucial element of the exercise is the family's emotional experience of not even having thought of it themselves until I pointed it out. It's as if those roles were behind some curtain when thinking about adult life. It is a visceral demonstration that family members are still very much "middle-class people" with only a veneer of "wealthy person" overlaid on top.
- During the exercise I watch the wealth creator(s) to see if they have already grasped this or not, in how they themselves participate. If they were ahead of the family and could see where this was going, it is illuminating for them to watch the rest of the family go through this exercise. They are usually pleased to see the light bulbs go on in heads around the room. If, however, they were with everyone else in forgetting about the list of wealth roles, the exercise is a vivid reminder they were blind to it as well. This is often shocking for them to realize.
- Once we deal with the reactions and insights of the family members in the room, we then brainstorm how the family's future "natives" of wealth can be much more attuned to the full set of wealth roles, compared to the "immigrants" in G1 and G2. It is another visceral, experiential way to drive the point home, underscoring the importance of Next Gen education. The family realizes that preparing themselves and the upcoming G3s is absolutely crucial. Otherwise, the G3s in particular will not know about, understand, or fulfill these multiple roles well. This energizes the family and puts financial and family education on a much better footing. Plus, family members who themselves were overwhelmed in the current exercise realize how much education they need as well. The family embarks on creating mechanisms to lead the way for themselves and for others (including spouses who marry in).

Throughout this exercise, I weave in the main purpose for preparation of the family, present or future: **To foster good decision-makers in all the roles and responsibilities they will have in adult life**. Each role or responsibility has multiple decisions connected to it, so being adept at the role means being able to make good decisions within it.

Which Families Do Best with This Exercise?

Experiential learning helps this exercise open the eyes of G1 and G2 about two things: (1) the added complexity of wealth compared to the economic world they came from, and (2) the need for education and preparation in so many areas of the family's new life together. The exercise is less effective with G3s and beyond if the family has done a decent job of creating family education or actively discussing preparation at its family assemblies. However, it can be good for a multigenerational family in G3 or beyond who has only run a family business as upper-middle-class people and not had a lot of liquidity directly in their hands. Near or just after a major liquidity event, the family may still see themselves as upper-middle-class people and be less experienced with the complex roles of significant wealth. The exercise can be instructive to show them how life is about to change.

If it seems the impact of the learning fades over time, I refer back to this exercise in subsequent family meetings to remind the family about the necessity and value of preparing each rising generation.

Useful Action Steps for Families

1. Retain the list of general and wealth roles. Incorporate it into the family meeting notes for the future of the family.
2. In subsequent family meetings, have some members lead the family in a deeper dive about the exercise: Were any roles not included in the final list? Which roles are broadly known and understood? What roles are less well known or confusing to many members? What competencies are needed for the major roles most family members will have? Some families derive great benefit from digging into the exercise on their own.
3. Form a family education committee or workgroup devoted to the learning mechanisms needed for the present and the future. Define the resources and processes the family will use, first to educate current family members and then for future members, including spouses and partners who will join the family. Most family education focuses on a few core domains—financial skills, ownership education, understanding governance, and estate planning/trusts. Families can start with these and expand later.
4. Some families take this exercise a step further by organizing likely roles according to category of family member, such as bloodline owner, non-bloodline spouse unlikely to have ownership, trust beneficiary, parents who have to do estate planning, etc. This matrix then guides the education committee in its mission to target education to the appropriate family constituencies.

Finally, the exercise is very useful in building understanding between G1s and G2s about the transition in the family from those to come *to* wealth (the "immigrants") and those who will come *from* wealth (the "natives"). Newcomers to wealth from lesser economic circumstances have either not learned certain roles or may have slowly learned things along the way, sometimes self-taught and sometimes learning from advisors. Those who are raised with wealth commonly prefer being proactive about learning. Roles and responsibilities are known elements the family can prepare for, using the resources of the family. This shift from reactively learning-as-you-go to proactively preparing in advance marks one of the central adaptations families must implement across generations. This exercise is a great method for starting the family down that path.

Additional Resources

Joline Godfrey, "Fundamentals of Financial Skills," In *Raising Financially Fit Kids,* rev. ed. (Berkeley, CA: Ten Speed Press, 2013).

Josh Baron and Rob Lachenauer, "Fundamentals of Owner Education and Family Business Roles," In *The HBR Family Business Handbook* (Boston MA: Harvard Business Review Press, 2021).

Hartley Goldstone, James E. Hughes Jr., and Keith Whitaker, "Fundamentals of Trusts, Trustees, and Beneficiary Roles," in *Family Trusts: A Guide for Beneficiaries, Trustees, Trust Protectors, and Trust Creators* (Hoboken, NJ: Bloomberg Press, 2015).

Jennifer Risher, "Growing into the Responsibilities of Wealth," in *We Need to Talk: A Memoir about Wealth* (Pasadena, CA: Xeno Press, 2020).

Biography

Dr. Jim Grubman is a senior consultant to multigenerational families and their advisors about the issues arising around wealth. He has over 40 years' experience in healthcare and financial psychology as a practitioner, educator, author, researcher, and speaker. He is the author of *Strangers in Paradise: How Families Adapt to Wealth Across Generations* and has published widely and been quoted extensively in various media. Jim has been recognized, along with his long-time collaborator, Dr. Dennis Jaffe, with the "Outstanding Contribution to Thought Leadership" award by the 2021 Family Wealth Report awards. His global consulting practice, Family Wealth Consulting, is based in the Boston, Massachusetts, area.

CHAPTER 13

Advancing Flourishing: A 10 x 10 Learning Roadmap

Stacy Allred, Joan DiFuria, and Stephen Goldbart

The number-one goal of successful, wealthy families is to foster thriving individuals and build a connected family. Financial wealth can be an amplifier that leads to flourishing or languishing. It can help to build well-being and self-esteem at each life stage or magnify ill-being and the potential of feeling lost. One way or the other, significant financial capital will have an impact.

LANGUISHING[1]	FLOURISHING[2]
Lack of well-being	Peak of well-being
Lack of motivation and self-esteem	Motivation/self-esteem
Inhibited by passivity and lack of purpose	Strong sense of purpose
Reticence to learn and grow	Meaningful contribution
Sense of stagnation and emptiness	Willingness to learn and grow
Feels like muddling through days	Positive relationships

> "My mission in life is not merely to survive, but to thrive; and to do so with some passion, some compassion, some humor, and some style."
>
> —*Maya Angelou*

As family advisors, we appreciate how each family is unique and different in their own right. But over the years that we've been helping families navigate wealth, we've experienced strikingly similar questions and concerns[3] of wealth creators:

[1]The term *languishing* was coined by sociologist Corey Keyes and popularized during the COVID-19 pandemic by Adam Grant's article "There's a Name for the Blah You're Felling: It's Called Languishing," *New York Times*, updated December 3, 2021.

[2]The definition of *flourishing* continues to evolve. The founder of Positive Psychology, Martin Seligman, defines flourishing as follows: PERMA: Positive emotions, Engagement, Relationships, Meaning and Accomplishment.

[3]Cognitive scientist and author Douglas Hofstadter developed the idea that many problems share a "conceptual skeleton."

- How much do we give our children so that the money doesn't undermine their motivation, well-being, or self-esteem?
- How can we live a life of purpose and meaning?
- How might we minimize the risk and divisiveness that money can bring to family unity?
- How can we steward our resources, finding the balance between personal enjoyment and sharing?

How Can Families Actively Navigate the Impact and Consequences of Wealth and Life Choices to Thrive?

In seeking to help families answer these questions, we created a comprehensive framework for family members of all ages to build capacity to effectively manage wealth and life choices.

The "10 × 10" roadmap comprises 10 core competencies across 10 life stages. It addresses financial, emotional, social, health, and wellness competencies required at specific life stages and sets a path for building these competencies.

This roadmap helps families protect against negative or destructive family cultures that can lead to indecisive, unmotivated, and entitled children. Instead, an active, ongoing engagement in the 10 × 10 Learning Roadmap cultivates life skills and competencies that help family members reach their true potential—and build strong learning families in the process.

The 10 × 10 is a framework for a comprehensive approach to planning and wealth management. It provides families and the advisors who serve them

- a self-authored approach that allows individuals to choose their own opportunities for learning (bolstering intrinsic motivation);
- a pathway to address needs and wants of both individuals and the family as a whole; and
- a catalyst to clarify important values and to define financial *and* lifestyle objectives.

10 Core Competencies across 10 Life Stages

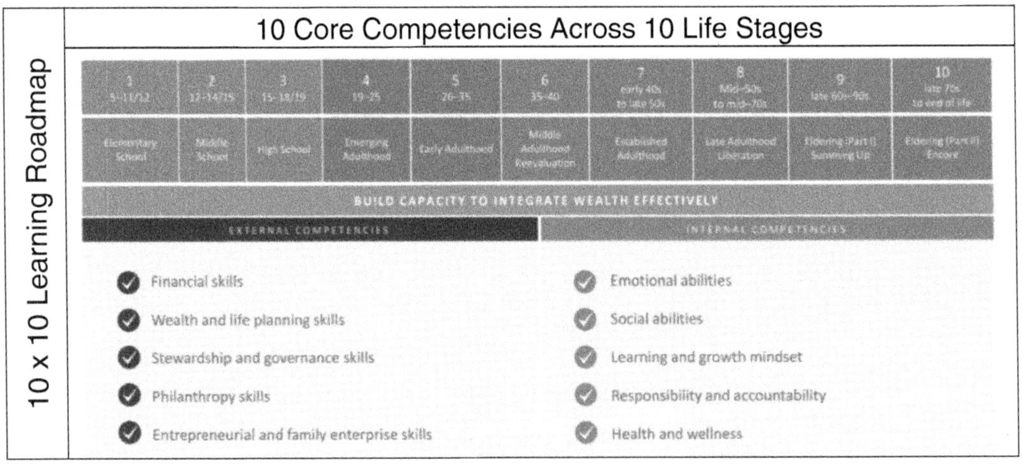

Ten Core Competencies

This 10 × 10 learning roadmap[4] comprises **five external** and **five internal competencies**, exercised over the course of life, from childhood to senior years. Each competency is paired with life stage specific activities and milestones.

The external competencies are the skills necessary for the development of a capable, educated person who gets things done (e.g., the knowledge, skills, and credentials we acquire). They are specific skill sets needed for ever increasing levels of responsibility in whatever pathway is chosen by each family member. Our understanding of the external competencies arises from work in the areas of leadership development, financial and estate planning, and family wealth consulting.

The internal competencies are the skills necessary for the development of a person who has a mature personality and well-being. These abilities surface, develop, and are exercised throughout a life-span. They are at the core of family members who have a solid sense of "character" . . . that special combination of emotional intelligence, social engagement, responsibility, and wellness. Our understanding of the internal competencies is culled from research in the disciplines of emotional intelligence, positive psychology, and adult development.

Working in synergy, these 10 core competencies

- build and elevate the overall capacities of every family member, enhancing flourishing, and protecting against languishing, and
- foster a more connected and resilient family unit.

Using the 10 x 10

The following chart will help you start the journey step by step and help you use the roadmap and move from awareness to action. Getting started is key! To paraphrase Isaac Newton, an object in motion tends to stay in motion.

To give you a taste of what choosing activities looks like, following is a **sample** of one activity per competency in each stage of life. *Please note:* This is approximately one quarter of the activities found in the full 10 × 10 learning roadmap. As you gain momentum and if you have the desire to go deeper, you can work on more than one activity at a time or dive into the full model.[5]

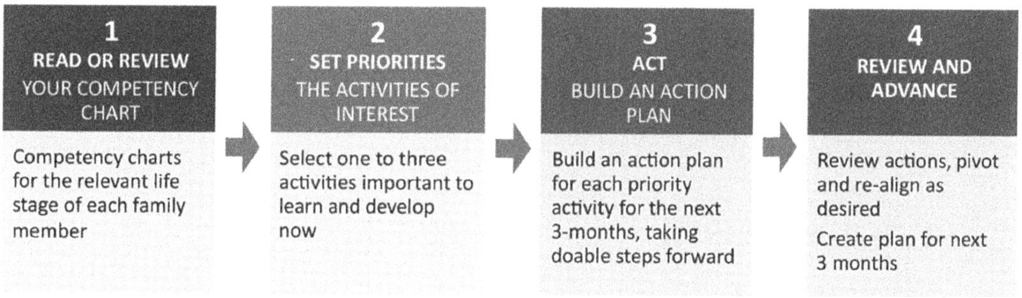

[4]For additional detail on the 10 × 10 Learning Roadmap, including the 10 key elements for each of the 10 competencies, tailored to wealth, see www.10 x 10LearningRoadmap.com or "Building a Strong and Connected Family of Wealth," *Trusts & Estates Magazine*, December 2021.

[5]For the full model, see www.10x10LearningRoadMap.com.

Stage 1 Elementary School

Ages 5–11/12

5 External Competencies

Financial Skills	Start an allowance, allocating parts to saving, spending and sharing
Wealth and Life Planning Skills	Explore different career paths through stories, movies, in-person experiences, etc.
Stewardship and Governance Skills	Focus on family life and financial values through role models and dialogue (e.g., family story illustrating work ethic)
Philanthropy Skills	Leverage online giving by supporting relatable causes
Entrepreneurial and Family Enterprise Skills	Start the practice of earning through a neighborhood activity, such as a lemonade stand

MILESTONES
Develop an understanding of saving, spending and sharing money

5 Internal Competencies

Emotional Abilities	Label and manage emotions, learn to set goals and be patient (e.g., delaying gratification)
Social Abilities	Develop interpersonal skills; establish friendships around common interests and activities
Learning and Growth Mindset	Foster interest in learning and enjoyment by taking on and completing small projects
Responsibility and Accountability	Offer experiences that help teach self control vs. acting on impulses (e.g., taking initiative and following through)
Health and Wellness	Make healthy food choices, exercise and practice self-control

MILESTONES
Experience a sense of accomplishment in learning activities and personal development

1	AGES 5–11/12	ELEMENTARY SCHOOL
2	AGES 12–14	MIDDLE SCHOOL
3	AGES 15–18/19	HIGH SCHOOL
4	AGES 19–25	EMERGING ADULTHOOD
5	AGES 26–35	EARLY ADULTHOOD
6	AGES 35–40	ESTABLISHED ADULTHOOD
7	EARLY 40s TO LATE 50s	MID-ADULTHOOD
8	MID-50s TO MID-70s	LATE ADULTHOOD
9	LATE 60s INTO 90s	ELDERING
10	LATE 70s TO END OF LIFE	ELDERING PART II

Ages listed are merely suggestions. Individuals may proceed through the stages faster or slower than ages listed. Authored by: Stacy Allred, MST and Money, Meaning & Choices Institute: Joan DiFuria, MFT and Stephen Goldbart, Ph.D.

Stage 2 Middle School
Ages 12–14

5 External Competencies

Financial Skills	Work with a mentor to research companies of interest and choose a few stocks to buy; open a bank account
Wealth and Life Planning Skills	Talk with a parent to develop an elevator speech to questions such as "Are you rich?"
Stewardship and Governance Skills	Look for ways to build shared decision-making skills, such as planning a family vacation within a set budget
Philanthropy Skills	Allocate part of an annual summer vacation to giving back, from a few hours to taking a volunteer vacation
Entrepreneurial and Family Enterprise Skills	Seek out skill-building summer experiences (for example, coding camp, improv classes, business plan competitions)

MILESTONES
Understand the purpose and limits of money; gain real world financial experiences

5 Internal Competencies

Emotional Abilities	Understand other people's perspectives, building the capacity for empathy and sympathy
Social Abilities	Manage increased tensions in social relationships (increased envy, jealousy, guilt related to having money)
Learning and Growth Mindset	Expand learning and new experiences in school and social groups outside the primary family
Responsibility and Accountability	Understand and manage the influence of social media; put a family social media policy in place
Health and Wellness	Recognize the need for privacy and time to relax the mind and body

MILESTONES
Develop abilities to handle personal situations (in and outside of the family)

1 AGES 5–11/12 ELEMENTARY SCHOOL
2 AGES 12–14 MIDDLE SCHOOL
3 AGES 15–18/19 HIGH SCHOOL
4 AGES 19–25 EMERGING ADULTHOOD
5 AGES 26–35 EARLY ADULTHOOD
6 AGES 35–40 ESTABLISHED ADULTHOOD
7 EARLY 40s TO LATE 50s MID-ADULTHOOD
8 MID-50s TO MID-70s LATE ADULTHOOD
9 LATE 60s INTO 90s ELDERING
10 LATE 70s TO END OF LIFE ELDERING PART II

Ages listed are merely suggestions. Individuals may proceed through the stages faster or slower than ages listed. Authored by: Stacy Allred, MST and Money, Meaning & Choices Institute: Joan DiFuria, MFT and Stephen Goldbart, Ph.D.

Stage 3 High School

Ages 15–18/19

5 External Competencies

Financial Skills	Involvement in a big-ticket item (car-buying process); develop a family car-driving policy
Wealth and Life Planning Skills	Discuss and plan for post-high-school life (university, trade school) and handling financial inequities with friends
Stewardship and Governance Skills	Invitation to family meetings to engage thoughts and opinions on family values, education and philanthropic activities
Philanthropy Skills	Increased commitment to local volunteering tied to interests
Entrepreneurial and Family Enterprise Skills	Consider a summer internship (perhaps at a family business) or a job outside the family enterprise

MILESTONES
Experiential learning and growth from the natural consequences of making choices

5 Internal Competencies

Emotional Abilities	Develop an identity that balances a sense of individuality with connection to family and community
Social Abilities	Bolster connection with friends by sharing ideas, feelings, mutual trust and understanding
Learning and Growth Mindset	Seek new experiences and greater independence, both at home and at school
Responsibility and Accountability	Develop personally meaningful moral standards, values and belief systems
Health and Wellness	Navigate physical and psychological changes through self-care (healthy eating, physical exercise and emotional well-being)

MILESTONES
Develop "who I am" and the abilities to make thoughtful and accountable decisions

Click on a life stage to get a quick look at activities for learning and growth, and milestones to achieving core competencies at a specific age.

1 AGES 5–11/12 ELEMENTARY SCHOOL	2 AGES 12–14 MIDDLE SCHOOL	3 AGES 15–18/19 HIGH SCHOOL	4 AGES 19–25 EMERGING ADULTHOOD	5 AGES 26–35 EARLY ADULTHOOD	6 AGES 35–40 ESTABLISHED ADULTHOOD	7 EARLY 40s TO LATE 50s MID-ADULTHOOD	8 MID-50s TO MID-70s LATE ADULTHOOD	9 LATE 60s INTO 90s ELDERING	10 LATE 70s TO END OF LIFE ELDERING PART II

Ages listed are merely suggestions. Individuals may proceed through the stages faster or slower than ages listed. Authored by: Stacy Allred, MST and Money, Meaning & Choices Institute: Joan DiFuria, MFT and Stephen Goldbart, Ph.D.

Stage 4 Emerging Adulthood

Ages 19–25

5 External Competencies

Financial Skills	Develop an annual financial plan for living on a budget while away at school
Wealth and Life Planning Skills	Make and manage young adult lifestyle choices, such as landing a first career job or renting an apartment
Stewardship and Governance Skills	Understand the family philosophy on prenuptial agreements
Philanthropy Skills	Explore opportunities for giving (time and treasure) to personally meaningful causes; join a volunteer group to expand your network and lens
Entrepreneurial and Family Enterprise Skills	Gain clarity on pathway and training for career development (within or outside of the family enterprise)

MILESTONES
Education and life/work experience fuels increased ability to make positive life decisions

5 Internal Competencies

Emotional Abilities	Develop self-confidence and sense of personal agency to live independently from parents
Social Abilities	Learn how to behave in romantic relationships; managing impact of money on close relationships
Learning and Growth Mindset	Strengthen problem-solving skills, including increased awareness of the positive and negative power of money
Responsibility and Accountability	Build self-agency to feel empowered to take on increasing levels of responsibility; set goals and finish what you start
Health and Wellness	Balance wellness practices with the challenges to physical and emotional health caused by lifestyle experimentation

MILESTONES
Enter emerging adulthood with self-confidence, humility and independence

1 AGES 5–11/12 ELEMENTARY SCHOOL
2 AGES 12–14 MIDDLE SCHOOL
3 AGES 15–18/19 HIGH SCHOOL
4 AGES 19–25 EMERGING ADULTHOOD
5 AGES 26–35 EARLY ADULTHOOD
6 AGES 35–40 ESTABLISHED ADULTHOOD
7 EARLY 40s TO LATE 50s MID-ADULTHOOD
8 MID-50s TO MID-70s LATE ADULTHOOD
9 LATE 60s INTO 90s ELDERING
10 LATE 70s TO END OF LIFE ELDERING PART II

Ages listed are merely suggestions. Individuals may proceed through the stages faster or slower than ages listed. Authored by: Stacy Allred, MST and Money, Meaning & Choices Institute: Joan DiFuria, MFT and Stephen Goldbart, Ph.D.

Stage 5

Early Adulthood
Ages 26–35 (as late as 40)

5 External Competencies

Financial Skills	Create strong working relationships with qualified financial advisors; develop a financial and investment plan
Wealth and Life Planning Skills	Develop long-range goals; manage impact of money on romantic partners
Stewardship and Governance Skills	Gain clarity on family financial values and related impact on life decisions (e.g., purchase of a first-time home)
Philanthropy Skills	Determine giving style and interests, causes; making funding decisions, working with peers with similar interests
Entrepreneurial and Family Enterprise Skills	Build leadership skills necessary for desired roles (inside or outside the family enterprise)

MILESTONES
Accept more responsibility in career, family and wealth-related decisions

5 Internal Competencies

Emotional Abilities	Greater importance for stable intimacy and increased ability for self-reflection and taking the long view for life choices
Social Abilities	Expand social circles that provide support and stability, including friends and colleagues
Learning and Growth Mindset	Increase openness to multiple perspectives, including ability to integrate the positives and negatives of financial capital
Responsibility and Accountability	Move toward establishing a "home base" and the selection of a life partner and/or career choices
Health and Wellness	Increase healthy practices that have a direct impact on emotional and physical health in later years

MILESTONES
Make decisions about work and love: solidifying who I am, who I want to be and who I want to be with

1	AGES 5–11/12	ELEMENTARY SCHOOL
2	AGES 12–14	MIDDLE SCHOOL
3	AGES 15–18/19	HIGH SCHOOL
4	AGES 19–25	EMERGING ADULTHOOD
5	AGES 26–35	EARLY ADULTHOOD
6	AGES 35–40	ESTABLISHED ADULTHOOD
7	EARLY 40s TO LATE 50s	MID-ADULTHOOD
8	MID-50s TO MID-70s	LATE ADULTHOOD
9	LATE 60s INTO 90s	ELDERING
10	LATE 70s TO END OF LIFE	ELDERING PART II

Ages listed are merely suggestions. Individuals may proceed through the stages faster or slower than ages listed. Authored by: Stacy Allred, MST and Money, Meaning & Choices Institute: Joan DiFuria, MFT and Stephen Goldbart, Ph.D.

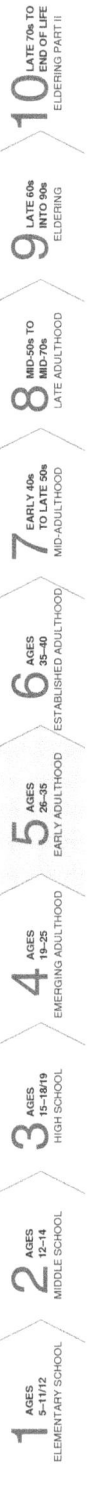

Stage 6

Established Adulthood
Ages 35–40 (as late as 45)

5 External Competencies

Financial Skills	Follow market activities and deepen investment knowledge
Wealth and Life Planning Skills	Put base estate planning documents in place — wills, revocable living trusts, power of attorney for healthcare and property
Stewardship and Governance Skills	Establish education trusts or plans for children (if applicable)
Philanthropy Skills	Invite younger generations to participate in family philanthropy
Entrepreneurial and Family Enterprise Skills	Become a mentor

MILESTONES
Start to share knowledge and experience with younger generations

5 Internal Competencies

Emotional Abilities	Learn to manage the emotional shifts that come with young children at home (if applicable)
Social Abilities	Understand and manage the impact of wealth on raising children (if applicable)
Learning and Growth Mindset	Identify long-term opportunities to stretch your comfort zone; explore "out-of-the-box" activities
Responsibility and Accountability	Increase responsibility and follow through for all domains of living; bolster awareness and reduction of risky behaviors
Health and Wellness	Commit to a health and wellness plan given competing time demands of established adulthood

MILESTONES
Handle the opportunities and challenges of life choices, deepen commitments, managing uncertainty and complexity.

1 AGES 5–11/12 ELEMENTARY SCHOOL
2 AGES 12–14 MIDDLE SCHOOL
3 AGES 15–18/19 HIGH SCHOOL
4 AGES 19–25 EMERGING ADULTHOOD
5 AGES 26–35 EARLY ADULTHOOD
6 AGES 35–40 ESTABLISHED ADULTHOOD
7 EARLY 40s TO LATE 50s MID-ADULTHOOD
8 MID-50s TO MID-70s LATE ADULTHOOD
9 LATE 60s INTO 90s ELDERING
10 LATE 70s TO END OF LIFE ELDERING PART II

Ages listed are merely suggestions. Individuals may proceed through the stages faster or slower than ages listed. Authored by: Stacy Allred, MST and Money, Meaning & Choices Institute: Joan DiFuria, MFT and Stephen Goldbart, Ph.D.

Stage 7 Middle Adulthood

Early 40s to late 50s

5 External Competencies

Financial Skills	Deploy a rigorous financial plan; participate in quarterly investment reviews
Wealth and Life Planning Skills	Planning for change at mid-life (e.g., career, travel, lifestyle, launching young adults)
Stewardship and Governance Skills	Collaboratively develop shared family decision-making (e.g., use of family vacation home, use of annual exclusion gifts)
Philanthropy Skills	Expand giving, elevating strategy and impact (increase alliance networks, involve family members)
Entrepreneurial and Family Enterprise Skills	Serve as a role model in the family and the community

MILESTONES
Share resources with your larger family and community

5 Internal Competencies

Emotional Abilities	Reevaluation: Assess life priorities and choices in the face of increased awareness of aging
Social Abilities	Seek and deepen involvement in personal and professional relationships, including support of close friends in the event of work or marital change
Learning and Growth Mindset	Focus on ability to forecast opportunities and challenges, with an expanded perspective on the complexities of life choices
Responsibility and Accountability	Guide rising generation in becoming mature, responsible and capable individuals
Health and Wellness	Optimize health and make best use of time and energy

MILESTONES
"Top of my game or ready to change": Deepen or end key relationships in work or love. Guide and launch rising generation.

1	2	3	4	5	6	7	8	9	10
AGES 5–11/12	AGES 12–14	AGES 15–18/19	AGES 19–25	AGES 26–35	AGES 35–40	EARLY 40s TO LATE 50s	MID-50s TO MID-70s	LATE 60s INTO 90s	LATE 70s TO END OF LIFE
ELEMENTARY SCHOOL	MIDDLE SCHOOL	HIGH SCHOOL	EMERGING ADULTHOOD	EARLY ADULTHOOD	ESTABLISHED ADULTHOOD	MID-ADULTHOOD	LATE ADULTHOOD	ELDERING	ELDERING PART II

Ages listed are merely suggestions. Individuals may proceed through the stages faster or slower than ages listed. Authored by: Stacy Allred, MST and Money, Meaning & Choices Institute: Joan DiFuria, MFT and Stephen Goldbart, Ph.D.

Stage 8 Late Adulthood

Mid-50s to mid-70s (typically late 50s to early 70s)

5 External Competencies

Financial Skills	Elevate financial knowledge and skills in order to review and make long-term decisions
Wealth and Life Planning Skills	Engage in new learning pursuits and hobbies
Stewardship and Governance Skills	Continue wealth transfer, with thoughtful gifting of personal items shared with stories and dialogue
Philanthropy Skills	Continue building collaboration with children and grandchildren as active participants in philanthropy
Entrepreneurial and Family Enterprise Skills	Support career development within the family business for the rising generation

MILESTONES
Making long-term decisions about distributions to family, philanthropy and future generations

5 Internal Competencies

Emotional Abilities	Deepen wisdom, including comfort with oneself — at ease and empowered with one's wealth, identity and impact of aging
Social Abilities	Seek meaningful and purpose-driven social activities; be more open and experimental in relationships
Learning and Growth Mindset	Focus attention on learning that enhances life enjoyment and fosters greater sense of meaning
Responsibility and Accountability	Understand the impact of wealth on future generations and create governance to minimize the risks of passing on assets
Health and Wellness	Increase attention to health maintenance, staying active and engaged and other wellness practices

MILESTONES
Liberation: Reevaluation of life priorities, with emphasis on quality of life.
Confronting what one can and cannot control; greater focus on well-being and legacy.

1	2	3	4	5	6	7	8	9	10
AGES 5–11/12	AGES 12–14	AGES 15–18/19	AGES 19–25	AGES 26–35	AGES 35–40	EARLY 40s TO LATE 50s	MID-50s TO MID-70s	LATE 60s INTO 90s	LATE 70s TO END OF LIFE
ELEMENTARY SCHOOL	MIDDLE SCHOOL	HIGH SCHOOL	EMERGING ADULTHOOD	EARLY ADULTHOOD	ESTABLISHED ADULTHOOD	MID-ADULTHOOD	LATE ADULTHOOD	ELDERING	ELDERING PART II

Ages listed are merely suggestions. Individuals may proceed through the stages faster or slower than ages listed. Authored by: Stacy Allred, MST and Money, Meaning & Choices Institute: Joan DiFuria, MFT and Stephen Goldbart, Ph.D.

Stage 9

Eldering Part I
Late 60s into 90s (typically late 60s through 80s)

5 External Competencies

Financial Skills	Engage in a financial "fire drill" with trusted family members and advisors; ensure significant other has necessary skills
Wealth and Life Planning Skills	Determine if you have the right network to develop and access meaningful opportunities for the next chapter
Stewardship and Governance Skills	Address unresolved conflict; revisit estate and gift planning and issues with current/future roles of family members
Philanthropy Skills	Document and communicate intentions for giving to promote deep family understanding; make legacy gifts
Entrepreneurial and Family Enterprise Skills	Share transition and succession plan with the rising generation and key stakeholders

MILESTONES
Stewarding succession and legacy: sharing your estate plan, mentor and transition

5 Internal Competencies

Emotional Abilities	Tend to unfinished emotional business, reframe the story to end on a better/more complete note; express gratitude and love
Social Abilities	Handle loss of peers and others by grieving without caving into despair
Learning and Growth Mindset	Continue to impart wisdom and experience with humility and open-mindedness
Responsibility and Accountability	Community: Increase participation in local/global issues, with money and time
Health and Wellness	Accept and manage some loss of physical and mental functioning and the passing of important relationships

MILESTONES
Make the moments count: Impart lessons learned with humility and grace; tell your story

1 AGES 5–11/12 ELEMENTARY SCHOOL	2 AGES 12–14 MIDDLE SCHOOL	3 AGES 15–18/19 HIGH SCHOOL	4 AGES 19–25 EMERGING ADULTHOOD	5 AGES 26–35 EARLY ADULTHOOD	6 AGES 35–40 ESTABLISHED ADULTHOOD	7 EARLY 40s TO LATE 50s MID-ADULTHOOD	8 MID-50s TO MID-70s LATE ADULTHOOD	9 LATE 60s INTO 90s ELDERING	10 LATE 70s TO END OF LIFE ELDERING PART II

Ages listed are merely suggestions. Individuals may proceed through the stages faster or slower than ages listed. Authored by: Stacy Allred, MST and Money, Meaning & Choices Institute: Joan DiFuria, MFT and Stephen Goldbart, Ph.D.

Stage 10 Eldering Part II

Late 70s to end of life

5 External Competencies

Financial Skills	Identify and mitigate financial risks, including potential cognitive decline; develop a plan and discuss with family and advisors
Wealth and Life Planning Skills	Take a fresh look at how you wish to spend time: self, relationships, productivity and community
Stewardship and Governance Skills	Continue dialogue: How will the rising generation fulfill their responsibility for wise and thoughtful use of what has been given?
Philanthropy Skills	Document family giving history and share with and mentor family members (stories, photos, letters)
Entrepreneurial and Family Enterprise Skills	Transition from an operating leader to a mentor; help successors build authority both in family and business

MILESTONES
Attain peace of mind, sharing contingency and continuity plans

5 Internal Competencies

Emotional Abilities	Foster a vitality of spirit and emotional equanimity that is not always of the body
Social Abilities	Seek closer connection to important people in one's life as social circle gets smaller
Learning and Growth Mindset	Continue to seek learning experiences: Make use of increased cross-hemisphere communication (wisdom) that comes with aging
Responsibility and Accountability	Say what needs to be said while it can still be said and heard
Health and Wellness	Employ those who can assist in areas that allow for freedom of choice and quality of time

MILESTONES
Come to terms with aging: exercising agility, resilience, acceptance and equanimity

1 AGES 5–11/12 ELEMENTARY SCHOOL
2 AGES 12–14 MIDDLE SCHOOL
3 AGES 15–18/19 HIGH SCHOOL
4 AGES 19–25 EMERGING ADULTHOOD
5 AGES 26–35 EARLY ADULTHOOD
6 AGES 35–40 ESTABLISHED ADULTHOOD
7 EARLY 40s TO LATE 50s MID-ADULTHOOD
8 MID-50s TO MID-70s LATE ADULTHOOD
9 LATE 60s INTO 90s ELDERING
10 LATE 70s TO END OF LIFE ELDERING PART II

Ages listed are merely suggestions. Individuals may proceed through the stages faster or slower than ages listed. Authored by: Stacy Allred, MST and Money, Meaning & Choices Institute: Joan DiFuria, MFT and Stephen Goldbart, Ph.D.

Choosing to Intentionally Navigate the Impact of Financial Abundance

If you choose to be strategic in navigating the opportunities, challenges, and risks of financial abundance, "You can't be that kid standing at the top of the water-slide, overthinking it. You have to go down the chute."[6] The 10×10 model provides a lifelong-learning roadmap for families to best steward and enjoy all dimensions of wealth. Using this model can help your family build the competencies essential to thriving with financial abundance, both individually and together. A potential bonus to this learning journey is that flourishing individuals create strong families who contribute to strong communities, making the planet better for all.

Additional Resources

Books

Gene D. Cohen, *The Mature Mind: The Positive Power of the Aging Brain* (Cambridge, MA: Basic Books, 2006).

Joan DiFuria and Stephen Goldbart, *Affluence Intelligence* (Cambridge, MA: DaCapo Press, 2011).

Joline Godfrey, *Raising Financially Fit Kids*, rev. (Berkeley, CA: Ten Speed Press, 2013).

Ryan M. Niemiec, *Character Strengths Interventions: A Field Guide for Practitioners* (Boston, MA: Hogrefe Publishing, 2018).

Andrew J. Scott and Lynda Gratton, *The New Long Life: A Framework for Flourishing in a Changing World* (New York: Bloomsbury Publishing, 2020).

Articles

Intentional learning in practice: A 3×3×3 approach, McKinsey & Company. Accessed January 17, 2022. https://www.mckinsey.com/business-functions/people-and-organizational-performance/our-insights/intentional-learning-in-practice-a-3x3x3-approach.

Allred, Stacy, Joan DiFuria, and Stephen Goldbart. "Building a Strong and Connected Family of Wealth: A 10 × 10 Learning Roadmap." *Trust & Estates Magazine* (December 2021).

Peppet, Scott. Creating a 5-to-10 Year, Five Capitals Family Learning Curriculum, 2019. Accessed January 17, 2022. https://scottpeppet.com/articles/for-family-members/creating-a-5-to-10-year-five-capitals-family-learning-curriculum/.

Staudinger, Ursula. "The Positive Plasticity of Adult Development: Potential for the 21st Century," *American Psychologist*, 75, no. 4 (2020): 540–53.

---

[6]Quote attributed to Tina Fey, comedian.

Biography

Stacy Allred consults on the qualitative priorities at the intersection of family and wealth. She began her career in public accounting. Armed with analytical training and thinking (master's degree in taxation), she addressed the structural questions of financial capital.

Twenty years ago, this all changed. While designing financial and estate plans, she experienced the tremendous energy behind the qualitative questions at the intersection of family and finances. Thoughtfully exploring these big questions led to adapting a holistic approach and dedicating her career to walking alongside individuals and families to effectively navigate the complexity and promise of wealth.

Grounded in the facilitation of family meetings, her practice spans the practical application of family governance and decision-making to creating a learning family. A curious, lifelong learner, Stacy is currently experimenting with the tools of foresight to elevate seeing around corners and identifying, planning, and shaping possible futures.

Joan DiFuria co-founded the Money, Meaning & Choices Institute (MMCI). She helps clients attain successful and lasting impact on their lives, their families, and their businesses. She is a globally recognized speaker and advises families of wealth, family businesses, family offices, corporate leaders, and wealth advisors. Bringing together expertise in business and psychology, she focuses on issues associated with wealth, such as the impact of money on children, succession planning, governance, legacy, and leading multigenerational family meetings.

Joan spent her first 18 years in business as the former director of strategic operations and national marketing director for the largest multinational metal distribution corporation in the world. After 18 years in that business, she went on to complete the Harvard Business School Program for Management Development. She then became a licensed psychotherapist, practicing in tandem with her business consulting work. She has been featured in the *New York Times, Financial Times, Wired,* MSNBC, CBS, and NPR.

Co-founder of MMCI, with over 40 years of professional experience, **Dr. Stephen Goldbart** is a licensed clinical psychologist, professor, author, public speaker, and organizational consultant. His professional interests focus on the opportunities and challenges of wealth, including the psychology of life transitions, adult development, depth psychotherapy, neuroscience, and strategic and succession planning. Stephen has a passion for working with complex family/organizational systems, helping to clarify purpose and establish structured procedures to find solution pathways. He has consulted with individuals, families, and organizations to help develop the fulfilling and sustainable balance of personal, professional, and philanthropic goals. He is co-author of *Mapping the Terrain of the Heart: Passion, Tenderness, and the Capacity to Love,* and *Affluence Intelligence* (Da Capo/Perseus 2012), as well as articles in both the professional and mainstream publications. Along with Joan DiFuria, articles on issues of money and meaning can be found on their Affluence Intelligence blog at Psychology Today (www.psychologytoday.com/blog/affluence-intelligence).

CHAPTER 14

Finding What's Next for Your Family

Barton Parrott

Families and their enterprises need ways to find what's next after a big change in the life of the family. That change could result from the sale of a business, the death of a patriarch or matriarch, a shift in the business landscape, or myriad other reasons. Change brings disruption, even when it results from positive events; with it comes the need to make sense of what's happening and take new action. After a big change we know that the future won't be the same as the past and that our old strategies and tactics won't work forever, but often we're not sure what do to about it. We need a process for moving forward.

One advantage of a big event in the life of a family, such as the sale of a business, is that it can push us to update our stories about what we do and how we do it. Too often we miss this chance and simply carry on with what worked before—even if it no longer succeeds in our new circumstances. It's part of the human condition that change is hard. But life is a cycle of endings and beginnings, of completion and renewal. Understanding how to master this cycle, instead of being mastered by it, is an essential practice for families who want to prosper together through multiple generations.

This chapter will describe a proven practice for actively engaging in this cycle of renewal, for finding what's next. The three-step practice involves asking a set of deceptively simple questions—What's true now? What's possible? What's our plan?—and following where they lead. These questions help us understand where we are, where we're going, and how we'll get there. They map to how we bring things into being and carry them through to completion, whether we're a family or a large organization. They can be used to plan our day or our decade. They provide a way to get moving toward what's next, no matter what situation we're in.

The Practice in Brief

1. "What's true now?"—This question launches a Discovery phase in which we take stock of our current situation, how we got here, and what matters most.

2. "What's possible?"—This question launches an Exploration phase in which we expand beyond incremental thinking to examine options and generate choices.
3. "What's our plan?"—This question forces us to narrow our choices, make decisions about Implementation, and create a written plan of action.

The Practice in Detail

1. *Discovery: What's True Now?*

   When thinking about what's next, many of us want to jump to solutions right away. We want to get on with it, perhaps to move past the anxiety of uncertainty. But decades spent working with families and their businesses have shown me that it always pays to begin by actively taking stock of the current situation, for better and for worse.

   Getting a shared, grounded view of reality is essential. How we see our situation shapes our possibilities. We must not only understand as many facts as we can about our situation, but also what narrative we're living inside of. What are our values, and what matters most to us, including financially, strategically, and interpersonally? What experience do we want to have—rather than what specific solution, form, or structure do we assume we need? This is a look inward within our organization and ourselves; it allows us to connect to our deeper truths. We connect to our legacy as a family and remind ourselves who we are. Rather than fighting the reality of our circumstances, we stop and acknowledge it fully: This is what is. When needed, we give ourselves permission to grieve what has been lost instead of rushing to fill the void with what's next.

   Sometimes acknowledging what *is* means acknowledging what has changed. One family business had a long and successful history as a construction firm; this shaped their story about who they were and what opportunities they pursued. Yet a deep dive into their business during Discovery revealed that their most lucrative opportunities were in real estate based on an inventory of properties accumulated slowly over decades. These opportunities were languishing because the family heir felt compelled to carry on their legacy as a construction firm; he could only picture a certain kind of success based on the family's identity, even though the situation in their market had changed. With a new perspective on their situation, the group of family owners saw new possibilities, tried on a different narrative, and made a shift.
2. *Exploration: What's Possible?*

   In the Exploration phase, we start with feet grounded in the realities of the Discovery phase and expand our view to the horizon. We look for ways to unhitch from incremental thinking and give ourselves permission to think big and divergently. The more ideas the better. We let go of being reasonable. We try on different stories. We ask what wild success would look like if we were to live our purpose, ideals, and values fully. This step is both liberating and harder than it looks, as we try to expand our focus beyond what *is* to imagine what *could be.* The aim is to generate options and to explore them freely.

This step is especially relevant in multigenerational families in which the accomplishments of previous generations cast a large shadow. Each generation must make sense of what they have inherited and decide how to apply it going forward. Giving themselves permission to do so is not a betrayal of the past; the family can remain true to who it is while reimagining what this might look like as the world continues to change. Indeed, this is the job of each rising generation. Bob Dylan sang that "he not busy being born is busy dying." The same applies to families as they look for what's next.

Exploration is an active process. We don't find the future by sitting in a conference room. One business-owning family came up with three scenarios representing possible futures. The scenarios differed in real ways from one another and from the family's current situation. Each was attractive in its own way and contained elements that the family knew from Discovery were important to them. They set about understanding what it would mean to live in each situation. This process of pressure-testing got them out in the world doing research and talking to people. Ultimately they decided on a path that combined elements of all three futures. Pay attention to that which doesn't change no matter what future you imagine—this will be the core of your story.

3. *Implementation: What's Our Plan?*

   If the Exploration phase is about *generating* choices, the Implementation phase is about *making* them. We make decisions about what to do and how. Writing down a plan makes it real; there is abundant evidence about the payoff of setting goals and listing specific next actions for moving forward. The crux of this phase is about choosing where to say no in order to say a bigger yes where it matters most. Power comes from focus. The Implementation phase defines the gap between where we are and where we want to be and provides a plan for closing it. This gap provides the creative tension for achieving our goals.

   The Implementation plan is often a learning plan. The members of one legacy family realized that they didn't know enough to launch their new idea. But their work in the previous phases had made it clear what they had to learn. They set out a clear roadmap about what they needed to find out and what assumptions they needed to test—which, after all, is the heart of any good business plan. They knew where to focus together, which gave them direction and momentum.

Getting Started

The beauty of this three-step practice is that it can be scaled up or down. It can work at the level of a committee, a company, or a country. You can take an hour or a year to answer these questions, depending on what scale of problem or opportunity you're addressing; in essence, they're the same questions at the heart of any strategic-planning process. To ask them, you don't need much to get started. You can use an existing family committee or pull together an ad hoc group. Facilitate a session to describe the process and brainstorm answers. When working with a group, hold at least one session for each of the three phases.

Individuals can do this practice as well, either as a way to prime the pump for group discussion, or simply to further their own thinking. Try this: Hold an hour on your calendar. Think of a situation where you're trying to decide what's next. Get some blank paper. At the top of a page write, "What's true now about this situation?" Set a timer for 20 minutes, and just start writing everything that comes to mind, big and small. Keep going. When the timer goes off, take a fresh page and write "What's possible?" Set your timer for 20 minutes and start writing. Follow the same process for the last question, "What's the plan?" and write for another 20 minutes, identifying as many specific possible actions as you can. At the end of an hour, you will have sharpened and organized your thinking about how to move forward.

To integrate the thinking of individuals back into a group, make a group version of each of the three lists, taking entries from each person. This could be in the form of sticky-notes on a wall or a digital list shown onscreen. Make sure to hear from each person before the loudest voice has a chance to dominate and close off other ideas. To get a shared sense of priorities, use small stickers to cast votes in a sticky-note gallery, or use an audience-participation app to cast votes on items in a digital list.

Outcomes

One family used an expanded version of the three-step practice to decide what's next after the sale of their business. Each of the siblings was now financially independent but wanted to stay engaged with the others. By giving themselves permission to think much more expansively about what they could do together going forward, they were able to pursue both individual and shared goals while also generating opportunities for the next generation in a way that honored their family legacy. What made their new creative solution possible was to start by acknowledging what had changed after the sale—both losses and gains—and what was true for each of them now. They brought their story up to date.

In another family in which the rising generation has been using this process to explore options for the future of their family, focusing on their values and understanding their current business in depth has been an essential springboard to their thinking about what's next. They are actively engaged in researching possible futures.

Change brings disorientation. The practices described in this chapter provide a way to get back in the driver's seat as we grapple with change and what to do next. Taking positive, thoughtful action brings a renewed sense of agency. It counters our evolutionary instincts to fight, fly, or freeze when we perceive a threat. In the face of change, acknowledging reality can be the hardest step, but it is always the place to start. It can lead to a sense of common purpose and shared meaning, even when the family is dealing with loss and crisis. It can bring people together. A good sign that the process is working is when people are acting curious rather than stuck or reactive.

When lacking effective leadership during times of disruption and change, families struggle. Individuals may fear that in order to lead, they must have all the answers at a time when there are no answers to be had. But leadership more often means having the right questions.

Additional Resources

Peter Senge, *The Fifth Discipline: The Art & Practice of the Learning Organization* (New York: Currency Books, 2006).

David Allen, *Getting Things Done: The Art of Stress-Free Productivity* (New York: Penguin Books, 2015).

William Bridges, *Transitions: Making Sense of Life's Changes* (New York: Lifelong Books, 2019).

Biography

Barton Parrott has spent more than 25 years focusing on learning in organizations and families. As a principal of Wealthbridge Partners, he has worked with many families and their enterprises on strategy, leadership, governance, succession, philanthropy, and family education and development. As a senior manager at CFAR, the Center for Applied Research, Inc., a privately held spinoff from the Wharton School, he worked with owner-led businesses and served as co-lead for the firm's strategy practice. Bart started his career instructing courses for the outdoor program Outward Bound, where he worked with management teams and boards to improve their ability to work together and learn from experience. Although he no longer works outside all year, he brings an experiential, active-learning approach to all of his work with families, executives, and organizations. Bart earned a BA with distinction from the University of Virginia and an MBA from the Wharton School of the University of Pennsylvania.

CHAPTER 15

Creating Impactful Learning Programs for Families

Greg Burrows and Ruth Steverlynck

When family relationships, love, and hopes overlay with money, control, and power, any future planning or contemplated transitions can easily get stuck in a quagmire of fear, lack of trust, and lack of transparency. These conditions can create anxious, dependent systems. But families can mitigate these forces by building openness, transparency, and capability through the work of learning together.

Building a family culture of learning and growing together does not just happen. It takes intention and planning and resources and consistency.

This chapter focuses on building an Impactful Learning Program (ILP). We will share some time-tested approaches and ideas that you can draw from to help evolve a family culture of learning and in so doing support the desired future for the family and for the financial engine of the family.

> *There is an old story from the Bible: two families build homes. One family chooses "quick and easy" and builds their house on sand. The storm comes and the house collapses.*
>
> *The other family chooses to invest in a solid foundation; they take the time to dig deep and build their home on rock. The storm comes and the house stands still.*

Build Your Foundation

Let's start with why Impactful Learning Programs (ILPs) are important for families. Motivations will differ but the overarching "why" is simple:

To minimize the gap between a possible negative future state and a desired future state

Any good learning program starts with an exploration within the family of a shared "*desired future state.*" We call this the **"Learning Anchor."**

Statements of a family's **Learning Anchor** could take these forms:

- "to foster meaningful Stewardship"
- "to bring to life the Trust Structures that hold our wealth"
- "to be responsible Owners"
- "to flourish as a family"

"Preparing for the privileges and responsibility of wealth is not unlike training for the Olympics. You cannot expect high performance from a child haphazardly trained to shepherd financial and human capital, any more than you can expect the weekend athlete to make it to the national trials for Olympic competition."

—Jolene Godfrey

Impactful Learning Program Framework

Design Principles for an ILP Framework

ONE: Engage all Participating in the Design
TWO: Build the Curriculum around your Learning Anchor
THREE: Design a Curriculum Reflective of Different Learning Styles
FOUR: Adopt a Continuous Improvement Mindset
FIVE: Ensure the ILP is Fun, Engaging, and Safe
SIX: Build in Accountability

Practical Steps

ONE: Identify Context Knowledge, Skills, and Abilities (KSAs)
TWO: Identify Family-Specific KSAs
THREE: Determine Delivery Platforms
FOUR: Select Subject Matter Experts/Resources
FIVE: Create your own Family Learning Resource Hub
SIX: Put Learning into Action

Design Principles for ILP Framework

PRINCIPLE ONE: Engage all Participating in the Design

All family members who are going to be participating in the learning should be invited to be part of the design of the curriculum.

"If people help build it, they will support it." Family Member

PRINCIPLE TWO: Build the Curriculum around your Learning Anchor

Ensure that desired KSAs support the Learning Anchor.

See more about KSAs under Practical Steps below

In an ILP, families ask,

To reach ***our desired future state. . . . . . .***

What are the observable, measurable, and specific ***KSAs*** *we need?*
Qualitative? Quantitative?
What will it look like for us if the ***KSAs*** *are present?*
What will it look like for us if the ***KSAs*** *are not present?*

PRINCIPLE THREE: Design a Curriculum Reflective of Different Learning Styles

Understand learning styles of those participating: verbal, visual, auditory, kinesthetic, social, solitary, combination.

Potential different: formats to reflect different learning styles

Conferences, subject matter workshops, articles, courses, research papers, blogs, events with guest speakers, family retreats, symposiums, personal development work.

PRINCIPLE FOUR: Adopt a Continuous Improvement Mindset

THE THREE "Rs"
In service of a **continuous improvement mindset,** the **three Rs** are a useful tool:

REFLECT: What is working well in our program ? What is not working well?
REVIEW: What new questions and areas of learning are emerging? What is changing in our thinking as a result of learning to date?
REFORM: What changes will we make? What new topics will we include?

PRINCIPLE FIVE: Ensure the ILP is Fun, Engaging, Dynamic, and Safe

Think about the following:

1. Creative ways to "experience" the learning rather than passively receiving it.
2. How to find peer groups, i.e., those in similar situations to learn with and from.
3. Ensuring a safe environment: When learners do not feel "safe" their ability to absorb learning is minimal.
4. Timing: be mindful of duration.

PRINCIPLE SIX: Build in Accountability

Use journaling to capture both learnings and application of learnings toward integration of knowledge and skill *to become able* (ability).

ACTIONABLE INSIGHTS: A LEARNING JOURNAL

DATE	NEW EXPERIENCE/ACTIVITY: *BRIEFLY OUTLINE*	REFLECTION/NEW IDEA *WHAT ARE YOUR INSIGHTS? WHAT NEW IDEAS OR MODIFICATIONS TO YOUR THINKING DID YOU GAIN?*	NEW ACTIONS *WHAT ACTIONS WILL YOU TAKE BY WHAT DATE TO ACTIVELY APPLY THESE INSIGHTS?*

Practical Steps for Building an ILP for Families

Step One: Identify Context KSAs These are learning topics that help the family better understand the problems and opportunities presented in the context of financial/business wealth. Some examples may include the following:

- Understanding "Wealth" in the fullest sense
- Understanding complexity of overlays of wealth, business, love, ownership, emotion, relationships
- Understanding risks of doing nothing
- Understanding the value of learning for self, for family, for system

Step Two: Identify Family-Specific KSAs These are learning topics that will specifically help the family reach their desired future outcome. When thinking through what these are, it is important to consider both the quantitative, i.e., technical, *head* topics as well as the qualitative, i.e., *heart,* topics.

Family-Specific KSAs

Quantitative topics may include deepening understanding of *legal structures, financial fluency, investments, tax, insurance, what does it mean to be a shareholder or a beneficiary or a trustee or a steward, cybersecurity, choosing advisors, philanthropy, charitable giving, working with boards, being a board member, choosing board members, etc.*

Qualitative topics may include deepening understanding in the following areas:

- *Individual, intrapersonal, interpersonal: effective communication, approaching conflict, resolving upsets, stress management, trust, forgiveness, gratitude, empathy, healthy boundaries, working with advisors, privacy, relationships in the context of wealth, parenting in context of wealth, psychology of wealth*
- *Health: mental, physical, emotional well-being*
- *Knowing self: values, purpose, meaning, what we stand for, how we show up, giving and receiving, life satisfaction, individual well-being*

Step Three: Determine Delivery Platforms

Delivery Platforms	
In-person tailored workshops	*One on one*
	Branch
	Family retreat
Print	*Articles*
	Books
Conferences	*Global and local conferences on topics relating to wealth, inheritance, life skills, etc.*
Courses	*Global and local courses on topics relating to wealth, inheritance, life skills, etc.*

Step Four: Choose Subject Matter Expert/Resources

- Who are the best subject matter experts to deliver?
- What do these experts know?
- Where/what are the best resources to achieve the learning desired?

Step Five: Create your own Family Learning Resource Hub Through archiving every learning experience, family members will have access to a library of content curated over the years which will be helpful as the family transitions through different stages and new members join.

Step Six: Put Learning into Action Each learning experience has an invitation for change:

- How will I use this learning in my life?
- What measurable changes will I see in my life because of this learning?
- What can I create with this learning?
- How will what I create with this learning enhance and transform this important area of my/our life/lives?

Successful learning happens when transformation occurs.

Lessons Learned from a Family

This family sold its 37-year-old family business, materializing several hundred million dollars of generational wealth for four generations of family members, ranging from infants to the first generation in their 80s. The liquidity event was followed by creation of a single-family office and several years of estate planning work. This resulted in a "family driven" estate plan, with disclosure given to family members and with expectations that the family begin a long-term learning and development program.

The family's learning anchor was that ***the wealth be a positive force in the individual lives of family members***. The ILP focused on ***helping build capacity, maturity, and skills to best prepare future inheritors for the transition of their family wealth***.

Using this **Learning Anchor** and applying the ILP framework, a long-term family learning and development plan was created and has been implemented over the last five years. The ILP targeted the second and third generations of the family with a primary focus on the third generation. It's also worth noting that given the **Learning Anchor**, trustee and beneficiary education is a significant area of focus within the plan.

Following we share the more significant reflections and lessons learned over the last five years:

> *Family leadership and commitment from older generations is critical for next generation role modeling.*
>
> *Generic content has limited effectiveness. Customizing content to be specific to individual circumstances has far greater impact.*
>
> *Include third-party speakers, presenters, and subject matter experts to keep the ILP dynamic.*
>
> *Use multiple delivery methods that layer over time (i.e., traditional in-person, or virtual family meetings; subject matter guest speakers; special events with spousal inclusion, online e-learning modules to bridge gap between meetings; capture all in a private family website/portal).*
>
> *Be intentionally repetitive in big, complex, and important topic areas (i.e., trustee and beneficiary education).*
>
> *Let the students (i.e., next-gen) become the teachers over time.*

In closing, the ILP framework and related lessons learned can be important tools to assist with meaningful family learning. In the absence of an active business or other vehicles for learning, they can be critically important tools to sustain an engaged and cohesive family over the long term.

Additional Resources

Bernice McCarthy, About Learning, https://aboutlearning.com.

James E. Hughes, Susan E. Massenzio, and Keith Whitaker, *Complete Family Wealth*, 2nd ed. (New York, NY: Wiley, 2022).

Carol Dweck, *Mindset: The New Psychology of Success* (New York, NY: Ballentine Books, 2007).

Nassim Talib, *Antifragile: Things That Gain from Disorder* (New York, NY: Random House, 2014).

Biography

Greg Burrows was the chief financial officer for the ARAM Group of Companies from 2005 to 2008, and after leading the family through a successful liquidity event, he transitioned to create and lead their Calgary-based single-family office. For the last 13 years, Greg has been the chief executive officer of the Mara Family Office, serving four generations of the Chamberlain family.

Greg serves on the steering committee for the annual Cambridge Private Family Office Forum. He also serves as a trustee on a family foundation and is on the local branch executive for STEP Calgary. In 2018, Greg was recognized with the Alberta Family Enterprise Advisor of the Year award.

Ruth Steverlynck is a principal at the Lovins Group. Ruth's great passion is working with families at the challenging intersection of family relationships, individual well-being, and significant financial assets. With an international background in law, dispute resolution, and governance, Ruth recognizes that no single approach works for all so draws upon her diverse experience and network of resources to help the families she works with.

Ruth has an honors Law degree, numerous certificates in mediation and conflict resolution, is a Fellow of Family Firm Institute and a long-term faculty member of the FEA (Family Enterprise Advisor) Program offered through Family Enterprise Canada (https://familyenterprise.ca/) and one of three lead adjudicators in the FEA Designation process.

CHAPTER 16

Developing a Family Wealth Education Plan

Kirby Rosplock

This chapter shares best practices and steps to build a family wealth education plan by first assessing and defining wealth education, developing a template, and assessing the challenges and process for implementing a family wealth education framework.

Defining Family Wealth Education

The first step is understanding a family's definition of wealth education. Wealth education may be defined as the "education, instruction, preparation and engagement of family members on the responsibilities of being an owner, inheritor, beneficiary, steward, fiduciary or other party to the wealth."[1] However, the process to craft a wealth education framework for a family is bespoke and requires engagement of family members at different ages and stages.

Most families start informally, with financial parenting, and using real-life experiences from shopping to banking as experiential opportunities to teach.[2] The early years of financial fluency training focuses primarily on financial awareness and money skills such as counting coins and bills, making change, evaluating potential purchases, bartering and trading, understanding the purpose of money, earning money, and creating small startups. Developing habits around saving, spending, investing, and giving may be followed by understanding cash needs, budgeting, and planning for purchases, impact investing, and understanding the differences between lifestyle and discretionary spending. Table 16.1 outlines money skills by developmental stage.

---

[1]Kirby Rosplock, "The New Frontier of Family Wealth Education," *The International Family Offices Journal* 5, no. 4 (2021): 12–18.

[2]Clinton G. Gudmunson and Sharon M. Danes, "Family Financial Socialization: Theory and Critical Review," *Journal of Family and Economic Issues* 32, no. 4 (2011): 644–67, doi:10.1007/s10834-011-9275-y.

Table 16.1: Money Skills by Developmental Stage[3]

Stage	Age (Years)	Money Skills to Master
1	5–8	Counts coins and bills. Understands the value and purpose of money. Learns to differentiate between wants and needs. Begins to develop an ethical compass.
2	9–12	Can make change. Shows initiating behavior and entrepreneurial spirit. Shows awareness of costs and earned money. Can balance a simple checking account and keep up with savings account.
3	13–15	Learns to shop comparatively. Understands the time-money relationship. Begins to earn money and initiates small ventures. Commits to saving goals. Has basic understanding of investment. Connects money and the future. Can read a bank statement. Understands interest and dividends. Understands philanthropy.
4	16–18	Actively saves, spends, and invests. Connects goals and saving. Experiences responsibility for others and self. Able to talk about money and plan future. Understands money as power. Can read a paycheck and complete simple tax forms. Shows a developing capacity for economic self-sufficiency.
5	19+	Manages cash flow. Designs and manages an annual financial plan. Commits and executes on saving and investing goals. Is cognizant of the responsibilities and obligations of paying taxes. Applies money, time, and talent to philanthropic contribution. Engages in productive financial conversations. Knows how to make a job, not just take a job. Understands the importance of credit.

Source: Joline Godfrey, "Raising Financially Fit Children: Tips from Joline Godfrey," More than Money, http://www.morethanmoney.org/articles.php?article=Raising_Financially_Fit_Children_Tips_from_Joline_Godfrey_447.

After high school, many families seek to formalize their learning plan. For wealth education plans to be successful, family educational milestones should be aligned with triggering events along the individual's age and stage. Most families recognize that a plan is only as good as the people who are accountable to implement it. This includes the learner, the mentors, the peers, and advisors who are all encouraging and inspiring a learner while on this path.

Devising an Education Plan

Many successful families who groom responsible beneficiaries recognize that great stewards are cultivated, not simply born.[4] So they don't leave it to chance. They lay out a roadmap for the educational needs of their offspring and hold education as a core value of the family. Table 16.2 illustrates a sample family education plan modified and adapted from *The Complete Family Office Handbook.* The grid assesses core functional areas a beneficiary may need or want in prioritizing their education goals.

Once these education needs have been assessed and mapped, advisors, fiduciaries and families should assess if they need to (1) build custom content; (2) hire a consultant, education firm, membership organization or institution to build content; (3) enroll beneficiaries in academic programs; (4) directly mentor beneficiaries; or (5) seek other innovative, progressive resources or experiences. With the reality of the global pandemic, many families are seeking online,

[3]For a more expanded version of this chart, see "The life/money map" in Joline Godfrey, *Raising Financially Fit Kids* (Berkeley, CA: Ten Speed Press, 2013): 6–7; "The Apprenticeship Years (ages 5–18)," The *Complete Family Office* (Boston, MA: Wiley, 2014).

[4]Kirby Rosplock, Tamarind Learning, www.TamarindLearning.com, 2020.

asynchronous learning that is private, secure, and accessible from anywhere at any time. Virtual learning is becoming more mainstream. A number of organizations have created curricula and programs to support family members, including Beewyzer in Europe and Tamarind Learning in the United States. Other next generation communities such as NEXUS and DIONZ are also creating opportunities for family members to get engaged and learn. The following learning case study demonstrates the possible application of the wealth education template with a fictionalized family.

Table 16.2:

Topic	Needs (Functional Requirements)	Wants (Nice to Have, but Not Required)	To Do What? (Map Topic to a Life Event)	Current Knowledge (Rate Weak to Strong, 1–10)	Priority to Learn (Rank Low to High, 1–10)
	I need education on:	*I want education on:*	*This topic will help me:*	*My knowledge is:*	*My desire to learn is:*
Budgeting					
Financial Planning					
Understanding Statements					
Career Planning					
Stewardship					
Estate Planning					
Trusts					
Working with Advisors					
Investing					
Entrepreneurship					
Direct Investing					
Saving					
Lifestyle Management					
Philanthropy					
Impact Investing					
Family Governance					
Wealth Transfer					
Family Office					

Source: © Tamarind Learning. All rights reserved.

Case Study

The Tannen family[5] had some basic education and governance building blocks in place, hosting family meetings and providing piecemeal education quarterly to generational cohorts in a just-in-time learning approach. The family brought in technical advisors and occasionally senior family members to lead instruction for different topics. The family began to realize that the younger family members (under 15) were losing interest in learning during these cohort education

[5]This is a fictional case study based on aspects of an actual affluent family. All identifying information has been modified to protect the client's privacy.

sessions when it was delivered as a teacher/classroom approach. Several of them shared feedback that the education was "boring," "not always applicable to me," or that "I feel lost but don't want to admit it."

Stepping back, the family noticed that as their young adult family members reached their later teens, twenties, and thirties, much of what they needed to know was related to their current life stage and age. For example, key milestones, like graduating college, purchasing a car, or signing a lease for an apartment, required a basic understanding of budgeting, capital sufficiency, lifestyle planning, and personal finance. Similarly, getting married or having children required other knowledge and skills as it relates to estate planning, marital agreements, trusts, tax, financial planning, and working with advisors. These were not your typical courses offered at university, nor were they always easy to learn in a 1- to 2-hour meeting or classroom-taught experience.

Learning Gaps and Approach

Even so, the family leaders were not convinced of the need for change and expressed confidence in the intelligence of the young adults and their ability to adapt to the traditional learning approach.

A consultant hired by the family proposed an experiment—an interactive game to test the young adults' knowledge, with senior family members present. So as not to put any one family member on the spot, the consultant divided them into two equal mixed teams composed of elders, adult children, younger family members, and spouses. Working together they had to answer correctly the questions posed during the game.

It was fascinating to watch the adult progeny reveal how they worked as a team, who appeared to lead their groups, and who did not participate. It was also telling to see how many basic questions they missed. For example, they could not identify what tax bracket the family fell into, the difference between short-term and long-term capital gains, the difference between health-care power of attorney and a power of attorney, what dispositive provisions of a trust meant, etc. These are just a few of the foundational aspects of wealth that were not clear to more than 20 beneficiaries born into a family enterprise worth more than $1 billion.

In reflecting on the overall family wealth education approach over the years, it was clear that the family had further to go. While they had made some strides using a traditional learning approach of classroom lectures, mentoring, and just-in-time learning, there was more to be done, especially given the realization that traditional classroom and one-on-one mentoring learners tend to only retain about 20 percent of what they learn 24 hours after the teaching experience. In fact, part of the challenge with traditional learning methods is that students are taught a concept but may not be able to experience or apply what they learn. This can make it difficult for the learner to reinforce and remember the concept. Further, if learners are too intimidated to ask a question, then they may not grasp what was initially communicated. Technical advisors may not be good educators, so they may miss the signs of when a learner is lost. When learners turn their attention to a device, such as a phone or iPad, it may signal the advisor who is teaching that the learner is disinterested, disrespectful, or insolent. In many cases, learners who feel lost will disengage because they feel they cannot keep pace or catch up on what was missed. The family began to realize that their traditional learning approach was not working the way they hoped it would.

Engaging Adult Family Members

The family decided to focus initially on the 18- to 35-year-olds who were grouped together to tackle discussions and issues on investing, finance, business ownership, and more as these individuals were coming into wealth or already had inherited. The consultant interviewed a sample of the adult family beneficiaries to determine their learning gaps in their perceived foundational knowledge and started to explain why the family office advisors were met by distant or befuddled stares when they were educating on complex planning. Many of the adult beneficial owners confided to the consultant that they were apprehensive to speak up or ask questions as it would reveal their vulnerabilities and lack of understanding. There were false assumptions that core technical areas such as reading trusts, understanding estate planning documents, and understanding financial and investment statements had been taught to them already. In their family, being ignorant or incompetent when it came to the enterprise and wealth was the greatest weakness of all. Despite most family members pursuing advanced degrees, the family beneficiaries found that many still felt very ill-equipped to manage their inheritance. Some also expressed that they wanted to learn more on their own before meeting as a family to discuss topics.

Outcomes and Takeaways

The consultant worked with the family to retool their learning approach. First, a design team of family members was formed, with representatives of different branches, ages, levels of knowledge, and roles. Second, a survey was crafted to gauge family members' knowledge and interest in a variety of learning areas and to prioritize what to learn. Third, they reviewed their current team of expert advisors and educators to determine any gaps. After their analysis, the family determined that they needed a virtual learning experience to support family member education goals.

The consultant worked with the family to assess feedback from the survey and consider the learning goals and needs of family members. Utilizing the wealth planning tool (Table 16.3), the family was able to map out its learning goals and needs. The consultant helped to design the curriculum and identify various resources from online education to mentors and advisors to map to the wealth education plan. Certain topics were conducive to teach in a cohort, others were better in a webinar format, while other topics could be addressed via a virtual learning platform.

Table 16.3:

Topic	Needs (Functional Requirements)	Wants (Nice to Have, but Not Required)	To Do What? (Map Topic to a Life Event or Need)	Current Knowledge (Rate Weak to Strong, 1–10)	Priority to Learn (Rank Low to High, 1–10)
	I need education on:	*I want education on:*	*This topic will help me:*	*My knowledge is:*	*My desire to learn is:*
Budgeting	Yes		Buying home	4	4
Financial Planning	Yes		Cashflow needs	2	5
Understanding Statements		Yes	Financial/investing	1	6
Career Planning		I have a job	I am in healthcare	10	
Stewardship	Yes		Role of a Steward	7	1
Estate Planning	Yes		Will, guardian, etc.	5	2
Trusts		Yes	How to read my trust?	3	3
Working with Advisors			Work well with advisors	8	
Investing	Yes		Understanding IPS	1	7
Entrepreneurship		No	No interest	0	
Direct Investing		No	No investments	0	
Saving	Yes		How much to save	5	8
Lifestyle Management	Yes		What can I afford?	6	9
Philanthropy		Yes	Want to give but when?	7	12
Impact Investing	Yes	Interesting to me	Yes, want an ESG lens to investing	4	11
Family Governance	Yes		Decision-making process	3	10
Wealth Transfer		Yes	How, when, how much, what do I need to know?	3	13
Family Office		Yes		3	

Source: © Tamarind Learning. All rights reserved.

The family's engagement shifted. Those who were reticent now leaned into participating. Younger family members started to see the learning progression and how it was leading to skill building and advancement within the family. Slowly, more family members began to ask questions as the shift in the learning culture progressed.

As the Tannen family case reveals, education planning requires time, intention, desire, engagement, and an understanding of not just what to learn, but how to learn at different ages and stages. Evolving learning approaches and employing learning education technology may help (1) streamline the time family is able to commit to in-person meetings and learning, (2) make family more self-sufficient, (3) create the appropriate expectations, interactions, and preparations for more meaningful family dialogues, and (4) empower the owner group to be prepared to make important decisions for wealth sustainability.

Conclusion

There are many hurdles to determining a learning plan for affluent families because education needs vary based on varying levels of knowledge, fear of setting false expectations, and the fear of entitlement. Yet, if families do not educate and prepare younger generations for inheritance, beneficiaries may create their own assumptions of what they believe will one day be theirs. As Warren Buffett famously said: "The perfect amount to leave children is enough money so that they would feel they could do anything, but not so much that they could do nothing."[6] Regardless of the amount a family wants to bestow, a beneficiary who is not educated and prepared for the responsibilities of wealth is at greater risk of mismanaging it, falling prey to financial predators, or spending beyond their means. Utilizing a wealth education framework to guide the learning needs and design may help a family to (1) engage family learners, (2) teach family members what they need to know, (3) create buy-in to continuous learning, (4) set a bar for learner achievement, and (5) demonstrate the value of investing in the family's human capital.

Additional Resources

Kirby Rosplock, "The New Frontier of Family Wealth Education," *The International Family Offices Journal* 5, no. 4 (2021): 12–18.

Susan Schoenfeld, "Tips for Raising Successful Children of Wealth," *Tamarind Learning Podcast* (January 28, 2021), https://www.tamarindlearning.com/resources/podcast/tips-for-raising-successful-children-of-wealth-with-susan-schoenfeld/.

Kirby Rosplock, "Jumpstarting Wealth Education with Families," *Tamarind Learning Webinar* (June 2021), https://www.tamarindlearning.com/resources/webinars/.

Charlotte Beyer, *Wealth Management Unwrapped* (Boston, MA: Wiley, 2017).

Kirby Rosplock, "6 Tips to Getting Conversations Started around Family Wealth Education," https://www.tamarindlearning.com/funnel-advisors/hurdles-and-solutions-to-getting-started/.

Joline Godfrey, *Raising Financially Fit Kids* (Berkeley, CA: Ten Speed Press, 2013).

Patricia Angus, "The Ten Facts Every Trust Beneficiary Should Know," *Private Wealth Management* (2003).

Biography

Kirby Rosplock, Ph.D., is the founder of Tamarind Partners, Inc., a leading family office consultancy named 2019 Best Family Office Management Consultancy and Best Family Wealth Counseling by the Family Wealth Report. Kirby is recognized by her peers as an innovator, trusted advisor, lauded author, and world-renowned speaker in the family business and family office domains. She is also co-founder and chief learning officer at Tamarind Learning, which provides wealth education and advisory. Born into a complex enterprising family, Kirby understands first-hand being a beneficial owner, inheritor, fiduciary, and an operator.

---

[6] Sam Ro, "Warren Buffett's Best Advice Ever May Have Been about Parenting," *Business Insider* (December 10, 2011), https://www.businessinsider.com/warren-buffetts-advice-to-wealthy-parents-2011-12.

Kirby combines her life experiences with her passions for research, client advisory, and her love of writing, which have culminated in many articles, research studies, and books, including *The Complete Family Office Handbook* and *The Complete Direct Investing Handbook.* Kirby received honors including the prestigious Family Wealth Industry Thought Leadership award in 2018 from the Family Wealth Alliance, and the Richard Beckhard Practice award for lifetime achievement and outstanding contributions to family business practice from the Family Firm Institute (FFI) in 2018.

Kirby earned her undergraduate degree from Middlebury College, MBA from Marquette University, and Ph.D. from Saybrook University. For more than 20 years, she has worked in the world of finance, family wealth, and family business, including working in the securities industry for a broker-dealer and more than a decade in a prominent multifamily office as the head of Research and Development. Kirby is dean of Family Office at the Purposeful Planning Institute, a fellow and family governance faculty of the FFI GEN Program, co-trustee of the Harbeck Family Foundation, and currently serves on the advisory board of Merton Venture Philanthropy and on the board of directors of Hope Trust.

CHAPTER 17

Practical Tools for Building Healthy Families

Christian Stewart[1]

If your family is going to succeed over time, it needs to make itself into a learning organization. But what should you learn, and how will you learn together? As an individual with significant financial capital, you are in a special, advantaged situation. You can deploy financial capital to help grow your family's qualitative capital. If you have not been doing this to date, you and your family can start a learning journey together of figuring out how to invest financial capital to grow the other forms of capital. Improving trust and communication and helping family members acquire related skills is a critical part of this investment and a key topic for family learning and development. This chapter summarizes specific skills, practices, and resources that can be included in your learning and development curriculum.

Work on Yourself

There are two perspectives to consider as you read this chapter. The first is your individual perspective.

What can you do as an individual to improve the way you communicate and collaborate? The best lever for change within a family is to change the one person you can control—yourself. As a family leader, if you put a focus on your change efforts, you will also provide a role model for everyone.

What would best support you in your own learning and development efforts? Options include reading, enrolling in external learning programs, and engaging a coach or a counselor who can teach you (and your spouse/partner) new skills and provide ongoing support on your interactions with others.

A Learning Family

The second perspective is the family perspective. You should start to think of your family as a learning organization requiring its own leadership, administrative support, and learning curriculum.

[1]The assistance of Mary K. Duke, Hartley Goldstone, and James E. Hughes Jr. is gratefully acknowledged.

What are some of the attributes of a learning family? A family that is committed to learning and growing its skill sets together will examine the collective assumptions of the family, periodically review decisions that have been made and whether they turned out as expected, adopt a growth mindset and not a fixed mindset,[2] and will periodically reflect on how effective the family members are when they are working together as a team.

What leadership will be required? Often a critical element of success is a family champion, a family member who is passionate and committed to raising the skill levels of the family, and if applicable, seeing family relationships healed.

What support will the family need? Individuals with wealth typically have an advisory team that can help with technical and quantitative issues. Who on your advisory team will provide professional advice on qualitative issues?

How can your family learn new skills? Options include a family book club; hiring external coaches, counselors and/or trainers to teach new concepts and skills; peer learning from other families; and providing funding for family members to seek personal or couples coaching or counseling or to attend externally run programs.

Curriculum

The following curriculum differentiates between individual and family learning; however, this is not a hard-and-fast division. A key to delivering family learning and development, both individual and family, will be family meetings (discussed in other essays in this book).

Curriculum Part A: Individual Skills

Learning Forgiveness Are you holding onto grievances toward your family members? Are you holding onto any grievances toward persons outside your family? If so, are there reasons that stop you from considering forgiveness as one of your options? Forgiveness is a practical tool to improve relationships, trust, and communication. Where there has been a breach of trust, forgiveness is the way to repair that breach.

Using Positive Emotion to Change Perspective When was the last time you experienced a positive emotion? What were you doing? How long did the positive experience last? Can you replicate that positive emotion? Do you know what kinds of activities bring you a positive emotional experience?

Positive emotion expands our perspective from "me to we," making us more open, flexible, and creative. Bringing positive emotion into our life, being mindful of it, being able to prolong the effect, helps us to flourish. Shifting our perspective from "me to we," to be more open to other family members, is a key part of improving family communication.

---

[2]Carol S. Dweck, *Mindset: The New Psychology of Success* (New York, NY: Ballantine Books, 2017).

One effective practice is to keep a gratitude journal, to list everything you are grateful for every couple of days. Another powerful practice is doing a Loving Kindness Meditation (LKM) on a regular basis.

Regularly practicing gratitude journaling and/or LKM literally rewires your brain. These are practices that you can do yourself, as part of working on yourself, that can have a positive impact on your relationships.

Working with Strengths Do you know what your strengths are? Do you know activities that allow you to experience a state of flow (where we feel and perform our best)?

Other essays in this book offer ways for you to identify your character strengths. Engaging these signature strengths is another way to bring positive emotion into your life. Identifying and engaging our signature strengths leads to an *engaged* life; engaging them in service of something greater than ourselves leads to a *meaningful* life. Although character strengths are about individual flourishing, engaging them will contribute to family flourishing.

Once you are familiar with your signature strengths, the next question to work on is whether you can recognize strengths in other family members.

Investing in Your Relationships Can you recollect a time when one of your family members shared news with you of a positive experience? How did you respond? Was your response typical of you?

Research has shown that a key element of satisfying relationships is how we react to positive events in the other person's life. The way a person responds to good news is classified based on two aspects: whether the response is active or passive, and whether it is constructive or destructive.[3] This means there are four basic ways of responding: active-constructive, active-destructive, passive-constructive, and passive-destructive. Of these four ways of responding, only one—active-constructive responding (ACR)—builds relationships. ACR means responding in a way that amplifies the positive news being shared with you.

Curriculum Part B: Family Skills

Where Is Your Family Today? When you think about your family and all its relationships, what is the overall trend? Is the trend toward growth or entropy (gradual decline), fission (conflict) or fusion (synergy)?

As a family leader, you need to think about the big picture and consider the direction of your family system.

The following exercise is taken from *Family, The Compact Among Generations* by James E. Hughes, Jr.:[4]

- On a whiteboard draw a large circle. Write the names of each of your key family members spaced equally around the perimeter.

---

[3]Margarita Tarragona, *Positive Identities: Narrative Practices and Positive Psychology* (Milwaukee, OR: Positive Acorn, 2015), who in turn quotes the work of Dr. Shelly Gable and team.

[4]New York: Bloomberg Press, 2007.

- Draw a line connecting each person to every other person.
- Label each relationship as trending toward entropy, fission, or fusion.
- Stand back and look at the whole.

What is the overall trend you can see in the system of family relationships? This is your starting point as a family.

Next, consider: *What would be one small change within the system that would have the biggest positive impact on the whole system?*

When you look at yourself and your relationships, which should you be working on to help improve the whole?

For a variation on the above exercise, reflect on which of the relationships are more colored by gratitude than resentment, and which are more colored by resentment than gratitude?[5]

Family Stories When you think about your family's past, what kind of narrative do you have?

- A descending narrative, e.g., "In the past we were a special family in some way, but then we lost it."
- An ascending narrative, e.g., "Look at where we are today when you compare to where we came from."
- An oscillating narrative, e.g., "We have had times when we were up and times when we were down, but we always managed to make it through the hard times."

The healthiest family narrative is the oscillating narrative because it teaches resilience through examples of overcoming hardship.[6] *Another question to think about is whether the story of any of your relatives or ancestors is a story from which you can draw strength.*

Sharing family stories of the past, going back as far as you can, is a powerful source of family connection and bonding. Including time for family storytelling should be an ongoing element of your family meetings.

A Thinking Environment How good are you at helping other people think for themselves, especially members of your own family? If someone comes to you with an issue, do you give them attention, do you hear them out, are you curious to see where their thinking will take them?

According to Nancy Kline in *Time to Think,*[7] the quality of the attention that you give a person determines the quality of another's thinking. "The most important factor in whether or not a person can think well for themselves is how they are being treated by the people with them."

---

[5]Dr. Kerry Howells, *Untangling You: How Can I Be Grateful When I Feel so Resentful?* (Melbourne, Australia: Major Street Publishing, 2021).

[6]Bruce Feiler, "The Stories that Bind Us," *New York Times* (March 17, 2013).

[7]Time to Think, *Listening to Ignite the Human Mind* (London: Ward Lock Cassell Illustrated, 1999).

The environment a person is in also affects their thinking. Your family meetings can be designed using Kline's Ten Components of a Thinking Environment. Kline's recommendations include the following:

- When someone has a turn to speak, no one is allowed to interrupt.
- Remind everyone to keep their eyes on the speaker and let their faces communicate respect for the speaker.
- It is okay to think out loud. You do not have to complete your thinking before you talk.
- Treat every person as your thinking equal.
- Give each person encouragement to do their very best thinking.
- Listeners should not compete with the thinker.
- Relax. Don't rush. Put the thinker at ease.

Difficult Conversations In a family enterprise, there will always be conflicts and difficult conversations. In any difficult conversation, there are always three underlying conversations going on:

- *The "what happened" conversation.* Each party will have their own story of events; each party will have made a contribution; you need to separate intentions (you can never know what their intentions really were) from the impact of what happened.
- *The "feelings" conversation.* There are always feelings present in such conversations and these need to be brought into your awareness.
- *The "identity" conversation.* It is very easy to be knocked off balance if your identity is challenged during a conversation. The key is to reflect in advance on how the conversation might impact on your identity so you can remain grounded.

The process includes thinking through and choosing your purpose in planning to have a difficult conversation, in choosing whether to raise the issue or not.

The Trust Matrix You also want your family to become adept with the topic of trust. Include the elements of trust, how to build trust, and what to do when trust has been broken, in the curriculum.

Is there anyone in your family that you would say you don't trust?

To say that you don't trust a person is a very broad statement. It is important to be able to narrow down what you mean when you think you don't trust someone. A useful practical tool for being more precise is the Trust Matrix.[8]

---

[8]Joseph Astrachan and Kristi McMillan, *Conflict and Communication in the Family Business,* Family Business Leadership Series No. 16 (Marietta, GA: Family Enterprise Publishers, 2003).

Trust Matrix

(Name)	*Individual*	*Team*	*Family*	*Company*
Honesty				
Intentions				
Skills and abilities				
Communication				

The Trust Matrix shows the need to be specific about both the different elements of trust and the context that you are referring to.

"Honesty" refers to being truthful. "Intentions" refer to whether the other person has their own interests at heart or the interests of others. "Skills and Abilities" means they have the skills and abilities to do their job or function effectively in the relevant group they are in. "Communication" means they tell you what you need to know when you need to know it. Your family can learn about the Trust Matrix together and use it to skillfully provide each other with constructive feedback.

Creating Your Own Curriculum

If you would like to design your own learning curriculum for your family, the first step is to come to a consensus on how your family defines its human, intellectual, social, and spiritual capital, or whether it will adopt its own different concept of wealth. Then what are the activities or experiences which that would help both the individuals and the family as a collective to grow its human, intellectual, social, and spiritual capital, in age-appropriate ways? What age appropriate skills and experiences will family members need to successfully integrate the financial capital into their lives?

The focus of this chapter has been on the family as a learning organization, intentionally investing in developing the trust and communication skills of its members. Families with shared ownership of financial capital are complex. Conflicts are an inherent part of such a complex system. Intentionally working to increase trust and to communicate more effectively is critical to ensure sustainability. In addition, the curriculum outlined in this chapter can also represent an investment by the family in enhancing family human and intellectual capital, teaching individual family members valuable life skills.

Additional Resources

Ian A. Marsh, *If It Is So Good to Talk, Why Is It So Hard? Rediscovering the Power of Communication* (Leicester, UK: Troubador Publishing, 2018).

Andrew Bernstein, *The Myth of Stress: Where Stress Really Comes From and How to Live a Happier and Healthier Life* (New York: Simon & Schuster, 2015).

Fred Luskin, *Forgive for Good: A Proven Prescription for Health and Happiness* (New York: HarperOne, 2002).

Barbara L. Fredrickson, *Positivity: Top-Notch Research Reveals the Upward Spiral That Will Change Your Life* (New York: Three Rivers Press, 2009).

Martin Seligman, *Authentic Happiness: Using the New Positive Psychology to Realize Your Potential for Lasting Fulfilment* (New York: Simon & Schuster, 2002).
Hartley Goldstone, James E. Hughes Jr., and Keith Whitaker, *Family Trusts: A Guide for Beneficiaries, Trustees, Trust Protectors and Trust Creators* (Hoboken, NJ: Wiley, 2016).
Nancy Kline, *Time to Think: Listening to Ignite the Human Mind* (London: Cassell & Co., 1999).
Douglas Stone, Bruce Patton, and Sheila Heen, *Difficult Conversations: How to Discuss What Matters Most* (New York: Penguin Books, 1999).

Biography

Christian Stewart is an independent family advisor based in Hong Kong and the founder of Family Legacy Asia. He assists family enterprises with family governance, succession, learning, and development. Christian is a fellow of the Family Firm Institute (FFI) and the recipient of the FFI's 2021 Interdisciplinary Practice Award. He has also received the Wealth Briefing Asia 2017 award for Leading Individual Advisor.

SECTION 3

PLANNING THOUGHTFULLY

"Plans are nothing, but planning is everything," holds a well-worn aphorism. It reflects the nature of reality: Things never turn out just as we expected. To quote a less-hopeful version, "Man plans, and God laughs." Despite the divine laughter, going through the work of planning helps prepare the mind for whatever fortune throws its way.

Planning is an essential component of managing financial wealth. Typically, that planning takes place under the auspices of various experts: financial planners, estate planners, investment managers, business succession experts, and so on. As a result, many times families feel that their plans are something external to themselves, not something they truly live. Sticking to a plan, or keeping it up to date, can be a real challenge.

The chapters in this section aim to address this challenge by providing exercises and tools in various aspects of planning that readers can easily apply, and reapply, to their own situations.

The section begins with John A. Warnick's guidance on "Expressing Purpose in Your Trusts." Families with significant wealth typically have a multitude of trust structures in which they hold their assets and transfer those assets to future generations. Far too rarely do they give any thought to the purpose of those structures, with often painful results for beneficiaries. Warnick's exercise gives trust creators a clear path for discerning their purposes and then incorporating those purposes into their trusts or their instructions for future trustees.

In the next chapter (reprinted from the first *Wealth of Wisdom* volume), Jamie Forbes describes steps to take to maintain shared ownership of a family vacation home. This is a topic that many families struggle with, given the great emotional power that a beloved family gathering place can have. Forbes uses the experience of his family's century-long stewardship of the island of Naushon, off Cape Cod, to offer practical guidance to any family seeking to preserve a home for generations.

Jay Hughes then turns our attention to the power of family financial assets to foster family members' abilities (especially in communication and entrepreneurship), through the mechanism of the "Family Bank." Though it doesn't require a charter, a family bank works best when it combines attention to each family member's needs and skills along with some formality of decision-making, whether that is in making loans or giving grants to family members for projects such as buying a house, starting a business, pursuing additional education, or the like.

Risk is a key element of planning, and yet it can often feel hard to evaluate. Linda Bourn offers readers a way to assess themselves regarding "What keeps you up at night?" in a variety of areas: cyber-risk, natural disaster risk, private collectibles, personal security, and so on. Her assessment then points to specific actions to take, whether in the form of asset retitling or relocation, expert consultation, or insurance.

Every community requires infrastructure—families too. For a family with significant wealth, that infrastructure takes the forms of effective monitoring of assets, financial controls, expense and liquidity management, human resource management, and reputation management—to name only a few items. Natasha Pearl gives readers a mechanism to evaluate their "infrastructure" and its needs, to see where it is crumbling or nonexistent, and then to determine what steps are necessary to upgrade the system.

A common challenge for family members is to learn and keep track of all the operational details of managing significant family wealth. Due to specialization and confidentiality, many important documents and reports can easily become lost or siloed, making information very hard to deploy in an emergency. In the next chapter, based on his own family's experience, Josh Kanter instructs readers how to create a "Family Owners' Manual" that consolidates this crucial information in one place, with flexibility to add to or change the manual as time goes on.

Clearly, the most important assets in any family are the family members themselves, and the last four chapters in this section deal with planning as it regards their health, well-being, and values.

Arden O'Connor helps families take on the difficult task of assessing behavioral health challenges (e.g., around alcohol, drugs, or mental illness) as well as guidance of what to do in a behavioral health crisis.

Given that so many family members are living longer than past generations, Susan Hyatt then offers readers a "Smart Aging Audit." Readers can think specifically about their medical information and needs, personal preferences and financial preparedness for the future, and end-of-life planning, by considering not only what they have in place now but "what if" different scenarios should come to pass.

Almost all families include members who suffer from diminished capacity as they age, a condition that can become even more challenging if the family member controls significant financial or business resources. Patricia Annino offers a list of steps to take before a family member's capacity diminishes, as well as guidance for opening up the conversation of diminished capacity with key family leaders.

Finally, planning often involves one's legacy—what one leaves behind. Most people consider their values to be a key part of their legacy, and yet they struggle with how to pass on those values. Scotty McLennan rounds out this section with a wonderful exercise—"Creating an Ethical Will"—that has stood the test of time and that gives parents or grandparents a way to express their most deeply held feelings and beliefs and to share those effectively with the people they love most.

CHAPTER 18

Expressing Purpose in Your Trusts

John A. Warnick

For the last decade or so of his active practice as a lawyer, my mentor James "Jay" Hughes would not take on a client to write trust documents if the client did not include in his or her trust some such statement as the following: "This trust is a gift of love. Its purpose is to enhance the lives of the beneficiaries."

Those sentences are not legal language. No court is going to seek to interpret what is meant by a "gift of love" or what sorts of distributions are necessitated by "enhancement" of a life. That said, including such a "Purpose Clause" is essential to ensuring that the trust fulfills the hopes you have for it and becomes a true benefit to your beneficiaries.

If trust creators fail to explain the *why* behind the creation of the trust, then beneficiaries are left to infer that purpose for themselves. Given that trusts are festooned with cold, impersonal, legal language, beneficiaries often wonder, "Did they not trust me?" "Did they think I'd blow it?" "What was more important to them—my well-being or keeping me away from the money?" These questions haunt far too many beneficiaries who struggle to see the positive side of their trust. Instead of viewing it as an opportunity, they consider it an obstacle.

The number of purposes for a trust are limitless. It is up to trust creators to decide what matters most—what they want to accomplish and what the impact of their trust will be. It can be helpful to consider some of the purposes for which other people have created trusts. Doing so opens vistas onto what the possible influence and outcomes of your trusts might be. I've had many clients say, "I never knew you could do that with a trust." Each trust is as unique as its creator. Each of us should make sure the light of our vision and purposes are captured in the trusts we create. Otherwise, they could be virtually anyone else's.

Initial Reflections

There is one thing that a trust creator should never forget to do: Spend at least 15 to 20 minutes reflecting on the two golden questions of trust creation:

1. Why am I creating this trust?
2. How would I want to be treated if someone were creating a trust for me?

If you do nothing else but answer those two questions with as much thought as possible, then your gift will be both positive and purposeful. If you put all sorts of other bells and whistles in your trust but neglect to reflect carefully about your hopes and dreams for what you will leave your family, your trust will not be as purposeful as it might have been.

Expressing Purpose in Your Trusts

Step 1

Once you have thought about why you're creating a trust, you can turn to the specific steps of expressing purpose in this trust.

To begin, carefully review the list of possible trust purposes in the following boxes. As you do, think about whether you would have wanted that as a purpose of a trust which might have been created for your benefit. After you have gone through the list completely, go through it once more, but this time circle the purposes that you feel are part of the hopes and dreams you have for your trust.

Which of these purposes is part of the gift you want your trust to be?

Provide Financial Security Enhancement—Make Life Better Encourage Education A Gift of Love, Faith, and Hope Guidance Contribute to Their Physical and Emotional Well-Being Let Them Know How Much I Love Them Preservation of Specific Assets Gift of Family Heirlooms A More Comfortable Life Than We Enjoyed Pass on Values and Life Wisdom Protect Assets against Creditors Promote Family Unity and Harmony Minimize or Avoid Taxes Legacy—Honor Our Heritage Encourage Volunteerism and Philanthropy	Teach and Encourage Stewardship Succession Planning—Preparing the Next Generation of Family Leaders Acquire Financial Planning and Wealth Management Skills Invest and Manage the Assets Prudently Safeguard Assets Create Mentoring or Coaching Opportunities Preparation of My Heirs for the Wealth Training the Next Generation(s) to be Excellent Beneficiaries Make Their Dreams Possible Incentivize My Heirs Create a Family Bank Help with Acquiring a Home or Starting or Expanding a Business Disinherit Specific Individuals Influence Career, Lifestyle, or Relationship Choices Restrict Freedom of Investment Choice

Now that you have circled some of the possible purposes for your trust, are there any other purposes that you would add to this list?

Step 2

If you circled more than 10 purposes, place a star next to what you feel are the five or six most important.

Step 3

Pretend for a moment that a law has been enacted that says that your trust can have only one purpose. Which would it be and why? Place three stars next to it and explain in the following space or on a separate sheet why this purpose is so important and what you hope its accomplishment would mean to your beneficiaries.

Step 4

After you have identified the most important purpose in Step 3, rank the other purposes that you placed stars next to or circled, and answer these questions.

Purpose 2—My Second Most Important Purpose:

- Why is this purpose important to me and how do I hope this purpose will be a positive influence in the lives of my beneficiaries?
- Is there an experience in your life that illustrates how important this purpose is?

Purpose 3—My Third Most Important Purpose:

- Why is this purpose important to me and how do I hope this purpose will be a positive influence in the lives of my beneficiaries?
- Is there an experience in your life that illustrates how important this purpose is?

Purpose 4—My Fourth Most Important Purpose:

- Why is this purpose important to me and how do I hope this purpose will be a positive influence in the lives of my beneficiaries?
- Is there an experience in your life that illustrates how important this purpose is?

Purpose 5—My Fifth Most Important Purpose:

- Why is this purpose important to me and how do I hope this purpose will be a positive influence in the lives of my beneficiaries?
- Is there an experience in your life that illustrates how important this purpose is?

Bringing It All Together

If you have followed the previous steps, you have a robust list of purposes for your trust, as well as several paragraphs describing why these purposes are so important to you, what you hope the trust dedicated to these purposes will do for your beneficiaries, and what experiences in your own life give you hope that the trust will have this effect. This is already a great accomplishment!

Now there are several directions in which you can go to inform your trust or trusts with these purposes. I will sketch them briefly here. For more on practical ways that you can use your statement of purpose in your trusts, I recommend reviewing the book: *Family Trusts: A Guide for Beneficiaries, Trustees, Trust Protectors, and Trust Creators.*

1. String together your statements about your purposes into a single paragraph, which can serve as a "Preamble" to your trust, like Jay's sentences, "This trust is a gift of love. Its purpose is to enhance the lives of the beneficiaries."
2. Develop your list of purposes and the paragraphs you've written about them into a Letter to Your Beneficiaries. This letter can accompany the trust and be given by the trustee (or by you) to the beneficiaries when they come of age. It is something that the trustee and beneficiaries can then return to each year in their discussions of how the trust can benefit the beneficiaries' lives.
3. Similarly, you can adapt your list of purposes and statements about those purposes into a Letter to Your Trustees. Trustees find any statement by the trust creator about his or her intentions for the trust extremely helpful in making informed judgments about future discretionary distributions to beneficiaries.
4. If you are technologically minded, consider making a video of yourself reading your Letter to Your Beneficiaries—even a brief smartphone video would be a powerful record not only of your words but of you, the person who willed this trust into being for these reasons. You could expand this video to include your talking about some of your own life experiences that led you to choose these purposes for this trust.
5. Many trusts include a list of preferences that the trust creator asks the trust to use in prioritizing future discretionary distributions. This list does not bind the trustee's hands, but it does give the trustee some guidance in choosing among distribution requests. You can take your list of purposes and, together with your trust attorney, use it to shape that list of preferences to guide future trustees.
6. Likewise, if you have trusts already in existence that lack purpose, you can confer with your trust attorney about the best ways to use your newly developed purposes to infuse them with purpose. Options range from attaching letters to these trusts all the way to "decanting" or reforming the existing trusts so that they better reflect your purposes.

Case Study

Perhaps the easiest application of your statement of purpose comes in how you choose to talk to the beneficiaries about the trusts and about money now. For example, once I helped two parents through this exercise, regarding some very large trusts that they had established for their three children and future generations. Their children were at this point already young adults. They knew that the trusts existed, but they had no idea what they were for, and so they avoided asking or talking about the trusts because they did not want to appear "greedy." Likewise, the parents avoided talking about the trusts because they did not really know what they wanted, except to avoid making their children feel "entitled." This mutual discomfort and silence meant that valuable opportunities to give purpose to this money were being lost.

Happily, the parents realized that their children had grown up with solid values and were not in danger of becoming entitled. So, first the parents went through this exercise to clarify their own wishes for the trusts. They realized, based on their experiences and values, that they wanted the trusts, first and foremost, to promote an entrepreneurial spirit in their children and future family members. They also wanted the trusts to give their family members the freedom to pursue their individual dreams. Finally, they wanted the trusts to afford their family members a certain basic level of financial security.

With these purposes in mind, the parents together wrote a brief letter to their children, which included these purposes and some stories from their lives that gave context to their hopes and wishes. They then convened a family meeting at which they read the letter to their adult children. In addition to their reading, they added further stories and reflections. They then gave their children an opportunity to ask questions, and a rich conversation ensued in which the children had a chance to begin to talk about their own dreams and hopes for how the trusts might play a role in their lives and their own children's lives eventually. One of the children also videoed the parents' reading and the conversation so that they could keep it as a record of this starting point.

For this was the initial step for this family, not the end. Based on the discussion, the parents further refined their letter. One of the things they added was the wish that each of their children would have the freedom, in the future, to add his or her wishes to the trust or trusts that would eventually benefit their own children. The parents then worked with their trust attorney to create a Statement of Wishes that accompanies their trusts and provides guidance for the trustees. The trustees review this statement every year in their annual meetings with each of the beneficiaries. The children feel clear about the purposes of the trusts and feel empowered to ask for trust funds to pursue those purposes. And the parents have the enjoyment of seeing the spirit of their gift play out in their children's lives.

Additional Resources

Hartley Goldstone, James E. Hughes, and Keith Whitaker, *Family Trusts: A Guide for Beneficiaries, Trustees, Trust Protectors, and Trust Creators* (New York: Wiley, 2017).

Hartley Goldstone and Kathy Wiseman, *Trustworthy: New Angles on Trusts from Beneficiaries and Trustees* (CreateSpace, 2012).

Biography

After practicing for 30 years as a tax and legal advisor to wealthy families, **John A. Warnick** left the large law firm he was a partner in to pursue his passion of assisting clients transition their wealth more purposefully. He works with clients, and their team of advisors, to ensure that the impact of their technical planning will be a positive force in the lives of the rising generations of their family. "John A" is the founder of the Purposeful Planning Institute and a fellow of the American College of Trust and Estate Counsel. He has served as the philanthropic editor of the *Journal of Practical Estate Planning* and serves on the Carter Center Philanthropy Council and the Multidisciplinary Teaming and Professional Collaboration Committee of the National Association of Estate Planners and Councils. John A received his BA *magna cum laude* from Brigham Young University and his JD from George Washington University with honors.

CHAPTER 19

Managing a Shared Family Property

Jamie Forbes

Legacy family properties can be a powerful grounding force. It's rare these days to have one place that remains constant throughout our lives. Many people move away for school, then to an apartment, and then to a larger house with the arrival of children. The average U.S. citizen moves more than 11 times in their lives.[1] Americans tend to move more than residents from other countries, but the fact remains that most of us move multiple times throughout life.

Having a home to which you can return through all those transitions provides a sense of place, a connection that remains unchanged amid all the other changes in life.

Such a place can be a huge gift. As someone with a shared family property that has been in my family for eight generations, I know firsthand that sense of belonging to a place and to the people who share it with me.

And yet, as anyone who has ever shared a property with other family members can attest, it takes work. There can be conflict that, if unresolved, can fester and upset family relationships. For this reason, many advisors recommend selling family properties instead of passing them on to your descendants and hoping they can figure out how to make it work.

Perhaps selling is the right thing to do for your family. But before you make that decision, it's worth considering what makes the most sense. This really needs to be a group discussion that includes everyone who will be responsible for the successful transition and ongoing decisions. Keeping a legacy family property while also keeping the family together requires clear communication, thoughtful planning, structure, and commitment. And it takes funding.

This conversation will take time. Depending on geographic and personal constraints, it could take several months or even several years to reach a decision and create a plan.

---

[1]Mona Chalabi, "How Many Times Does the Average Person Move?" FiveThirtyEight (January 29, 2015), https://fivethirtyeight.com/features/how-many-times-the-average-person-moves.

It is useful to think of the process as three different steps or phases. Each of the steps can result in a decision to sell, or it can progress to the end with a specific plan for transitioning ownership, according to decisions made along the way.

- *Step 1.* Owner discussion—Hold the property or transition out
- *Step 2.* Family discussion—Interest and willingness
- *Step 3.* Family discussion—Creating a working plan

Step 1. Owner Discussion—Hold the Property or Transition Out

This is a discussion among those who currently own, manage, and control the property, and your advisors. Often the owners are a couple who acquired the real estate. Sometimes it's more than one couple, as when the owners are siblings or even friends who decided to buy the property together. Key considerations for this discussion include the following:

1. Will you need the proceeds for another use?
2. Do family members have an attachment to the property?
3. Do family members enjoy the property together?
4. Have family members expressed interest in keeping the property?
5. Do you think the property would help maintain family relationships?
6. Do you have any specific concerns about whether it would work?
7. Are some family members more interested than others?
8. If so, do you have a way to make your decision seem fair for those not interested in keeping the property?
9. Would keeping the property put a financial burden on your family that may create stress?

There are likely other questions you'll want to ask yourself that relate to the property itself or to the specific dynamics of your family. The main objectives in this step are to become clear about what your vision is for the property and to understand what the major challenges are to achieve your vision for future ownership.

Step 2. Family Discussion—Interest and Willingness

Whether you plan to keep the property in the family or sell it, the next step is to meet with family members. This step begins with outlining what you think makes sense: what is your vision for the future of the property you plan to sell? Explain why that makes sense to you so everyone understands. If you'd like to explore the possibility of keeping the property in the family, let everyone know you want their input. The goal in this step is to understand what family members want to do and begin exploring how that might work. You may come to an agreement in Step 2 that it is time to sell. Or the discussions may lead you to create a specific plan in place for transitioning the property to family members.

Step 3. Family Discussion—Creating a Working Plan

This step requires a lot of detailed discussions and generally takes the most time. The objective of Step 3 is to develop a clear understanding of what will be required for each owner/family member. You need to create a structure and process for management, usage, decision-making, and capital investments. You should discuss how family members will resolve conflict (because there will be conflict!). If there is no endowment or revenue that fully supports the annual expenses, consider how family members are to deal with financial disparity among themselves. In other words, what happens when some are more able to contribute to the property's upkeep than others? And you need to discuss how you plan to add new family members as owners (through marriage or new generations) and how ownership will transition (because of divorce, death, or for financial reasons).

Things to Consider throughout the Process

Don't force the discussion. Being patient can be very challenging, and it's not always possible. Sometimes a death in the family or terminal illness creates a sense of urgency that is unavoidable. But ideally this conversation should begin well before any decisions are required. You can move the process forward by creating agendas for meetings and clarifying next steps. Consider using a professional facilitator for larger families or more complex properties so that everyone can participate fully.

Be open. You may have a vision that you're really excited about, but if it's not shared by others, it will not be successful. The more flexible you are about the outcome, the more likely it is that everyone will feel good about the process and support the eventual decision.

Don't feel you have to go it alone. Families often find that hiring an outside facilitator is helpful. It can make the process feel a bit more formal at times, but it is generally more efficient and allows everyone to participate rather than letting family dynamics interfere with the discussion.

Observe behaviors. Conversations about emotionally charged topics such as money and cherished family properties can be very revealing. Use the discussion with your family to anticipate how well they will work together on the property.

Talk about the things that might go wrong. Things *will* go wrong, whether it's from a natural disaster, mechanical failure, or accident. Some of these are easy to discuss. Others may be more difficult. You won't be able to anticipate everything, but the more you are able to talk through, the easier it will be to think in practical terms about what you will do.

Document the vision. It's useful to document why you are choosing to work with your family members to preserve the property. This does not need to be a lengthy document. In fact, it can even be a short paragraph. It simply needs to state why the property is important to you as a family. You might start this with your personal vision and have your family add their vision, so the result is collaborative. This statement can be a reference point for decisions and to resolve conflict.

Tricky Issues

The following is a list of common things that can cause conflict over time with legacy family properties. Talk through them during Step 3 and think of any others that may be more specific to your family or to the property itself.

Communication. Strong communication is an essential ingredient in keeping the property in the family. Create a process that supports consistent communication. Family members should meet at least once a year to discuss financial details, make decisions, discuss usage, and address any challenges. I suggest you meet once a year in person and, in addition, have quarterly conference calls. The quarterly discussions enable you to address any issues that came up in the previous season and address topics about future needs. It is essential to create a process for raising and resolving disagreement because conflict is inevitable in group ownership.

Financial burden. It is easy to enjoy a place that someone else is funding or has endowed. When there is no mortgage on the property, and there's a funding plan to support whatever is needed in the way of capital expenses, real estate taxes, and property management, there is one less major source of conflict. But these situations are extremely rare. Typically, there are at least annual expenses that need to be covered. There are too many options for a complete discussion on the different ownership structures and the implications for each. These details also vary by state and country. Find good advisors who specialize in these matters to help you understand what type of ownership structure and financial model makes sense for both your property and your family. Make sure the model is sustainable for whatever time horizon you think is reasonable for your family's ownership. Consider how to make it affordable for everyone.

Financial disparity. Sooner or later this will be an issue for family members if the property remains in the family for a long time. It first appears in discussions about upkeep or the question of whether it's time to renovate the kitchen. Then it creeps into conversations about annual fees or dues. Think about how you will handle these issues. In general, families that find ways to successfully accommodate financial disparity are also able to sustain their collective ownership longer than families that have more rigid "pay-to-play" rules. The most straightforward way to do this is by establishing an endowment or using an earned revenue stream, such as rental income, which can be set aside for current or future use. Some families also find it useful to create a process for buying out family members who no longer wish to participate. Others focus more on creating a process to ensure that the property is available to all family members, regardless of their ability to pay.

Usage disparity. The more users there are, the faster this will become an issue. Some family members may live within driving distance to the property while others may require lengthy travel. Those who live close-by are more likely to be frequent visitors while those who live further afield may visit fewer times during the year and for longer stretches of time. It's important to be aware of these differences, discuss them, and find ways to accommodate them. Creating a scheduling, reservation, and time-allocation process can be a useful way of ensuring everyone understands and follows the process.

Ownership perception. This issue can be closely tied to usage disparity. Ownership perception is different than actual ownership. It describes the perceived difference in ownership among family members. In general, the objective is to prevent differences in ownership perception within the family. It's not easy because more frequent users often participate more in property management and maintenance needs. For example, imagine you cut, split, and stack the three cords of wood needed for the fireplace each winter while other family members use their time on the property to relax and enjoy the view. Over time, recurring patterns like this can translate into some family members feeling like their hard work should give them more say when decisions need to be made. Those who spend just one week on the property may begin to sense over time that their vote doesn't count as much on decisions because they aren't as active in ongoing management details. All these challenges can be addressed and mitigated, but they need to be discussed and aired.

Management burden. The size and scope of the property will dictate how much time it takes to manage and steward it. If a lot of hands-on work is required, consider including property management fees or other staffing costs into the annual expenses. Sometimes family members decide to rotate the management responsibilities, so every member shares the burden over time. If that's not practical, be clear about what makes the most sense and discuss whether the "manager's" time commitment should be recognized in some way, whether in a reduction of annual fees or some other gesture. If you decide to create exceptions, be mindful of how it might impact everyone's ownership perception.

House rules. House cleaning, food stocking, storage space, and even parenting styles can all come into play here. It is no fun to arrive to a house that isn't clean or has no food in the pantry when you left it fully stocked on your last visit. Establishing clear expectations for these details can go a long way toward family harmony. If there are discrepancies between family members about what it means to leave the house "clean," create a checklist and guidelines. That way, when there is conflict, you can have a specific conversation about how to address it.

Legacy family properties can build long-standing family connections, provide a lifetime of memories and create continuity through generations that establishes a unique sense of belonging and identity. When families are intentional with how they make it work, it can be magical. It's worth taking the time. That will make all the difference.

Additional Resources

James Hughes, *Family: The Compact Among Generations* (New York: Bloomberg Press, 2007).

James Hughes, Susan Massenzio, and Keith Whitaker, *Complete Family Wealth* (New York: Bloomberg Press, 2018).

Charles W. Collier, *Wealth in Families*, 3rd ed. (Cambridge, MA: Harvard University, 2012).
Roy Williams and Vic Preisser, *Preparing Heirs* (Bandon, OR: Robert D. Reed Publishers, 2011).
George Howe Colt, *The Big House* (New York: Simon & Schuster, 2004).

Biography

Jamie Forbes grew up in an old New England family imbued with a strong sense of belonging, good fortune, and a clear understanding that with privilege comes responsibility. This experience taught him the importance of family culture, tradition, mentoring, and stewardship.

As founder of Forbes Legacy Advisors, Jamie works with individuals and families on all aspects of family culture. He believes that sustaining a healthy family culture is an essential element of creating resilient families. Jamie advises clients in the areas of family culture, governance, and philanthropy.

When he is not at work, Jamie can be found with his wife and two daughters or enjoying time with friends. Jamie is a Charter Advisor of Philanthropy (CAP), holds a BA in economics from Connecticut College, and has also studied at the Wharton School and Babson College.

CHAPTER 20

Creating a Family Bank

James E. Hughes, Jr.

The family bank is a practice that provides a means for a family's wealth to be leveraged by making loans available to family members on terms not available commercially. These are loans that would be considered high risk by commercial bankers but are low risk to the family because of their contribution to the family's long-term wealth preservation plan.

Loans from a family bank are usually for two purposes: *investment*, to increase the family's financial capital, or *enhancement*, to increase the family's qualitative capital, that is, the family's long-term well-being.

Investment

In the case of loans for investment, the family's purpose is to take advantage of opportunities brought by individual family members for financial gain. The loans give the family opportunities to grow its financial wealth while also enhancing the intellectual growth of individual members. These are frequently investments in businesses founded by individual family members.

Such business loans should follow these basic rules:

1. The borrower prepares a business plan and a loan application equivalent to that required by any commercial lender.
2. The borrower discusses the project's feasibility with the family bank's board and advisors.
3. When a loan is granted, the borrower provides proper business reports on the investment.
4. The borrower ultimately repays the loan.

This process gives the family borrower excellent business training and the highest possible chance of a successful financial outcome. It also allows the family the chance to reap a financial reward from the individual family member's initiative.

Enhancement

With enhancement loans, the family's purpose is to increase its qualitative capital by increasing the independence and growth of individual family members.

As with investment loans, proper lending procedures for enhancement loans are critical to the growth of each borrower's qualitative capital. When seeking an enhancement loan, the borrower should be encouraged to state how such a loan will increase his or her independence and growth, as well as how the loan will add to the family's human, legacy, family relationship, structural, or social capital. When family members explain to their peers and advisors on the family bank board how a loan will be enhancing, they must be certain that their individual qualitative capital will really be enhanced. With enhancement loans, repayment comes in the form of the increased independence of the individual borrower and his or her increased qualitative capital.

Common varieties of enhancement loans include funds for education or for the down payment on a primary residence. Such loans may be made on an interest-free base, or on an interest-only payment plan, with the balance to be forgiven at a future date. As a result, enhancement loans may turn into grants or gifts, which requires careful consultation with competent tax advisors. That said, the goal of enhancement loans is never simply tax mitigation but rather the increase of the individual's independence and the family's qualitative capital.

It may seem like a surprising point, that a *loan* could increase individual *independence.* The surprise is natural. Entered unwisely, a loan can create terrible dependence and resentment. It is for this reason that many family members react instinctively against the notion of a family bank: "Never a lender or a borrower be!" Never, indeed—without a clear focus on the enhancement of family members' true well-being.

That is why families striving to preserve their complete family wealth quickly grasp that a family bank is not primarily about financial capital. While having a friendly lender gives an enormous competitive boost, it is the growth of qualitative capital that is the true reason for forming a family bank.

Practical Considerations

Managing a family bank is a delicate business. Here are the beginnings of some guidelines for setting one up:

- The family bank should not be a formal institution. It isn't a bank in the normal corporate sense. It is important that it be informal so that its activities remain private and so that it can evolve a system of governance that meets the unique circumstances of the family that creates it.
- While it is not a formal institution, the family bank must have formal rules for meetings. It should have officers, directors, and, if needed, advisory boards. It should have procedures for receiving and processing loan applications. That said, the rules and procedures will vary considerably, depending

on who will fund the loans. For example, parents who create a family bank from their own funds will likely have much more latitude than trustees who seek to use a trust as a family bank, even one with a broad mandate for distributions.

- The family bank must have a mission statement explaining its philosophy and reason for being. The lenders and borrowers must understand the family bank's purpose—to be a high-risk, low-interest lender—and the consequences of that policy. The bank's mission statement should also contain a values section incorporating the overall family mission statement and should explain how the bank will assist in carrying out that mission.
- Because family trusts are potential lenders and borrowers, it is particularly important that trustees understand and agree to participate in the family bank. Even if you don't have a family bank right now, if you believe that your family would someday want to use the family bank concept, it would be wise to include the requisite powers and permissions for future trustees in any trusts or successor trusts you create.
- It is important to have concurrence of all family members, both lenders and borrowers, with the terms of the bank's mission statement.

It is particularly important that all family members who agree to participate in the family bank be given copies of all loan applications. Personal financial data may be withheld for confidentiality, but all members should receive the qualitative capital portions of the applications.

Conclusion

Without being named as such, the family bank concept has formed the core of the creation and growth of family fortunes from the days of the Medici and Rothschilds to the present-day creation of many "tech" fortunes. But beyond its financial power, the family bank offers a way for family members to articulate and practice the skills of communication and decision-making that lie at the heart of individual and family flourishing. If qualitative capital is a family's true wealth, the family bank is a paramount means of preserving and growing that capital for generations to come.

This article has been adapted from *Complete Family Wealth,* 2nd ed. (Wiley: New York, 2022).

Additional Resources

James E. Hughes, Jr., *Family Wealth,* 2nd. ed. (Wiley: New York, 2004).

James E. Hughes, Susan E. Massenzio, and Keith Whitaker, *Cycle of the Gift* (Wiley: New York, 2012).

James E. Hughes, Susan E. Massenzio, and Keith Whitaker, *Complete Family Wealth,* 2nd. ed. (Wiley: New York, 2022).

Biography

Widely considered the father of the field of family wealth, **James "Jay" E. Hughes, Jr.**, is a retired attorney and author of *Family Wealth: Keeping It in the Family* and *Family—The Compact Among Generations.* Jay is co-author of *The Cycle of the Gift, The Voice of the Rising Generation,* and *Family Trusts: A Guide for Beneficiaries, Trustees, Trust Protectors and Trust Creators.* Jay was the founder of a law partnership in New York City. He is a member of various philanthropic boards and a member of the editorial boards of various professional journals. Jay is a graduate of the Far Brook School, which teaches through the arts, the Pingry School, Princeton University, and the Columbia School of Law.

CHAPTER 21

Undertaking a Family Risk Assessment

Linda Bourn

A family risk assessment typically has three objectives:

- Understand each family's unique risk profile.
- Develop a plan to manage risk across generations and family holdings.
- Integrate risk planning into annual wealth and financial management discussions.

This process should include the family's relevant advisors, including the family office, wealth management advisor, estate planning attorney, accountant, and insurance advisor.

Using an established process like the one shown in Figure 21.1 may help families and their advisors to develop an integrated risk assessment and management plan.

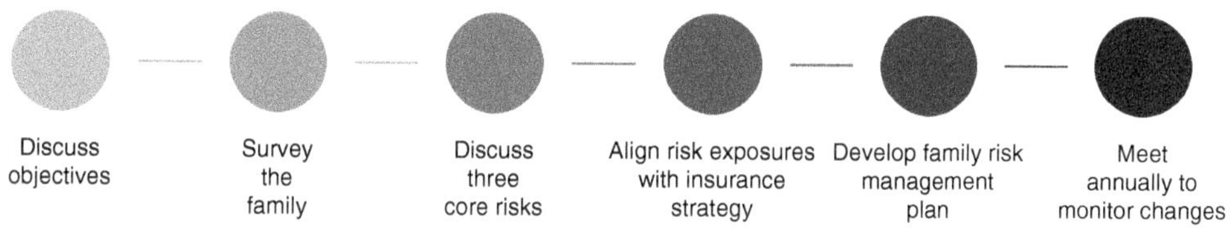
Discuss objectives
Survey the family
Discuss three core risks
Align risk exposures with insurance strategy
Develop family risk management plan
Meet annually to monitor changes

Figure 21.1 Family Risk Assessment

Source: Alliant Private Client

Family Risk Awareness Survey

Families today are facing ever-more-diverse risks, from a global pandemic to hurricanes to cyber incidents. A short risk assessment survey can help family members understand and participate in the risk planning process. It may also help them develop a sense of their own risk concerns and their individual unique risk exposures.

Family Risk Assessment Ranking
What Keeps You Up at Night?

	Rank 1 (highest) to 10 (lowest)
Personal Cyber Risk (Data breaches, malware and viruses, fraudulent credit and bank transfers, phishing schemes, etc.)	__________
Natural Disasters Impacting Tangible Property (Wildfire, hurricane, earthquake, flood, tornado, etc.)	__________
Liability from Outside Board Position (Serving on nonprofit boards and associated liability)	__________
Liability from Serving as Trustee of Family Trusts	__________
Employment Practices Liability (Discrimination, sexual harassment, wrongful termination, etc.)	__________
Liability Resulting from Dependent Children (Young drivers, recreational sports, social networking, etc.)	__________
Travel Risk (Medical [e.g., pandemic], international travel, emergency response planning)	__________
Damage or Loss of Value to Collections (Fine art collection, jewelry, wine, etc.)	__________
Ownership, Operation, or Charter of Aircraft or Yachts	__________
Hosting Events at Home or Public Venues (Liquor liability, subcontractors, etc.)	__________
Other (specify):	__________

Source: Alliant Private Client

Recognize Core Family Risk Landscape

In order to understand the family risk landscape, Figure 21.2 can be an effective tool to help identify various risks during annual wealth planning discussions. To begin the dialogue, focus on the four key risk areas in your planning discussions:

1. Asset Profile: What is owned and how are they owned
   The range of tangible assets such as residences, collections, and unique assets such aviation, yachts, farms, or ranches and how they are owned (e.g., LLCs, trusts).
2. Social Media: Social and digital footprint
   This includes information security as well as the evaluation of cyber risk.
3. Roles: Personal and professional
   Evaluation of roles and potential liability (director, trustee, employer).
4. Locations: Residence locations and travel profile
   Residence locations have their own unique risks of natural disasters (wildfires, hurricanes, earthquakes). Travel requires emergency preparedness for medical and security situations.

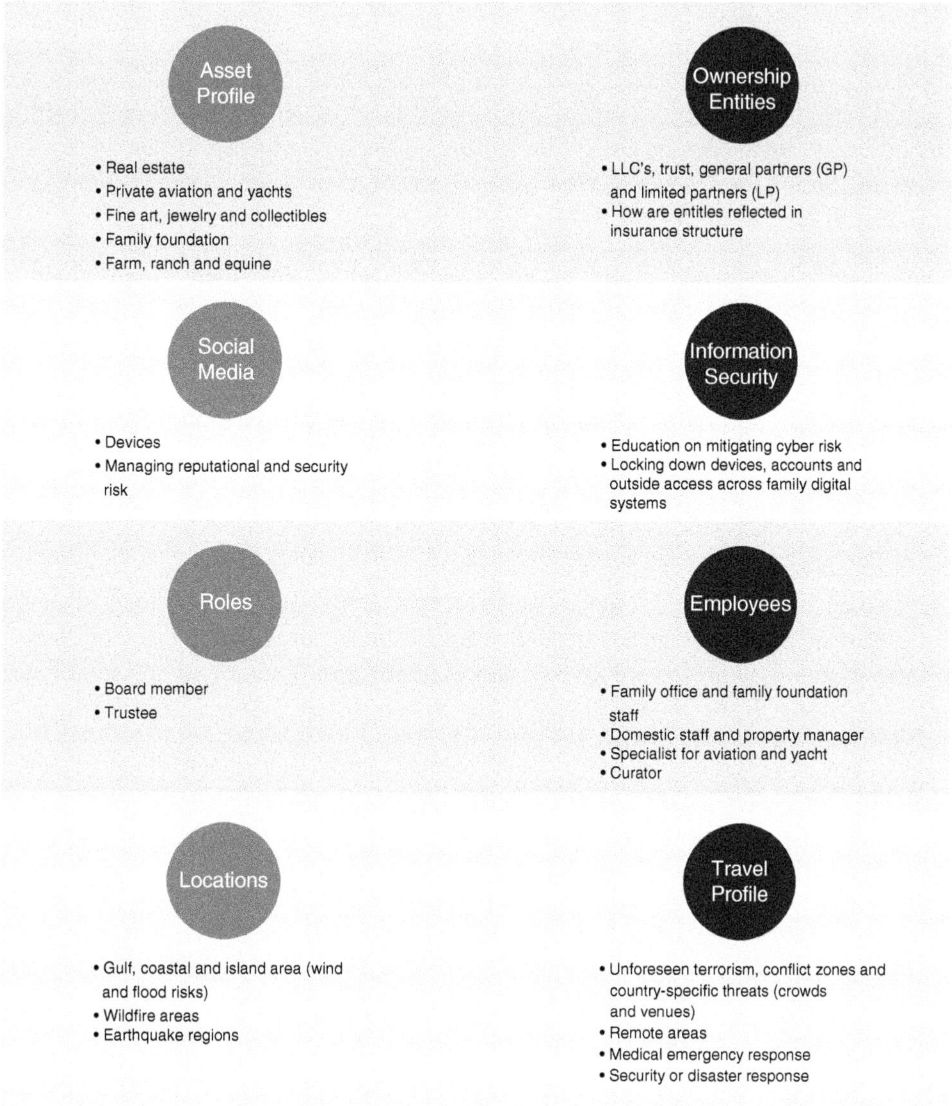

Figure 21.2 Family Risk Discovery Areas

Source: Alliant Private Client

Discuss Core Family Risk Areas

Two main risk categories are persistent for most wealthy families and can have a substantial impact on one's lifestyle: cyber and natural disaster.

Personal Cyber Risk

Our personal data are exposed to potential cyber criminals through our use of numerous websites, apps, and organizations on various devices—phones, tablets, or computers. Unfortunately, cyber criminals exploit PII (personally identifiable information). Examples of PII as defined by the Department of Homeland Security include Social Security numbers, driver's license numbers, and financial or medical records.[1]

As an example, in 2020 the Consumer Sentinel Network, a secure online law enforcement database, received 4.8 million reports, including 2.2 million of fraud (46 percent of all reports), 1.4 million reports of identity theft (29 percent), and 1.2 million other reports. The report[2] indicated more than $3.3 billion was lost to fraud.

According to Chubb,[3] personal cyber risk includes the risk of financial loss through examples such as cyber extortion and ransomware, unauthorized credit card charges, cyber breach of personal information and identity theft, cyberbullying, and fraudulent funds transfer.

Family Risk Discovery Questions:

1. Are you enrolled in an ID theft monitoring service of your credit files, social media, and personal information to quickly address criminal activity?
2. Have you installed antivirus and malware protection software on all of your devices?
3. Have you properly secured your devices and app purchases, such as purchasing password protecting app, limiting tracking of data and location, or protecting your data if your device is lost or stolen?
4. Have you explored cyber insurance to reimburse various expenses and provide access to specialists to resolve identity theft events?

Natural Disaster Risk

Family homes, whether primary residences, vacation properties, or family vacation compounds, are often located in ever-changing catastrophe-prone areas (wildfire, hurricane, earthquake, flood). The National Oceanic and Atmospheric Association and its National Centers for Environmental Information 2020 overview[4] of U.S. billion-dollar natural disaster events included a record seven disasters linked to tropical cyclones, thirteen to severe storms, one to drought, and one to wildfires.

These types of events can impact family homes and valuable contents (e.g., high valued furnishings, fine art, jewelry, heirlooms, autos, or collector vehicles garaged at the location).

---

[1] Department of Homeland Security, PII definition, https://www.dhs.gov/privacy-training/what-personally-identifiable-information#:~:text=%E2%80%9D%2C%20or%20PII%3A-,DHS%20defines%20PII%20as%20any%20information%20that%20permits%20the%20identity,U.S.%2C%20or%20employee%20or%20contractor.

[2] Federal Trade Commission, Consumer Sentinel Network Data Book 2020, ftc.gov/data.

[3] Chubb, Personal Insurance website, www.chubb.com.

[4] NOAA, Billion-Dollar Weather and Climate Disasters: Overview, www.ncdc.noaa.gov/billions.

Family Risk Discovery Questions:

1. Describe your emergency preparedness plan. Does it allow access to residential properties for wildfire defense services? Does it have a hurricane preparation or evacuation plan—people, animals, valuable personal property? Does each family member have a plan?
2. What type of plan is in place for fine art or other collections, e.g., storage, packing, shipping?
3. How have you utilized complimentary risk mitigation services from your insurance advisor? (See Figure 21.3.)

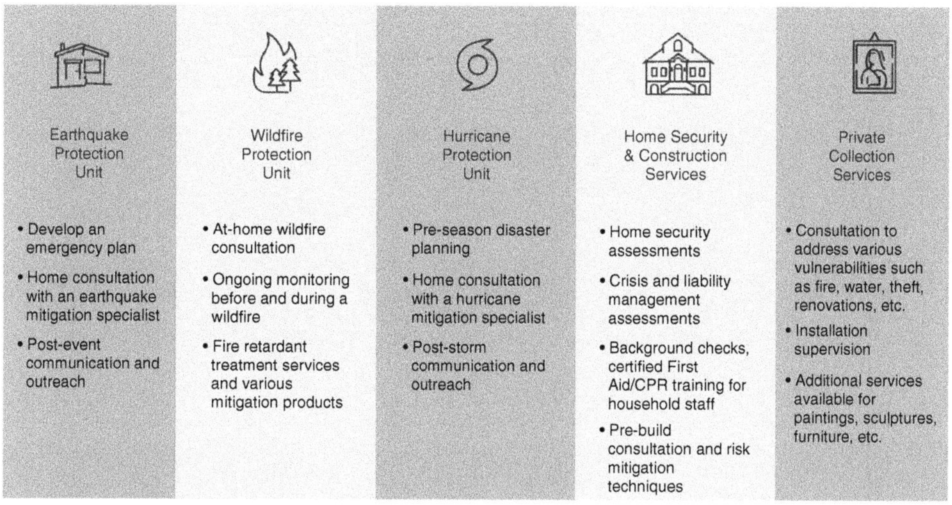

Figure 21.3 Risk Mitigation Areas

Source: Alliant Private Client

Develop an Action Plan

The framework detailed in Figure 21.4 is a tool that can help families begin thinking about the impact of risks on their lifestyle and how they want to address them accordingly. Some risks such as natural disasters have the biggest impact on personal lifestyle as well as tangible assets and require risk management tools such as insurance to help manage that risk.

Other risks such as serving as a trustee or director require managing governance practices to successfully address the duties of the role.

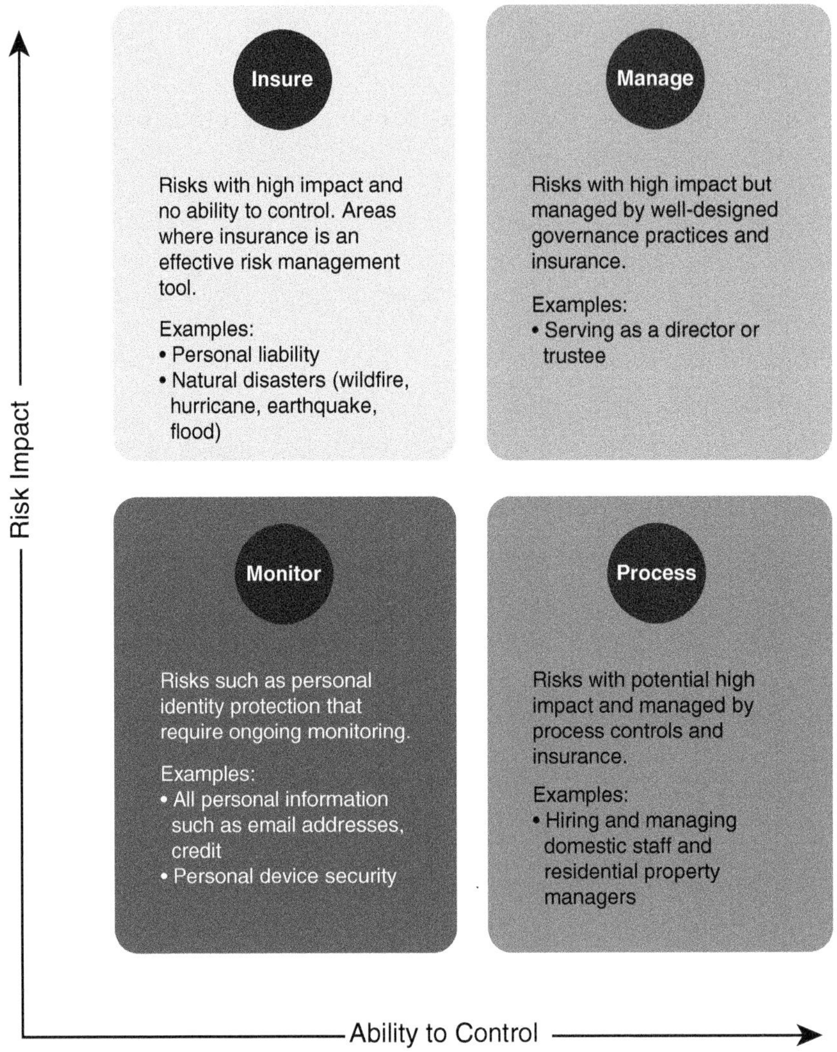

Figure 21.4 Risk Decision Framework

Source: Adapted from 2015 Crystal & Company, an Alliant-owned company, Family Enterprise Risk Index and Family Office Metrics risk review framework

Utilizing Insurance as an Effective Planning Tool

Insurance is an effective risk management planning tool that can help address a range of risk exposures that have a high impact on the lifestyle of the family. Complimentary risk assessment services such as natural disaster mitigation can be coordinated through an insurance advisor, as described previously. The process can also track limited liability corporations and trusts that own assets and should be properly reflected within the appropriate policy. The insurance review process shown in Figure 21.5 can be integrated into annual planning discussions (See Figure 21.5).

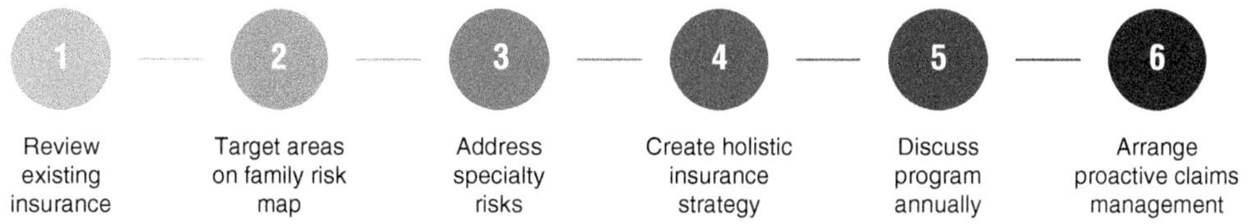

Figure 21.5 Insurance Review Process

Source: Alliant Private Client

Summary

Although personal risk management can seem overwhelming, the first step is to begin a family risk assessment. The assessment can help identify your family's risk landscape and help provide insight into unique risks that require a more detailed plan.

Having informative discussions with the help of professional advisors can help families develop awareness of their risks, implement a plan to address their risks, and annually monitor their plan to keep pace with changes that occur throughout the year.

Additional Resources

IdentityTheft.gov: Report identity theft and get a recovery plan

uhnwinstitute.org/resource-library: Risk Management Domain. Education about the major risks impacting wealthy families, with strategies for integrated risk and insurance planning

CoreLogic, 2021 Wildfire Report

CoreLogic, 2021 Hurricane Report

Biography

Linda Bourn leads the Family Enterprise Risk practice of Alliant Private Client. She specializes in guiding generational families through a holistic risk assessment to help them align risk exposures with insurance strategy. She advises family office boards on directors and officers liability, and evaluates insurance for complex family holdings held in trusts, limited liability corporations, and partnerships.

She is a fellow of the Family Firm Institute, an advisory board member of Babson College Institute for Family Entrepreneurship, and risk management domain chair of the UHNW Institute. She holds an MBA from Babson College, BA from California State University at Long Beach, and the FFI GEN Advanced Certificate in Family Business Advising.

CHAPTER 22

Is Your Infrastructure Resilient?

Natasha Pearl

Mr. Bluebird (not his actual name) sold his successful operating business some years ago. He owns estates in three different locations. Upon arriving at his Colorado ranch for a much-needed vacation, he confronted three unpleasant surprises. First, he discovered that the dishwasher, motorized shades, and heating system were broken. He texted his estate manager, but she was on vacation (not visible on his calendar). Second, the pool and landscape vendors called Mr. Bluebird on his cell phone (how did they get his number?), stating that their unpaid invoices were more than 90 days past due. Third, he received an urgent e-mail (fourth request) from a private equity fund manager stating that 24 hours remained to wire substantial funds (which exceeded his cash on hand) for a capital call.

Mr. Bluebird serves as his own chief investment officer, selecting investment managers as well as making direct investments in private companies. He is planning to create a consolidated investment statement where he can view the cost basis and current valuation of his investments, but he hasn't gotten around to it just yet. In addition, he hasn't created an investment policy statement (IPS) and spends considerable time evaluating myriad opportunities that range from commodities, to tech start-ups, real estate, and cybercurrency. Tax season brings a flurry of K-1s and other documentation, which sometimes arrive at the wrong physical or e-mail address and have to be traced.

It's clear that Mr. Bluebird faces multiple risks. Certainly his time and quality of life are negatively impacted. But his lack of personal and administrative infrastructure threatens to reduce the value of his home, makes it impossible to determine his asset allocation much less rebalance if needed, and may reduce his net worth, perhaps drastically.

Like Mr. Bluebird, a surprising number of the wealthy lack infrastructure. Not bridges, roads and harbors, but rather personal and administrative infrastructure—the processes, systems, and resources that enable consistent service levels, improve quality of life, reduce risk, and avoid surprises. Consolidated investment reporting, up-to-date cybersecurity measures, and residential preventative maintenance checklists are all examples of essential infrastructure.

Some point to their personal assistant or chief of staff or their attorney and insist that "all is under control" due to that person's excellent work. But resilient infrastructure is not dependent on any one specific person; rather, it consists of processes and systems that operate in the absence of any specific person.

Why does infrastructure matter? Infrastructure prevents disasters, such as careless spenders depleting their inheritance, residential maintenance breakdowns causing leaks or fire, cybersecurity breaches, compliance issues, and lawsuits. Without infrastructure, wealth preservation becomes a game of chance. What may be less obvious are the positive impacts. Infrastructure enables opportunities, including participation in sophisticated investment and estate planning strategies. Further, it enables peace of mind and sleeping well at night, providing time for strategic and creative thinking.

While it is certainly true that every wealthy individual, and their single-family office (SFO), is unique, it is also true that fundamental infrastructure components must be present in order to maintain a high quality of life, reduce risk, and to preserve wealth.

For these reasons, whether you are an advisor or principal, you need to know: Is the infrastructure robust and state-of-the-art? Or crumbling. Decayed. Nonexistent.

What follows is the Infrastructure Self-Assessment Tool, which enables wealthy individuals and their advisors to quantitatively assess the status of their infrastructure, and to prioritize improvements.

Infrastructure Assessment Instrument

		Excellent = 1, Terrible = 5	Low = 1, High = 5
Core Infrastructure Area	**Definition**	**Status (1–5)**	**Priority (1–5)**
1. Health and Wellness	Oversight and monitoring of physical and mental health; preventive measures including nutrition, exercise, and stress management		
2. Legal Entity Structure Optimization	Strategic selection of the best possible entity or entities (e.g., LLC, foundation, corporation, trust) for real estate and other assets, to achieve objectives related to tax, estate planning, efficiency, and effectiveness		
3. Decision-Making and Conflict Resolution	Knowledge of techniques to efficiently reach decisions and resolve conflicts or ability to source this expertise externally if needed		
4. Human Capital Management	Age-appropriate education and training in key areas including finance, budgeting, and investing; career coaching; skill-building including staff management, creation of high-performing teams, etc.		
5. Compliance	Support and expertise to ensure compliance with laws and regulations related to tax, investing, human resources, vehicles, etc.		
6. Financial Controls/Fraud Prevention	Ensuring segregation of duties, dual control, periodic audits, mandatory vacations, etc.		

Core Infrastructure Area	Definition	Excellent = 1, Terrible = 5 Status (1–5)	Low = 1, High = 5 Priority (1–5)
7. Consolidated Investment Reporting	Systematic tracking of cost basis, performance, and current valuation of all assets by entity		
8. Expense Management	Analysis of spending by entity and category; comparison to contract terms, prior periods, and budget estimates		
9. Liquidity Management	Proactive management to ensure funding of living expenses, philanthropic commitments, capital calls, gifting, etc.		
10. Risk Management	Proactive identification of potential risks and liabilities; periodic property/casualty insurance review		
11. Residential Service and Maintenance Processes	Documentation of steps to be taken, diagrams, frequency and specific techniques, for all aspects of maintenance for all structures owned, including up-to-date contracts and contacts for vendors		
12. Human Resources Procedures for Private and Single Family Offices Staff	Policies for compensation, benefits, time off, and complaint handling; documented processes; regular performance reviews; termination protocol		
13. Security—Physical and Cyber	Residential security including alarms, gates and cameras; cybersecurity including social media and dark web monitoring		
14. Family Reputation Management	Ensuring that the principal, family, businesses and other entities are represented accurately on LinkedIn and other media; proactive monitoring for mentions; crisis public relations resources accessible on short notice		
15. Emergency Planning and Business Continuity	Plans and training for staff and principal in the event of medical, weather, pandemic, or other unexpected crisis		

Scoring

- Add up the entries in the "Status" column. A score greater than 32 indicates serious risks to wealth preservation and a critical need for improvement. Keep in mind, however, that a score lower than 32 may still reveal individual weaknesses that could cause serious damage if not corrected.
- Add up the rows: Status plus Priority. Any scores greater than 7 per area indicate a critical need to improve that specific area.

There are at least five negative consequences of deficient infrastructure.

- Inconsistency and workarounds. The Merriam-Webster dictionary defines a "workaround"' as "a plan or method to circumvent a problem without eliminating it." A common workaround is to hire more people, but this does not address the root cause. Staff may be working hard, but the client's requirements are still not being met. Service levels may be excellent one day and terrible the next because the processes are not systematic.

- Distraction. Infrastructure issues described above are unpleasant distractions that impair quality of life, but they also prevent clients from focusing on their most important priorities, including wealth preservation and strategic thinking.
- "Communications blizzard." Inadequate infrastructure prompts a flurry of urgent e-mails, texts, and calls to resolve issues, preventing clients from focusing on their priorities. What's more, these communications are unstructured, so it is not possible to track, analyze, and systematically address the underlying issues.
- Noncompliance. Lack of infrastructure can lead to missing deadlines, errors on tax returns and other filings, labor law violations, followed by penalties, sanctions, and lawsuits.
- Collapse. The client's existing infrastructure may collapse entirely. Excessive spending, deferred maintenance, lack of controls, and lack of disaster planning can have profound negative consequences.

Why would intelligent, wealthy clients risk these negative consequences? Rarely is this a conscious, deliberate decision. More often, deficient infrastructure is a result of plans not made and actions not taken, of negligent rather than malicious intent. Moreover, there is typically not one reason, but rather a combination.

Reasons for Infrastructure Deficiencies

Reason	Example
Accumulation	"We started with two residences, three cars, and a boat; now we are up to five residences and have lost count of all the rest."
Short-term-ism	"We have so much to do today and can't take the time to plan long-term infrastructure." OR "Let my successor worry about it."
Focus on cost reduction	"In our single-family office, we minimize expenses; 'infrastructure investments' will not be approved."
Lack of expertise	"There isn't anyone in this single-family office who is capable of developing and implementing the infrastructure that we require."
Fear of change and its consequences	"This is the way we have always done things, and if we changed, we would have to terminate some family office staff and/or it would upset our parents."
An underlying feeling that it is wrong to invest in personal comfort and quality of life	"Surely there must be higher priorities than my personal comfort."
Wealth creator or entrepreneurial mindset	"I am laser-focused on my operating company and anything else is a waste of time."
"One time thing-ism"	"I don't need a 'process' for bill pay, tax administration or home maintenance because of a few isolated errors or unfortunate incidents."

How to Build Infrastructure: The Seven-Step Plan

Step 1: Identify the areas that require infrastructure improvement.

First, identify what is working well and why. This will provide insights in improving the problem areas and help ensure that changes made to address problems do not inadvertently damage the areas that are high-functioning.

Step 2: Prioritize on a 5-point scale with the Infrastructure Assessment Instrument (above).

Rank each area by its current status (1= Excellent; 5= Terrible). For each area requiring improvement, rank it by impact (1 = Least impact; 5 = Highest impact). Prioritize those with the highest combination score (7–10).

Step 3: Quantify current resource allocation and document current processes.

Who is doing what? Are resources available but not allocated toward the priorities? Are resources insufficient? Are skills missing? Which activities are the most staff-intensive, error-prone, and high impact? Focus on these.

Step 4: Identify the infrastructure gap and add a third score for ease of implementation.

Compare the current status versus the desired outcome. Rank each desired improvement based on ease of implementation, on a 1–5 scale (1 = Easiest to implement; 5 = Very difficult to implement) and reprioritize based on level of impact but incorporating ease of implementation.

Focus on the quick wins—those that are highest impact in Step 2 and easiest to implement in Step 4.

Step 5: Create a plan and obtain agreement from stakeholders.

Develop a strategic and tactical plan to implement the improvements. Ensure that stakeholders (e.g., family members, SFO and private staff) are in agreement to move forward. Document these agreements in writing.

Step 6: Implement.

- Organizational change is challenging, and many forces will try, consciously or otherwise, to stop it. Change management expertise is essential.
- Identify an implementation "owner" who will lead the process and ensure accountability.
- Convene an implementation steering committee consisting of principals, staff, and qualified experts to oversee and manage the implementation process, ensuring milestones are set and met.

Step 7: Maintain ongoing monitoring, measurement, and accountability.

Ongoing monitoring is needed to ensure accountability. Specific actionable metrics should be tracked, such as "preventable maintenance issues." **Since an important goal is to prevent distractions, any high-impact issues that arise must be tracked and analyzed to determine root cause, and to be prevented in the future.** It is also vital to measure positive financial impacts such as tax reduction, reduced insurance premiums, and staff expense, to help justify the cost of the infrastructure investments. One SFO reported that annual savings from their infrastructure implementation more than paid for the annual cost of the SFO.

In summary, building and maintaining resilient infrastructure is essential for quality of life as well as wealth preservation. While an investment in time and money is required, the payback will be swift, in the form of higher quality of life, reduced risk, and increased likelihood of sustainable wealth preservation.

Source

Natasha Pearl, "The Essential Infrastructure for Wealth Preservation," a chapter in *Advising the Wealthy Client* edited by Barbara R. Hauser (United Kingdom: Globe Publishing, 2020).

Additional Resources

Atul Gawande, *The Checklist Manifesto: How to Get Things Right* (New York: Metropolitan Books, 2009).

Aston Pearl Tracker, a proprietary, low-tech tool to identify and manage projects.

Tracking software such as Zendesk or ServiceNow, which can be customized to enable root cause analysis of "incidents" indicative of infrastructure issues.

Biography

Natasha Pearl founded Aston Pearl in 2003. The firm provides objective and confidential consulting to single-family offices (SFOs), family enterprises, and private clients, with a focus on SFO structure and start-up, and residential operations. Aston Pearl has developed a proprietary approach and significant intellectual capital in the area of Wealth Preservation Infrastructure®. In 2015, Natasha was named one of the "50 Most Influential Women in Private Wealth." In 2021, she was named by *Business Insider* as "one of the 21 people powering the huge growth in family offices." She received her undergraduate and MBA degrees from Harvard University.

CHAPTER 23

Creating a Family Owner's Manual

Josh Kanter

We're all familiar with the cliché, "You get an owner's manual with a toaster, but you don't get one when you have a child." I've always found that to be true and insightful, but it never stared me in the face quite as clearly as on my father's death. So I've expanded the cliché to add: "You don't get an owner's manual with a family of wealth either."

But you should! In the book *Cycle of the Gift*, the authors analogize the sudden transfer of great wealth to a meteor strike. I suggest that is equally true of the sudden need for knowledge and information at the illness, incapacity, or death of a member of the family's elder generation.

Too often, we talk about succession planning in the context of a person or role—who will take over, what are the qualifications they need, etc. To our detriment, we often don't consider the succession of information. How can I identify my informational and planning blind spots? How can I communicate with, and educate my family and advisors about, various matters as part of my stewardship of my wealth? How will my partner, heirs, or advisors know what they need to know in the event of my absence?

These are not abstract questions—unfortunately, despite our best efforts, illness, incapacity, or death is coming for us all! Families of wealth spend enormous amounts of time and money on planning, communication, education, and governance. Yet at each generational transition, families spend more time and money than should be necessary on things that fall under the heading, "I wish I knew that."

As my father's death approached, we thought we were prepared. He was a world-renowned trust and estate lawyer turned venture capitalist. Our structure was complex. We were litigating a 30-year tax controversy matter. We were filing nearly 750 tax returns per year. I was a nearly captive employee and had all the requisite training—a law degree that included taking my father's class (big mistake), a career as a transactional lawyer with an outside firm, time running one of our portfolio companies, and 18 months at his side before he succumbed to cancer.

What came next, and hasn't stopped for 20 years, was the "I wish I knew that" phase. In an effort to stop history from repeating itself, the Family Owner's Manual (FOM) was born, a single-source document that would dramatically expand on the traditional "emergency file." The document would not only tell the family where to look, but what to look for, why to look for it, and what to do when they found it.

The FOM is something I recommend to families I work with and, frankly, to all families of wealth. It is a tool that, if used with care, will improve a family's current planning, can provide an educational roadmap for family members and advisors, and will help preserve the legacy that the family has worked to create.

There are many ways to embark on the creation of your own FOM. You might reach out to your estate lawyer, investment advisor, or multifamily office to ask for a checklist. A number of books are available on the subject of "preparation." Whatever your preferred method of getting started, however, the real value in the process is to get beyond the "what and where" to the "how and why." Think about it—a checklist of the parts in your toaster might be nice, but it's the instructions that tell you how to use the thing!

And so it is with the concept of the FOM—we need to think not just about the parts, but the transfer of knowledge about important history, rationale, and priorities that will need to be considered when making timely and strategic financial and nonfinancial decisions. Failing to do so can too often result in unnecessary expenses, time, lost opportunities, and more. In a typical FOM process, we want people to think about categories, roughly as follows:

- Demographics. Who are your family members? Who is in your "sphere of responsibility"? Think broadly. Maybe you're paying a nephew's rent. Maybe you want to provide for a long-term household employee. Who are the people that might not be in your formal planning but play an important part in your life? Consider at least these categories:
  - Family Members
  - Pets
  - Advisors
  - Friends, Mentors, and Confidants

  And these questions:
  - How do you know, and how are you involved with, these people?
  - In the case of your advisors, what are their specialties and for what purposes should your family call on them?
  - Do you have family trees, documentation of family history, accounts such as Ancestry.com?
- Personal Information. Explore things like your medical information, and your wishes in case of your illness, incapacity, or death. Collect information about your clubs, programs, and digital assets. What does everyone need to know about your personal properties, whether that is your primary residence or your waterfront or ski-in, ski-out family vacation home. Consider at least these categories:
  - Medical information, including providers and records
  - Information about your incapacity or death
  - Information about your travel and leisure programs and accounts

- Your noninvestment properties, including information about associated liabilities, vendors, and accounts
- Your digital accounts, including the location of all password or other access information

And these questions:

- Have you prepared any letters of wishes for your family, trustees, or advisors?
- Have you considered the inheritability of any of these assets or accounts?
- Have you thought about the ownership or governance structures surrounding any legacy assets?

• Estate, Tax, and Insurance. Press yourself to think beyond the basics—explain not only *what* was done, but *why* it was done. After all, a good deal of this will only matter when it's too late for you to explain it all. Consider at least these categories:

- Your basic estate documents
- Your identification and other important documents
- Your tax information
- Your insurance information

And these questions:

- When was your last insurance or estate review?
- Have your children reached important age milestones for legal or insurance purposes?
- Have you explained the purpose of any trusts created or to be created by your estate?
- Do your beneficiaries have effective relationships with your current and successor trustees?
- Are you maximizing the use of your annual exclusions and lifetime/generation-skipping estate tax exemptions?
- Do you anticipate a taxable estate?
- Have you considered the family dynamics and governance that your planning will cause or require?

• Financial and Investment. What kinds of accounts do you have? What kinds of investments do you have? How are your investments structured? What does that mean to your expectations for the investments? For their ultimate liquidation? Will your family know to liquidate this before that, why, and with whom, to maximize value? Will they know how to meet an estate liability? Consider at least these categories:

- Bank, brokerage, retirement, and related financial accounts
- Investment assets
- Appraisals and valuations
- Guaranties and liabilities
- Philanthropic structures

And these questions:

- Do you sit on boards? Have stock options or the like?
- Have you thought "beyond the numbers"? What does my family, and do my advisors, need to know? Who are my partners? Why were these investments made? How can they or should they be liquidated or unwound?

- Have you outlined your enterprise structure and why it was structured in that way?
- Have you provided for your philanthropic wishes?
- Have you reviewed your beneficiary designations? Named successor donor advisors?

Because our lives are ever-changing, your FOM should be continually evolving and updated.

Every family that creates their own FOM will undoubtedly learn something new and will discover a solution—a gift, if you will—that will benefit every member of the family. Such a gift is more than an organizational tool, though it can certainly provide that function.

A FOM is unique to your family. As such, it is impossible to pinpoint where you will find the most value, but here are just a few examples of things typically uncovered by this process:

- A client retained personal ownership of two personal residences, thus assuring an unnecessary visit to probate court. In two states.
- A client was encouraged to provide a detailed explanation of a complex second-to-die insurance structure so the beneficiaries would know how the transaction was structured, why, and importantly, how to unwind it after the matriarch and patriarch were gone.
- A client discovered the strict conditions of inheritability of a valuable vacation club membership.
- A client modified an insurance program to meet their philanthropic goals, while more efficiently addressing their taxable estate, resulting in an increase in the benefit being left to the next generation and philanthropic recipients, while reducing the amount being paid to the IRS.

In similar fashion, we recently worked with a client who was a retired senior executive with a real estate investment and development firm in the Midwest. He was well organized but hadn't connected the dots between the paper records and information in his head. Through our process, he highlighted his most important contacts, how he knew them, and when they should be called on to help the family.

In reviewing his investment portfolio, and the myriad investment partnerships with different sponsors, time horizons, and expectations, he was able to impart more information about these deals so his family would know more about where to turn in the event of his absence and would have a better roadmap to think about future values, liquidation priorities and expectations. This client has a close relationship with his four adult, well-launched children, but he had never imparted this level of knowledge to any of them. After doing so in a family meeting, the children were "wowed," and everyone realized what a gift he had given to the family by embarking on this process.

We all know that each passing year seems to add complexity to our lives. When complexity and wealth are combined, the need for, and benefit of, such a process grows exponentially. This process is valuable for every family enterprise or family of wealth. This is equally true for the single young professional, the successful nuclear family unit, and even the family enterprise that has grown significantly enough to justify a single family office.

Whether you get started with a call to your estate lawyer, investment advisor, a bookstore visit, give your family this gift: Get started. Once you're started, we hope that adding and updating your information will become second nature, but if not, consider setting yourself a schedule to review your manual quarterly or annually to consider what has changed, what should be added, and what should be deleted.

Additional Resources

www.leafplanner.com.

Visit www.leafplanner.com/wealthofwisdom for special resources for Wealth of Wisdom readers.

Chanel Reynolds, *What Matters Most: The Get Your Shit Together Guide to Wills, Money, Insurance and Life's "What-Ifs,"* HarperWave, 2021.

Free Checklists: https://www.fidsafe.com/resources/checklists-organizers/.

Biography

Through **Josh Kanter** Wealth Advisory Services, Josh provides thoughtful, personalized multigenerational family wealth advisory services to his clients, including family meeting facilitation, structuring, governance, trust, estate and tax planning, "blind spot" review, philanthropy, and more. Josh founded **leaf**planner, to offer families a tool to develop a personalized family owner's manual. **leaf**planner brings the deliberateness of a family office to a family's organization, education, communication, and decision-making.

Josh is involved with numerous nonprofit organizations and is a frequent speaker on family, family office, political, economic, and philanthropic topics.

Josh received his JD from the University of Chicago in 1987.

CHAPTER 24

Family Behavioral Health Wellness Assessment

Arden O'Connor

"I barely recognize my own son. Where did we go wrong?"

Their sobbing and desperation fill the room. We want to respond with reassurance that their son will turn out as they hoped, eventually become "normal." We know better—we know that the journey toward "wellness" will challenge these parents to their cores and force them to examine their preconceptions, hopes, and plans for their son. We respond, "There are strategies to improve the issues you describe, and qualified professionals to help. The path is not easy, nor straight or simple. Your son's issues will likely impact your family system, and we will want to take a holistic approach to maximize our chances for success."

Affluent families are not immune or protected from experiencing behavioral health challenges. Stigma, shame, and entitlement often accompany clinical diagnoses, making them hard to treat. While money allows families to afford best-in-class care, it also allows natural consequences to be avoided and families to remain in denial in even the most acute situations. Our clients need help determining how to support loved ones with mental health or substance abuse issues, while simultaneously holding them accountable for their behaviors and maintaining their own realistic expectations.

Our questions in this chapter aim to promote self-reflection, exploration into issues ignored or avoided, and uncomfortable conversations. Silence protects the status quo of dysfunction. The first crucial step in addressing behavioral health issues is talking to professionals and each other.

Section I. Warning Signs of Behavioral Health Issues

Purpose: To explore whether a loved one is showing signs of or experiencing a behavioral health issue

Identifying signs of behavioral health issues and knowing when to seek help can be challenging even for the savviest and most psychologically sophisticated families.

1. Do you notice a sustained change (more than two or three weeks) in appearance/hygiene, personality, behavior, interests, performance, ability to think, motivation, sleeping patterns, and/or appetite with a loved one?
2. Is there a genetic predisposition toward substance use, mental health diagnoses, eating disorders or autism in your family system?
3. Have you or has someone else commented on a loved one's maladaptive coping strategies (i.e., excessive drinking, sleeping, eating, spending)?
4. Has a loved one had a medical, vocational, legal, or financial crisis as a result of a behavioral health issue (i.e., DUI, school suspension, job loss, psychiatric hospitalization, debt)?
5. Did the concerning person suffer trauma in the past? If yes, did they receive treatment?

Conversation starter: What would it take for you to believe that a loved one's behavior has crossed the line from acceptable to problematic, i.e., behavior that may warrant clinical investigation and intervening measures?

Section II. The Family Toll

Purpose: To assess how a loved one's maladaptive behavior impacts others who love them

Family members often respond to a loved one's plight by engaging in coping strategies that compromise not only their own personal well-being but also the overall integrity of the family system.

- I regret lowering my standards of what I consider to be normal and acceptable.
- I am exhausted by the pretense I maintain that everything is okay.
- I feel isolated from friends and family.
- I am resentful toward my loved one.
- I am afraid to leave or change the relationship with my loved one even though I have thought about doing so for years.
- I used to dream of the future; now, I just want to make it through the day.
- I feel like this couldn't possibly be my life but have felt unable to do anything about it.
- I no longer expect that my feelings will matter.
- I dwell on my loved one's plight continuously.
- I feel drained because I sleep poorly at night due to my constant worrying.
- I am satisfied if a conversation with my loved one or other family members doesn't turn into an argument, even if nothing changes.
- I am disturbed by the negative impact my loved one's behavior has on other members of the family and the tension it causes in our family.
- I have made excuses to stay away from home rather than admit my loved one is making home uncomfortable for me.

Conversation starter: How can family members work together to create the healthiest dynamic possible?

Section III. Protecting the Status Quo

Purpose: To assess the level to which you may be protecting the problematic behavior

Family members often engage in activities that alleviate the natural consequences of a loved one's behavior, which results in a family dynamic that not only promotes dysfunction but also increases the odds of high conflict between other family members.

- I have canceled social plans with a false excuse at the last minute because of my loved one's poor behavior/intoxication.
- I have forgiven insulting behavior, i.e., aiming disrespectful language at me, being dishonest, stealing from me, manipulating, or bullying me.
- I have made excuses for my loved one's failure to follow through on personal or professional obligations.
- I have kept my loved one's behavior a secret from people close to me, even when they express concern.
- I have called in sick to work or school for my loved one.
- I have anticipated my loved one's neglect of household duties and filled in the gaps.
- I have paid my loved one's bills or taken care of other financial obligations despite his active substance use.
- I have reminded my loved one to eat, sleep, or perform other basic activities of living.
- I have provided excuses for my loved one's absence when she has failed to come home.
- I have made emotional excuses for my loved one's behavior, such as "he had a rough childhood" or "she is under a lot of stress."
- I have minimized, rationalized, or justified the actions of my loved one, such as by believing her stories even when my instincts told me she was lying.
- I have avoided discussing any problems with my loved one.
- I have bailed my loved one out of jail.
- I have asked for help from police or lawyers to avoid criminal charges.

Conversation Starter: Can you envision anything positive that might come from allowing a loved one to experience the negative consequences resulting from poor behavioral choices?

Section IV. Managing Crisis

Purpose: To assess whether your family has supports in place for managing a crisis

Notwithstanding ample wealth to afford best-in-class care, knowing what approach to pursue and which treatment professionals to trust can be a confusing and overwhelming process when a family member experiences a behavioral health crisis.

1. How equipped are you to navigate the systems that exist to help with behavioral health issues in the event a family member experiences a crisis?
2. Are you able to name a qualified professional to whom you would go for advice and guidance in the event of a crisis, someone who would handle these types of delicate issues discreetly and competently?
3. Would you be able to identify the most beneficial use of financial resources to allocate toward resolving a behavioral health crisis and supporting a loved one's immediate and future needs?
4. Would family members agree on which of their loved one's behaviors they would be willing to support versus which behaviors they would distance themselves from, both in the short term and the long term?
5. Would your estate planning benefit from including additional contingencies focused on substance use, mental health, or other related disorders?

Conversation starter: How can you best preserve both the short- and long-term interests of your family in the event of a crisis?

Note that these questions should help you think about your family's holistic wellness; they are not meant to replace professionally facilitated assessments or advice from qualified medical or behavioral health practitioners. If these questions raise any concerns about your loved one's health or of any family member, please seek medical or clinical attention. We do not accept liability for failure to follow this instruction.

The Chinese character for crisis is said to be composed of two characters: "danger" and "change point" (which some read as "opportunity"). Daily, we remind families that while all crises are anxiety-provoking by their nature, they also may be the very thing that interrupts the status quo of dysfunction and propels a family and their advisors to have frank discussions and make necessary shifts.

There are even unforeseeable upsides to this discomfort. The very same parents who fill our offices with words of hopelessness and despair regularly reflect a few months later that they feel like they can breathe for the first time in a very long time. They now feel hopeful for their family's future—such a simple statement on the surface, yet so impactful when taken in context and measured against the depths of where this family has been. There is no fanfare or shouting from the rooftops, only the simple satisfaction of peace in this moment. While fraught with bumps along the way, steps forward and steps back, this family has traveled the distance from dysfunction to the road to recovery.

Following, you will find resources for continued exploration.

Additional Resources

Behavioral Health Clinical Support

- O'Connor Professional Group, Private Concierge Behavioral Health Treatment Service Provider: Services for Addictions, Eating Disorders, Mood and Personality Disorders, Autism Spectrum Disorders, and Other Behavioral Health Concerns, https://oconnorpg.com.

- ZENCARE: Therapists Directory, https://zencare.co/.
- NAMI: Mental Health Support and Treatment Options, https://www.nami.org/Home.
- SAMHSA: Treatment Directory, https://www.samhsa.gov/.
- MEDA: Eating Disorder Resource, https://www.eatingdisorderhope.com/information/help-overcome-eating-disorders/meda.
- AANE: Asperger/Autism Network, https://www.aane.org/.
- SHATTERPROOF: "ATLAS," Substance Use Treatment Directory, https://www.shatterproof.org/find-help/locate-a-high-quality-provider.

Online Screening Tools

- Mental Health America, Array of Screening Tests for Addiction, Depression, Psychosis, PTSD, Postpartum Depression, Bipolar, Anxiety, and Eating Disorders; for Individuals and Parents; for Adults and Youth, https://screening.mhanational.org/screening-tools/.

Resources

- Podcast: Beyond the Balance Sheet, O'Connor Professional Group, https://oconnorpg.com/podcast/.
- Podcast: Let's Talk Addiction and Recovery, Hazelden Betty Ford Foundation, https://hazeldenbettyford.org.
- Podcast: Sharon Spano, "Raising Resilient Adults in the Age of Entitlement with Diana Clark" (January 27, 2021), https://www.sharonspano.com/raising-resilient-adults-in-the-age-of-entitlement-with-diana-clark/.
- Webinar: Collegial Conversations with Diana Clark, O'Connor Professional Group, https://oconnorpg.com/oconnor-professional-groupwebinars/; see in particular, the webinar entitled "Family Dynamics and Family Recovery."
- YouTube: "Family Roles When Addiction Takes Hold," William Moyers (February 20, 2019), https://www.youtube.com/watch?v=C_qtatC0UeU.
- YouTube: "Mental Health Moments: Family Systems and Addiction," Dr. Holly Daniels for the Sober College (March 6, 2017), https://www.youtube.com/watch?v=eCJL_Bkwn2c.
- Book: Diana Clark, *Addiction Recovery: A Family's Journey* (2014). This book offers guidance to family members of those struggling with substance use disorders and mental health concerns.

Behavioral Health and Family Articles

- "Helping a Loved One Cope with a Mental Illness," American Psychiatric Association, https://www.psychiatry.org/patients-families/helping-a-loved-one-cope-with-a-mental-illness.

- Alexandra Helfer, "How to Spot Alcohol Use Disorder in a Family Member," *Psychology Today* (August 28, 2020), https://www.psychologytoday.com/us/blog/addiction-recovery/202008/how-spot-alcohol-use-disorder-in-family-member.
- Dan Meyer. "Addiction as a Family Affliction," *Psychology Today* (May 2, 2016), https://www.psychologytoday.com/us/blog/some-assembly-required/201605/addiction-family-affliction.
- Allen Frances, "Advice to Families Coping with Psychiatric Problems," *Psychiatric Times* (October 21, 2019), https://www.psychiatrictimes.com/view/advice-families-coping-psychiatric-problems.
- "Boundaries in Addiction Recovery," Hazelden Betty Ford Foundation (August 24, 2018), https://www.hazeldenbettyford.org/articles/boundaries-in-addiction-recovery .

Family Office and Advisor Articles

- Arden O'Connor, "Family Office Solutions for Physical and Mental Health Issues: Understanding and Utilizing Care Management for Families," UHNW Institute (March 2021), https://oconnorpg.com/wp-content/uploads/2021/03/Family-Office-Solutions-for-Physical-and-Mental-Health-Issues_030521.pdf.
- William Messinger and Arden O'Connor, "Rethinking Trustee Responsibility for Addicted Beneficiaries," *Trusts and Estates Magazine* (March 2018), https://www.wealthmanagement.com/estate-planning/rethinking-trustee-responsibility-addicted-beneficiaries.
- William Messinger and Arden O'Connor, "When Addiction Surfaces in Beneficiaries and Client Offspring," *Trusts and Estates Magazine* (August 2015), https://oconnorpg.com/wp-content/uploads/2018/12/When-Addiction-Surfaces-in-Beneficiaries-and-Client-Offspring-Trust-Estates-Magazine-August-2015.pdf.

Biography

Arden O'Connor founded the O'Connor Professional Group to address the needs of families and individuals struggling with an array of behavioral health issues, including addiction, mental health disorders, eating disorders, learning, and other developmental challenges. With several relatives in recovery, Arden is passionate about helping families and individuals navigate the highly fragmented treatment system in a way that creates positive outcomes and allows families to heal. Arden is a graduate of Harvard College and Harvard Business School. She remains involved in community activities as a board member of Winsor School Corporation, and Massachusetts Association of Mental Health.

CHAPTER 25

Building a Smart Aging Plan

Susan Hyatt

We are in the midst of a longevity revolution. Baby Boomers are hitting retirement age in ever-increasing numbers. We are living longer and getting older. Once we retire, we may live another 35 or 40 years. Have you considered what it means to live and age well post-retirement?

Jane Fonda, the well-known American actress, coined the term *Third Act* to describe the last three decades of her life. Now in her 80s, she views her life in 30-year blocks, recognizing that she changes her views as she gets older. She summarized her research and thoughts in a TEDx Women Talk (New York 2011).

How do we envision our own Third Act? Most of us would probably say we want to live well with purpose and live life on our own terms—safe, secure, and independent. The key question is how do you plan to get there?

How do you want to live well at 80 or 100 years of age?

Your family's financial success has been built on your ability to see ahead, plan, and manage ahead. These same insights apply equally to creating a plan for your own Third Act. In the same way your chief financial officer (CFO) or family office manager takes a coordinated approach to your family's wealth, a smart aging advisor takes an integrated approach to your life, health, and well-being. How will your financial resources be used to support your plan? If you become ill and unable to speak for yourself, who will make decisions about your physical and emotional needs? What types of care might be needed and how much will it cost?

Let's begin planning with a smart aging audit. The goal is to think through how you want to "live life on your own terms" and audit what you already have in place. The next step is to document your preferences related to life and future health needs, your wishes at end-of-life, and how you want to live with purpose. Your plan is a written declaration of your wishes and a roadmap that can be shared with family members, and those who may have to make trusted decisions for you.

One Scenario:

Charlotte is a 65-year-old lawyer and partner in a large law firm. She lives alone in a house in central Toronto, has a cottage in Ontario's Muskoka Lakes region, and a condo in Naples, Florida. She is a widow. She has one son who has Down's syndrome, and he lives in a private group home in Caledon, Ontario. All other immediate family members have passed away from early onset Alzheimer's disease, and she is concerned this may happen to her. She has a wealth manager advising her on estate planning and acting as her CFO. With the unexpected death of a close friend, she has turned her attention to her own personal health and well-being and that of her son with special needs. These are the questions she asks herself: Where do I go to get the best medical assessments? What happens if I do get Alzheimer's and need to hire personal help? What are the alternatives if I want to stay in my own home? How long can I travel to my cottage and condo in Florida? How does that get organized? Who will manage all of this? Who will manage my son's care if I cannot do so?

Charlotte decides to start with a smart aging audit so she can begin to sort out possible scenarios, her own priorities, and start assessing what decisions should come first. Ultimately, she decided to do a full planning exercise, including detailed costing on future care options for both herself and her son.

Getting Started

In our practice, we often see family disputes emerge when people are guessing about what a parent or family member might wish if they become ill or cannot speak for themselves. By creating a personalized plan, you take the guessing out of the equation and start to be specific about your wishes.

Take some time to consider the future from your perspective. Think about what you want in your life plan as you get older or what your wishes might be should you need assistance. Where do you want to live and with whom? Is it short term or longer term? Do you have preferences for a country or certain location? Would you be happy living in a multigenerational household? What are your goals for life-long learning? With whom do you want to share a meal or attend a concert?

Once you have thought through your preferences, you can start building your smart aging plan. The following section provides an initial outline to get started. You might also find it helpful to have a smart aging advisor or coach to help you build a more comprehensive plan and to pinpoint your preferences.

Once your smart aging plan is completed, we suggest you keep it in a binder in a safe place at home. In case of an emergency, you can take the binder with you to the hospital to share as baseline information. Also keep an electronic copy so you can easily update information and review it in its entirety at least every year.

Smart Aging Plan—Initial Outline

Part 1: Primary Contacts

- List primary family contact details, including cell phone, work phone, e-mails, etc. List emergency contacts who are within 5 minutes of your home.
- In case of a health emergency, create a notification tree—primary contact names, powers of attorney (POA), lifeline, or emergency pendant details etc.

Part 2: Health, Medical, and Personal Living Information

- List your normal routines for daytime and nighttime. Where do you eat meals, and what are your preferences? Do you exercise daily? How do you relax?
- What are your future living preferences? What location(s) do you prefer? If you are unable to care for yourself, do you prefer care in your own home with a live-in caregiver or someone who comes in each day? Would you consider going to a retirement home with assisted living services, if needed?
- Document a current list of your medical and health care providers and their contact details. Examples include family doctor, dentist, physical therapist, podiatrist, etc.
- Medical and surgical history: List any medical issues. List surgeries. Include all relevant data and contact physicians. Include allergies.
- Prescription medication: List all medications including dosage, renewals, referring doctor.
- Over-the-counter medications: Include herbal remedies. Some may cause drug interactions.
- Eyeglasses, hearing aids, mobility aids, and other aids: Include copies of prescriptions, supplier, etc.
- Vaccination records: Include official receipts for COVID-19 vaccinations.
- Other sections could include medical coordination services, home care companies, etc.

Part 3: Financial Preparedness Related to Future Costs

- Determine ranges for future care costs and discuss funding strategies with your wealth manager. For example, compare staying at home with 24-hour care versus assisted living facility options, etc.
- Review relevant tax planning items related to care situations, depending on your jurisdiction, for example, disability tax credits, home renovation credits, etc.
- Review health and dental insurance benefits coverage related to care costs, mobility aids, etc.

Part 4: End-of-Life Planning

- Document your preferences and advance care directives you may wish to put in place.
- Include information about medically assisted death, depending on jurisdiction.
- Supply information on funeral preplanning and prepayment.

Part 5: Review with Designated Attorneys

- Discuss overall plan. Are your attorneys able and willing to carry out your plan?
- Do your attorneys understand your preferences and estimated costs for services and accommodation?

Part 6: Next Steps

- Discuss your plan with advisors, family members, and designated attorneys. Seek buy-in and integrate information such as cost estimates with financial strategies.
- Identify priority actions, set timelines, and services to assist you.

Thinking about our Third Act in life takes time and reflection. Many of us have not considered how we would define living well as we age. By using the smart aging plan approach, you can begin to document your wishes for family and substitute decision-makers. This is especially important if the unexpected occurs and you are not able to speak for yourself.

This process also gives you the opportunity to explore a few "what-if" future scenarios regarding your health and well-being. With a well-thought-out and written plan, it gives you an opportunity to cost out different options and to integrate the funding of those options into your financial plans.

Imagine living to 100 years! For the first 60 years we focused on education, building wealth, and planning for retirement. For the next 30 years, we will focus on living our lives. It's worth rethinking our priorities and planning for our own Third Act with a focus on living a purposeful and fulfilling life beyond retirement.

Additional Resources

Joseph F. Coughlin, *The Longevity Revolution* (Cambridge, MA: MIT Age Lab, 2017).

Lynda Gratton and Andrew Scott, *The 100 Year Life* (New York, NY: Bloomsbury Business, 2016), www.silversherpa.net.

Silver Sherpa Inc., www.silversherpa.net.

Biography

A leader of the "smart aging" movement, **Susan J. Hyatt** is the CEO and co-founder of Silver Sherpa Inc., a professional services company delivering confidential planning, coordination, and crisis management services for high-net-worth individuals and families planning for or in transition in their later stages of life. With over 40 years of industry experience, Susan is an expert in transforming healthcare systems and is widely quoted on elder management, "smart aging," and estate planning issues. Susan has served on numerous public and corporate board of directors and commissions in Canada, Australia, Ireland, and the United States. She is a member of the Canadian College of Health Service Executives and the International Federation on Ageing. Susan holds a postgraduate certification in negotiations from Harvard Law School/MIT and a master's in business administration with a specialty in international business from Griffith University, Australia. She also holds a bachelor of science degree in physical therapy specializing in critical care/trauma from the University of Toronto, Canada, where she taught in the Faculty of Medicine.

CHAPTER 26

Managing the Risk of Diminished Capacity

Patricia Annino

Many families undertake planning to alleviate the common risks, such as death, divorce, out-of-date governance or documents, lack of liquidity, lack of proper estate planning, and lack of succession planning, to name a few. Risk management for diminished capacity is as important as any of those and yet less often considered.

Diminished capacity in the years prior to death is also common enough that families should prepare for its risk—yet few do. Even the families that one would think would understand its importance (such as Sumner Redstone, Donald Sterling, Lilianne Bettencourt, and Brooke Astor) faced major obstacles when the question of diminishing capacity arose. Advanced planning can mitigate the risk of fraud, loss of financial resources, possible litigation, family stresses, reputation risk, business failure, and thwarted life and estate plans.

The Risks of Not Planning to Mitigate the Risks Associated with Diminished Capacity

Given the severity of the consequences and the benefits of advance planning to mitigate these risks before the crisis occurs, why do so few families properly prepare for diminished capacity?

Here are some of the most common rationalizations that keep this in the "maybe someday" category versus "do it today" priority:

- Procrastination kicks the can down the road.
- Money—No one wants to pay for planning if there is no current compelling need to plan.
- Denial/narcissism—This will never happen to me (or any family member). It does not run in my family.
- Fear—I don't want to think about what will happen if my cognitive ability fails or if a key family stakeholder I depend on loses his/her cognitive ability.
- Ignorance—Not knowing how or when to have the conversation until there is no alternative or it is too late.

- Uncertainty—I'm unsure what it entails and how to think about it.
- Shame—Although it should not be that way, mental health and diminishing capacity issues are more embarrassing than physical health issues, such as cancer.
- Naiveté—Many families believe the standard clauses in their legal documents are sufficient to handle the issue, should it arise.
- Discomfort—Wanting to avoid an uncomfortable discussion with an obstinate or stubborn patriarch or matriarch.
- Lack of knowledge—Not knowing where to turn or how to begin the process.

A Complex Situation with Unique Qualities

By definition, it is better to plan in advance of a family crisis. When the slow, creeping crisis of diminishing capacity hits, the family is forced to make decisions when emotions are running high. If there are conflicts within the family, planning is even more difficult.

Even without family drama, the onset of dementia is the most difficult phase. When a family member's capacity diminishes, the crisis can have a long, slow initial deterioration as abilities and insight dissipate. Often, capacity ebbs and flows, sowing confusion for everyone involved. It is very difficult to address diminishing capacity with a person who may be slipping.

Emotionally, it is natural for us to hide our weaknesses, so minimization, excuses, and denial are common. Self-awareness and judgment are the first cognitive casualties of dementia. These losses are more deadly than the obvious impairments of memory or language and denying them can become increasingly hard-wired in the brain.

Denial is common for those closest to the person suffering initial signs of dementia too. It is human nature for those closest to put off acknowledging someone's decline until the evidence becomes undeniable. It is also very difficult to grant someone dignity and autonomy while recognizing he/she may be increasingly impaired in decision-making, with positions and livelihoods in the balance.

Personal biases come into play. You may not want the patriarch or the matriarch to be diminished and instead focus on the lucid intervals to justify that it is not happening—until it is too late. Those who have known the person for a long period of time may have emotional biases that cloud their ability to view what is happening rationally. Those who have an emotional and/or financial stake in the outcome may not always act in good faith, either intentionally or unintentionally. That is human nature.

Sorting through the complex symptoms and possible causes often overwhelms anyone not professionally trained in neuropsychological assessment, like the family and most of their trusted advisors.

Getting a neuropsychological evaluation can be helpful, but it may be neither easy nor conclusive. Those who are still competent enough may fight the attempt to be evaluated or have their control taken away—and they may prevail, sometimes with retaliatory consequences. When an evaluation does occur, the findings can make things murkier instead of clearer. A medical determination of borderline capacity six months ago may not accurately reflect the situation three months ago, today, or three months from now.

This Difficult Situation Requires Advance Planning and Risk Management

Like other foreseeable problems, proactive risk management is better than crisis management. Planning well in advance of any capacity issues includes multiple elements that must be properly implemented in concert. A risk-managing incapacity plan involves three dimensions: financial, personal (family and relationships), and medical (mental and physical health).

A good starting place is to review where the family is now by answering questions on this checklist. Some of the issues, terms, and solutions may vary depending on the jurisdiction of the family. The references in this chapter are U.S. based. It is important to consult with a knowledgeable advisor in the relevant jurisdiction.

Action Checklist

1. **Review the current financial and estate plan.**
   - Gather all financial documents—bank accounts, brokerage accounts, life insurance, deeds, investments, long-term care insurance, disability insurance, other investments, etc.
   - Review the title on each financial asset. Whose name is it in—one person, joint, joint with a right of survivorship, in trust?
   - Review the primary and secondary beneficiary of any contractual asset (life insurance policy, IRA, annuity, deferred compensation plan, etc.).
   - Gather all passwords to guarantee access to digital assets.
   - List all advisors with their contact information, and identify the role played by each advisor.
   - Organize all legal documents and inform key people of where the documents are located. Note the date that the most recent version of each document was signed.
2. **Inventory the legal documents that are in place to determine what may be missing or out of date.**
   - **Healthcare Proxy**—This document, sometimes known as a *healthcare* durable power of attorney, names one person (in some jurisdictions) to make healthcare decisions for the person executing it. It is important that only one person be named at a time because doctors and hospitals want to rely on the judgment of only that person and do not want to be involved in a dispute.

- Who is the primary healthcare agent? Is that person's cell phone number and address on the document? Does that person know that he/she has been named in that capacity?
- Does the principal's primary care physician have a copy of the healthcare proxy?
- Do the primary healthcare providers know who the person's health care agent is?
- Does the healthcare agent know the person's primary healthcare providers?
- Has the person discussed with the named healthcare agent if the agent is willing to participate in the medical care decisions?
- Has there been a discussion that incorporates the person's religious beliefs and thoughts on terminating life?
- Has there been an open and full discussion as to the person's intent, such as their wishes for medical care, desire to live at home or have private care, or wishes to terminate life if advised by a physician?

- **Durable Power of Attorney**—The durable power of attorney is a financial document in which the principal nominates one person (or a team of people) to handle the financial aspects of his/her life. Unlike a healthcare proxy, the named person (the "attorney-in-fact") can act whether or not the principal agrees, and more than one person may be named to serve concurrently. It is a lifetime document. The principal may revoke it at any time (while competent), and it is automatically revoked at death. In the document, a principal can also state a preference as to who should serve as his/her guardian or conservator of the property upon the commencement of protective court proceedings.
  - When was the durable power of attorney signed?
  - Who is named?
  - If more than one person is named, how are decisions made?
  - What are the powers outlined in the document?
  - Is a successor attorney-in-fact named?
  - Is there a mechanism for appointing a successor attorney-in-fact?
  - Is there a nomination for a guardian/conservator in the document? If so, does it coordinate with the person named in the healthcare proxy?
- **HIPAA Waiver**–HIPAA (The U.S. Health Insurance Portability and Accountability Act of 1996) allows an individual to sign a waiver allowing the individual's health information to be used or disclosed to a third party. This document allows the healthcare agent to speak to physicians and stay informed.
  - Is there a signed HIPAA waiver?
  - Should the attorney-in-fact named in the financial durable power of attorney also hold a HIPAA waiver?
  - Should a trustee and successor trustee under the individual's trust hold a HIPAA waiver?

- **Revocable Trust**—A revocable trust is one established by a person, known as the grantor, settlor, or donor. Typically, the same person will serve as the initial trustee. A revocable trust (and transferring assets to it) will avoid probate. If the person is married, it may also reduce estate taxes the family will have to pay. It sets up a mechanism by which the assets titled to the trust can be managed for the person establishing it if that person becomes disabled or incapacitated and the trust assets can avoid probate and continue to be held in trust past the person's death.
  - A revocable trust is continuous. It is in effect when it is signed, continues through any disability or incapacity a person may have, and continues past death until by its terms the assets are distributed to the beneficiaries. (This contrasts with the health care proxy and powers of attorney, which are only lifetime documents and end at death.)
  - When reviewing the trust document ascertain the following:
    - Who are the successor trustees?
    - What are the circumstances by which successor trustees may be appointed or removed? Who has that power?
    - How is the disability or incapacity of the donor determined? What is the triggering mechanism?
    - To whom must the trustees (and successor trustees) account?
    - If there are unusual assets, such as a business, vacation home, or other illiquid assets, are there special provisions that address the management of those assets?
    - If it is a blended family or a tricky family situation and the donor becomes disabled, who are the beneficiaries (including the donor)?
    - Is there a confidentiality clause?
    - Is there an arbitration clause?

3. **Consider and review the choice of fiduciaries.** When establishing legal estate planning documents, the choice of the fiduciary is critical to the implementation of any plan. There are two key components to good planning: what the documents say (the organizational component) and how the documents are operated (the operational component). Both are equally important.

   The fiduciary for the healthcare proxy is the healthcare agent. The fiduciary for the durable power of attorney is the attorney-in-fact or agent. The fiduciary for any trust is the trustee.

   When choosing and reviewing the fiduciary selections, remember that asking a friend or family member to serve in that capacity is asking him/her to perform a difficult job. The responsibilities associated with the complexities of someone else's life can be daunting.

   When selecting the fiduciary for the healthcare decisions, only one person should be named at a time so that there is clear authority when dealing with doctors and hospitals. Successors may be named. For all other fiduciary capacities, the questions to consider are whether there should be one person or professional fiduciary (with successors or a mechanism for successor fiduciaries), or a team of fiduciaries (that may include friends, family members, professional fiduciaries and/or trust companies). It may also be important that the healthcare agent be aware of the person's religious counselors and thoughts on serious illness and termination of life.

Establishing a team of fiduciaries has some benefit. If, as time progresses, one of them has an issue in his/her life and is unable to pay the appropriate level of attention, there will be at least one other person or professional who will know that and address that issue.

If more than one person is named, it is important to determine whether the actions are by majority or unanimous. It is also important to consider specifying in the document that, whether it is by majority or unanimous decision, the signature of only one fiduciary is necessary to effectuate any transaction.

When selecting fiduciaries, it is important to be cognizant of potential conflicts of interest and think through how the fiduciaries named in different capacities will communicate and work with each other. As an example, if a parent names a second spouse as healthcare agent (and authorizes the spouse to make the medical care decisions) and names the two oldest children from a prior marriage as attorneys in fact under the durable power of attorney, will that work? The person making the healthcare decisions does not have the authority to write out checks for the care. Conflicts also arise if there is business ownership. Naming a child who is in the business and has a vested interest may present future issues pertaining to valuation, trigger of buyout, etc.

- The choice of suitable fiduciaries can evolve over time due to several factors:
  - Aging of fiduciaries
  - Fiduciaries encountering overwhelming stress in their own lives—divorce, financial difficulties, caring for an elderly parent, change in health, change in spouse's health, etc.
  - Changing relationships—A child may marry a spouse who is not liked; divorce and/or remarriage may happen, etc.
  - Changing advisors over time—stronger and more suitable advisors in different phases of life
- If your ability to make your own decisions is compromised, others can assist you through supported decision-making (as opposed to surrogate decision-making, a process by which the legal documents are implemented and/or the court has appointed a fiduciary to act on the person's behalf). When decision-making is supported, others may be enlisted to assist with decisions, such as a marriage or divorce, major purchases, sales or gifts, or changing an estate plan or fiduciaries.

  - If the need arises, a person will need to decide who should be named to provide support, how formal the supported decision-making should be, and whether the supported decision system is backed up with legal documents in case additional protection is needed.
  - It is also important to ensure that the people involved are coordinated rather than in conflict and that they have accountability. (See Toomey, James, "Understanding the Perspectives of Seniors on Dementia and Decision Making," *AJOB Empirical Bioethics* 12, no. 2 [2021]: 101–112.)
  - It is also important to determine if the family has "common wealth." This includes shared family or business assets that should be governed by documents, such as a partnership agreement, operating agreement, articles of organization, by-laws, shareholder agreement, or employment contracts, or corporate and partnership confidentiality agreements, privacy clauses, and arbitration clauses.
  - At the end of the day, it's important to understand that life is a movie, not a snapshot. Ongoing annual review of these documents is crucial to the success of any plan.

4. **Prepare for changes in physical and mental health.** In addition to the above discussion addressing the legal documents, it is important to have access to physicians across a spectrum of specialties. A competent internist or general practice physician is important. It is also important, long before there is a crisis, to line up who the physicians and mental health professionals will be who can assess and deal with diminished capacity concerns.
   - To be proactive, consider implementing a family risk rule that whenever a family member attains a certain age, that person should undergo a neurological assessment baseline.
     - Add a neurologist to the medical team before an issue occurs or when any mental or behavioral red flags begin to appear.
     - Set a standard of regularity to help determine and demonstrate when a person begins to decline.
   - Regular updated testing—perhaps annually once a person reaches a certain age.
     - There should be a system of regular evaluations. This can be a long process, and it may be years before this system pays dividends. (See Somers, Moira Ph.D., "When Dementia Takes Over the Corner Office," *Journal of Financial Planning* [November 2020]).
   - Medication—put a medication management system in place to ensure prescriptions are consistently and properly filled and taken.

Privacy and Confidentiality

Behind all the practical issues are those that deal with dignity, privacy, and confidentiality. Questions to ponder include the following (especially if the person in question is an owner of a business or in control of family "common wealth"): When is a person's right to medical privacy outweighed by the necessity or duty to keep others informed? Who are the stakeholders (other family members, business owners, etc.)? When should they be informed? Who should inform them? What are the conditions on that discussion? What is the duty to inform versus duty of privacy? These are complicated issues that underscore the importance of putting the planning and mechanisms in place long before there is any reason to bring the issues public.

Facing the Risk, Like Any Other

We all know the best time to plan is before it becomes necessary. We also know that being proactive is hard because other issues can always seem more pressing. With global increases in longevity, families should address and prepare for the inevitable possibility of a family member's diminishing capacity, and they must do so with the same level of attention, thoughtfulness, and intelligence they bring to the other risks that confront their family.

Additional Resources

Keith Drewery, "Managing Declining Capacity—The Role of a Family Office," *The International Family Offices Journal, Global Law and Business* 6 (2017).

Eugene J. Fierman and Janet B. Fierman, *Family Enterprise Guide to Major Mental Illness* (Boston, MA: Sheehan, Finney, Bass & Green, 2016), https://www.sheehan.com/wp-content/uploads/2016/12/Family-enterprise-guide-to-major-mental-illness-2016-JBF.pdf.

RBC Wealth Insights, Preparing for the Expected: The Financial Impact of Cognitive Decline (2020), https://www.rbcwealthmanagement.com/us/en/cmp/managing-the-financial-risk-of-dementia.

Steve Parish, "What If a Business Owner Loses Cognitive Ability?" Forbes (2016), https://www.forbes.com/sites/steveparrish/2016/06/06/what-if-a-business-owner-loses-cognitive-ability/#7771a1351d89.

Laura Zeigler, "Of Minds and Money: The Donald Sterling Case and Mental Capacity," *Bessemer Trust Newsletter* (2014).

Lucy Warwick-Ching, "How Can I Manage the Succession of our Family Business?" *Financial Times* (Dec. 10, 2019), https://www.ft.com/content/.

Biography

Patricia M. Annino is a partner with the Boston office of global law firm, Rimon, P.C. She is a nationally recognized authority on estate planning with more than 30 years of experience serving the estate planning needs of families, individuals, and owners of closely held and family owned businesses.

Patricia has been voted by her peers as one of the Best Lawyers in America (trust and estates), a Super Lawyer, a top 50 Massachusetts Female Lawyer, Boston

Estate Planning Council's Estate Planner of the Year, and the initial recipient of EuroMoney/Legal Media's "Best in Wealth Management—USA" award.

Patricia has written six books, including *Women & Money: A Practical Guide to Estate Planning, Women in Family Business: What Keeps You Up at Night? It's More Than Money: Protect Your Legacy,* and *Power, Strength & Perseverance: What Women Know about Other Women but Search for in Themselves.* She is the author of the chapter, "How You Can Prepare for Longevity and Mental Incapacity among Family Members" in *Wealth of Wisdom: The Top 50 Questions Wealthy Families Ask* (Wiley).

She is a frequent speaker and has been quoted extensively on estate planning topics for national publications, including the *Wall Street Journal, Bloomberg, Barron's, Chicago Tribune,* MarketWatch, and Investors.com.

Patricia is a graduate of Newton Country Day School of the Sacred Heart, Smith College (A.B.), Suffolk University School of Law (J.D.), and Boston University School of Law (L.L.M. in Taxation). She is a fellow of ACTEC (American College of Trust and Estates Council), and a fellow of the Family Firm Institute (F.F.I.).

CHAPTER 27

Creating an Ethical Will

Scotty McLennan

One's "last will and testament" generally deals with material things, with property, rather than passing on a vision of the qualitative dimensions of life that matter to one personally. An "ethical will"—a values-based letter to your loved ones that accompanies your legally drafted will—is concerned with relationships, with love and friendship, and with the profoundly human aspects of living a good life. It is about your legacy in terms of your life's deepest purpose and what you would most want to be remembered for.

Such a document can be produced in a single sitting of a half hour or so, or it can be drafted and re-drafted over weeks, months, and years. It can be all on one page, or it can take the form of a larger composition. It could be a place to clear the air, especially if you think there are significant misunderstandings with others or if you want to acknowledge shortcomings of your own that you regret and would like to make amends for. It can be used as a vehicle to express gratitude for the positive elements of your life, including people and experiences that have really made a difference for you. It can move from acknowledging the past, through celebrating the present, to anticipating the future—bestowing hopes and dreams and blessings on those who will remain after you die.

Description

Ethical wills go back to biblical times. A classic example is found in Genesis 49:1–33 when the patriarch Jacob "called his sons, and said: 'Gather around, that I may tell you what will happen to you in days to come.'" It violates many of the modern "do's and don'ts" of drafting: for example, telling his eldest son that he shall not excel in life henceforth because he "defiled his father's bed" by sleeping on it with his concubine. Or cursing two other sons for their anger and violence. Jacob commends one son as a great ruler to come and another as a "strong donkey." He uses epithets for others of his children like "viper" and "ravenous wolf." Finally, he showers his next-to-youngest with praise and asserts that for him "the blessings of your father are stronger than the blessings of the eternal hills."

From my perspective, ethical wills at their best relate to one's moral and spiritual legacy. They pass on a sense of what matters most in life. They express beliefs, guiding principles, and ideals. They can tell important stories about one's own life and the recipient's. They can describe how you want to be remembered in a qualitative, not quantitative, way. They can instruct, hopefully gently, about life's true purpose, about what is worth living and dying for, about personal and family mission, about wishes for how things could come to be at their best.

Don't use an ethical will to blame, condemn, make others feel guilty, or preach demands to the recipient. Don't try to dictate the future by stating specific requirements of those to whom it's directed. Instead, seek to inspire and enlarge, comfort and bolster, nurture and bless. Ultimately, an ethical will is not about you, the writer, but about those who will remain in this world trying to navigate it well and with fulfillment.

Process

Ethical wills do not necessarily need to be composed for one's offspring. These letters can be written to a partner or spouse, siblings, nieces, nephews, and cousins, friends, or anyone else, including the larger community. They can be written at any time in one's life and then revised and changed in the future—just as one's last will and testament may look very different when written as one attains the age of majority at 18, as one gets married, as children and grandchildren are born, after losing a spouse and remarrying, and generally as one accumulates life experience and wisdom.

One way to begin the process is described in a book by Jack Riemer and Nathaniel Stamper entitled, *So That Your Values Live On: Ethical Wills and How to Prepare Them.* They suggest starting with an outline that is constructed by finishing sentences like these:

- These were the formative events of my life. . .
- These are the people who influenced me the most. . .
- These are the mistakes that I most regret having made in my life. . .
- I would like to ask your forgiveness for. . .
- This is how I feel as I look back over my life. . .
- I want you to know how much I love you and how grateful I am to you for. . .

Then, treat each of these completed sentences as an outline topic. Expand it into a written paragraph or more. Arrange and rearrange the topics in the order that feels best to you, reading them through for coherence and editing as necessary. To personalize your ethical will and to strengthen the links between topics, Riemer and Stamper counsel thinking of words and expressions that are loaded with special meaning for you and for those referenced in the document. There may also be favorite sayings to be preserved. Some of your points may then be best illustrated by short anecdotes. And there may be key dates to remember in writing.

Another way to create an outline is suggested by Barry Baines in his book *Ethical Wills.* He proposes these five elements:

1. Opening thoughts
2. Statements of values and beliefs
3. Meaningful and personally instructive life experiences
4. Hopes for the future
5. Concluding thoughts

Baines recommends using each section as an opportunity for specific writing exercises. For example, for opening thoughts, one might explain why you're writing the ethical will. It could be to leave lessons learned in life, convey what is most personally important, or simply express love. The section on values and beliefs could describe virtues that seem essential, meaningful aphorisms, and compelling stories. Life experience is, of course, a broad category; you could write about relatives and friends, events happening in the larger world, childhood memories, education, work stories, influential people, critical decisions, transitions, and so much more (or less!). Regarding hopes for the future, the horizon is wide open and could run the gamut from family matters to furthering world peace. Concluding thoughts might include expressions of gratitude, what you'll miss most, and how you would like to be remembered.

Baines also suggests avoiding certain areas in the process of writing because then you could produce an "unethical will." Don't try to "reach out from the grave" to instill guilt or blame, denounce survivors, or attempt to micromanage and control people's lives. One can steer clear of this by trying to stick to "I" statements rather than using "you" statements. Aim for a cherished personal legacy rather than being coercive of others.

Outcomes

In her book, *Creating the Good Will,* attorney Elizabeth Arnold insists that good estate planning is the process of determining last wishes regarding both values and valuables. As she puts it, "How well you understand the human side and incorporate it into your decision-making can make the difference between leaving a legacy of warmed hearts or heated heads." Writing an ethical will before thinking about how to distribute property will lead to much better estate planning results. Although an ethical will is "qualitative, rather than objectively quantifiable or legally enforceable," it can be "essential to creating goodwill." It may be critical to helping loved ones understand why certain choices were made in the estate plan, along with fathoming your life's purpose, what you stand for, and how you want to be remembered. It can be "the glue that binds families together, particularly in times of grief and hardship, or when children start to quibble over the fine print in your will."

Some people choose to share their ethical wills well before their death. This can have real positive outcomes as well. Barry Baines explains how ethical wills can be used as the basis for stating family values clearly. It may lead to improved communication between children and parents. Children can come to appreciate what is really important to their parents—perhaps hold them to it in the future! Riemer and Stampfer tell the story of certain parents reading their ethical wills to their children, who then responded with surprise upon learning things that they didn't know were of such significance to their parents. In turn, the parents were surprised to discover that their children didn't realize how strongly they felt about these matters. Children and parents were brought closer together and developed a much better understanding of each other.

Noam Zion in his three-part series on ethical wills for the Purposeful Planning Institute even suggests intergenerational co-authoring of family ethical wills. If children can add their own expressions of gratitude for what they think they received from their parents, often their parents learn things that they actually imparted of which they were never aware. As a further step, children can add new dimensions to the family legacy, yet to be crystalized, as in philanthropic goals that are important to them but not yet known to their parents.

In any case there's a "now or never" dimension to writing an ethical will. Missing the opportunity can deprive family members and other possible recipients of knowing what you think is most important about your life on earth and the legacy you're leaving. Reimer and Stampfer state that "if we don't tell our children our stories and the stories of those from whom we come, no one else ever will." Barry Baines explains that an ethical will puts what one values the most "on the record," not to be forgotten or lost. It is also a vital exercise in self-reflection on the big questions of personal meaning and purpose.

Example

For several years I co-taught a weeklong summer seminar called "What Happens Next"—for people thinking about retirement—at the Tufts European Center in the French Alps with the former university rabbi, Jeffrey Summit. One of the exercises that he brought to participants was creating an ethical will. In our case, Jeff encouraged us to follow this outline:

1. Opening Thoughts
2. Values and Beliefs
3. Lessons and Reflections about Life
4. Hopes for the Future
5. Love
6. Forgiveness
7. Requests
8. Concluding Thoughts

During the first couple of years that he introduced it to attendees, I also followed his instructions to go out into the large garden for 20 minutes, find a private spot, and begin doing some writing, or at least fill in some bullet points on his outline. Yet, I never got very far. It seemed like an overwhelming task. In the third year, though, I decided to try to write something quickly for each of the eight topics. Somehow, I was prepared now, and the writing flowed. That fall, on my 70th birthday, I shared it with my two children, then in their mid-30s. Here's what I was able to say. (By the way, I would advise setting yourself a time limit, at least for a first draft, and then just doing it. Otherwise, you may never get started!)

1. Opening Thoughts

FOR DAN AND WILL: You are the greatest treasure of my life. I'm so glad that you came into Mom's and my world and we have had the chance to spend so many years with you. Lucky us. Blessed us. I love you so much.

2. Values and Beliefs

My values and beliefs, as I think you know, at least from my mouth, always come back to *love*. I fear I haven't manifested it or shared it clearly enough for each of you, demonstrated it in action, and just have held you, literally and figuratively. But I love you not only unconditionally but eternally.

3. Lessons and Reflections about Life

Life is hard. All life is suffering, as the Buddha said. I am so pained, and always have been, when I see either of you two suffering, as you both have: in your health, in social dynamics of various sorts, in trying to be fully with others in ways they haven't appreciated, in your academic and work lives. But the antidote is letting go, getting beyond your ego, not being attached, and being radically open to the present moment: Not looking back with regret or forward in desperate anticipation or fear.

4. Hopes for the Future

I hope for each of you love freely given and freely shared and received, not only with your wives and children and your parents, but also with your friends and colleagues, and ultimately even with your enemies. I've had my own, and I hope I've responded lovingly, even if they did things I didn't like.

5. Love

Love is all.

6. Forgiveness

There are so many ways I've fallen short. So many things I hope you can forgive me for:

- **a)** Not being more obviously loving.
- **b)** Not spending more time with you.
- **c)** Not always understanding you as you are and need to be, rather than as I hope and want you to be (always happy, fulfilled, value-driven).

7. Requests

Please take good care of your Mom, if I die before she does. Please take very good care of each other. Love your wives through thick and thin. Be there for your children unconditionally. Always think about saving the world, and keep your oar in the water, doing that where you can.

8. Concluding Thoughts

I am so grateful for all I've had and all you've meant to me. Gratitude is also the balm for all ills. I give thanks for all we've ever shared together. I love you forever.

The experience both of writing and of sharing this brief ethical will was one of the most powerful and poignant of my life. The tears flowed freely. My sons seemed genuinely moved. It has brought us closer together in an entirely new way. I feel it has had a lasting impact for all of us. You can do something like this too, and perhaps much more. It will be worth it, I promise.

Next Steps

Now, take out a piece of paper and list six to eight topic areas. Begin by filling in a few bullet points for yourself in each of the areas. Then, take some time to reflect—10 minutes, perhaps—and scribble in additional thoughts and feelings that come to you. Then, put it aside overnight. Within the week, though, come back and give yourself a time limit, perhaps a half hour, to write at least a few lines for each of the topic areas. You have a first draft!

You can take a longer time, if you want, perhaps by journaling regularly, to work on the draft and expand it as you choose. You can begin sharing it—if not immediately with the intended recipients, with a close friend or partner. Talk about it and begin honing what you want to say. Once you think you have it in shape to share with the recipients, go ahead and do so. Or you may feel, as many do, that you want to lock it away in a safety deposit box to be shared only after you die.

You have only begun, though. Come back to it for annual reviews, just as you would with other aspects of your estate planning. Your life circumstances will keep changing, and so also might what you want to say in your ethical will or wills. The crucial thing is to be able to share what matters most to you in your relationships with those you care about the most.

Additional Resources

Elizabeth Arnold, *Creating the Good Will* (New York: Penguin, 2005).

Barry K. Baines, *Ethical Wills: Putting Your Values on Paper,* 2nd ed. (Cambridge, MA: Da Capo Press, 2006).

Jack Reimer and Nathaniel Stampfer, *So That Your Values Live On: Ethical Wills and How to Prepare Them* (Woodstock, VT: Jewish Lights Publishing, 1991).

Noam Zion, *Ethical Wills* (Jerusalem: Purposeful Planning Institute, 2020).

Biography

Scotty McLennan is a minister, lawyer, teacher, and author. He is a lecturer in political economy at the Stanford Graduate School of Business. His primary research interests are in the interface of ethics, spirituality, and the professions. Scotty served as the dean for Religious Life at Stanford University and the university chaplain at Tufts University. He was also a senior lecturer at the Harvard Business School. Scotty is the author of *Finding Your Religion: When the Faith You Grew Up With Has Lost Its Meaning* and *Jesus Was a Liberal: Reclaiming Christianity for All*, as well as co-author of *Church on Sunday, Work on Monday: The Challenge of Fusing Christian Values with Business Life*. Scotty received a B.A. from Yale University and M.Div. and J.D. degrees from Harvard Divinity and Law Schools.

SECTION 4

INVESTING WISELY

Investing is a huge topic with a vast literature devoted to it. The goal of this volume is not to offer tools or exercises aimed at making money through investing. Instead, we approach investing here not from its quantitative perspective but from the qualitative one: What should family members be thinking and talking about to make sure that their investment process enhances their lives together as a family?

Perhaps the most fundamental skill with regard to financial wealth is to identify and track the factors with the largest impact. In the first chapter in this section, Scott Peppet shares a graph that families can use to provide themselves a "stewardship snapshot" of their portfolio, in the face of the "Four Horsemen" of fees, taxes, spending (including charitable giving), and inflation. This graph allows families to keep track of their financial wealth as well as to talk specifically about what is (and is not) in their control when it comes to stewarding that wealth well.

In the next chapter, Joe Calabrese moves us from tracking wealth to setting goals, by leading readers through the simple but powerful exercise of "Capital Sufficiency Analysis." Since families have only four options with regard to financial wealth—create it, consume it, charitably give it away, or convey it to heirs—Calabrese's exercise prompts members to think about which of those goals they want to pursue (and how to prioritize them), and then whether their current investment plan provides an expected balance of risk and return to achieve those goals (or whether they are likely to under- or overshoot them).

For families who want to pursue this line of thinking in even more detail, Jean Brunel and Voyt Krzychylkiewicz then expand on this framework with an exercise that allows readers to assign probabilities to the different types of goals they want to pursue (needs, wants, wishes, and dreams), as well as timelines for pursuing these goals. They then introduce the concept of dedicating subportfolios to these different classes of goals.

Many families seek to help their members become better stewards of their financial wealth through offering some sort of investment education. Our contributors share various tools and exercises related to family wealth education in the section entitled, "Becoming a Learning Family." In this section, however, we have included a contribution by Jim Garland specific to family learning about investments. In it, Garland describes in detail the series of seminars that the Jeffrey family devised over several decades to educate family members about their financial assets, along with the methods of instruction and outcomes. This program provides an excellent blueprint for other families to consider and adapt to their specific needs and situation.

CHAPTER 28

Monitoring Financial Capital with the "Four Horsemen" Graph

Scott Peppet

A family's "wealth" is not limited to or primarily about its financial capital. Much more important than its dollars are its members' physical and emotional health (human capital), relationships and decision-making (social capital), intellectual momentum (learning or intellectual capital), and purpose and service (legacy or spiritual capital).

At the same time, financial capital does matter. If a family hopes to succeed over multiple generations, thoughtful stewardship of its financial capital is critical to support these other types of wealth. What does such thoughtful stewardship require, and how can a family's success with its financial capital be measured?

In this chapter, I offer a simple graph that can help a family monitor its stewardship of financial capital over time. The goal of this graph is to create a "stewardship snapshot" on one page by condensing a great deal of information into a simple visual. In particular, the graph shows how a family's financial capital is performing—in terms of investment gains or losses—against the effects of four factors that typically deplete a family's financial capital in the long term: taxes, fees, spending, and inflation. I call these factors the "Four Horsemen of the Apocalypse" because of their often-devastating effect on financial capital. Thus, the graph is called the "Four Horsemen Graph."

To use this graph, a family must track the following categories of information on at least a yearly basis:

1. Investment gains or losses (shown in light gray shading): For families with highly liquid assets, such as marketable securities, this is relatively easy. For others with more illiquid assets, such as an operating business or real estate holdings, this may require internal or external valuations. Regardless, the graph depends on an accurate yearly assessment of the family's increase or decrease in equity.
2. Fees (shown in dark gray shading): Next, a family must track the fees paid to achieve that investment return. This should include fees to outside managers,

family office investment professionals, and embedded fees in hedge, private equity, or other funds that the family holds. The goal is to accurately summarize the total cost of managing the investment portfolio.

3. Taxes (shown in vertical lines): Investment generates taxes, and different investment approaches create different tax burdens. Taxes can be hard to represent simply because often tax obligations are shifted from one year to another by various tax strategies. But the goal here is to report the total cash outlays for taxes paid in a given year (not the obligations incurred).
4. Spending (shown in dot pattern): This category reports funds that a family distributes from its corpus or operating business for spending. It is not necessary to track each family member's actual expenditures, although that would be most accurate. For our purposes, it suffices to show the total amount removed from the family investment portfolio—whether those funds are actually spent on purchases or are saved elsewhere (e.g., in an individual family member's personal estate).
5. Charitable giving (shown in diagonal lines): This is a component of spending but it can be useful to break it out separately. This category should show funds removed from the investment portfolio and donated to either a public charity or a family foundation in a given year but should not include funds housed in that foundation and then donated to charity. The purpose of this graph is to show how the family's corpus of financial capital has been stewarded; it would be "double counting" to show a dollar leaving the portfolio to a family foundation and then show that same dollar again when it left the foundation when granted to an ultimate charity.
6. Inflation (shown in black): This is perhaps the hardest metric to include. A family must decide how it wants to represent inflation. In Figure 28.1, inflation is shown as compounding over a five-year period.

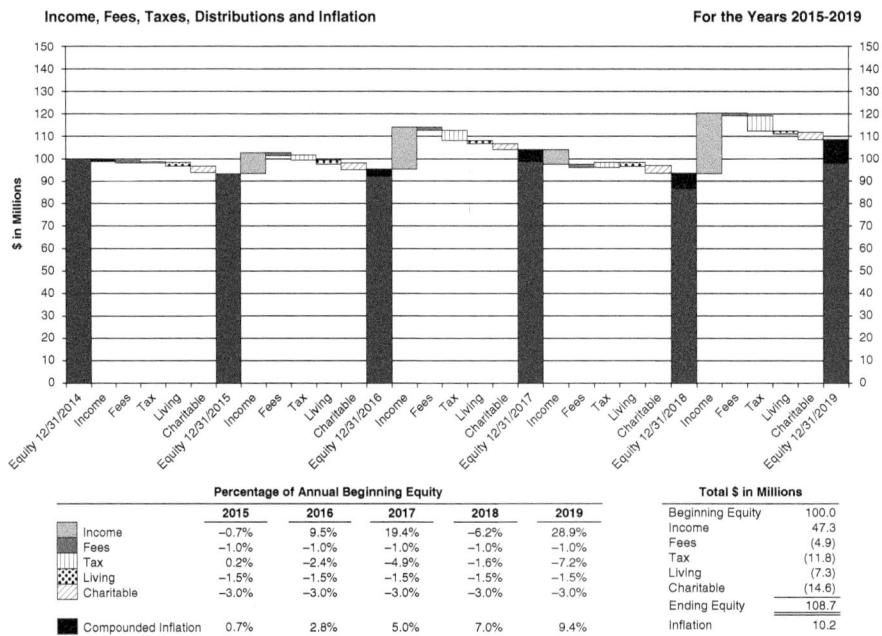

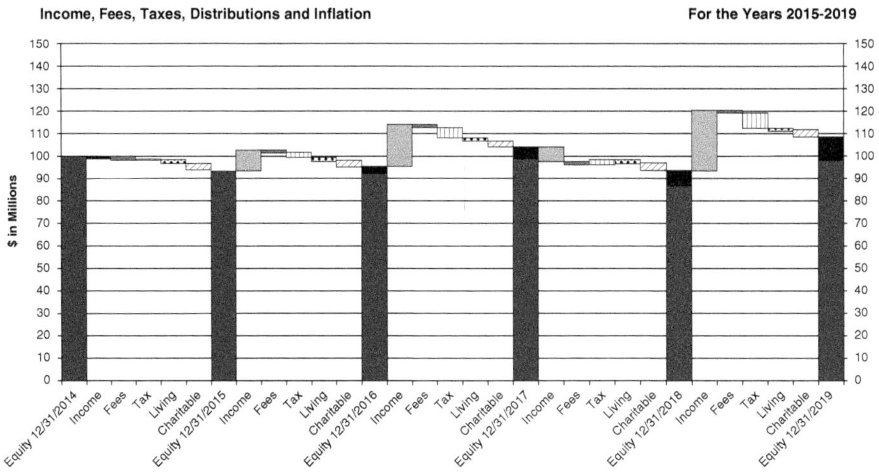

Percentage of Annual Beginning Equity

	2015	2016	2017	2018	2019
Income	–0.7%	9.5%	19.4%	–6.2%	28.9%
Fees	–1.0%	–1.0%	–1.0%	–1.0%	–1.0%
Tax	0.2%	–2.4%	–4.9%	–1.6%	–7.2%
Living	–1.5%	–1.5%	–1.5%	–1.5%	–1.5%
Charitable	–3.0%	–3.0%	–3.0%	–3.0%	–3.0%
Compounded Inflation	0.7%	2.8%	5.0%	7.0%	9.4%

Total $ in Millions

Beginning Equity	100.0
Income	47.3
Fees	(4.9)
Tax	(11.8)
Living	(7.3)
Charitable	(14.6)
Ending Equity	108.7
Inflation	10.2

Figure 28.1 A Sample Four Horsemen Graph

Armed with these categories of information, it is relatively simple to make the bridge graph shown in Figure 28.1, (You can download a sample Excel spreadsheet here: https://scottpeppet.com/articles/for-parents/the-most-important-financial-stewardship-graph/.)

This graph shows, on one page, how a family is stewarding its financial capital. In particular, it answers one question: Is the family preserving its purchasing power by beating inflation after accounting for taxes, fees, spending, and charity? For most families, this is a baseline definition of success—if a family is not preserving its purchasing power in this way, it is hard to see itself as stewarding financial capital for future generations. (This may not be the case if a family has a very large corpus and has decided that it can intentionally "spend down" some of its assets while still having sufficient resources for the future, but it is generally true of most families.) I am referring to a "leave no trace" type of stewardship, where the idea is to leave the family's financial capital in as good shape as you found it.

It is relatively easy for a family to say, "Yes, our goal is to beat inflation after accounting for taxes, fees, and spending or charity," but it is remarkably hard to do. Few families, in my view, actually do it. Thus, this graph is often quite revealing. The example in Figure 28.1 illustrates why: At the end of the five-year period, the family in question has less—adjusted for compounding inflation—than it did at the start.

When a family first compiles the Four Horsemen Graph, the following are the most common reactions:

- *"How can taxes and fees be so high?"* Both taxes and fees are often hidden in financial reporting. Many financial products show gains after fees or taxes, which leaves these expenditures out of the picture. When a family really tracks its taxes and fees, it may be surprised by what it is paying to invest its financial assets.
- *"But we don't spend that much!"* It is useful to aggregate all distributions or dividends to the family in one place, particularly charitable donations, and show the total outflows from the family's portfolio. A family may not realize the impact that such expenditures have had on the family's financial capital.
- *"Does inflation have that much impact?"* In the last decades, inflation rates have been at historic lows. Nevertheless, inflation compounds over time, and even low rates of inflation have massive effects on the actual purchasing power of a family's financial capital. Very few families seem to track this corrosive threat to their stewardship.

Each of these reactions can prompt useful discussion between a family's members or with its advisors. A family may dig into their taxes and fees and try to make their portfolio more efficient. Or they may revisit their distribution policy and engage on the difficult questions that surround how much spending and donation makes sense in their context. Or the Four Horsemen Graph may lead a family to focus on increasing their investment returns by reallocating their portfolio.

More fundamentally, the exercise of squarely confronting the four horsemen of the apocalypse may lead a family into the most meaningful conversation it can have about its financial capital: What is the purpose of that capital, and what is the family's shared definition of successful stewardship?

This may lead a family to revise its goals. Perhaps maintaining purchasing power over many generations *isn't* its idea of success. This is the purpose of the graph: to show, simply and succinctly, how the family's financial capital is performing against these factors, so that a family can thoughtfully engage around the purpose of its financial wealth.

Personally, I find this the most important financial graph that a family can use regularly. It sums up the stewardship problem in one simple sheet of paper by showing both income and expenditures, as well as inflation's slow effects. I hope that it proves useful in your work and discussions.

Additional Resources

Jean L. P. Brunel, *Goals-Based Wealth Management: An Integrated and Practical Approach to Changing the Structure of Wealth Advisory Practices* (Hoboken, NJ: Wiley Finance, 2015).

Greg Curtis, "Numeracy, Innumeracy and Hard Slogging" (Whitepaper 29, Greycourt, April 2003), http://www.greycourt.com/wp-content/uploads/2019/09/WP-No-29-Numeracy-Innumeracy-and-Hard-Slogging.pdf.

Biography

Scott Peppet is the president of a family-centered office, a writer and speaker on family learning, and an evangelist for stewarding human capital, not just financial capital. In a past life, he was a law professor who taught conflict resolution, contract law, and how to counsel family enterprises. He lives in Boulder, Colorado, with his wife, children, and a terribly coddled horse named Copper. He loves to ski and hike and is an ordained Soto Zen priest.

CHAPTER 29

Keeping Goals in the Spotlight with Capital Sufficiency Analysis

Joe Calabrese

In managing and preserving significant wealth, investors and their advisors typically make use of every financial tool available to them that is appropriate for their situations. However, one important tool is often overlooked: capital sufficiency analysis. This can play an important role in a goals-based investment strategy for an ultra-wealthy family.

Why Capital Sufficiency Analysis Is Critical

Capital sufficiency analysis is the process of determining whether a family's existing and estimated future financial resources will enable them to achieve their financial goals. For most investors, it helps them determine if they will be able to meet their retirement goals. In contrast, ultra-high-net-worth investors don't generally have the same type of concern. If a family has $25 million or more, for example, it's generally not worried about the risk of running out of capital. As a result, they may dismiss the importance of undertaking a capital sufficiency analysis.

That's ironic because ultra-wealthy families stand to gain the most from this process. While they may not be concerned about being able to retire comfortably, they typically place a high priority on goals involving charitable giving, business continuity and succession, and wealth transfer to subsequent generations. Without careful capital sufficiency planning, they may fall short of achieving all their financial goals.

Markowitz and Risk-Adjusted Returns

To put capital sufficiency analysis in perspective, it helps to examine how portfolio construction using goals-based investing differs from the traditional risk-return approach. For years, the majority of investors—small and large, private and institutional—have been designing and managing diversified portfolios using a risk-based approach. But while the benefits of diversification had been known for ages, it wasn't until the 1950s that the groundbreaking work of Harry Markowitz provided the math behind optimizing a portfolio's risk-return profile.

The problem Markowitz wanted to solve was how to create and maintain a portfolio that would minimize the risk required to generate a targeted return of a portfolio—in other words, how to maximize risk-adjusted returns. To do that, an investor needs to estimate both the expected return and volatility (or risk) of various portfolio alternatives. Projecting the expected return of a portfolio is straightforward. The investor merely needs to calculate the weighted average of the expected returns of each investment. But portfolio volatility cannot be computed in the same way—the volatility of each investment cannot simply be aggregated to determine a portfolio's overall riskiness.

To properly estimate the volatility of a portfolio, Markowitz concluded that an investor must impute the effect of the covariance of the returns of each investment with those of the others. This revelation led to the popularization of what is now the traditional mean-variance asset allocation approach for building portfolios.

The basic idea is that investors seeking higher returns must be willing to hold higher-volatility portfolios, whereas those desiring safer, predictable returns would hold lower-volatility portfolios. While there are advantages to this approach, there are also shortcomings. When a standard risk-adjusted approach is used, the primary goal is to simply maximize returns at any given level of risk. What the money is used for is inconsequential, making goals largely irrelevant. The shortcoming of this approach is the investor's portfolio may not be optimized to fund all of an investor's goals, possibly leaving the portfolio short or exposing the investor to unnecessary risk.

Bringing Goals into the Planning Picture

As its name indicates, goals-based asset allocation puts an investor's life goals exactly where they should be: on center stage. Capital sufficiency analysis plays a vital role in goals-based investing. It is the process used to determine the likelihood that an investor's current and future financial capital will result in meeting all their financial goals, which may range from satisfying lifestyle requirements to fulfilling legacy aspirations.

The purpose of goals-based investing using capital sufficiency analysis is not to maximize capital growth but to reverse-engineer an outcome designed to meet consumption, charitable giving, and conveyance goals. Capital sufficiency analysis helps an investor answer several key questions:

- How much **core capital** is required to satisfy lifestyle needs?
- How much **excess capital**—the amount in addition to core capital—will be required to support additional goals for charitable giving and wealth transfer?
- How likely is it that appropriate levels of core and excess capital will be reached?
- Is the amount of wealth transferred to beneficiaries at the time of the investor's death too high, too low, or just right?
- Is the risk being taken in the portfolio too much or too little?

Calculating Capital Sufficiency

Wealth managers commonly use two methods to evaluate capital sufficiency:

- Deterministic forecasting
- Stochastic modeling

Deterministic forecasting involves estimating portfolio growth in a straight-line manner using inputs such as the investment portfolio's current value, investment horizon, annual return assumptions, contributions to and outflows from the portfolio over the investment horizon, inflation, taxes, and investment management fees. While straightforward and easy for investors to understand, these models don't accurately reflect real-world volatility and risk.

Stochastic modeling, or Monte Carlo simulation, attempts to quantify the likelihood of achieving a future outcome by incorporating uncertainty into the mix. By generating random results based on assumed probability distributions for key variables, a stochastic model produces a large number of potential outcomes— typically hundreds or even thousands—over the investment horizon. The outcomes of these various trials are compiled to help an investor determine the probability that a goal will be met.

After identifying an optimal asset allocation and risk profile using a capital sufficiency model, investors can determine if they are comfortable with the level of risk required to meet their goals. Iteration and calibration will yield a result consistent with investors' risk capacity and goals. Wealth managers who prepare capital sufficiency analyses typically recommend an investment strategy that has a high probability of success, e.g., at least 75 percent to 85 percent.

The Four Cs

A family can do four things with its wealth, which can be thought of as the four Cs:

- **Create** more of it.
- **Consume** it.
- **Charitably** give it away via donations or make gifts to family members during the investor's lifetime.
- **Convey** it upon death to loved ones, future generations, charitable causes, and the community.

Capital sufficiency analysis helps an investor determine how much capital is needed via the investment portfolio to support consumption needs, charitable giving goals, and the desire to leave a legacy. Investors may find that they are in a sufficiently strong position to achieve additional goals, add to existing ones, or reduce the portfolio's risk. In situations where one or more goals cannot be met, capital sufficiency analysis provides a framework for a family to address shortfalls by making changes in one or more of the four Cs.

Addressing Shortfalls through the Four Cs	
Wealth Options	**Possible Changes**
Create more of it.	• Modify the strategic asset allocation to take more risk. • Establish credit facilities and draw on them for spending during market downturns. • Work longer than originally planned. • Incorporate tax planning into the process, e.g., move to a jurisdiction with lower income-tax rates.
Consume it.	• Consider establishing or modifying household spending patterns to reduce expenditures.
Charitably make gifts to family members or charities.	• Reduce gifting during the investor's lifetime. • Delay the timing of gifts.
Convey it upon death.	• Prioritize beneficiaries to reduce end-of-life wealth transfers.

Capital Sufficiency Analysis and Clients: A Case Study

To see how capital sufficiency analysis enhances planning for ultra-wealthy families, it helps to look at a case study involving real clients.

Goal Setting and Assumptions

Sam (68) and Louisa (69) Dalton live in the United States and have two children: Sara (18) and Derek (15). The couple has $41 million in their investment portfolio and two homes valued at $6 million. The Daltons met with their wealth management team to clarify their long-term investment strategies. The first step in the Daltons' capital sufficiency analysis involved the articulation of their aspirations. Sam and Louisa had three specific goals:

Goals	Type of Capital Required	Description
Lifestyle	**Core**	Maintain their current annual spending of $1 million (in current dollars) for the rest of their lives.
Wealth Transfer	**Excess**	Bequeath $1 million each to Sara and Derek upon the death of the second spouse. ($2 million is estimated to be $3.9 million in 2052 dollars.)
Charitable	**Excess**	Make additional charitable contributions of $200,000 per year from 2021 through 2030.

Projecting Outcomes

In the stochastic model used for this analysis, the investment rate of return was randomly altered 1,000 different times in each analysis to provide a large-enough sample size of outcomes to make a sound forecast of the probabilities of success for the period ending 2052.

The model required numerous assumptions, including investment returns, inflation rate, standard deviation of investment returns, federal and state tax rates, timing of distributions for spending needs, percentage of portfolio income taxed, timing of charitable distributions, percentage of taxable portfolio income taxed as qualified dividends, and portfolio turnover.

The modeling focused on addressing two important questions:

- What is the likelihood that $3.9 million or more will be available in 2052 to bequeath to their children if Sam and Louisa fulfill their lifestyle (spending) goal?
- If the Daltons make additional annual charitable contributions of $200,000 through 2030 and maintain lifestyle spending plans, what is the probability that they will have $3.9 million or more to bequeath?

Projected Outcomes—1,000 Trials

	Lifestyle Spending Goal Met		Lifestyle Spending Goal + Charitable Goal Met	
Year-End 2052 Asset Levels	**Number of Trials Achieving Desired Outcome**	**Cumulative %**	**Number of Trials Achieving Desired Outcome**	**Cumulative %**
Over $43.4 million	500	50.0%	500	50.0%
Between $3.9 and $43.4 million	440	94.0%	326	82.6%
More than $0 but less than $3.9 million	28	96.8%	33	85.9%
$0	32	100.00%	141	100.0%

Sufficient assets (at least $3.9 million) at 2052 to meet wealth transfer goal.

The Daltons' capital sufficiency analysis indicated that there is a high probability (94 percent) that they will be able to satisfy their needs for lifestyle spending and for bequeathing $3.9 million to their children in 2052. They also have a high probability of success (82.6 percent) of meeting their goal of making additional charitable contributions—$200,000 per year in donations from 2021 through 2030—while also meeting their lifestyle and wealth transfer goals.

Identifying the Threshold Return

The wealth management team also helped the Daltons determine that their investment portfolio needed a minimum risk-adjusted return of 4.2 percent to achieve their lifestyle and wealth transfer goals. Based upon long-term historical rates of return for equities and bonds over a period going back to January 1900, they found that a 70 percent/30 percent equity/fixed income portfolio would be expected to earn 8.1 percent in risk-adjusted returns—nearly twice the threshold return—suggesting they could consider scaling back the risk in their portfolio and still be in a strong position to meet their goals.

Adding Value with Capital Sufficiency Analysis

By considering a wide range of scenarios and risk, and incorporating the interaction between the four Cs, capital sufficiency analysis provides the basis for a rich conversation between the family and its wealth advisor. Capital sufficiency analysis tools can also be used to explore what-if scenarios, e.g., another event like the Great Financial Crisis (2008). Of course, the analysis is not a one-and-done exercise. It must be updated regularly to measure progress, assess the effectiveness of any adjustments, and incorporate changes in a family's situation. *While the process may sound daunting, it's well worth the effort. It is the clearest path to providing investors with peace of mind—equipped with the knowledge their portfolios are built to meet their financial goals in lieu of some arbitrary benchmark.*

Additional Resources

Jean Brunel, *Goals-Based Wealth Management* (Hoboken, NJ: Wiley, 2015).

Kurt N. Schacht, James C. Allen, and Robert W. Dannhauser, *Elements of an Investment Policy Statement for Individual Investors* (Charlottesville, VA: CFA Institute, 2010).

Mark Haynes Daniell and Tom McCullough, *Family Wealth Management* (Hoboken, NJ: Wiley, 2013).

Biography

Joe Calabrese is executive vice president and chief operating officer at Key Wealth Management. He is responsible for overseeing the development, integrated delivery, and strategic development of a full range of financial planning, investment, fiduciary, and banking capabilities for Key's clients. Joe has more than 25 years of experience in the financial services industry. He joined Key in 2016 and lends his knowledge and expertise to affluent individuals, families, business owners, and institutions. Before joining Key, Joe held a wide range of executive roles including president and chief executive office of Geller Family Office Services, a New York based registered investment advisor (RIA) and multifamily office, and president of Harris myCFO, which focused on serving clients with a net worth in excess of $100 million. Joe graduated from McGill University in Montreal, Canada, with a joint honors degree in economics and finance and holds a Chartered Accountant designation. Joe actively serves on the advisory board of the UHNW Institute and the Gaples Institute for Integrative Cardiology. He is a past president of the Goodman Theatre Board of Trustees in Chicago and also served as chairman of the board of overseers for Lewis College of Human Sciences of the Illinois Institute of Technology. Joe has three children and resides in Bronxville, New York, with his wife.

The author thanks Jeff Getty, Joel Redmond, and Justin Tantalo for comments on this chapter. The views expressed are my own and do not necessarily reflect the views of KeyBank National Association or any of its affiliates. KeyBank National Association assumes no responsibility or liability for any errors or omissions in the content of this chapter.

CHAPTER 30

Constructing an Investment Portfolio to Support Family Goals

Jean Brunel and Voyt Krzychylkiewicz

Traditional finance has trouble dealing with the needs of individuals. Most investment solutions have been developed for the institutional client with the relatively simple objective of maximizing risk-adjusted returns. While institutions typically have this singular goal, individuals and families tend to have multiple goals with different horizons and with multiple different stakeholders in mind (including children and charities among others). Furthermore, not all goals are equally important, nor do they all cost the same amount.

It is typical for families to think through their goals early on, particularly when a liquidity event transforms concentrated single security wealth into more liquid financial assets. However, goals are dynamic, and the passing of time and underlying investment performance may require families to periodically revisit their goals and the resultant financial asset allocation.

As a result, there is often more than one opportunity to consider the following twin questions:

1. What are our financial goals, their time horizons, and the requisite certainty of attaining these goals?
2. Does my current asset allocation align with these goals?

Note that many goals-based discussions focus largely on the first of these questions, but it is important to tackle the approach from both perspectives. Further, when considering how to adjust your current asset allocation to align with goals, it is important to factor in costs, most notably taxes, which may impact how, and even if, this can be executed efficiently.

The purpose of this chapter is to explain the process of constructing an investment portfolio that supports your family's specific goals. At times, the exercise itself can become quite technical and may require the help of an investment advisor, but our aim is for you to understand the process and put you in a position to ask yourself, as well as your advisors, better questions about your portfolio construction.

Setting Goals

Though some families find it relatively easy to set out their major financial goals, they do not always appreciate that setting goals must be done in an iterative fashion to reflect both their available current (and future) assets as well as the risk tolerance that is required to achieve their goals. It may even become obvious that no reasonable strategy, short of purchasing the proverbial lottery ticket, will do the trick to meet all of a family's goals.

Let's use common language to separate family goals into four categories: Needs, Wants, Wishes, and Dreams. First, let's define these four items before considering how you may practically convert your goals into an investment strategy.

- **Needs** include fixed expenses to maintain your current standard of living and for which you require a very high level of certainty. However, you do not have to restrict your thinking to the basics of survival—for example, food and shelter. For some people, they may have a "need" for tithing or charitable giving, maintaining a second home, or an annual trip to visit children. The principle is to identify items that are a necessity or key obligation where you have little tolerance for failure. In our following statistical analysis, we express needs as a goal that requires a greater than 90 percent probability of success.
- **Wants**, by contrast, may include more discretionary items where you have a desire for something but are comfortable absorbing greater risk of these not being met (perhaps greater than 80 percent probability of success).
- Similarly, your **Wishes** and **Dreams** include items that are less critical to achieve. This does not necessarily mean that Wishes or Dreams are "less important"; it may be just that they are more aspirational in nature and so are less likely to be achieved. For our following statistical analysis, we use a greater than 70 percent probability for Wishes and greater than 50 percent for Dreams.

Clearly, the goal-setting process is highly personal. You may even have your own language to describe the ranking of your goals, but the aim is to develop a hierarchy of goals considering the relative necessity to achieve them.

After developing this hierarchy, the next step is to understand the financial implications of the various goals as well as the respective time frame for each. This may involve your financial planner or family office building more detailed cash flow forecasts that also factor in other items such as expected income or sizable one-off purchases. This approach of starting with your goals contrasts with that taken by many wealth managers (and indeed, regulators), which seek to set a single risk rating based on the individual or their level of knowledge of investment products. In truth, the risk sits with each goal, and of course a single individual or family will have multiple goals with differing risk appetites.

The following table may provide a useful framework as you map your goals. We have included several examples of types of goals, although these are not intended to be prescriptive since this process is highly personal to each family and may also include nonfinancial goals that could be addressed through planning work beyond investments (e.g., tax structuring, philanthropy planning, succession planning).

Let's consider the example of the Patel family. The Patels are a couple with adult children who have $50 million of investable assets and net annual expenditure of $1 million per year. In our example, the family has four goals, which we have included in our table:

- They *need* to maintain an emergency reserve sufficient liquidity to meet lifestyle expenses for the next three years.
- They *want* to maintain the same lifestyle for the next 15 years.
- They *wish* they could give $10 million to their children in 5 years.
- They *dream* about funding a foundation with $20 million in 20 years.

	Value	Time Horizon	"Probability of Success" Requirement
1. Needs			
1.1 Maintain sufficient liquid capital for next 3 years	$1 million p.a.	0–3 years	95%
1.2 Financially support children until independence			
1.3 Financially support parents or broader family			
1.4 Other			
2. Wants			
2.1 Maintain current standard of living	$1 million p.a.	3–15 years	80%
2.2 Acquire art or other collectibles			
2.3 Complete home renovation			
2.4 Other			
3. Wishes			
3.1 Provide a gift to children in future	$10 million	5 years	70%
3.2 Purchase additional vacation property/second home			
3.3 Purchase luxury asset such as a yacht/aircraft			
3.4 Other			
4. Dreams			
4.1 Set up and fund own family foundation	$20 million	20 years	60%
4.2 Fund family's entrepreneurial ventures			
4.3 Donate to charity			
4.4 Other			

Identifying Subportfolios to Support Each Goal

For each of these goals (or other goals you want to include, with their own distinct required probabilities of success), we need to develop a unique subportfolio of financial assets to support each unique goal. The key point is that the mix of financial assets will likely be very different for each goal due to the underlying risk of the investment assets and time to realize the goal.

Generally speaking, a Need in the near term (say, less than five years) should likely be backed with low-risk financial assets where there is greater certainty of the outcome. These financial assets may include cash or short duration bond portfolios. By contrast, Dreams and Wishes or goals in the distant future may be backed by higher risk assets, such as public or private equity. The reason we can use higher risk portfolios to back longer-term goals is that there is time to recover from short periods of underperformance. Effectively, the variance (or volatility) of investment outcomes reduces over long-term horizons, making long-term performance more predictable than short-term performance.

Returning to the Patels, let's assume they have the option to invest in six distinct investment portfolios running from conservative (Portfolio A—low return and low volatility) to aggressive (Portfolio F—high return and high volatility). The illustrative six subportfolios have different underlying asset class exposures as outlined below.

	A	B	C	D	E	F
Cash	80%	26%	3%	1%	1%	1%
Investment Grade Bonds	20%	44%	45%	25%	0%	0%
High-Yield Bonds	0%	5%	11%	25%	34%	4%
Low Volatility Alternatives	0%	9%	13%	0%	0%	0%
Real Estate	0%	5%	5%	3%	3%	0%
Equities	0%	11%	15%	22%	35%	60%
Equity Alternatives	0%	0%	8%	24%	27%	35%

These six subportfolios create something that resembles a reasonable efficient frontier[1] as can be seen in the following chart.

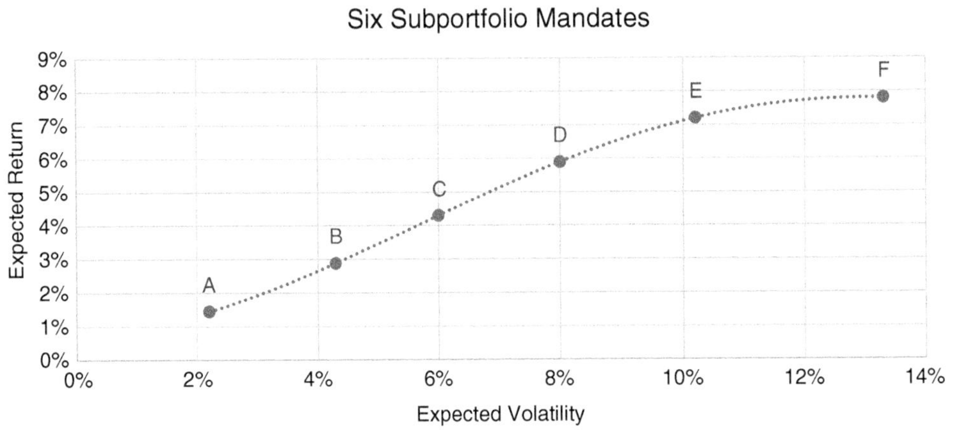

Now that we know the investment alternatives, how do we decide which portfolio to invest in for each goal? Recall our earlier comment that shorter term goals

[1]An efficient frontier is a set of optimal portfolios that each offer the highest expected return for a defined level of risk.

or those requiring high levels of certainty (i.e., Needs and, perhaps, Wants) will typically be invested in more conservative portfolios. Long-term goals or goals with lower levels of required certainty (i.e., Dreams and Wishes) can typically be invested in higher risk/return asset classes.

While this "rule of thumb" may be useful, we can be more specific by looking again at the expected investment returns and expected volatility of our six portfolios[2] shown below.

	A	B	C	D	E	F
Expected Return	1.5%	2.9%	4.3%	5.9%	7.2%	7.8%
Expected Volatility	2.2%	4.3%	6.0%	8.0%	10.2%	13.3%

When looking only at expected returns, it is tempting to suggest that all capital should be allocated to the portfolio with the highest return potential—portfolio F in this case. However, remember that there is a 50 percent chance of doing better than the expected return and a 50 percent chance of doing worse. Obviously, the concern for many families is performing significantly worse than the expected returns and, as a result, potentially jeopardizing the family's goals.

This is where volatility comes into it. Portfolios with higher expected volatility have a wider range of expected potential outcomes and so may not be suitable for certain goals. Your advisor can carry out some statistical analysis looking at what impact the volatility has on returns based on certain probabilities.

The following table shows that there is a 95 percent probability that the expected return of Portfolio A will be –2.2 percent or better in any single year. By contrast, there is 95 percent probability that Portfolio F delivers –14.1 percent or better. This suggests that Portfolio A provides a higher expected return where a family requires a 95 percent probability of meeting its goal (i.e., a Need). To simplify matters, we have bolded the portfolio with the highest expected return based on differing levels of probability. As you can see, as the required probability of a goal diminishes, portfolios with higher expected return and higher expected volatility become more suitable.

Annualized Minimum Expected Return (1 year)

Probability	**A**	**B**	**C**	**D**	**E**	**F**
95%	**–2.2%**	–4.2%	–5.6%	–7.3%	–9.6%	–14.1%
90%	**–1.4%**	–2.6%	–3.4%	–4.4%	–5.9%	–9.2%
80%	**–0.4%**	–0.7%	–0.7%	–0.8%	–1.4%	–3.4%
70%	0.3%	0.6%	1.2%	1.7%	**1.9%**	0.8%
60%	0.9%	1.8%	2.8%	3.9%	**4.6%**	4.4%
50% (i.e., the expected return)	1.5%	2.9%	4.3%	5.9%	7.2%	**7.8%**

[2]Note that expected investment returns and expected volatility are calculated based on historical performance.

The table shows the expected minimum return for one-year periods only, so we need to do a similar exercise for longer-term horizons (e.g., 5- and 20-year horizons). You can see that as the time horizon is extended, the higher risk portfolios deliver higher expected returns even at higher levels of required probability of achieving your goals. Again, this should be intuitive—if we have a long investment horizon, we are able to take more investment risk as more volatile and high return investments have more time to recover from any periods of weakness.

Annualized Minimum Expected Return (5 years)

Probability	A	B	C	D	E	F
95%	–0.2%	–0.3%	–0.1%	**0.0%**	–0.3%	–2.0%
90%	0.2%	0.4%	0.9%	1.3%	**1.4%**	0.2%
80%	0.6%	1.3%	2.0%	2.9%	**3.4%**	2.8%
70%	0.9%	1.9%	2.9%	4.0%	**4.8%**	4.7%
60%	1.2%	2.4%	3.6%	5.0%	6.0%	**6.3%**
50% (i.e., expected return)	1.5%	2.9%	4.3%	5.9%	7.2%	**7.8%**

Annualized Minimum Expected Return (20 years)

Probability	A	B	C	D	E	F
95%	0.6%	1.3%	2.1%	3.0%	**3.4%**	2.9%
90%	0.8%	1.7%	2.6%	3.6%	**4.3%**	4.0%
80%	1.0%	2.1%	3.2%	4.4%	5.3%	**5.3%**
70%	1.2%	2.4%	3.6%	5.0%	6.0%	**6.2%**
60%	1.3%	2.6%	4.0%	5.4%	6.6%	**7.0%**
50% (i.e., expected return)	1.5%	2.9%	4.3%	5.9%	7.2%	**7.8%**

Going back to the case of the Patels, recall that they had a Wish of providing their children with $10 million of capital in five years. Using the table for five-year returns and a 70 percent required probability, we can see that subportfolio E provides the highest expected return of 4.8 percent per annum. Similarly, for their 20-year Dream of setting up a family foundation (using a 60 percent required probability), we can see that subportfolio F would be optimal, providing a return of 7.0 percent per year.

Combining Subportfolios to Develop Your Investment Portfolio

Once the optimal subportfolios have been identified for each unique goal, they can be combined to develop the overall investment portfolio as shown in the following table. In the case of the Patel family, the good news is that they have sufficient capital to meet all four of their goals and would even have excess capital ($26.2 million).

This excess capital can be used to increase current goals, such as boosting the amount of the gift to their children or adding additional goals in the future. They could also increase the required probability for some of their goals. Similarly, if they did not have sufficient capital to meet all their goals, they would need to extend the time horizon, reduce the amount, or reduce the required probability.

For our purposes, we have assumed the Patels are comfortable with the current goals and have decided to invest their excess capital into a "moderate" subportfolio while they evaluate any changes to their goals (Portfolio D).

	Goals				Surplus	Total
	1	2	3	4		
Investment Horizon	3	15	5	20		
Required Success	95%	80%	70%	60%		
Optimal Subportfolio	A	E	E	F	D	
Required Capital ($'000)	3,039	7,667	7,907	5,124	26,263	**50,000**
Required Capital (as a % of total)	6.1%	15.3%	15.8%	10.2%	52.5%	**100.0%**
Asset Mix						
Cash	80%	1%	1%	1%	1%	**6%**
Investment Grade Bonds	20%	0%	0%	0%	25%	**14%**
High-Yield Bonds	0%	34%	34%	4%	25%	**24%**
Low Volatility Alternatives	0%	0%	0%	0%	0%	**0%**
Real Estate	0%	3%	3%	0%	3%	**3%**
Equities	0%	35%	35%	60%	22%	**29%**
Equity Alternatives	0%	27%	27%	35%	24%	**25%**
Total	100%	100%	100%	100%	100%	**100%**

Additional Considerations

While the process just outlined shows how to convert your goals into an investment portfolio, there are several other practical considerations and questions which you should ask yourself and any relevant advisors:

- How different is the optimal portfolio from our current portfolio?
- What would the transaction costs be (such as taxes or costs to unwind structures) if we rebalanced the portfolio immediately and is it feasible to carry this out?
- Is our investment portfolio sufficiently liquid such that we can easily rebalance?
- Can we make use of derivative strategies that could help in rebalancing the portfolio?
- Can we use other strategies such as insurance to mitigate certain risks (e.g., longevity) and support specific goals?
- Outside of return objectives, do we have any other goals that relate to investments, such as impact or lifestyle investing?

- How do our transition or succession plans impact our goals and resultant investment portfolio?
- If we have capital in excess of what is required to meet our goals, do we want to increase or change some goals?

Conclusion

It can be daunting to decide how to invest your hard-earned wealth, particularly given the ever-growing list of asset classes and complex, yet intriguing, alternative products that exist today. However, it is important to remember that you are not seeking to optimize your financial assets. Your financial assets are only a tool as you seek to achieve your goals, which may indeed mean that you forgo potential returns in order to increase certainty of achieving your desired outcomes.

The process just described highlights how each family, with its own unique goals and circumstances, will ultimately require a unique investment portfolio to support the realization of these goals. It is also worth remembering that this process is not static and that it is necessary to reflect on your goals periodically to ensure your portfolio still supports these goals.

Additional Reading

Franklin Parker, "Goal-Based Portfolio Optimization," *The Journal of Wealth Management* (Winter 2016): 22–30.

Jean L.P. Brunel, "Extending the Goals-Based Framework to Comprise both Investment and Financial Planning," *The Journal of Wealth Management* (Spring 2020): 21–46.

Daniel Kahneman, "Thinking Fast and Slow" (New York: Farrar, Straus and Giroux, 2011).

Jean L.P. Brunel, "What Should Your Asset Allocation Be?" In *Wealth of Wisdom,* Tom McCullough and Keith Whitaker (Hoboken, NJ: Wiley, 2018).

Biography

Jean Brunel is the managing principal of Brunel Associates, a firm serving ultra-high-net-worth families. Prior to 2001, Jean spent most of his career with J.P. Morgan, becoming, in 1990, the chief investment officer of J.P. Morgan's global private bank. He has been the editor of the *Journal of Wealth Management* since its 1998 founding and authored two books—*Integrated Wealth Management: The New Direction for Portfolio Managers,* by Euromoney (2002, 2006), and *A Practical Guide to Goals-Based Wealth Management* by John Wiley & Sons (2015). In 2011, Jean received the C. Stewart Sheppard award from the CFA Institute, was named the 2012 Multi-Family Office Chief Investment Officer of the Year by Family Office Review, and was the first recipient of the J. Richard Joyner Wealth Management Impact award from IMCA in 2015. He is a graduate of HEC in France and holds an MBA from the Kellogg School of Business.

Voyt Krzychylkiewicz is a vice president at Northwood Family Office and chairman of its Investment Committee. Prior to joining Northwood, Voyt led the investment function as an executive at a global publicly traded investment holding company where he concluded more than $1 billion of direct private transactions. In addition, he was the CEO of its real estate investment subsidiary and chaired the group's investment committee. His investment career started as an equity analyst in South Africa where he was the top-rated analyst covering banks and specialty financial sectors. He has sat on the boards of 13 private and public companies within the financial services and property sectors and is president of the Young Directors Forum. He is a CPA, CA, and a CFA Charterholder and completed his executive MBA at the University of Toronto's Rotman School of Management.

CHAPTER 31

Investment Education for Family Members

Jim Garland

The Jeffrey family is large (over 400 family members) and is widely scattered across the United States and overseas. Furthermore, our pooled investment vehicle—known as The Jeffrey Company—uses an unorthodox approach to investing. We have long sent traditional quarterly and annual reports to family members. However, due to the family's size and the company's unusual investment objectives, something more was needed. As a result, in 1990, we began holding seminars so that family members could meet each other and could learn about the Company's investment practices. This is the story of those seminars.

* * * * * * *

The Jeffrey Company has been family-owned ever since its founding in the 1870s. It manufactured mining and road-building machinery. In order to diversify the family's investments, the company sold its operating businesses for cash in 1974 and used that cash to create in effect a private mutual fund. The company's shares (i.e., shares of the mutual fund) were held in a generation-skipping trust, one that sheltered the family's capital from estate taxes for over a century until the trust terminated in 2017.

When that trust terminated, the 62 remainder beneficiaries became direct Jeffrey Company shareholders. Today, because of gifts to spouses, children, and grandchildren, there are more than 150 investors. That number will continue to grow.

The Jeffrey Trust was income-only, meaning that the beneficiaries could not withdraw principal. As a result, the company had focused on generating long-term distributable cash flows, ones that kept pace with inflation. It acted like a perpetual endowment fund. This focus on income made us unusual: We cared very little about market values and very much about corporate dividends and profits—the sources of the cash we distributed to our owners.

From 1914 until 2017, the beneficiaries were trapped inside the trust. Now that the trust has terminated, however, the beneficiaries-turned-shareholders are free to leave—i.e., to sell their Jeffrey shares and go elsewhere. Today most Jeffrey shareholders are still interested in income, but some are now interested in market values as well.

Goals and Expected Outcomes

We had several objectives in establishing these seminars.

The first was to help family members understand the company's unusual investment objectives. The investment community is obsessed with market values. On the other hand, because we act like a family endowment fund, we are obsessed with income—specifically, with our assets' ability to generate distributable cash. That requires a different mindset. We welcome bear markets, for example, because lower prices mean lower manager fees and lower capital gains taxes when we have to refresh our holdings.

A second objective of the seminars was to enable cousins to meet each other and to meet company management. Only a few family members live in Ohio, where our office is located. We occasionally host regional family dinners, but these don't permit extended contact. The seminars allow family members to spend much time in small groups with their cousins and with the people running the company. We also allow a few participants to attend Jeffrey Company board meetings, with the hope that they'll appreciate the efforts that the directors spend on the shareholders' behalf.

The third objective—an outcome of the first two—was to keep the company intact. An understanding of our unusual objectives, and familiarity with and confidence in company management, were keys to keeping the family together following termination of the Jeffrey Trust.

In addition, we wanted to inculcate family members with the values that matter to us. One is a sense of the family's extreme good fortune—of our situation being a blessing rather than an entitlement. Another is treating the Jeffrey capital as a family heirloom, something to pass down from one generation to the next.

Finally, now that the trust has terminated, senior family members can give away their capital to charities or to outsiders and, even if family members try to keep their capital intact, estate taxes will take a bite. We remind younger family members that they'd be wise to plan on getting nothing. "Get a good education, get a good job, and spend less than you earn." One new objective of the seminars is teaching younger family members how to invest on their own.

Description of the Seminars

We offer three classes. Seminar 101 covers both the company and general investment topics in basic terms. Most of the reading material (other than items we wrote ourselves) is taken from newspapers and magazines. Seminar 201 again covers the company plus general investment topics, but in more depth. Much of the reading here comes from professional journals. Seminar 301 covers just two topics—taxation of limited liability companies (LLCs) and estate planning. Seminars 101 and 201 comprise four sessions each. Seminar 301 is only two sessions. All sessions last for three hours and either begin or end with lunch.

The classes are small, usually four or five participants per class. That way, there's no place to hide. If too many people apply, we'll sometimes offer two different sections. The seminars are taught jointly by the former and current Jeffrey CEOs. Due to the time involved for study, travel, and the seminars themselves, we pay participants a modest meeting fee.

Only Jeffrey family members can apply—no boy/girlfriends or fiancées. Generally, we prefer that participants be several years out of college and have some work experience. We don't teach basics such as the differences between dividends and interest, etc.

We run these seminars on a calendar-year schedule. We e-mail invitations in mid-November so that family members can discuss signing on when they meet over Thanksgiving dinner. Individual seminar sessions are scheduled at least two months apart. We distribute reading materials three to four weeks before each session. Too early, and they may forget the material. Too late, and they may not have time to read it.

What We Teach

We cover seven subjects.

a) **Jeffrey-specific subjects.** For example: how the company is structured; our unusual (income-focused) investment objectives; our strategies for achieving those objectives; and how we keep score.
b) **Investment fundamentals.** The trade-off between risk and return; the behavior of common asset classes; market efficiency; etc. We assume participants understand basic concepts such as the differences between bonds and stocks and between realized and unrealized capital gains.
c) **Owners' responsibilities.** Setting objectives and understanding oneself (see (d)).
d) **Behavioral finance.** Overconfidence; following the herd; confirmation bias; use of heuristics; anchoring; mental accounting; loss aversion; etc.
e) **Agency conflicts.** Dealing with brokers and financial planners; conflicts at corporate and governmental levels.
f) **Taxes.** The corrosive effect of capital gains taxes. Also, taxation of pass-through business entities, i.e., S-corporations and limited liability companies (LLCs).
g) **Estate planning.** Wills; revocable and irrevocable trusts; powers of attorney; healthcare directives; selecting trustees; etc. We discuss "soft" issues such as instilling in children a sense of financial discipline and self-respect, and how to prevent them from turning into "trust fund babies."

How We Teach

Whenever possible, we tell stories. Stories are more memorable than abstract models and theories.

We teach history. We want participants to understand how markets and investors have behaved in the past, in order to understand how they might behave in the future.

Whenever possible, we use metaphors and analogies—again, because they are more memorable. We have our own language. Our most potent metaphor has been that of chicken-famer investors and egg-farmer investors. Chicken farmers raise chickens to sell them; the market value of chickens matters very much. On the other hand, egg farmers hold chickens for the eggs that they produce. Chicken-farmer investors, such as those saving for retirement, care a lot about the market values of their "chickens" (stocks). Egg-farmer investors care a lot about the "eggs" (dividends) that their "chickens" can produce, but very little about the market value of those "chickens." We tell Jeffrey family members that we (and they) are egg-farmer investors, that the investment community is dominated by chicken-farmer investors, and that family members should pay little attention to what others say.

Whenever possible, we use articles from newspapers, magazines, and professional journals. Markets don't change much over time, and people don't change at all—they keep making the same mistakes. Some of our articles are almost 50 years old. (As a practical matter, getting permission to copy articles from American newspapers and magazines is easy and inexpensive due to a company called The Copyright Clearance Center.) We also use a few books.

Collecting good newspaper, magazine, and journal articles will take time. Some books to consider would be *The Random Walk Guide to Investing* by Burt Malkiel, *The Little Book of Behavioral Investing* by James Montier, and *Wealth of Wisdom* by McCullough and Whitaker.

We call our classes "seminars" because we want the participants to answer and ask questions. These aren't lectures. We provide reading material plus questions designed to spark discussions. The rest is up to the participants.

What Have Been the Results?

In the four years since termination of the Jeffrey Trust, only one family member has cashed out. Several others have redeemed shares to buy homes or to make charitable gifts, but these redemptions have been smaller than we expected. And we've not heard any significant grumblings about the company's direction or the way it's been managed. These signs suggest that the family is content. At least some portion of this success may be attributable to our seminars.

More than 170 family members have participated in Seminar 101 so far (the numbers for 201 and 301 are less because those are newer), and we often receive more seminar applications than we can accept. These, too, suggest that the significant efforts we've devoted to these seminars have been worthwhile.

Additional Resources

Our office subscribes to a few professional journals, such as *The Journal of Portfolio Management* and *The Journal of Investing*, and we sometimes use articles from those journals in our seminars. However, the hit rate—the proportion of articles that are of practical value to us—is rather low. Generally, we have better success in the popular financial press, meaning *The Wall Street Journal, Financial Times, The Economist,* etc.

Many investment firms share their insights on the internet. These are often just tactical insights (for example, whether stocks are over- or undervalued), but sometimes you'll spot useful pieces on strategic matters, or on behavioral or family issues.

Look for others who are doing the same thing. Northwood Family Office, for example, posts an excellent reading list on its website.[1]

The bad news is that the internet has made available an almost limitless number of investment articles and papers. Separating the wheat from the chaff takes time. The good news is that, because human nature doesn't change, and because markets don't change very much, once you've found good materials, you should be able to continue using those materials for a very long time.

Biography

Jim Garland is former president of the Jeffrey Company, a family office based in Columbus, Ohio. A Maine native, he graduated from Bowdoin College in 1969 with a degree in music history. He worked for seven years at NASA's Goddard Space Flight Center in Greenbelt, Maryland, then returned to Maine in 1976 to join an investment advisory firm, and finally moved to Ohio in 1995 to work for the Jeffrey Company. He has written papers dealing with endowment spending and taxable investing that have appeared in the *Financial Analysts Journal, The Journal of Portfolio Management,* and *The Journal of Investing.*

[1]Full disclosure: Tom McCullough, one editor of this book, is chief executive officer of Northwood.

SECTION 5

SEEKING SOUND ADVICE

Family wealth management is not a do-it-yourself activity, though many family members derive great satisfaction (and are quite skilled at) investing, managing companies, or having fun together. Nonetheless, the wide variety of expertise needed to manage all aspects of a family's financial wealth outstrips even the most dedicated family members' knowledge base. As a result, all families make use of advisors of some sort, which means that knowing how to select, manage, and evaluate advisors is a key qualitative skill for family members.

A fundamental question is, of course, what sorts of advisors a family needs. To help readers think through that question, Scott Hayman and Tom McCullough begin this section with a Family Self-Assessment Tool that allows families to rate their comfort with their organization and planning, their investment management, risk management, tax planning, estate planning, reporting/document management, philanthropy, family communication about various risks, and their advisors. The results from this assessment should give readers a clear sense of which areas a family should seek sound advice in and whether they need someone with a very specific skill set or an integrated holistic advisor.

Kathy Lintz and Ned Rollhaus then put the focus on selecting a comprehensive wealth manager. They offer a worksheet that families can use to think through that choice, involving evaluating prospective advisors in the areas of culture, people/resources, alignment of interests, scope of services, fee structure, and typical client profile. They also offer recommendations on how to be a good client to the right advisor.

As time goes on and financial wealth transitions from one generation to the next, most families find that much of that wealth comes to be held in trusts. As a result, one of the most important choices family members must consider is that of trustee. Kim Kamin educates readers about the responsibilities of trustees and the different types of trustees—along with their respective pros and cons. She also offers extensive questions that readers can use when interviewing prospective trustees.

A key challenge for many enterprising families is leadership development. In the first *Wealth of Wisdom* volume, Susan Massenzio contributed a chapter to help readers think through what to look for in the choice of a coach or consultant to work on leadership. In this volume, Greg McCann offers a worksheet for readers to evaluate their own readiness for leadership coaching—a key measure if such coaching is going to prove effective.

No advisor works for free, and so understanding the fees that advisors charge and being able to discuss those fees effectively are additional skills needed by wise stewards of family wealth. To help in developing these skills, Mark Pletts rounds out this section with a series of observations regarding fees charged by attorneys, certified public accountants, institutional wealth advisors, independent wealth advisors, life insurance agents, and family dynamics consultants. This chapter gives readers questions to ask their advisors, to better understand their fees, to make sure that the advisors' interests are aligned well with the family's, and to ensure the family is receiving value from the relationship.

CHAPTER 32

Assessing Your Family's Financial and Family Management Needs

Scott Hayman and Tom McCullough

Most wealthy families have a lot going on—in all the diverse components of their lives, including their financial, tax, and legal affairs, businesses, investment activities, family interactions, and administration. Many families find it a challenge to stay on top of all these elements and, if they are honest with themselves, don't always feel confident that every aspect is handled properly or is managed in an integrated, internally consistent manner.

This can cause a whole series of issues:

- Concern that something important will be missed, which could cost money or throw off other decisions
- Worry that they have not done sufficient due diligence and will make a poor decision
- A lack of integration where decisions need to be aligned
- Concern that a particular component of the family strategy is not being properly managed
- Uncertainty about the appropriateness and longevity of some of the family advisors
- Worries about succession and transition
- Poor coordination and communication in the family about important issues
- Anxiety about the appropriateness or transparency of fees
- Dropped balls among various advisors
- Poor governance and decision-making structures and process
- Family conflict due to differing expectations and communication
- A general lack of confidence about the overall management of their affairs, or a vague sense of unease and uncertainty that everything is not "alright"

Every once in a while, it is a good idea to do a complete review of where you are at in the management of your family and financial affairs, reassess your requirements, and determine if there are any gaps. It is helpful to treat the self-assessment as if you were starting from scratch and setting up a system that will help you to meet all your goals and objectives. You can find the best way to fill in those gaps to give you the confidence that your family is in the best position possible. Of course, this can be quite hard to do since many families have structures in place, have worked with the same advisors for years, have investments that are illiquid, and have family members who are set in their ways and not open to change.

To that end, Northwood Family Office developed a Family Self-Assessment Tool. It helps families identify the areas of their family and financial lives (1) where they feel things are in good shape; (2) where they believe there are gaps and they don't feel confident that they, or key advisors, are fully on top of them; or (3) where they are just not sure.

There are 52 self-assessment statements in 10 sections. Typically, a family leader or other family member will review each of the statements, and rate themselves on their level of comfort and confidence in each area. This is not a purely technical assessment and doesn't require 100 percent accuracy. Rather, it is intended to point out how confident they feel about each issue. The person taking the assessment simply answers Yes ("I feel confident that this area is in good shape for our family"), No ("I don't feel confident"), or Not Sure ("I'm just, well, not sure").

FAMILY SELF-ASSESSMENT TOOL

ORGANIZATION AND PLANNING	
I know what my family's long-term goals are.	Yes ☐ No ☐ Not Sure ☐
We have quantified the family goals and have a good idea what they will cost.	Yes ☐ No ☐ Not Sure ☐
Our personal financial situation is straightforward and relatively easy to manage.	Yes ☐ No ☐ Not Sure ☐
I enjoy managing our financial affairs, and feel I am doing a good job.	Yes ☐ No ☐ Not Sure ☐
Our financial affairs are well organized and in good order.	Yes ☐ No ☐ Not Sure ☐
I can safely say that very few financial details fall through the cracks in our life.	Yes ☐ No ☐ Not Sure ☐
CASH FLOW MANAGEMENT	
I know clearly how much capital we will need over the long term to maintain our standard of living and meet all of our goals.	Yes ☐ No ☐ Not Sure ☐
I know what our family expenses are and feel confident that they are manageable over the long term.	Yes ☐ No ☐ Not Sure ☐
I have a clear plan in place to prepare for a liquidity event, such as a business sale or inheritance.	Yes ☐ No ☐ Not Sure ☐
I understand the most tax-effective way to fund our expenses.	Yes ☐ No ☐ Not Sure ☐
INVESTMENT MANAGEMENT	
I know what rate of return we need from our investments to ensure we meet our family's objectives over the long term.	Yes ☐ No ☐ Not Sure ☐
I am confident that our asset allocation is appropriate based on our financial goals.	Yes ☐ No ☐ Not Sure ☐
We have a clear process in place to select our investment managers and/or investments.	Yes ☐ No ☐ Not Sure ☐
Our investment managers are reviewed on a periodic, timely basis, and I am confident we have the right ones in place and in the right combinations.	Yes ☐ No ☐ Not Sure ☐
We have a written Investment Policy Statement for our overall investment portfolio that clearly lays out the objectives, limitations, review process and accountability.	Yes ☐ No ☐ Not Sure ☐
We have a regular, consistent review process in place to evaluate the success of our investments and other financial issues against relevant benchmarks.	Yes ☐ No ☐ Not Sure ☐

RISK MANAGEMENT	
I am comfortable that we have the appropriate level of risk in our overall family balance sheet.	Yes ☐ No ☐ Not Sure ☐
We are well-diversified and not overly reliant on a few particular asset classes.	Yes ☐ No ☐ Not Sure ☐
We have a clear process in place to select, monitor and review all of our advisors.	Yes ☐ No ☐ Not Sure ☐
We have management processes in place regarding our family properties including their staffing and their use.	Yes ☐ No ☐ Not Sure ☐
I understand all our insurance policies and am confident that they are appropriate and up-to-date. If there is no insurance in place, I am clear as to why it isn't a good fit for our family.	Yes ☐ No ☐ Not Sure ☐
TAX PLANNING AND STRUCTURING	
I am comfortable that we are taking advantage of all the tax efficiencies available to us in each of the jurisdictions where we have assets/ reside.	Yes ☐ No ☐ Not Sure ☐
I understand how the use of trusts or other structures could be beneficial in our planning.	Yes ☐ No ☐ Not Sure ☐
I am confident that we have the right structures in place to meet our family objectives and that it is no more complicated than it needs to be.	Yes ☐ No ☐ Not Sure ☐
I am confident in the advisors that we use for our tax and structure planning.	Yes ☐ No ☐ Not Sure ☐
ESTATE PLANNING AND SUCCESSION	
I have a clear idea of our estate objectives and how much our heirs will receive and when.	Yes ☐ No ☐ Not Sure ☐
Our wills have been updated in the past three years. We have properly executed powers of attorney (or other appropriate documents) for financial and healthcare purposes.	Yes ☐ No ☐ Not Sure ☐
I am confident we have used all appropriate and available estate planning strategies that would be appropriate for our family.	Yes ☐ No ☐ Not Sure ☐
I am confident that we have appropriate trustees and executors in place.	Yes ☐ No ☐ Not Sure ☐
I feel comfortable that our children are financially well-educated and sufficiently responsible to inherit the assets that are likely to be left to them.	Yes ☐ No ☐ Not Sure ☐
We have a solid transition plan for our financial assets and family enterprise, if applicable.	Yes ☐ No ☐ Not Sure ☐
I am comfortable that I am leaving the legacy I want to.	Yes ☐ No ☐ Not Sure ☐
REPORTING AND DOCUMENT MANAGEMENT	
We receive regular, easy-to-understand, consolidated reporting on all our family holdings across all of our entities and family members.	Yes ☐ No ☐ Not Sure ☐
Our technology and data management systems are in a modern format that could be easily taken over by someone else if necessary.	Yes ☐ No ☐ Not Sure ☐
We have a very good document records system that allows us (or our heirs) to quickly put our hands on whatever is needed.	Yes ☐ No ☐ Not Sure ☐
Our financial and personal information is well-defended against cybersecurity intrusions and frequently upgraded.	Yes ☐ No ☐ Not Sure ☐
PHILANTHROPY	
I understand the objectives we want to achieve by giving.	Yes ☐ No ☐ Not Sure ☐
Our family has a strategy in place for our philanthropy that outlines how we make donations.	Yes ☐ No ☐ Not Sure ☐
I understand how much I can give away to philanthropic causes and over what time period given other financial goals.	Yes ☐ No ☐ Not Sure ☐
I know the most tax-efficient way to donate given my current structure.	Yes ☐ No ☐ Not Sure ☐
FAMILY ISSUES	
Our family has frequent, open, healthy dialogue about money and financial issues.	Yes ☐ No ☐ Not Sure ☐
We have regular family meetings where key issues are addressed.	Yes ☐ No ☐ Not Sure ☐
I am comfortable that my spouse and children will be able to manage if something happens to me.	Yes ☐ No ☐ Not Sure ☐
Our family has protections in place for our assets in the event of divorce, disability, and other family events.	Yes ☐ No ☐ Not Sure ☐
We have discussed mental incapacity and aging issues in the family and have a plan in place that is reviewed regularly.	Yes ☐ No ☐ Not Sure ☐
Our family has good methods for making decisions, now and for the future if I were not around.	Yes ☐ No ☐ Not Sure ☐
Our family has discussed our shared values and they are evident in our financial decisions.	Yes ☐ No ☐ Not Sure ☐

ADVISORS			
Our family has one or more advisors who are trusted, knowledgeable, and objective regarding all of the issues listed above.	Yes ☐	No ☐	Not Sure ☐
Our advisors are proactive and regularly anticipate the key issues that need attention in our life.	Yes ☐	No ☐	Not Sure ☐
I know all the fees we are paying to our advisors and understand the value we receive and the impact on our net worth.	Yes ☐	No ☐	Not Sure ☐
I successfully act as the coordinator and manager of our advisors or have a family office/integrated advisor who does.	Yes ☐	No ☐	Not Sure ☐
TOTAL			

We see the Family Self-Assessment as a living document. We have edited and added to it over the years as issues have arisen and as our scope of services has expanded to meet family needs, and it will probably continue to morph over time.

If you respond with "No" or "Not sure" to six or more of the statements, there is room for improvement and progress.

One of the main benefits of our Family Self-Assessment Tool is that it helps families identify the gaps in the management of their financial affairs and where they may want to take action. In some cases, it can be something they can fix or improve on their own, or simply begin to educate themselves on so they can see what best practices exist. In other cases, they may want to engage a professional advisor to help them make course corrections.

It can also be beneficial to see if the areas where there is low confidence are narrowly focused issues that can be dealt with on a one-off basis or by a single specialty advisor. On the other hand, it may be that the list of "No" or "Not Sure" answers is broad, and there is a need for a more holistic review of the family strategy. This may also be the point where a family office or other integrated advisor is required.

Another benefit of the Family Self-Assessment is that it highlights areas that are in good shape and don't need to be addressed at the current time. That helps to declutter the radar screen and allow the family to focus on the areas of greater risk or concern.

It can also be helpful to have several members of the family (or close, unconflicted advisors) complete the Family Self-Assessment independently, share their results with each other, and identify what they believe the common priority issues are. Dad may feel comfortable that some key areas are in-hand, whereas Mom or the kids may not. It may expose some gaps that need to be addressed in the family management, or it could simply be a need for better family communication.

It is important to answer the Family Self-Assessment as honestly as possible and get help and input where you need it to answer the questions well. Frequently, a family member may be confident about a component of their financial affairs where they actually *shouldn't* be. A discussion among family members or advice from an independent external source can be an even more reliable and objective judge of how well the particular area is being managed.

Following are two case studies that demonstrate how the Family Self-Assessment might be used:

Sam and Julie Jones

Sam and Julie Jones have four adult children and two grandchildren. They sold their manufacturing business eight years ago and have been addressing the various components of their family and financial management as they have come up. They have several advisors, multiple tax-driven structures, and diverse investment holdings. They have been working hard at all the various aspects of this project but have had a vague feeling of uncertainty that all of the key elements are not properly managed and are certainly not integrated in a strategic and holistic way. The couple recently sat down to go through the Family Self-Assessment.

Upon completing the exercise, they saw a lot of "Nos" and "Not Sures" on the page, and their feeling of uncertainty was confirmed. They decided they needed to implement the following changes to achieve the confidence they wanted in their financial situation:

1. A clear understanding of their structure and why it is the way it is
2. An objective review of everything (advisors, investments, estate plan, etc.) to ensure they can properly achieve all their goals and objectives, and regain a sense of order and control
3. A system to organize themselves so that their children would not be left with a burden when Sam and Julie pass away
4. A plan to integrate future generations into the management of the wealth the family has accumulated

Because there were a large number of gaps in diverse areas (versus just a few specific ones), the family decided to engage a multifamily office to undertake a holistic review of their affairs. They focused on meeting the family's four main goals and put together a strategy to accomplish them. Meeting regularly led to a comfort level that the plan was being implemented and the family was progressing toward achieving their objectives. "To do" lists were created and prioritized, and items on the list started to be checked off, including launching regular family meetings. The Family Self-Assessment Tool began the journey for the Jones family and two years later they were able to check the "Yes" box on almost all of the questions.

Cindy Wilson and Ravi Patel

Cindy and Ravi are both high-earning senior executives at large public companies. They have no children but several nieces and nephews they are very close to and would like to support. Cindy is highly competent financially and has the time and interest to manage their own personal financial affairs, including investments. Their lives are not particularly complex, except when it comes to their investments. They both completed the Self-Assessment and found that they had "No" and "Not sure" answers primarily in the investment section. They decided to engage an advisor with specific expertise in this area and felt confident that they should keep moving forward as they have been in all of the other areas, at least for the time being.

Our Family Self-Assessment is designed to help families identify gaps and determine what the best ways are to close them and develop confidence that each component of their family and financial management is solid and well in hand. There are many benefits to completing the Family Self-Assessment.

- Being able to say yes to all 52 questions (it is possible!). This will give you the confidence that you are well prepared in the key areas and have made the very best choices you can.
- Being able to focus on the gaps and not waste time with things that are already in good shape. This brings efficiency to where you are spending your time.
- Knowing that someone is on top of each area and responsibility is assigned. This tells you that you have the right skill sets internally and the right advisors to help you.
- Having a clear strategy and an integrated plan to ensure everything gets done and fits together. This can boost your confidence and provide clear direction for the future.

Conclusion

Every family wants to have the confidence that they are making the best decisions they can about their overall financial and family management. The starting point is an honest assessment of where you are at and what gaps you have. The next step is to find the solutions to the gaps that you have identified. We hope our Family Self-Assessment is as helpful a tool for you as it has been for our client families.

Additional Resources

A complementary tool is the *Ten Domains of Family Wealth* from the Ultra High Net Worth Institute, which lays out the key components of family wealth in helpful categories and offers a useful case study to show how these components show themselves in families and are interconnected.

https://www.uhnwinstitute.org/content/2020/6/26/the-10-domains-of-family-wealth-supplement-1.

Biography

Scott Hayman is president, chief operating officer, and co-founder of Northwood Family Office and is the senior partner at the firm responsible for client relationships. He has been providing advice and counsel to private clients on all aspects of their financial affairs for more than 30 years. Scott is a chartered professional accountant (CPA, CA), a certified financial planner (CFP), and a trust and estates practitioner (TEP). Scott is a lecturer for "The Management of Private Wealth" course in the MBA program at the University of Toronto's Rotman School of Management. Northwood Family Office is the leading multifamily office in Canada.

Tom McCullough is the chairman, chief executive office, and co-founder of Northwood Family Office. Northwood was established in 2003 to provide integrated and holistic family office services to Canadian families of wealth. Tom is the co-author of *Wealth of Wisdom: The Top 50 Questions Wealthy Families Ask* (Wiley, 2018) and *Family Wealth Management* (Wiley, 2013). He is an adjunct professor and executive-in-residence at the University of Toronto's Rotman School of Management MBA program where he teaches "The Management of Private Wealth" and is a faculty member in Rotman's Family Wealth Management program for families. Tom also serves on the board of directors for the Ultra High Net Worth Institute, and was recently awarded Best Individual Contribution to Thought Leadership in the Wealth Management Industry (North America) by the *2020 Family Wealth Report Awards.*

CHAPTER 33

Finding an Advisor Who Will Help Your Family Thrive for Generations

Kathy Lintz and Ned Rollhaus

If you aspire to have a family that will thrive for generations, selecting a trusted advisor to guide you through this process is one of the more important decisions you will make as you embark on your journey. As the universe of wealth advisory firms is large and complex, our purpose here is to highlight some practical considerations to help families evaluate to what degree a potential advisor is likely to be a good match for your family. In this chapter, we focus on the few areas that we feel are most likely to reveal the characteristics of an advisor that a family would want to know before making a decision. It is important to note that this is never a question of who is the "best" advisor and always a question of who is the "right" advisor for your family.

Culture: The famous quote from Peter Drucker that "Culture eats strategy for breakfast" most certainly applies to advisors who serve families. Culture is everything in our field as it permeates through all areas that will directly affect the quality of service and advice families receive. Recruiting and retaining top talent, commitment to innovation, customization of services available to families, level of collaboration to tackle complex problems, chemistry with family, ability to manage conflicts, etc. all are critical elements of a good partnership that are deeply rooted in firm culture.

People and Resources: As with most professional service businesses, people are the only meaningful asset of advisory firms. Without the people who have dedicated their careers to serving families, there is very little value to any advisor. A good indication of how well a firm will take care of your family is how well they attract and care for their most precious asset.

Alignment: For our purposes, we define alignment as how much you and your advisors are working toward the same goal, which generally encompasses some form of serving the family's best interests ONLY and helping your family flourish. Misalignment occurs when there are conflicts between advisor objectives and family objectives, such as fee structures for pushing particular products, accountability to owners far removed from the client (e.g., large corporations or outside investors), lack of transparency on potential conflicts, firm emphasis on adding new clients versus serving current clients, grooming the firm for sale so owners can "cash out," etc. While strong alignment between advisor and client should be a given in a partnership that may last for generations, it is always surprising to us how many families fail to properly evaluate this in their selection process.

Scope of services: In the selection process, a family will need to get down to the brass tacks of what services they want to source externally. Families should carefully identify what services are important to them, prioritize their needs, and ultimately match them to the pool of advisors they are evaluating.

Fee structure: Understanding how a firm gets paid will speak volumes and provide important insights to all of the areas mentioned previously (culture, people, alignment, and scope of services). Families tend to focus more on the level of fees (and note there may be hidden fees depending on the firm) at the exclusion of how they are being charged, which is a missed opportunity to uncover important information.

Typical family profile: For good reason, families tend not to want to be the outlier in the stable of clients of a firm. Advisors who have deep experience working with families similar to your own will be able to add more value more quickly than those who are unfamiliar with nuances of your particular situation.

One Reminder: Look Inside before Looking Out

In order to find an advisor who will be a good partner for your family over generations, we recommend that you take a good look inside and explore the fundamental questions of what matters most to you. This will enable your family to start the search for an advisor with purpose and intent, which will likely lead to better outcomes. This is covered very well in Section 1 of *Wealth of Wisdom: The Top 50 Questions Wealthy Families Ask* (Wiley 2018), so we will not go further into this here other than to bring this very important part of the process to your attention.

A sample list of questions are grouped within a few core areas for families to ask potential advisors:

Sample Questions	Notes	Family Impression? (+ or –)
<u>Culture</u>		
How does the advisor represent their culture?	Look for consistency of representations throughout the entire process as well as how closely this aligns with your experience of the firm and its people.	
The "why" of their existence?	Consider alignment with the values of your family. Consider the potential impact if they plan to ultimately sell the firm.	
Culture of retention versus acquisition?	Are they more concerned with finding new clients or serving existing clients? Are they evaluating how good a fit your family is for their firm?	
Culture of learning versus production?	Where are they investing within employee training? Sales training versus skill development? Is the focus on individual or team development?	

Sample Questions	Notes	Family Impression? (+ or –)
Culture of innovation versus self-preservation?	Can they innovate to meet evolving client needs? Level of bureaucracy and red tape in the firm?	
Quantitative versus qualitative approach to family balance sheet?	Are they focused mostly on the financial assets or do they take a broader view of the family balance sheet? Compare with what your family is looking for.	
Is the process of getting to know them one of persuasion or inquiry?	Evaluate the questions they ask of you. Is the firm trying to persuade you into a choice or does it feel like an authentic exploration of the mutual fit?	
People and Resources		
Experience and qualifications?	Education, experience, reputation and credentials are important in our field so look at them closely.	
Employee development, retention and turnover?	How is the firm stewarding its most important asset? Look at recent job descriptions to get a sense of what kind of people they look for. Has there been turnover? (Note not all turnover is bad but excessive amounts are a red flag.)	
Background checks, reputation checks, job postings, social media posts, and regulatory filings	Trust but verify.	
Have any members of the firm walked in your shoes?	Are there members of the firm who look like members of your family (e.g., wealth creators, entrepreneurs, inheritors, divorced spouses)? While it is unrealistic that many employees will have had a path similar to their clients, having a few that have the capacity to offer empathy and a unique perspective based on experience is helpful.	
Does the firm have sufficient resources and financial stability to serve your family for generations?	Financial statements and strategic plans will help in the evaluation.	
Alignment		
Ownership structure and who is the firm ultimately accountable to?	Understand who ultimately drives the ship.	
Standard of care	Fiduciary versus suitability standard? If fiduciary, how long have they been held to the standard?	
Conflicts of interest	How do they handle conflicts of interest? Are these plainly and proactively disclosed? Look carefully as misalignment here is indicative of more problems ahead.	
Employee compensation structure	Does it support the culture of the firm? Does it incentivize the types of behaviors your family is looking for?	
Scope of Services		
Chief investment officer services	Open or closed architecture? What is their "edge"? Can this be demonstrated or quantified? How have they performed? Are they benchmarking returns and risk against standard industry benchmarks?	
Chief financial officer services	Do they provide all of what the family will need? Sample reports are helpful here.	
Chief learning officer services	Is this important to the family? How is this delivered to the families?	
Chief risk officer services	Do you get a sense that they have a multidisciplinary approach to effectively identify and help you manage risk?	
Chief fiduciary officer services	Is this important to the family? Evaluate pros/cons of individual, corporate, and private trust company trustees. Evaluate potential conflicts (e.g., serving as both trustee and investment manager).	

Sample Questions	Notes	Family Impression? (+ or –)
How integrated are the services they provide?	Level of integration of all of the above. Does the team have a more siloed or collaborative approach? Who is responsible for the "big picture" for the family, and what are their qualifications?	
Fee Structure		
What is the fee structure? Bundled or broken out by service?	Compare to industry standards.	
How many ways do they get paid?	Evaluate potential conflicts and look carefully.	
Are they proactively disclosing all fee arrangements and conflicts?	Are they actively bringing this up in a clear manner in addition to being in the disclosures?	
How do you feel about the fees?	Are they in line with industry standards? Will it feel like an expense, investment or honorarium?	
Typical Family Profile		
Similar in net worth, complexity, scope of service needs, stage, source of wealth to your family?	Is your family going to be an outlier?	
Number of clients?	Evaluate the pros and cons of small versus large firms.	
Ratio of clients to employees?	Compare to other firms.	

Final Words of Wisdom

Make an effort to be a good client: The most successful relationships with an advisor are a true partnership, which means both parties have to commit to making it work. For families, this includes being curious, reading materials and documents, responding to questions in a reasonable time frame, trusting your instincts, challenging the advisor if something doesn't seem right, and not being afraid to ask the "dumb" questions.

The pain and cost of switching advisors: The direct and indirect costs of switching advisors is significant, and it is much better to get it right the first time. Higher fees (legal, tax, transfer, etc.), administrative complexity, the pain of going through the process a second time, the loss of confidence of the family members in the decision-making process, the loss of historical data, the loss of institutional knowledge, and the time to train a new advisor are just a few of the reasons to invest the time and energy on the front end of the process to lower the chance that you will be doing it again.

Additional Resources

Tom McCullough and Keith Whitaker, *Wealth of Wisdom: The Top 50 Questions Wealthy Families Ask* (Hoboken, NJ: Wiley, 2019): Section 1.

Gregory Curtis, *The Stewardship of Wealth: Successful Private Wealth Management for Investors and Their Advisors* (Hoboken, NJ: Wiley, 2013): Chapters 5 and 6.

Courtney Pullen, *Intentional Wealth: How Families Build Legacies of Stewardship and Financial Health* (Wheatridge, CO: Pullen Consulting Group, 2013); Chapter 10.

Dennis Jaffe, *Borrowed From Your Grandchildren: The Evolution of 100-Year Family Enterprises* (Hoboken, NJ: Wiley, 2020): Chapter 6 and Appendix: Tools for Families.
James E. Hughes, Jr., *Family Wealth: Keeping It in the Family* (Princeton, NJ: Bloomberg Press, 2004).

Biography

Kathy Lintz is the founding partner of Matter Family Office and began her career in financial services at Chase Manhattan Bank in New York in the 1980s. She had the opportunity to help develop and deliver one of the first financial education and planning programs in the country at the Chase Exchange. This experience led her to become an early certified financial planner designee and build fee-only, multi-family offices in St. Louis, Denver, and Dallas. As founder, her role is to align Matter's values, capabilities, and future efforts with the firm's core purpose of helping successful families thrive for generations.

Ned Rollhaus is a partner in the Denver office of Matter Family Office and has more than 25 years of experience in management, investments, and advising families. Ned's personal and professional experience has fostered a passion for helping families navigate the complexities and responsibilities of wealth across generations. Ned graduated from Trinity College with a BA in economics and received an MBA from Northwestern University's Kellogg School of Management. He is also a CFA charter holder and serves as chair of the beneficiary relations committee for a private family trust company.

CHAPTER 34

Choosing Trustees with Care and Wisdom

Kim Kamin

One of the most crucial decisions you make for a trust is selecting the best available trustee. In approaching this decision, you should consider all the circumstances surrounding the trust and its structure and then do the analysis to identify the most desirable trustees under the circumstances.

For jurisdictions that permit private trusts, all such trusts will generally have certain elements in common. They are designed and established by a *settlor* to hold assets in trust for the benefit of the trust *beneficiaries* by the *trustee* who holds legal title to the assets subject to certain fiduciary duties.

Before addressing the question of trustee selection, you should first discuss with your advisors (1) certain preliminary inquiries about why the trust is being established and its fiduciary structure; (2) the roles and responsibilities of the trustee; and (3) the full extent of your options for trustee. Only then should you begin to work through the process for selecting the best trustee for your situation.

Preliminary Inquiries about the Trust

There are numerous reasons for setting up a trust, such as tax, asset protection, future control, and future flexibility. There are also many different kinds of trusts. In the United States, for example, you will see revocable living trusts, irrevocable gift trusts, grantor retained annuity trusts, and charitable remainder or lead trusts. Trusts can be designed for a short term (e.g., a two-year GRAT), or trusts can be designed to last forever (e.g., a perpetual Dynasty Trust). Other jurisdictions will have different laws and types of trusts. It is essential for your advisors to work with you to determine why this particular trust is being created.

Here are suggested preliminary questions to tease out this information:

1. Where is the trust being created, and what are the parameters/restrictions of the governing law in the country and/or state or locality?
2. Why is the trust being created? What is its purpose? Who are the intended beneficiaries both currently and in the future? Spouse? Descendants? Other family members? Other individuals? Charities?
3. What are your values? What are your goals? What are your fears about the assets in the trust or the needs and competencies of the trust beneficiaries?
4. To what extent are you willing to release control? Are there essential aspects of the trust that need to remain in place, even for future generations, that should not be able to be changed?
5. Have you considered that changes might be desirable in the future and have you built in sufficient flexibility for the fiduciaries to modify the trust provisions as deemed necessary or desirable in the future?

Understanding the Trustee's Role and Responsibilities

A trustee has three primary functions.

Hold and Invest Trust Property. First, trustees must be responsible stewards of the trust assets. Trustees need to preserve capital and protect assets by maintaining and insuring them appropriately. The trustee must invest liquid assets to ensure growth that outpaces inflation and provides sufficient liquidity to support the trust's cash flow needs. The trustees need not hold and invest the property themselves; these functions are often delegated to custodians and wealth management firms. But the trustee must responsibly select and supervise those who custody and manage the trust investments.

Administer the Trust. The second aspect of a trustee's job is to handle the day-to-day administration of the trust, such as preparing and communicating periodic accountings, maintaining the trust records, preparing tax returns, and the like. As with investments, these responsibilities do not need to be personally executed by a trustee, but the trustee has responsibility for making sure that the trust is administered properly and that all these activities are done and properly communicated to the beneficiaries or their representatives.

Make Distributions. The third aspect of the trustee's role is to make appropriate distributions from the trust to or for the benefit of the trust's beneficiaries. This is an essential function that generally cannot be delegated by the trustee to a third party, especially for distributions to be made at the trustee's discretion. There are different kinds of distributions, and it is important to understand the types of distributions that will be the trustee's responsibility, as well as the cadence of when distributions are likely to be made. For example, is it intended to be an accumulation trust that isn't expected to make distributions in the near term, or are some distributions of income and principal mandatory while others are at the trustee's discretion?

In fulfilling these three responsibilities, a trustee must follow settlor intent, administer the trust by its terms, and execute on this role while strictly adhering to the trustee's fiduciary duties of loyalty, impartiality, confidentiality, information, and prudence—among others. The duty of loyalty means avoiding self-dealing and conflicts of interests. A trustee also has a duty to be impartial among beneficiaries. In addition, the trustee has duties of confidentiality and to provide the beneficiary with sufficient information about the trust in order for the beneficiary to protect their interests (such as providing copies of the trust instrument and sharing trust statements and other financial records). The duty of prudence suggests taking a cautious and risk-averse approach. It involves the obligation to act wisely and carefully to preserve and protect property, and it requires that any delegation is done cautiously and thoughtfully only as necessary and appropriate and with proper supervision.

Trusts are about human relationships. Most trusts are created out of love and a desire to promote the well-being of the beneficiaries. When considering potential trustees, do not underestimate the interpersonal aspects and the potential for the trustee and beneficiaries to have a positive and life-enriching relationship built on respect and trust. The wrong trustee selection can instead lead to years of conflict and ill-feelings.

Description and Process

Once the preliminary trust purposes and the trustee's role and responsibilities are fully understood, then you will be positioned to consider all your options for a trustee and how to select among them, as outlined next.

Types of Trustees. There are essentially two types of trustees—individual and corporate. Individual trustees are people that you trust to handle the responsibilities of the trustee role. Corporate trustees are legal entities that are authorized to serve as trustee and are typically regulated. Within each of these two types, however, there are subcategories of options, each with their own advantages and disadvantages.[1]

<u>Individual Trustees.</u> There are four possible options:

1. *Family Members.* Ordinarily for an irrevocable trust, if you are the settlor, you should not be trustee. You can, however, usually serve as trustee for a trust created by your spouse (subject to certain restrictions and limitations, at least in the United States). In addition, descendants or other family members, even if they are beneficiaries, can also be trustees. Family members who are beneficiaries or closely related to the beneficiaries might serve for no fee, but naming family members like siblings to act for each other can lead to conflicts and disputes.

---

[1]While the examples used are U.S. and are likely different in other jurisdictions, many of the key questions and principles apply across all common law jurisdictions. In all cases, it is important to consult a qualified local tax and estate lawyer to understand the specific issues and requirements for each family.

2. *Friends and Business Associates.* For expanded flexibility, you might want to ask a personal friend or business partner to serve in the role. As an independent party, they can make distributions subject to a broader discretionary standard in their sole and absolute judgment. Close friends also may be a comfortable choice for working with the family and understanding your intentions for the trust and its investments. If the trust holds closely held business assets, a business partner may be a well-positioned and efficient option to help the trust manage that asset. Friends may be limited in time or experience to serve as trustee, and it is not appropriate to expect them to serve for no compensation.
3. *Independent Advisors.* Sometimes your personal advisors (such as attorneys, accountants, financial advisors, or insurance advisors) may be willing and able to serve as trustee. If the professional is knowledgeable about trusts, investments, and tax laws, this can be an ideal selection if they are permitted to serve. For professionals who bill by the hour, they can charge their normal fee for the time they spend working on trust matters.
4. *Professional Individual Trustees.* Sometimes individuals act professionally as trustees. These individuals may be trust professionals who worked for corporate trustees for many years; others are retired attorneys or investment professionals who have realized there is demand for high-quality individual trustees. The professional trustee can also be selected to create *situs* within a desirable jurisdiction. While the professional might need time to get to know the family, often their experience, objectivity and professionalism can make them a good choice.

Corporate Trustees. One advantage of a corporate trustee is that the corporation (or its successor) theoretically will outlive any individuals. The four possible options are:

1. *Large National Bank with Trust Powers.* The most traditional form of corporate trustee are the large name brand national or international banks. These may seem attractive if you prefer one-stop shopping and want to have your deposit accounts, lending relationships, investments, and trusts all under the same roof. Some concerns may be conflicts of interest, high-turnover, lack of flexibility, and cost.
2. *State Chartered Bank with Trust Powers.* Smaller regional or community banks work much like the large money-center banks and can pose the same concern about conflicts of interest. They may have lower minimum account sizes and lower fees than the big banks. They may also have fewer investment options and fewer specialized services. But they may be more flexible and be able to provide more personalized attention than the larger banks.
3. *Independent Public Trust Company.* Independent corporate trustees are an exciting and newer option in the trust management space. They are often chartered in the most desirable jurisdictions such as Delaware and South Dakota. They avoid conflicts of interest by outsourcing the investment of trust assets.
4. *Private Trust Company.* If your family has sufficient assets (typically at least $1 billion U.S.), forming a private trust company may be the best solution.

These come in both regulated and unregulated versions and are established to serve only one family, as that term is defined by a state statute.

Attached as Addendum A is a Trustee Decision Tree that illustrates these trustee options.

Consider the Individual's Personal Qualities. When selecting an individual trustee, there are certain characteristics that will be desirable. Trustees must be honest, trustworthy, wise, and have good judgment. In addition, consider if the individual is well-organized and able to pay attention to details. Does the individual have sufficient bandwidth to take on the commitment and will they be able to devote the necessary time to successfully do the work as trustee? Will they be accessible and a good communicator with the beneficiaries? Also consider their location as that will impact the situs of the trust. If the trust is a U.S. trust, naming a trustee in another country could make the trust a foreign trust. If the trustee resides in a state with income taxes that taxes trusts based on the identity of the trustee, it could cause undesirable income tax consequences. On the other hand, selecting a trustee in a desirable jurisdiction could be a positive aspect.

Attached as Addendum B and Addendum C are lists of questions to ask when you are considering appointing an individual trustee or a corporate trustee to help you evaluate whether or not they might be a good fit.

Because there will be advantages and disadvantages to each trustee option, you might determine the best option is to name co-trustees. For example, a common choice is to name a spouse or adult primary beneficiaries as trustee, but then to also name a professional individual trustee or a corporate trustee as the independent co-trustee.

Avoid Bad Reasons for Naming Trustees

It can help to do a negative screen to make sure you aren't naming an individual for one of the following bad reasons listed. Some red flags include the following:

1. Appointing trustees simply based on birth order (e.g., the oldest child is always automatically named first).
2. Appointing all of the children to act together as trustees. Even in families where the children get along well, it is simply not reasonable to expect adult children to have to agree on all the decisions a trustee needs to make regarding investments, trust administration, and distributions.
3. Appointing someone as trustee simply out of concern that they will feel insulted if not appointed.
4. While cost is important, you shouldn't be selecting a trustee simply because it is an individual that you know would be willing not to charge a fee for their work. Being a trustee is a tremendous amount of responsibility and work. Other than family members who serve as trustee while also being beneficiaries of the trust, it should be standard to expect the trustee to be paid reasonable trustee fees for acting as trustee.

5. Another bad reason to select a trustee is because someone on the advisory team (like the drafting lawyer) has suggested themselves for the role to you. Many law firms won't permit their attorneys to act as trustees for clients, and others have hurdles such that an attorney can act only if the client has explored all other options and can't find another suitable alternative. When an advisor (especially the drafting attorney) suggests themselves as trustee, that is certainly a conflict of interest.

Next Steps. The structure and selection of trustees is a personal decision, and different people may come to different conclusions. Your advisors should be poised to help you ask questions that will get to the heart of what you want to accomplish, help you to analyze whether your current or proposed trusts succeed in accomplishing your goals, and help you to design and establish each trust to achieve the maximum likelihood of success. After thinking about the process just described, it is time to review your existing and/or proposed trust documents and ask yourself: Now that I have a better sense about what is involved, am I comfortable with who is appointed as trustee and the process for the appointment of successors?

When you engage in the trustee selection process carefully and wisely, you can design the appropriate structure and select the best individual or corporate trustees to ensure success. It requires a bit of thought but can be well worth it for the trust to serve generations to come.

Addendums.

- Addendum A: Trustee Decision Tree
- Addendum B: Questions for Individual Trustees
- Addendum C: Questions for Corporate Trustees

Addendum A: Trustee Decision Tree

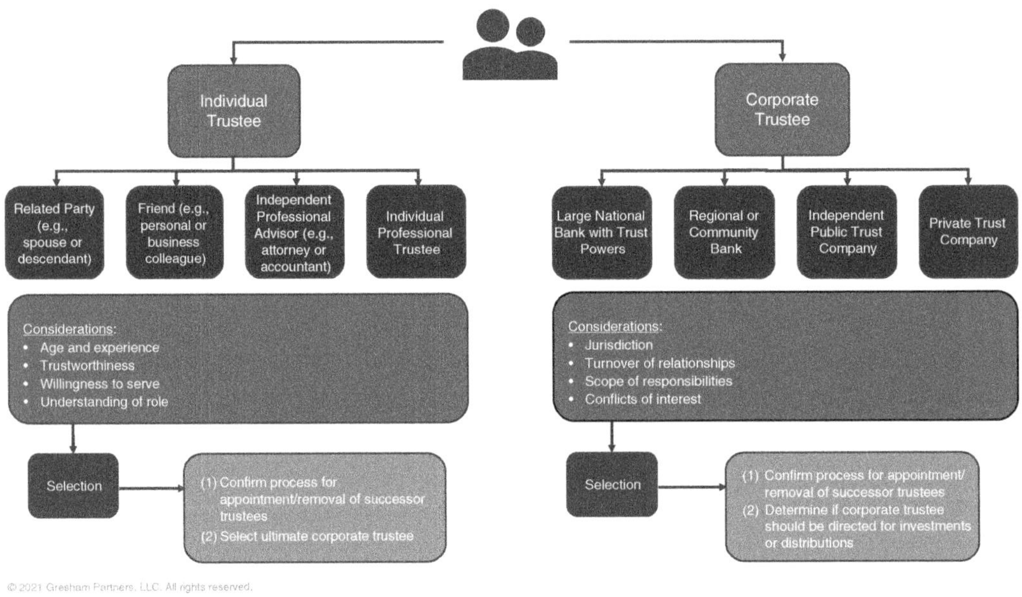

Addendum B: Questions about Individual Trustees

- Do you know this individual well enough to have confidence and trust in them?
- Has this individual had opportunities to demonstrate that they are trustworthy and have good judgment? Consider specific examples of this.
- Has this individual ever served as a trustee before?
- Why do you believe this person is trustworthy?
- Does this individual have the temperament and characteristics to be a good trustee?
- Is this individual:
  - Patient?
  - Wise?
  - A mentor?
  - Impartial?
  - Competent?
  - Well organized?
- Does this individual have the requisite skills to invest and administer the trust?
- Will this individual be able to communicate effectively with the beneficiaries and diplomatically say no to requests for excessive distributions?
- Will this individual understand family dynamics?
- Do the beneficiaries know and respect this individual? If not, can you arrange for them to get to know each other prior to the time that the individual begins acting as trustee?
- Does this individual fully comprehend what is expected of them to serve in the role as trustee?
- Have you confirmed that there are no structural conflicts?
  - If there are structural conflicts, have those conflicts been sufficiently addressed to reduce the change of problems?
- Have you confirmed there are no inherent relationship conflicts of the kind described above?
  - If there are relationship conflicts, have those conflicts been sufficiently addressed to reduce the change of problems?
- Have you discussed the appropriate compensation this individual will receive?
  - If the individual is a professional, will they receive their regular fee?
  - If the individual is a trust beneficiary, will they forgo trustee fees and instead take trust distributions?
  - If the individual is a parent or relative of the beneficiaries, will they forgo fees for familial reasons?
  - If the individual is a friend or business partner, appropriate compensation should be paid and agreed to in advance.

Addendum C: Questions about Corporate Trustees

- Number and characteristics of similar trusts for which they serve as trustee?
- Will they serve as directed trustee with regard to investments? Or do they want to manage investments?

- If investing, what is their investment approach used for similar trusts?
  - Asset allocations among traditional and nontraditional asset classes?
  - How are investment services and products selected?
  - Are *internal* or other proprietary investment services or products used? If so, how is it disclosed and how does it impact trustee fees?
  - Are *external* investment services or products used? If so, how is any revenue or other economic benefit received by the institution for those services or products disclosed and how does it impact trustee fees?
- What process is used to determine discretionary distributions and other exercises of discretion? Examples?
- How do they handle special characteristics of the trust:
  - Coordinating with an investment direction advisor and/or special trustee on concentrated positions in the trust's investment portfolio?
  - Coordinating with any investment direction advisor and/or special trustee on nontraditional assets in the trust's investment portfolio?
  - Unequal treatment of current beneficiaries?
  - Conversion to a "total return" approach?
  - Communications with beneficiaries who have adverse interests?
- Descriptions and examples of the reporting capabilities and investment performance assessments that will be used for the trust?
- Any trust-related litigation or regulatory problems in recent years?
- Background of the people who will provide trustee services for the trust, those to whom they report, and how long they have been in their current positions?
- How does the institution use external firms to provide trust-related services, including insurance, tax compliance and estate planning services?
- How will the trust be charged for services provided by the institution and external firms it expects to use?
- How will interest paid on cash balances in the trust accounts be calculated?

Notes for Analysis of Corporate Trustee Answers

- *What are the motivations and priorities of those providing trustee services?*
- *Will the institution's receipt of revenue from the internal or external investment products or services affect its ability to be loyal, impartial, and prudent?*
- *Does the institution's history, stated priorities, and current delivery of services model indicate the following:*
  - *The trust will receive on a continuing basis the desired level of resources and personal attention from the people who will be providing the trustee services?*
  - *Transitions to new resources and new people within the institution will be handled effectively?*
  - *Trustee discretion will be exercised on a continuing basis with the desired level of flexibility?*

Additional Resources

Hartley Goldstone, James E. Hughes, Jr., and Keith Whitaker, *Family Trusts: A Guide for Beneficiaries, Trustees, Trust Protectors and Trust Creators* (Hoboken, NJ: Wiley, 2016).

Biography

Kim Kamin is a principal at Gresham Partners, an independent wealth management firm serving select ultra-high-net-worth families. As the Chief Wealth Strategist, she leads Gresham's estate, wealth transfer, philanthropic, educational, and fiduciary planning activities. Previously she was a partner at a large law firm where she practiced in trusts and estates for many years.

Kim teaches at the Northwestern University Law School and the University of Chicago Business School. She is on the Editorial Advisory Board of *Trusts and Estates Magazine*, a Regent with the American College of Trust and Estate Counsel, immediate past president for the Chicago Estate Planning Council, and on the Advisory Board for the UHNW Institute.

Kim was executive co-editor and co-author of the Leimberg Library book, *Estate Planning for Modern Families.* She received her BA from Stanford University and JD from the University of Chicago Law School. She is an AEP® and a 21/64 Certified Advisor.

CHAPTER 35

Assessing Your Readiness for a (Family Enterprise) Leadership Coach

Greg McCann

Some of the most well-respected and successful business leaders have help from a coach behind the scenes. Taking on a leadership role formally or informally within your family or family enterprise is exponentially challenging given the complexity of family relationships, history, and systemic dynamics. Are you ready, willing, and able to engage a leadership coach?

In my experience, coaching is perhaps the best way to accelerate your development as a leader. These reflective questions will help you understand what coaching is (and isn't), what to expect from coaching, and the proper mindset for working with a coach.

		Definitely Yes	Maybe	Not Sure	Maybe Not	Definitely No
1	Are you currently a leader or striving to become one?	1	2	3	4	5
	It sounds simplistic, but nonetheless true. If you want to know if you are leading, see if anyone is following you. Leadership is not a title or a position but rather an ability to set a vision, gain alignment or buy-in from key people, and commit resources. You can lead in your family, its enterprises, its philanthropy, or anywhere in your life. "Do you want to lead?" is the question.					
2	Do you want a safe, neutral place to process ideas, challenges, and opportunities?	1	2	3	4	5
	This is a precious resource. Especially in the overlapping, complex, and interdependent roles of a family enterprise, it is as difficult as it is valuable to have someone who can listen to you say something such as "*I feel inadequate for this new challenge*" and not have them become anxious (such as your employees), try to immediately reassure you (such as your spouse), or fix it (most people default to this approach whenever stress arises). Do you want someone objective who can help you explore the challenge, dig deeper to see if it is a pattern, help you explore if you have options you haven't considered, or even help you reframe your perspective?					
3	Do you want someone to guide you to your truth rather than tell you what to do?	1	2	3	4	5
	A leadership coach is not, as so many people assume, like an athletic coach from school who tells you what to do. A coach trusts that you have the answer and helps explore your patterns, assumptions, and perspectives so that you gain insight into who you are and how you might move toward success, as you define it. Are you ready to take greater ownership for your career and ultimately, your life?					

4	Are you courageous and willing to be challenged and vulnerable to build on your strengths and work on your shortcomings?	1	2	3	4	5
	Coaching is working on the thing you can most change: yourself. A counterintuitive truth I have found in coaching (and consulting) is that virtually every breakthrough with a client arises when he or she gets vulnerable. A truth arises. At the same time, most people struggle far more to own their strengths than their weaknesses, so you can lean into achieving your potential. Do you want to truly own your strengths and learn to better navigate your weaknesses? "All of humanity's problems stem from man's inability to sit quietly in a room alone." — Blaise Pascal, Pensées					
		Definitely Yes	**Maybe**	**Not Sure**	**Maybe Not**	**Definitely No**
5	Do you value and seek out objective feedback?	1	2	3	4	5
	According to the Center for Creative Leadership, the number one risk to derail your career as you move up in an organization is lack of *objective* feedback. I believe there is an even greater risk in a family enterprise where conflict is so often avoided. All good leaders seek out feedback from others and are generous with giving feedback. Do you want to hear from those you are leading? Do you want to offer them the same gift?					
6	Do you want to work ***on*** your career and life, not just ***in*** it?	1	2	3	4	5
	If your life feels like Indiana Jones running ahead of that boulder, you may gain some satisfaction from striving, suffering, and feeling stress, but it takes a toll on you, your business, and your life. As one client of mine says: *We don't reward suffering, just performance*. Are you ready to work ***on*** your life and career?					
7	Do you want more whitespace to think and process deeply?	1	2	3	4	5
	Every one of my clients holds the goal of creating whitespace (i.e., time and space for deep thinking) as a priority. If you are trying to change a system (i.e., leading), it is vital. Are you creating enough whitespace for what you and your family enterprise need? Are you willing to let go of an attachment to feeling busy being a measure of your importance or worth?					
8	There are predictable stages leaders evolve through. Do you know where you are now and where you want to be?	1	2	3	4	5
	Few people can articulate what a good leader is and therefore struggle to see where they want to evolve as a leader. Do you want a roadmap for where you are, where you want to be, and how to get there?					
9	Is self-care a priority for you?	1	2	3	4	5
	If these recent years taught us anything it is that we must take care of ourselves, body, mind, and soul. The tank must get refilled. Would being accountable to a coach help you with this?					
10	Can you define what success looks like for you?	1	2	3	4	5
	You, not the coach, have to answer this. For example, the year I retired from 27 years in academia, I sought out a coach with one primary goal: to not fill up all that time with work. I am proud to share that success was achieved! Though it can and should evolve, can you articulate what success looks like for your career and life?					
	Total each column then add them up = _____ • If your score is 26 (or higher), you may want to wait, reflect, and check back in three to six months. • If 15–25, at least take the next step and set up a call to explore things with a coach. • If under 15, what are you waiting for?					

Client Stories

One coaching client who has been working with me for almost two years shared that as she stepped into the role of being president of the family office she had worked with for years, things were just not working. She needed help. She realized she had been educated and trained for her other roles, but not in leadership per se. She also said she would've scored under 15.

Another coaching client and leader in a second-generation family business was motivated to reconnect with a coach as he faced several upcoming transitions. His motivation was to frame more clearly his intention, then working on making the implementation effective. He believed that by seeking professional guidance from a coach who had experience in the field and knew him well, he would maximize his chances of success.

A third client recounts, "As I returned to the workplace after earning a master's degree, I felt as though something was missing. It became evident when people would ask 'What is it that you really want to do as a leader?' I had some vague idea of what I wanted to do. I could see the peak of the mountain, but the next steps on the path were covered in fog.

"I decided to reach out to a leadership coach to guide me through this process. With a coach, I took a step back to understand myself at a deeper level. The gift of knowing myself is making it easier to be my best self, to go for positions and show up in ways that fit my values and passions in a way that positively affects others and the future. Now, I can choose what unique language, framework, or role that I need to use for each meeting or conversation. Having a coach is a gift that has helped me to lead with confidence and self-awareness, to maximize my influence for good, to unlock human potential on my teams."

Conclusion

Leaders today face greater complexity, change, and interdependencies than ever before. This is especially true when you are a leader in a family enterprise. Investing in your leadership development is essential to give yourself, your family, and its enterprises the best possible chance of success. In my experience, working with a professional leadership coach is a tremendous resource to do this, when you are ready, willing, and able. Hopefully you now have a clearer sense of how ready, willing, and able you are to start this journey.

Additional Resources

Diane Coutu and Carol Kauffman, "The Realities of Executive Coaching," *Harvard Business Review Research Report* (January 2009).

Diane Coutu and Carol Kauffman, "What Can Coaches Do for You?" *Harvard Business Review Research Report* (January 2009).

Greg McCann, "How Coaching Can Help Deepen Your Awareness and Drive More Effective Action," *Tharawat Magazine* (March 2020).

Greg McCann, "The Benefits of Coaching for Rising Gen Leadership," Family Office Exchange, published March 26, 2000, https://www.familyoffice.com/insights/benefits-coaching-rising-gen-leadership.

Biography

Greg McCann is the son of a serial entrepreneur and has been involved in his family's business since he was 12 years old. These experiences growing up have led Greg to consulting, speaking, coaching, teaching, and writing two books on family enterprise.

Greg works with family enterprises in the areas of leadership, succession, communication, and conflict resolution, with a special emphasis on leadership. Greg has coached leaders and executives for more than 20 years and is certified in Leadership Agility and Myers-Briggs Type Indicator.

Now retired from Stetson University after 27 years in academia, Greg was founder and director of the Family Enterprise Center, where he led the effort to develop the nation's second minor and first undergraduate major in Family Enterprise. He also was the executive MBA director and cohort coach.

Greg has served on the board of directors of the Family Firm Institute (FFI) from 2005 to 2008. He was awarded the institution's 2016 Interdisciplinary Award for outstanding achievement in the advancement of interdisciplinary services to business families and the 2006 Barbara Hollander Award acknowledging him for a lifetime of achievement in family enterprise education.

CHAPTER 36

Understanding Advisors' Fees

Mark Pletts

Do you know *all* of the costs for the financial services and products you own? When we ask this question to affluent families, most of the time we can tell by their responses that the answer is "not really."

Successful families have many options when they seek out financial services and products. The myriad solutions that exist to guide families today and for future generations can be intimidating. As consumers we are constantly running cost/benefit analyses (sometimes formal, sometimes informal) of everything we purchase. The problem in the financial services industry is a lack of transparency.

To be better consumers of these services, we need to reframe the questions we ask. Most families prioritize relationships and perceived competencies when they enter an advisory relationship or purchase investment products. Price, although a topic of discussion, is not always a priority—often because it is so difficult to clarify the true costs of products and services.

Why Is What You Pay So Important?

Understanding the jargon is a good starting point. The investment industry uses "basis points" (bps) as a unit of measure, where 100 bps equals 1 percent. Therefore, 60 bps equals 6/10ths of 1 percent, or 0.6 percent. On a $10 million portfolio, a price reduction of 60 bps would equate to savings of $60,000 a year, or $600,000 over 10 years. Although savings of this magnitude may only have a nominal effect on a successful family's lifestyle, it can have a big impact on their kids, grandkids, or the charities and causes they support. To be good stewards of the wealth that has been entrusted to you requires you to know what you are paying, and saving any "bps" you can is part of that analysis.

Following is a great starting point to get your mind around some of the questions you can ask your family's advisors. These questions are meant to be used in the service of being a good steward and not meant to be a challenge to the advisor; however, if an advisor gets defensive when asked these questions, it may be a red flag for the family.

The list of trusted advisors that support families may include attorneys, certified public accountants (CPAs), wealth advisors (both institutional and independent), life insurance agents, and consultants. As it relates to compensation in any industry, a good rule to remember is, "If you know how someone is compensated, you can predict their behavior."

Attorneys

These seem like simple questions but it's worth asking them of the various law firms you interview. You should never be surprised when you get a bill. Also keep in mind that a higher or lower fee shouldn't always be the determining factor. A great attorney with a high hourly rate who can cut to the chase and provide efficient advice may be better than one with a lower hourly rate who needs to take twice as long to complete the project.

- Will you charge me per project or by the hour?
- Why do you charge this way?
- Can you estimate what my total cost will be?
- Can you provide examples of why the total cost would be higher or lower?

CPAs

You want a proactive accountant who can collaborate with your other advisors. In a perfect world your CPA would have other clients with similar balance sheets, so as to be accustomed to the complexities associated with affluence. In all your advisor relationships, great advice goes beyond the numbers.

- How many other clients do you have who are like my family?
- What is your typical fee for a tax return preparation engagement? What services are covered by those fees?
- What are some examples where you have collaborated with other advisors? What were the outcomes of those collaborations?

Institutional Wealth Advisors

Wealth advising is a murky world where everyone professes to be different yet offers similar services. The key to remember is that when you work with a team from a large institution, brokerage firm, insurance company, or a household-name entity, your advisor serves two masters. They may have corporate production requirements that dictate their compensation (the firm is the master) and they have you as a client (you are the master). A trusted advisor may be able to navigate this dual loyalty and the opaque nature of the pricing model. Still, to be a good steward, it is still important to know the costs.

There are two types of fees hitting your account:

1. The fee the advisor gets all or a portion of and
2. The fee charged by the products they purchase on your behalf (the advisor may or may not get a portion of that fee).

- What is the fee you as an advisor charge for the relationship I have with you?
- Do you get all that fee? (This question clarifies what the other master—the firm that employs them—is receiving.)
- Can you show me exactly what each product you have placed in my account is charging?
- Do you get any compensation from product providers?

Independent Wealth Advisors

Alongside wealth advisors in institutions, there are many independent advisory firms. This is also the structure most multifamily offices take. One of the priorities for most independent advisors is to harness the collective knowledge of all your advisors on your behalf. There is only one master in this world and that is you, the client. Still, it's sometimes hard to get to the bottom of what you are paying. In a perfect world, your fee would be on every quarterly statement you receive. It usually is a basis point charge for the assets the firm manages for your family, an approach to fees that may be similar to the institutional advisor described previously.

The financial services world has moved away from a commission-based model to charging a fee for assets under management (AUM). The premise of this change is, "When you do better (i.e., achieve better returns) your advisor does better." While true at the surface level, a bit of a conflict arises for affluent families who are considering large charitable donations, gifts to children, or a sizable real estate purchase. Anything that reduces the assets an advisor manages reduces the AUM-based fee. A more recent and less common pricing model that reduces the opportunity for conflicts of interest is a flat fee not tied to the value of the portfolio but based on the complexity of the family's financial affairs. Many advisors are less inclined to use this method as it removes the built-in growth of fees related to asset growth (market performance), which is often unrelated to the work the advisor is doing with the family. It can also be challenging to properly evaluate the family's needs and complexity until the engagement is underway.

Here is a starting point to that discussion with your independent advisor:

- Are you able to charge me a flat fee? If yes, how would you calculate it?
- Can you outline where there may be conflicts of interest in your business model?
- If you can't charge a flat fee, how do you handle conflicts of interest when they arise?
- How often do you review my fees?

If the answer is no to using a flat fee, then ask the set of questions that are outlined above for the institutional advisor.

Life Insurance Agents

Many affluent families need life insurance. In the United States most of the policies one would purchase are filed with the state's insurance commissioner. That means the commission scales that are paid have also been filed and are nonnegotiable.

There is private placement insurance for larger policies where commissions and cost can be negotiated, but that is the exception, not the norm.

If your advisor is selling you life insurance, this can create a conflict of interest that you should be aware of. It may be more prudent to consider buying insurance when it is suggested by someone (i.e., an attorney, your CPA, or your wealth advisor) who is not going to sell it to you. You should make sure the life insurance discussion starts with a dialogue around objectives and a clear planning-based need, and not a solution in search of a problem.

Some questions for your insurance advisor include the following:

- Are you able to sell me both whole life as well as universal/variable life policies? Could you illustrate both for my family?
- Do you have access to all the top life insurance carriers?
- Do you get paid more to sell me one contract over the other?
- What would be the total amount of your commissions on this product?

There are benefits and risks to all types of insurance contracts and by seeing them side by side you will be able to discern what makes the most sense for your family.

Consultants[1]

The world of family wealth abounds with a variety of consultants: security consultants, educational consultants, art advisors, aircraft and watercraft consultants, real estate advisors, home staffing consultants, and on and on. For the purposes of this chapter, however, we're going to focus on the group of consultants who advise families regarding family enterprise or family dynamics.

These consultants often come from a background in psychology, education, or law. They help families enhance their communication, plan smooth leadership transitions, and make other important decisions in an effective way. Some of these consultants may also help families develop learning plans to help rising generation family members integrate their wealth into their lives in healthy ways.

In general, consultants in this space are paid on a project basis. That means that the consultant will present you with a proposal that includes a scope of work, a timeline, and a proposed fee for the project. Most consultants develop their project fees using an estimate of the time involved and multiplying that time by a daily rate. Daily rates can vary greatly, anywhere from $2,500 to $10,000 per day or more. Few consultants will agree to work on an hourly basis.

Some questions to ask consultants with whom you're thinking of working include the following:

- In addition to the scope of work and timeline, what do you see as tangible deliverables for this project?
- How do you come up with a project fee?
- How does your daily rate compare to other consultants in your field?
- How should we review the fee, in case the work turns out to be more involved—or less involved—than expected?

---

[1]The author expresses his thanks to Keith Whitaker for contributions to this section.

Conclusion

Most families are hesitant to do deep discovery around what they are paying for the products and services they purchase. Knowing the costs of what you are paying may not be the final arbiter in your decision, but engaging in these dialogues will make you a better steward of your wealth. This is an easier discussion when you are first interviewing advisors. If you've already been working with an advisor for a while, you can simply reopen the pricing conversation with the following bridge statement: "When we first started working together, I know you went through all the costs with me, but it's been a while. Could we do that exercise again?" You will find that there is a simple math calculation to many of these discussions. More importantly, you will find that how your advisors handle these questions should affirm and build confidence in trusted relationships.

Relationships/ Providers	Compensation	Questions to Ask (You should never be surprised)
Attorneys	Hourly, per Project	• Do you charge per project or by the hour? • Which way will you charge me? • Why do you do it that way? • Can you estimate what my total cost will be? • Can you provide examples of why it would be higher or lower?
CPAs	Hourly, per Tax Return, per Project	• How do you charge? • What is the estimated cost of my engagement? • If I consolidate more of my tax work to you, will the cost go down? • Can you provide examples?
Institutional Wealth Advisors	Commission Based, Percentage of AUM, Company Bonus Plans	• How are you paid? • Can you show me how those fees are broken out? • Will I see them on my statements? • Can you show me an example? • Do you get paid more to sell me your company's sponsored products? Are you able to show me all the costs for products in my portfolio?
Independent Wealth Advisors and Multifamily Offices)	Paid directly by the client, usually via an assets-under-management fee or an annual flat fee.	• Are you paid based on a percentage of assets under management? • What is the fee? • Are you able to charge a flat fee? • Can you show me the internal fee of the products I have purchased from you? • Am I able to see these on my statements?
Life Insurance Agents	Commission pre-filed with state insurance departments.	• Are you able to illustrate whole life, universal and variable life contracts for my family? • What percentage of those various contracts do you sell each year? • Can you show me how much you get paid annually on those contracts?
Family Dynamics Consultants	Paid directly by the client. Often a project fee, based on a daily rate.	• What do you see as the scope of work, timeline, and tangible deliverables for this project? • How do you come up with a project fee? • How does your daily rate compare to other consultants in your field? • How should we review the fee, in case the work turns out to be more involved—or less involved—than expected?

Additional Resources

David C. Bentall, *Dear Younger Me. . . Wisdom for Family Enterprise Successors: 9 Character Traits to Transform Your Leadership* (Burlington, Ontario, Canada: Castle Quay Books, 2020).

John Rinehart, *Gospel Patrons: People Whose Generosity Changed the World* (Reclaimed Publishing, 2013).

James E. Hughes, Jr., Susan E. Massennzio, and Keith Whitaker, *The Cycle of the Gift, Family Wealth and Wisdom* (Hoboken, NJ: John Wiley & Sons, 2013).

Biography

Mark Pletts is the co-founder of Waypoint Capital Advisors LLC (WCA), a flat fee multifamily office with offices in Minnesota and Arizona. WCA harnesses the collective knowledge of a family's advisory team to help them navigate the nuances associated with affluence. Mark has held senior positions in sales and marketing at organizations such as Fidelity Investments and AllianceBernstein.

Mark graduated from Lawrence Academy in Groton, Mass and Bowdoin College in Brunswick, Maine in 1980 with a B.A. in Government. Mark sits on the Board of Directors of Matter, a Non-Governmental Organization that works globally to provide health and educational service to those in need.

SECTION 6

RAISING THE RISING GENERATION

Most parents see their children as their greatest gift, and accordingly look at the task of raising happy, independent young adults as their most important work. At the same time, the special risks and concerns that raising children amid significant wealth brings cause many parents to doubt themselves, procrastinate taking action or communicating, and miss opportunities for passing on important life lessons.

The chapters in this section aim to resolve this dilemma, as much as possible. We begin with two chapters devoted to instituting new "rituals" in your life with your children.

In the first, Joline Godfrey describes steps that parents can take to introduce discussion of responsibilities and maturity into a "pre-birthday" ritual for each child. Starting even with young children, parents can connect the benefit of getting presents with the importance of taking on new responsibilities as a child ages. It is a ritual that can resonate powerfully when children are faced with receiving much larger gifts as part of parents' estate planning.

Next, Andrew Doust outlines a college "sending" ritual that families can use to mark the special transition from life at home to life at college, which for many children marks the true beginning of adult life. This ritual involves inviting the young-adult child to reflect on what he or she wants to get out of the college experience and creating an agreement of expectations of what the college student will do and communicate with parents in exchange for the "scholarship" of family funds that are covering tuition. As with the pre-birthday ritual, this ceremony aims to connect the opportunity that wealth affords with responsibility, to militate against entitlement.

Much of the work of effective parenting takes place through offhand conversations that make the most of "teachable moments." But as the two prior chapters show, intentional communication can be very powerful. This is the point of the next chapter as well, in which Bo and Suzanne Huhn relate the lessons they imparted to their grandchildren, using a thoughtful plan of written notes, humorous conversations, structured family dialogues, and video testimony. Over the course of years this intentional process of imparting "life lessons" deeply shaped their grandchildren's character.

In many families, raising the rising generation also involves the practical consideration of whether members of the rising generation will join the family business. The next two chapters take up this dynamic, first from the standpoint of the rising generation member who is considering this choice and then from the standpoint of the senior family member who is trying to prepare his or her successors to succeed.

In the first, Josh Baron and Rob Lachenauer offer a checklist for the rising generation family member who is considering joining the family business. This list prompts reflections on everything from the young adult's motivation, to past experience, to the nature of the ownership structure, to the alignment of the young adult's goals with the current owners' and managers', and much more. The results of this self-assessment will help the prospective member of the family business decide whether, and at what speed, and with what support, to move ahead in this choice.

In the next chapter (reprinted from the first *Wealth of Wisdom* volume), Dean Fowler offers guidance to family business leaders on how to mentor their successors and prepare them to succeed. The checklist for these mentors includes ensuring that successors have developed their own sense of independence, that the family has enhanced its ability to talk about difficult topics, that there is a transition strategy in place that (among other things) addresses the liquidity needs of various family members, and that the successors have developed their own ability to assess, take, and manage financial risk.

If there is one ability that is central to long-term family success, it is the ability to communicate effectively among generations. The greatest obstacle to this communication very often is the belief that it has taken place. As a result, families commonly need to make time to foster intergenerational communication in an intentional manner. In the final chapter in this section, Susan Massenzio offers a simple but extremely powerful exercise for structuring an "intergenerational dialogue," which family members can use to share their most important messages with each other, to learn from each other, and to practice communicating effectively *within* each generation as well.

CHAPTER 37

Balancing Entitlement and Responsibility in Children's Birthdays

Joline Godfrey

Most parents say that they want to make their kids happy and raise happy kids. These goals sound the same, but they are not—the outcomes are often very different. "Making your kids happy" may mean praising the most insignificant achievements and offering a new toy or treat for any event. "Raising happy kids" is a mindful process of constancy, helping children develop the capacity to *make themselves* happy, no matter the challenges life offers up.

Children train their parents from their earliest months: with a smile, a clap of the hands, a gurgle of joy. So satisfying are these moments (coming as they may between long bursts of fussiness and the agony of sleeplessness) that parents reasonably do what they can to replicate small satisfactions that keep them going; they try to find ever more ways *to make kids happy.* This attempt is understandable, and it is no use judging parents for doing their best to make it through the marathon of childhood.

A New Rite of Passage for Children 5 to 15+

Still, seizing small opportunities to go beyond the quick thrill of making kids happy can have a bigger pay-off for both kids and parents. The Birthday Eve offers one such possibility. Consider making this rite of passage a new family tradition.

The Set-Up. It's the night before the child's birthday. You go out as a family[1] with the one child (no siblings unless perhaps they're twins) to a restaurant that's a little more special, a little quieter than say Chuck E Cheese or McDonald's.

[1]*Family* is used mindfully here to encompass whatever constellation is real in your system. Mom, grandmother and Aunt Susan may be one family; Dad and young Rex another; blended families; families of affinity; temporary families; these are all 21st-century families.

The goal is to communicate by your choice that *"This is important."* For little ones, it might be any place they think of as special; for teens the setting should signal "grown-up." White tablecloths would not be inappropriate.

The Message. *"Honey, we're excited! Tomorrow is your birthday. We'll have cake [or whatever], you'll see your friends [if a party is in the works] and you'll have wonderful surprises [assuming gifts will be forthcoming]. It will be fun! But tonight, we're here to talk about the changes that come with being a year older."* Your message is simple: The privilege of each birthday is balanced with attention to responsibility. Gifts, fun, and celebration are not the whole story. Nor does responsibility crowd out fun. Responsibility is not offered as a punitive after-effect of fun, but as a means of paying respect to the privilege of celebration. The point is to recognize that the pleasures of the day come thanks to the efforts of others and to acknowledge that becoming a year older is part of the process of maturing.

The Conversation. While the message is essential, the conversation is critical. *"We're celebrating the fact that you're another year older. It's exciting because it reminds us you are maturing—and are ready for new responsibilities. Now that you're another year older, what new responsibilities do <u>you</u> think you're ready to handle?"* The question tells the birthday child you recognize their new status and respect it. Now, such a question can be challenging for a five-year-old. You may have to offer examples: Can you make sure the dog has water in her bowl at all times? Can you brush your teeth without being reminded? Can you put your toys away at the end of the day? The 10-year-old may be proud as punch or puzzled (especially if this is a new rite of passage) and may also need help identifying new responsibilities. For example, making your bed, setting the table a couple of times a week, keeping track of a first allowance, etc. The 15-year-old may be suspicious of an unfamiliar attachment to a formerly unencumbered celebration. For them, responsibility may equate to giving a percentage of their birthday cash to a philanthropic cause, managing a financial report once a month, or volunteering in a program the family supports. It might mean a monthly clean-up of their closet or taking over the role of primary dog walker. New tasks can be anything that sends the message that your child is maturing. Acquiring skills, becoming part of a community (family, school, or the larger village), maturing itself is an intentional journey, not an accident.

The Repetition. Introducing new traditions is rarely a breeze. Suspicion, misunderstanding, even fear are natural responses to new behavior on the part of parents. This is why starting very early (4–6 years old) and normalizing expectations for young children is often easier. This is not to say starting later isn't effective; better late than never! But later starts may require more grit and determination on the part of parents. Repeating the message and the question (what responsibilities are you ready to take on?), year after year—for little ones and older children—is essential.

In year one, children may be surprised or puzzled by the exercise but go along with the novelty. In year two the response might be an indignant, "You told me this last year!" In year three you may get a rolling of the eyes (old news, ho hum). But by year four the tradition is set. This will be the story your kids tell their kids, "When I was growing up, every year . . . ." Obviously the conversation that links privilege and responsibility gets reinforced between birthdays. But linking key values to a significant annual event is an organic and effective way to build family culture that children carry within, throughout their lives.

This activity lends itself to engaging extended family members, the great invisible treasure in so many families: aunts and uncles, grandparents and godparents. But those "treasures" have a dark side when one (or more) claims the dreaded "right" to spoil [my grandchild, nephew, niece, etc.]. Intentional parents trying to pass on an ethic of generosity, only to be undermined by relatives showering excessive gifts on kids, are often at their wits' end trying to enlist the cooperation of that loving grandparent who ignores their pleas. Invite those relatives to the dinner; include them in the conversation; practice a little surreptitious teaching across the generations.

The Case Study

The Browns (not their real name) were in the audience for a talk I gave at a Harvard Business School Reunion. The couple met at the Business School, eventually married, and by then were parents of an 8-year-old boy and a 10-year-old girl. In the talk I shared the Birthday Eve Dinner idea and the two were first in line at the conclusion of the talk. "We've done well," Jeff, the dad, began, "which means our kids live very comfortable lives. We don't want to deprive them in some artificial way to make a point, but we want them to grow up with an appreciation for the benefits of making do, sharing, and using family resources thoughtfully. Our challenge is that both kids attend fancy schools and while the staff—and fellow parents—talk a good game, what our children see is birthday and holiday gifts closer to game show winnings. Also, my father is adamant that it's his right as a grandparent to give his grandkids whatever he feels like, which is an endless stream of "surprises." Jane's [the mom] parents are better at checking before giving anything too major to the kids. But we're feeling discouraged about my dad and won't be surprised if we wake up in five years to see a car for sitting in the driveway our daughter. What can we do?"

I invited the couple to call me for a longer conversation, which we had a few weeks later. There was not so much to teach as to support their good instincts and offer strategies for navigating the culture—and family—in which they were immersed. This is often the case. Most parents *know* what to do; but peers, relatives, Instagram, and even the cacophony of competing experts conspire to challenge the good sense of smart parents.

A few weeks later we met to talk about their goals: setting boundaries on the grandfather's "generosity" and offsetting the impact of the school culture.

Putting kids in a bubble is no solution. And expectations of changing grandparents' behavior can border on magical thinking. Behaviors, family patterns, and power issues are often so entrenched that emphasis is better placed on the actions one *can* control rather than tackling those likely to be intractable.

Instilling financial values in kids is economic self-defense—and the most effective way to help children acquire identity and a moral compass. With this as the first goal, we returned to the Birthday Eve dinner and how to use it to give their kids grounding. I offered some loose "scripts" to adapt as appropriate; a few weeks later they called to report on the experience.

It had, according to them, been a fun night—the little boy was excited to be at a special dinner at a fancy restaurant—without his older sister. And they had done their best to keep the conversation focused (reconstructed here as they told it):

"Are you looking forward to the party tomorrow?" the mom asked. *"Sure!"* the little boy responded. Then went on to speculate about what he was going to get for presents.

At this point the dad broke in with, *"Tomorrow will be a great day Adam, and we're looking forward to it. But tonight, we want to talk how important birthdays are. You're growing up. We're proud of how many things you've learned to do this year. You helped me paint the porch floor, you do a much better job of putting your Legos away, and you seem to be leaving your sister alone when her friends come over. These are all signs you're growing up and taking on new responsibilities."* He continued, *"Adam, tomorrow you will be nine. What can you do this year to show how you're growing up?"*

According to both parents, Adam was a little befuddled, but finally offered that, *"I can walk the dog when I get home from school."* The parents agreed this was a good task for a nine-year-old and wondered if there was anything else he could think of. Adam is a smart kid and like most children, caught on quickly that another year of age might be a double-edged sword. He volunteered to stop complaining about haircuts, and the parents took that as a victory and ordered dessert.

The family didn't call me again until after their second dinner with Adam. Though he was getting wise to the seriousness of the Birthday Eve Dinner, it was going well. At 10, Adam was beginning to see the dinner as an opportunity to negotiate with his parents: If another year of age meant new responsibilities, what new privileges would he also get?! It was not an easy process, but a learning and growing conversation that was becoming part of family tradition.

They were also ready to report on the experience with Rachel who had had her own Birthday Eve event. As the older sister, she had initially been offended she was doing something her little brother had done first. But in her case, her mother had launched the conversation with, *"Rachel, we're proud of the way you're growing up and showing more maturity every year. The party you're having tomorrow will be a great celebration. But tonight, we'd like to hear what you're looking forward to and what growing up means to you."*

This was a sophisticated way to frame the question for a now 12-year-old girl and would not work with every child; but parents know their kids, and Rachel's mom knew her daughter was up to it. Rachel talked about looking ahead to middle school; about wanting an Apple Watch and a horse. Her mother didn't want to frame those desires as rewards for taking on new responsibilities, so she responded with, *"Those are exciting goals—and they tell us you're thinking about more grown-up things now. Becoming another year older opens new doors to things you can do and achieve, but it also means demonstrating good decisions, judgement, and readiness to take on more responsibility. Where would you like to begin?"* By being less prescriptive ("This is what we want you to do"), and more curious ("How will you demonstrate these capacities?"), Rachel's mother made a pivot from rewards for new chores to a way of thinking. Both parents offered suggestions for what demonstrating new behaviors might look like:

Her dad said, *"You might volunteer to help your brother at least once or twice a week. You know he gets frustrated when he can't reach something and if you gave him a hand without being asked that would show both empathy and maturity. And showing him how to look through your bird binoculars would be another way to show you're being more grown up—anything that demonstrates you're thinking about his needs."* Her mother then asked, "*Does this give you any other ideas?*" Rachel thought for a minute and said, "*If I do those things and feed the dogs every night, can I get an allowance?*" Jane and Jeff had considered the implementation of an allowance but weren't sure their daughter was ready. This opened the door.

Adam and Rachel's stories both started out well. But it didn't ensure an easy process. Rachel was "in transition," showing signs of maturity one day, regressing to her childish self another. And Adam reveled at every opportunity to "bargain" with his parents. Had it not been for the parents' fortitude, the outcome for Adam and Rachel might have been less satisfying than it is. The secret sauce was parental persistence and clarity of goals.

In the early years, our check-ins were largely about supporting Jeff and Jane's goals and good instincts. "Repetition," I repeated to them, "is essential to helping children internalize responsibility as a family expectation." The Birthday Eve Dinner was the beginning of an ongoing conversation, not a one-and-done trick.

The Browns stayed in touch with me for the next six years. Rachel was getting ready for college and her parents reported they were confident she would handle her college allowance responsibly. Adam was 12 when I last heard from them, but his entrepreneurial spirit had kicked in: Jeff and Jane had already coached him through a couple of "business plans." The Birthday Eve Dinner was not a silver bullet. But it was an effective mechanism to engage their kids and help nurture a family culture that embraced an operating value of balancing privilege and responsibility.

Additional Resources

Ron Lieber, *The Opposite of Spoiled: Raising Kids Who Are Grounded, Generous, and Smart about Money* (New York: Harper, 2016).

Joline Godfrey, *Raising Financially Fit Kids,* rev. (San Francisco, CA: Ten Speed Press, 2013).

Biography

Joline Godfrey is an innovator in financial education for children and the financial novice. She has served more than 400 of the world's wealthiest families and launched a range of innovative financial education programs. She is the author of *Raising Financially Fit Kids* and other books on financial fluency in families.

CHAPTER 38

A Ritual to Send Children off to College

Andrew Doust

Leaving home for college is without doubt one of the most formative and challenging experiences of life. It's up there with marriage, having children, and getting your first job.

Away from the constraints and familiarity of home, college offers a rare opportunity to redefine ourselves. There is freedom to try new experiences, pursue new interests, to choose new friends, and to decide who we want to be in the world.

Our college years reveal and shape our identity. Our worldview, our character, and our values are all tested in new ways, and the decisions we make in those years have lifelong implications.

Perhaps like me you've seen too many young adults head off to college without a solid grounding, unprepared for the choices and challenges they will face, sometimes with tragic consequences.

Some time ago I was engaged by a family to help prepare their G3 children for college life abroad. Raised in a sheltered culture, the family was concerned that their children would be overwhelmed by their new culture and could quickly lose their way. I recalled my own experience of being sent by my family, which inspired this simple College Send-Off Ritual.

The following ritual assumes that the family is funding the tuition costs, although you'll find elements of it useful even if that is not the case. In families where there is an expectation that college fees are automatically paid by the family, I have found there is great value in creating a scholarship process like the one described next. It reduces the risk of entitlement and creates a healthy performance dynamic.

The Big Idea behind the Ritual

While academic goals are important, they are not sufficient to thrive at university. The aim of this ritual is for the college candidate to intentionally commit to who they want to be at college and to help them feel emotionally and relationally supported by the family.

What's Involved?

1. **Questionnaire and preparatory conversations**
   The college candidate completes a questionnaire (see the following example) and discusses the results with a trusted family member, education coordinator, or coach. The questions are designed to get them thinking about the challenges they may face at college and the values they want to hold on to. For most, these are not easy questions, and they may not yet have clear answers. That's okay. Through healthy conversations you will be able to help them to form a view and an intention for each question. The emphasis here is on helping the college candidate think about and be grounded in their values and be intentional about who they want to be at college. The goal is to start a conversation rather than to have all the answers.
   The output of these conversations forms the basis of the scholarship application, scholarship agreement, and the letter to the family, which is part of the sending ceremony.
2. **Scholarship agreement**
   Rather than simply pay for college fees, treat it as you would any other scholarship. There's an application, evaluation, and an agreement, which includes performance provisions.
   The responses to the questionnaire form the basis of the application. The college candidate should present their application for scholarship to the family. There should be as much emphasis on their ambition to grow in character as there is on academic achievement.
   I appreciate that this may seem like an unnecessary formality as the family is likely to pay for tuition in any case. The point is to be intentional and use this pivotal moment to build family culture and personal character. For the college candidate, the point is to see this gift of education as a privilege and to be intentional about who they want to become as they step into the next season of their life. For the family, it's a way to remind everyone that the opportunities created by abundance are sustained by healthy relationships and by our commitment to character and values.
3. **Sending ceremony**
   I remember when my older siblings left home. We would have a special family dinner and my father would give an emotional speech reminding them that they were loved, that they were always welcome home, and that they should stay true to our family values. And then, as was our family custom, we would pray.
   As the youngest, I was the last to leave. Dad invited me for a bike ride. It was the first (and last) time ever, so I knew it must be serious. He encouraged me to be confident in my identity and not compromise my values to conform to the expectations of others. Looking back now, I can see these sending rituals were my father's way of intentionally sending his children out to the world and to prepare us for our new independent season of life. His words continue to be a guiding force for us all.
   I encourage you to create a sending ceremony that is an authentic expression of your family.

Here's an outline I've used with families which can help get you started. This is a great opportunity to involve different generations and branches of the family.

Sending Ceremony Outline

	Key Talking Points
Introduction Led by senior family member or parents	• Leaving for college is a significant milestone. • In leaving for college, you leave home and continue your journey toward independence—taking responsibility for yourself. Many things will change. • It's good to take time to recognize and celebrate the new chapter of life you are entering. • It's also good to acknowledge the family scholarship which has made this possible.
College reflections and wisdom Contributions from older generations, mom, dad, aunts, uncles, etc.	• Older family members share three reflections/wisdom on thriving at college. • Note that there will be bumps on the way. Times of struggle and discomfort and even failure. Struggle is an important tutor and is how we grow. Don't give up.
The scholarship Led by the parents and the scholarship administrator	• A fully funded college education is only possible because of the wealth created by previous generations. • Using wealth to educate future generations is important to the family. • The family has established a scholarship fund to enable family members (and some nonfamily members too) to continue their education. • Brief overview of the agreement—highlights only—focus on the expectations and responsibilities section and discuss that preparing for leadership and managing wealth is about more than academic achievement, which is why we include contribution to others and living out family values as well. • Our desire is for you to have a holistic learning experience.
Letters from the college candidate Prepared by the college student	• The scholarship recipient prepares and reads a letter for the family. See following guidance.
The family affirmation	• Family members each briefly affirm and encourage the college candidate. It's important to affirm the commitment of the family to love and support the student no matter what.
Ceremonial gift	• Some families have a family emblem, wise quotes, or some other way to communicate what matters to the family. Consider creating an artifact that encompasses this to give to all those who leave home.

What Next?

If you have not tried "ritualizing" milestone moments in your family, I believe you are missing out on an important way to build individual character and family culture. While this College Sending Ritual has worked well with families I've worked with, it's vital that you make it your own. Use this example as a starting point to create this and many more family rituals. It's never too late to start.

Templates

Questionnaire—Completed by the College Candidate

Thriving at college: Preparing for new challenges and opportunities College is a formative time of life that impacts who we become as a person and as a professional. A good college experience will help prepare you as a future leader in society and the family and as a steward of family wealth.

Beyond your academic education, there is much more to learn at college. Think about what else you want to learn and how you would like to grow while at college.

During college you will be faced with many choices, the results of which will shape your character. You will need to decide before you start college whether you wish to shape the culture around you or be shaped by it. Much of this depends on the friends you choose from the day you arrive.

The following questions are designed to get you thinking about how you want to live and what you want to achieve at college.

1. Why did you choose your major? What are you hoping to do with it?
2. What would you like to achieve academically?
3. Beyond your academic education, what else would you like to achieve or do while you are at college?
4. What personal skills would you like to develop while at college?
5. What is your picture of a successful life?
6. What are three important character attributes/values that you want to be known for at college?
7. Beyond financial resources, what support would you like from the family while you are at college?
8. When making new friends at college, what attributes or qualities will you look for?
9. Describe the type of person who you think will be a poor influence on you (they will not bring out the best in you) and with whom you should probably not be close friends.
10. What do you think an appropriate allowance should be while at college? What ideas do you have to work part-time to earn more living allowance?
11. What will be the warning signs that you are not staying true to yourself and your values at college? What steps will you take?
12. What ideas do you have for how you would like to use your summer holidays to learn and to grow?
13. How will you keep the family informed of your progress at college?
14. Generosity and serving is a key family value. What opportunities will you look for to serve those in need while at university?
15. How will you respond when asked to participate in an activity that you feel is contrary to your values?

Family Education Scholarship Agreement—Example

The family mission supports ongoing education The financial wealth of the family was first created by [NAME]. The Family Office has been established to sustain and grow this wealth over multiple generations. The family desires to use this wealth not only to help those in need through the family foundation but also to educate future generations of the family.

The Family Education Scholarship Family members are eligible to receive a comprehensive education scholarship for the continuation of their education. An education scholarship is a privilege that is awarded at the discretion of the family and is conditional on meeting certain expectations and responsibilities that are detailed next.

Adjusting to campus life is challenging and the family commits to supporting you personally and emotionally as you start this exciting new chapter of your life.

What is included in the scholarship? The following table details what is included in the scholarship. The family will fund your first undergraduate level degree after which you will be eligible for a scholarship to undertake a master's degree or equivalent professional qualification.

Category	What the Scholarship Covers	Estimated Value per Year
Tuition fees	Tuition fees for the academic institution. The scholarship does not cover the cost of re-taking failed subjects. The cost of re-taking a failed subject is subject to family approval.	
Academic resources and activities	Purchase of required academic resources and participation in essential field trips—reimbursed based on receipts. Optional field trips to be evaluated on a case-by-case basis.	
Accommodation and meals provided by the university		
Living allowance	A discretionary living allowance paid monthly to cover offsite meals, entertainment, clothes, and college social activities. It is expected that this will be supplemented with income from part-time work.	
TOTAL ANNUAL VALUE		

What are the expectations and responsibilities associated with the scholarship? The family believes that academic achievement is just one part of your education. Equally important is the formation of character and growing in the virtues that will help you succeed not just in your profession or life generally but as stewards of family wealth and legacy.

	Expectations and Responsibilities—EXAMPLE
Academic achievement	• Apply yourself as your first priority fully to the completion of your studies. • Maintain an agreed-upon cumulative GPA, while taking subjects which are a mix of familiar and challenging. • Seek help and advise the family as soon as possible if falling behind in academic attainment.
Contribution to others	• Serving others is deeply enshrined in the family culture. • While campus life offers many opportunities for personal enjoyment, you are expected to seek opportunities to serve others on and off campus through volunteering, through giving financially, and through acts of kindness in day-to-day life. • During summer break, you will have an opportunity to visit and participate in projects that help others.
Personal development and growing independence	• Beyond academic studies, you are encouraged to develop personal (such as music, art, outdoor, media) and leadership skills through involvement in extracurricular activities as long as these do not compromise your academic goals. • During summer break you are encouraged to take on internships and participate in programmatic experiences that will help you grow personally and professionally.

	Expectations and Responsibilities—EXAMPLE
Living out family and personal values	• Campus life away from home presents temptations and opportunities that may not be consistent with your own or our family's values. • You are expected to live in a manner that represents your best self and the values of the family. Your desire should be to shape the culture around you rather than be shaped by it. • We encourage you to choose your friends wisely as this often has the most significant impact on your values. • This doesn't mean being perfect. We all make poor decisions and mistakes at times. We ask that you quickly acknowledge these and where necessary make changes.
Family communication	• It is expected that you report your grades and other volunteering and development activities to the family at the end of every term in a formal e-mail. • It is expected that you report to the family board at least annually relative to the expectations outlined in this agreement. • When facing challenges and struggles, we invite you to promptly seek the wise counsel and support of the family.

Performance

We recognize that you will face many challenges and setbacks and the family is here to support you to do your best. We invite you to seek support and guidance at any time.

It is important to communicate quickly and openly with the family if you feel you are struggling in any way or are unable to meet the expectations of the scholarship.

The scholarship may be withdrawn if, after attempts to improve your performance and after discussions with the family, you consistently fail to meet the expectations outlined previously.

Questions

The education scholarship is administered by [NAME] on behalf of the family. Any questions or comments regarding the scholarship together with regular reports should be directed to [NAME].

Scholarship Agreement

The family congratulates [NAME] on attaining admission to [COLLEGE] to study [DEGREE] and is pleased to offer a comprehensive scholarship as detailed here. The scholarship is subject to meeting the expectations and responsibilities outlined in this document.

Recipient Commitment

I gratefully accept this comprehensive education scholarship and commit myself to faithfully honoring the expectations and responsibilities detailed above.

Signed by recipient.	Date

Family Commitment

The family commits to supporting you financially, personally and emotionally throughout this scholarship and your academic studies. We are available to provide support and guidance at any time.

Signed (On behalf of the family)	Date

Guidelines for Letter Prepared by College Candidate for the Family

It is good to honor and thank your family for providing your college scholarship. One way to do this is by writing a letter to older generations before you head off. You will be invited to read this at the Sending Ceremony and provide copies to family members.

Your letter is an expression of what you feel. You may wish to include the following:

- Your appreciation and gratitude for the opportunity to continue your education made possible by the family scholarship
- Your commitment to try your best and apply yourself to your academic studies
- Your desire to honor your family and values
- Your personal values that will shape how you live at university and the friends you will make (reference your responses to the questionnaire)
- Beyond your academic studies what else you would like to achieve and the skills you would like to develop while at the university
- A commitment to update the family with your progress
- The warning signs that you feel may indicate that you have drifted off course and or away from your values

Biography

Too many families succeed financially but fail to thrive where it matters most—in their relationships. Through his advisory practice, Plenitude Partners, **Andrew Doust** helps families globally lay the foundation for intergenerational flourishing, preparing each member to enjoy more of what matters most in life and to navigate the complexities and opportunities of wealth.

In addition to his advisory work, Andrew has been instrumental in creating and leading KORE Venture's programming, a unique nonprofit organization that helps young leaders to grow in character, forge their identity apart from wealth, and find their unique path to purpose and fulfillment.

CHAPTER 39

Developmental Life Lessons for Grandchildren

William (Bo) and Suzanne Huhn

This chapter describes a process to be used by grandparents to convey personal development lessons to their grandchildren. Our specific effort was aimed at teaching the kids certain tools to protect them from substance abuse and addiction, but the process could be used to achieve other goals.

As we all know, wonderful things sometimes grow out of the most painful experiences. In our case, the disaster involved a daughter who lost her adolescent years to drug addiction. This was a horrible experience for her and our entire family. Fortunately, she fought her way to recovery, and we are very proud of her professional accomplishments and, even more important, her success as a wonderful mother.

As a result of the nightmare, we pondered a way to help protect our grandchildren. As the idea of developmental life lessons crystalized, we realized that our attitude and the process was more important than the specific lessons. We started with confidence and optimism. We decided to use a lot of humor and personal interaction. We figured this would be a long-term effort, requiring different media and much repetition. The goal was to slowly pound the lessons into the kids' bones over the course of years.

Before listing the lessons, it is important to describe the specifics of our process. This involved our four daughters (10-year age spread), their husbands, and 13 grandchildren (18-year age spread).

For six months in 2004, Bo wrote a one-page story each day and sent it to each of the grandchildren in the U.S. mail. He had four rules for the stories: Each daily installment had to be a maximum of one page, include humor, move the plot forward, and end on a note of suspense. The supposedly "true" story involved our family, our fearless Maltese dog, a tiger, a mongoose and a young prophet from India.

The story appeared to be pure entertainment, but the real goal was to teach the six life lessons. At the end of 186 days, we compiled the daily stories into an elegant, illustrated volume, which we gave to each grandchild at Christmas.

Then, starting in 2006, we gave each of the grandchildren a gift of $200 in cash and a Christmas letter containing the life lessons. They would focus on the cash first, but they always read the letters, and we would discuss the lessons.

In 2010, we purchased a nearby house as an investment, and for the next two summers, six of the grandchildren worked with us on the restoration. As we worked, we sought teaching opportunities for the lessons. We used a light touch, but kept at it. The kids teased us, especially Bo, but they understood that we were serious.

During the summer of 2012, our entire family spent a weekend in Hyannisport. Between outings and adventures, our 13 grandchildren worked in teams to teach the six lessons to each other and to their parents. The methods they chose to teach the lessons were very creative and funny.

In 2014 most of our grandchildren attended a forum at Bo's 50th college reunion at which he described the life lessons and their positive impact on the kids. Several years later, we and three of the grandchildren participated in a video about the lessons created by Don Opatrny, CEO of the Lovins Group Family Business Consulting Center. These were wonderful teaching opportunities.

We used a new game at Christmas in 2014 instead of a cash gift. We deposited $1,000 for each grandchild in a brokerage account. The kids had complete freedom to seek advice and decide how to invest (or not) their individual $1,000. At the end of the five years, each child would keep their investment. Our annual Christmas letters analyzed how the six life lessons applied to that year's game. There was much angst and humor as each year passed, and we discussed the success or failure of the various investing strategies. One of the youngest cousins was the overall winner; another lost his entire $1,000 on a bankrupt biotech bet.

We have described our process in detail to illustrate that a sustained effort is required to have a significant impact. Such an effort could be compared to one by a multinational corporation to create and teach a set of corporate values to all employees.

The Six Lessons (somewhat abridged):

Over the course of two years, we compiled a list of more than 30 ideas from many sources. These are the six we chose from that list:

1. You alone are responsible for your life. Not your parents, your teachers, your friends, or the government. They can help you or hurt you, but it is up to you to choose your path. You can choose the easy way or the hard way. Surprisingly the path of strength is the easy way.
2. Make conscious choices. There are inner reasons that motivate all behavior. For example, when children go out and ride around in a car destroying mailboxes with a baseball bat, they are not angry at mailboxes. If you are hurting and acting badly, consider what is really bothering you. Identify what you really want or need, and what will help you get it. This sounds easy but it is very, very hard.
3. Opportunities to learn are a blessing. School is not punishment. It is supposed to be hard. The happiest adults continue to learn throughout their lives.
4. Work to build on your strengths and to overcome your weaknesses. You are not a loser if you have flaws. Children aren't supposed to be finished at age

8 or age 21. (You won't be perfect until age 65!) Consider your flaws to be opportunities for growth. Pick the weakness that bothers you the most, and think about it. Ask for advice on how to overcome it. Work on it for several years. When you have changed yourself, pick the next self-improvement project. Continue this throughout your life.

5. Risk. Taking risks is an important part of growth and independence, but illegal or criminal risks should be avoided.
6. Peer pressure. Like many other animals, humans are genetically coded to run in packs. We live in communities and work in teams. This is a great strength, but beware of occasions when the pack is on the wrong path. Practice standing up against your peers. This can be of great value as an adult.

The most effective part of the teaching process has been informal, not the planned initiatives. Throughout the year, we watch for teaching opportunities to reinforce the six lessons, and gently introduce them into our conversations.

For example, in our stock market competition, our cautious oldest grandchild held her $1,000 in the account for more than a year. As the stock market went up her mother urged her to make an investment. Soon after she did, the market plummeted. At a family dinner, Emily began to blame her mother for the loss. We then teased her unmercifully about Lesson One: "You are responsible for your life, not your mother!" We all laughed, yet it was a good reminder.

A final comment on the process. We did not ask the grandchildren to memorize the lessons, and most of them could not recite all six when asked. We discussed this with one of our granddaughters, Mary, who was a high school sophomore at the time. She was embarrassed that she couldn't recite the exact lessons. We reminded her that Lesson One is: "You are responsible for your life, not your parents, your teachers, your friends, or the government. . .." Mary said: "Of course I'm the one responsible—that's fundamental. I don't understand why so many people don't know that." If you knew Mary, you'd know that is an intrinsic part of her personality. Did the life lessons contribute to her strength? We are sure they did. We also discussed the peer pressure lesson. Mary said: "No one can make me do something I don't want to. Why are so many kids afraid to be different than their friends? It's stupid." The peer pressure lesson also is deeply ingrained, a part of her core strength.

In conclusion none of the grandchildren used alcohol or drugs in their teens; several didn't drink alcohol in college; and those that did, in moderation. No one has used drugs, including marijuana. The older cousins have been instrumental in teaching the younger ones, and the younger group has loved being included as equals in the discussions and activities. There has been a lot of teaching from one family group to another. The life lessons have definitely been something that brought all the cousins together, providing a unique shared experience.

Additional Resources

For more details, check the community website at www.itsworthitguilford.org.

Go to the "for grandparents" tab on the left side of the website for a few sample letters from BEAU DOG, THE TIGER, THE MONGOOSE AND THE PROPHET, A GRANDFATHER'S TRUE STORY, and our Christmas letter with the six life lessons. Don Opatrny's video can be found at: https://vimeo.com/lovinsgroup. Questions? Call us at (Home) 203 453-2872, e-mail whihn@snet.net, or text Suzanne at 203-928-9931.

Biography

Bo Huhn received a BA Yale 1964 and LLB Yale 1967, and **Zanne Huhn** a BA from Wellesley in 1966. She is currently pursuing a masters in environmental studies from Southern Connecticut. Bo worked as a lawyer for IBM (antitrust) and Pfizer (general law and environmental law), and Zanne as a Lamaze educator and OB/GYN nurse. We have four daughters and 13 grandchildren and have lived in Guilford, Connecticut, since 1972. We focused much energy and thought on our family and are blessed to have strong and close relationships.

CHAPTER 40

Deciding If You Should Join the Family Business

Josh Baron and Rob Lachenauer

Working in a family business, whether it's your immediate family, a family that you've married into, or someone else's family, brings its own forms of challenges and rewards. The decision to accept *any* full-time job offer can be stressful. But with family businesses, the choices can be far more complicated: It's as much an unspoken social contract as an employment one—and the consequences can last far longer. Even the most highly qualified family members have a hard time navigating the emotional mix of expectation, obligation, uncertainty, and desire for professional success when faced with the decision.

When bright, ambitious young people talk about career prospects with a prospective employer, they are typically full of questions about how that company will support their professional growth. But remarkably, the same young people will confess that the prospect of joining their own family business leaves them tongue-tied. In families whose culture has been one of deep respect for those who are in the day-to-day trenches of the business, young family members often worry that asking too many questions might make them seem presumptuous or pushy. We get it. Asking too many questions can seem entitled. But we have seen many family relationships fractured from poor communication at the start of a family business job. This is *your* career. And *your* family. Making the wrong decision because you're afraid to ask good questions can lead to heartache for everyone.

When deciding whether to join your family business full-time, **consider the following 10 questions and then rate your responses in the scorecard**. It's important that you effectively navigate the emotional mix of expectation, obligation, uncertainty, and desire for professional success when faced with the decision. As with any such complex decision, there will be pros and cons. We urge you to explore both. The following questions will help you articulate what's driving your decision, what you need to understand and accept about your family business, and what the road ahead might look like if you decide to join.

1. Assess your motivation: First, you should consider *why* you are interested in joining. Check that your motivations are healthy ones. How does what you can contribute to your family business compare with what you might bring to any other potential career options? Be sure to articulate your own reasons and ensure they are compelling enough to make your single largest career decision. Rank your key motivators (1, lowest, to 10, highest) to joining your family business:

A. I'm excited about my career potential in my family business. __
B. I believe I have the ability to contribute to the success of my family business. __
C. The financial rewards relative to other career opportunities are acceptable to me. __
D. I always wanted to work in my family business since I was young and I'm clear why. __
E. I want to make sure I help protect the ownership of my family branch. __
F. I'm excited about working in the industry of my family business. __
G. I want to live up to the expectations of others. __
H. It may be the best job I can get. __
I. I love working with my family. __
J. I feel an obligation to my family. __
K. Other motivators you may have. __

Evaluating your top three to five motivators above, do you think they are appropriate for your career decision? What concerns do you have?

____

____

Is this your "highest and best use"? Is this the career path that will make the best use of your talents, interests and ambitions? Or could you be happier and more successful elsewhere?

____

____

Get a second opinion. Discuss with people who have your best interest at heart and ask if they see your motivations as you do and whether, with those motivations, they'd advise you to join your family business.

2. Do you already have significant outside experience? In most cases, we recommend that family members get a college degree and then work in another company for at least three to five years. Demonstrating to your family business leaders, managers, and employees that you're capable of earning a genuine promotion for your work outside the company helps ensure that you're appropriately valued in your own family business.

3. Is this a real job? When you enter the family business, make sure it's for a real job, not one that has been made up for you.

4. How ready are you for the commitment? Joining your family business requires you to be all-in. Your family life and business life will be conflated. Your personal identity will be more tied to your work than it would be if you go elsewhere.

5. Are the personal relationships among the family leaders healthy enough? Do you see evidence that the leaders can make good decisions together about the future of the company? Can your own relationships in the family withstand the pressures of working together in the future?

6. Do you understand how ownership in the business works? Who are the current and future owners? Will you be required to work in the business to be eligible for future ownership? Who gets to decide who can be owners in the future?

7. Do you know who will make decisions about your career? Will you be treated differently than nonfamily employees? Who will be helping you develop and grow? How will the decisions about your career be considered? Who gets to weigh in? Don't assume you will have a typical career path—ask.

8. Are your goals and priorities aligned with the current owners? Do you actually know the goals of the current owners? Do they prioritize growth, liquidity, or control? A combination of two? If you don't know their goals, you should consider raising this topic with the current owner group.

9. Will you be in the loop on critical conversations? Just because you're family doesn't mean you'll be in the inner circle. Do you understand how much information about the business will be shared with you? Are you okay with the answer?

10. Will leadership succession take place in a way that works out for you? Are you hoping that joining the business means you're on the path to the C-suite? Is that a realistic hope? Do you know how the current owners plan to transition business leadership in the future? And are you okay if that's not a likely path for you?

Family Employment Scorecard

Having thought about the previous questions, assess yourself on the following statements as a way to gauge whether you are ready to join the family business (and whether the *business* is ready for you to join). For each statement, determine if you are "red" (there's danger here), "yellow" (there are some concerns but can proceed with caution), or "green" (no concerns, good to proceed). If you are unsure, you can mark "don't know."

	Green	Yellow	Red	Don't Know
1. Are you clear about your motivation for joining the family business? The right motivations?				
2. Do you have enough outside experience work already? Do you know what it is to be known by your first name and not just your last name?				
3. Is this a real job or one that has been made up just to provide you work?				
4. Are you ready for the commitment?				
5. Are the personal relationships among family leaders healthy enough for career success?				

	Green	Yellow	Red	Don't Know
6. Do you understand how ownership in the business works and is that attractive to you?				
7. Do you know who will make decisions about your career and are you okay with the approach?				
8. Are your goals and priorities aligned with the current owners?				
9. Will you be in the loop or a voice on critical career conversations?				
10. Will leadership succession take place in a way that works out for you?				

After you've completed your analysis, check your assumptions and expectations in a conversation with the family business leaders about what lies in store for you if you do join the business. It may feel awkward to have this conversation, but your ability to have a candid conversation about these issues is one of the best indications that your employment will be well accepted.

Use our "scorecard" to think through what you need to understand about your family business before joining. The point of the questions and the scorecard is not to get to a single "right" answer, but rather it is to help make sure you are making a thoughtful choice. If you see a significant number of "red" or "don't know" answers, you probably have a lot more homework to do. Are the "red" answers long-term impediments or challenges that can be overcome with appropriate conversations and planning? If you see mostly greens and yellows, you're probably heading in the right direction. We hope this exercise will help guide the necessary conversations you should have with yourself and with family members about whether joining the family business is a good decision for you.

This is an adapted excerpt from the "Family Employment Policy" chapter of the Harvard Business Review Family Business Handbook.

Additional Resources

Sam Bruehl and Rob Lachenauer, "How Family Business Owners Should Bring the Next Generation into the Company," *Harvard Business Review* (July 24, 2018), https://hbr.org/2018/07/how-family-business-owners-should-bring-the-next-generation-into-the-company.

Josh Baron, "The Common Traps of Working in Your Family's Business," *Harvard Business Review* (November 6, 2017), https://hbr.org/2017/11/the-common-traps-of-working-in-your-familys-business.

Biography

Dr. Josh Baron is a co-founder and partner at BanyanGlobal. He is co-author of the *Harvard Business Review Family Business Handbook.* For the last decade, he has worked closely with families who own assets together, such as operating companies, family foundations, and family offices. He helps these families to define their purpose as owners and to establish the structures, strategies, and skills they need to accomplish their goals. Josh is also an adjunct professor at Columbia Business School, where he teaches MBA courses on family business management and managing conflict in family business. He also teaches in the Enterprising Families Executive Education Program.

Rob Lachenauer, a co-founder and managing partner of BanyanGlobal, has been an advisor, business leader, and writer throughout his career. He is co-author of the *Harvard Business Review Family Business Handbook.* As an advisor, he was a partner at the Boston Consulting Group, where he helped family-controlled and other businesses set and implement growth strategies. While at BCG, he co-authored *Hardball: Are You Playing to Play or Playing to Win?* with George Stalk. Rob has worked closely with scores of family businesses throughout the world, helping them navigate the decisions they face as owners while strengthening family relationships.

CHAPTER 41

How Can You Ensure the Success of Your Successors?

Dean Fowler

How can a mentor help to ensure the success of a family enterprise successor? One effective way is by encouraging successors to emulate behavior that fosters continuity of the business from one generation to the next. In consulting with numerous family businesses over the past 40 years, I have identified seven habits of highly successful successors (with apologies to Stephen R. Covey, author of *The 7 Habits of Highly Effective People*). Good mentors promote these best practices and guide their protégés in adopting them.

These seven habits encompass the three distinct roles of successors in family enterprises: family membership, company management, and business ownership. The first two—establishing independence and reshaping communication dynamics—nurture healthy family relationships and typically develop during the protégé's 20s.

The next three—demonstrating competency, participating in strategic decisions, and clarifying boundaries—provide the framework for management responsibilities and growth during the protégé's 30s.

Finally, by developing liquidity strategies and assuming financial risk, successors are transformed from passive shareholders into proactive participants in ownership of the business. This final stage of mastery typically occurs during the protégé's late 30s and 40s.

Many of these principles can also apply to families who don't have operating business, but who still operate together as a group, such as families with holding companies, substantial financial liquidity and combined philanthropic activities.

Nurture Healthy Family Relationships

1. Establishing Independence

The first habit—establishing adult independence—serves as the foundation for the other six by transforming the relationship between the two generations. Mentors should encourage their protégés to establish their own adult lives, separate from and independent of their family and its business. In many cases, this means working outside the family firm. Outside experience helps a young adult to gain technical competency and business experience. More important, this experience helps next-generation members to overcome emotional dependence on their parents and to prove to themselves that they can function independently of their parents' financial resources.

As an alternative to working outside the family enterprise, mentors can help their protégés to identify key projects over which the protégé may exert leadership. Taking charge of a project enables young people to succeed in their own independent efforts. For example, one successor identified an opportunity to provide additional services to customers of the family business. Under the tutelage of the chief financial officer, she developed a formal business plan that outlined the financial viability of her business proposal. Using family venture capital, this successor started a separate business. As president of this venture, she had full authority and responsibility for future success.

2. Reshaping Family Communication

It's the successor's responsibility to reshape communication dynamics within the family and to break the patterns of childhood. Two skills are critical to achieving this new pattern of interaction. The first is the ability to avoid what's known as triangulation. This unhealthy communication pattern often occurs when conflict, anger, resentment, or frustration has built up between two people. To alleviate this build-up, one of the people "downloads" the negative feelings by sharing them with a third person instead of discussing the conflict directly with the other party. For example, if a daughter disagrees with a decision made by her father, she might complain about the situation to her mother, although the issue would be best resolved if she raised the issue with her father.

Nonfamily employees and managers are often caught in the dangerous pull of triangulation. Rather than be drawn into this scenario, a mentor can impart a valuable lesson by refusing to participate as a triangulated party. Instead, the mentor should encourage the two people in conflict to address their issues in an open and straightforward manner.

The second communication skill is active (or empathic) listening. The power of this skill rests in the listener's ability to really understand the perspective of another person. Family members must recognize that everyone needs assurance that he or she has been understood. Mentors must master active listening in order to really understand the needs of their protégés. For example, one daughter was frustrated because she felt that her father didn't really listen to her. Her mentor, the vice president (VP) of human resources, helped her to develop her own listening skills. Building on the communication principles the VP taught her, she created a code—A or O—and presented it to her father. When she wanted his acceptance, she told him the conversation was an A; when she wanted his opinion, she told him it was an O. With the help of her mentor, she took the responsibility to reshape communication dynamics with her entrepreneurial father.

Framework for Management Responsibilities and Growth

3. Demonstrating Competency

The third habit to teach your protégé concerns competency. This habit has two dimensions: technical competency in some area of the business and demonstrated leadership capability.

Training and development programs for successors are often designed to give them limited exposure to several different aspects of a company. Although this broad-based exposure is helpful, it doesn't enable the successor to develop any detailed technical expertise. More significantly, the successor isn't given the opportunity to develop as a leader by managing direct reports.

To become competent, successors should assume long-term responsibilities that require leadership. Initially, this may involve the responsibility of overseeing a significant project and heading the project team. As experience grows and develops, successors should take on departmental leadership roles or divisional responsibilities, where profit and loss results may be measured and evaluated. In one family firm, the vice president of operations was asked to develop a comprehensive training program for the family successor. The president of the company considered mentoring to be an important part of the VP's responsibilities. These duties became part of the VP's primary goals and objectives and were measured as part of his annual performance review. Working closely with his protégé, the VP developed a four-year program that culminated in the protégé's ascent to management responsibility for a major division of this international business.

In addition to financial measures, a "360-degree" leadership performance review is an effective tool to identify strengths and weaknesses as protégés develop their leadership capabilities. In this review process, managers, peers, and direct reports of the protégé all complete a questionnaire that evaluates the next-generation member on several key dimensions of effective leadership. The questionnaires are compiled anonymously in order to ensure frankness and pinpoint areas of leadership development where the protégé needs additional mentoring.

4. Participating in Strategic Decisions

The fourth habit mentors teach their protégés relates to the development of business strategy. Successors are frequently involved in day-to-day operational issues without participating in strategic decisions. They must learn about strategy early in their careers by defining how their own projects fit into the broader strategy of the business. Typically, one of the senior executives who participates in the corporate strategic planning process helps the successor to develop project management skills. The mentor guides the protégé in determining how best to align the successor's projects with the strategic goals of the business, rather than simply to develop day-to-day tactics in reaction to business circumstances.

Successful successors take the strategic process one step further; they partner with the senior generation to define future strategies that fit the passions and competency of the successor generation. In one family business that specialized in long-haul trucking, a successor recognized that the company's communication technology and logistics expertise could also serve other businesses in managing their own private fleets. The vice president of operations helped him to prepare a strategic plan that outlined how these core competencies could be leveraged to create a separate profit center for the business.

5. Clarifying Boundaries

Perhaps one of the greatest challenges facing business successors involves clarifying the boundaries separating operational responsibilities, the development of strategy, and corporate financial decisions. Effective mentors help their protégés negotiate these boundaries, which are typically complicated by role confusion between family membership and company management. Parents, as the primary shareholders of the business, usually maintain control of the major strategic and financial issues that affect the company while delegating operational responsibilities and accountability to their direct reports, including their children with management positions in the company.

Conflicts between the generations are often rooted in two distinct issues. First, the senior generation will delegate operational responsibilities without defining clear expectations and performance measures and then will step back in to take control when the outcomes don't meet their undefined expectations. Second, the senior generation is often risk-averse, whereas the successor generation wants to implement strategies to grow the business for the next 20 years.

When conflict and tension exist between parents and their children working in the business, mentors play a very important role as mediators between the two generations. One nonfamily president was given the challenge of balancing two alternative strategic solutions to a current business situation. With sales declining, the father wanted to reduce overhead expenses in order to bring the company back to profitability. The son, on the other hand, wanted to hire a sales manager to build future business opportunities. The mentor worked with both the father and the son to objectively evaluate the pros and cons of each alternative. The alternatives were then presented during the formal strategic planning process, so that the entire executive team could determine the best strategy to pursue.

Transforming from Passive Shareholders into Proactive Participants

6. Developing Liquidity Strategies

The first five habits that protégés must master define key characteristics of any successful manager (family or nonfamily) who may be considered for executive responsibilities and leadership of a company. The next two habits—developing liquidity strategies and assuming financial risk—involve areas where family membership, management expertise, and ownership dynamics intersect.

Although most family businesses have an estate plan that addresses financial issues in the event of the death of the majority owner(s), very few develop liquidity strategies to restructure the capital of the business while the senior generation is still alive. With life expectancy now in the late 80s to early 90s, more successors are recognizing the need to design a mechanism for buying the business from their inactive siblings or cousins, as well as from the senior generation.

Mentors must discuss with their protégés various approaches to financing a smooth intergenerational transition. Successors should take a proactive role in learning about effective strategies for recapitalization of the business. For example, one family is wrestling with the question, "Should we sell our business to a strategic buyer?" A nonfamily president manages the day-to-day responsibilities of the business and has explicit instructions from the board of directors to serve in a mentoring capacity to the successor generation. As part of their quarterly board meetings, the successors have been investigating several alternative scenarios. Under the guidance and direction of the nonfamily president, they have explored an employee stock ownership plan (ESOP) to create diversification and liquidity for the senior generation, new buy/sell agreements among siblings to structure future redemptions, funded nonqualified retirement programs for the senior generation, and finally, the pros and cons of selling the business to a strategic buyer. Guided by the nonfamily president, the successors have been given the responsibility of meeting with their parents' advisors, and other experts to identify the best possible options and then make their recommendations to the board of directors. The board will take the successors' recommendations under advisement and make a decision about the future ownership of the business.

7. Assuming Financial Risk

In most family businesses, successors are owners by virtue of being gifted nonvoting stock. In this respect, the successors are essentially participating in estate planning tactics rather than assuming the responsibilities of ownership. Mentors must encourage their protégés to become involved in the financial aspects of the business as a way of transforming themselves into responsible owners. Early in a protégé's career, this involves teaching the young person how to read financial statements and explaining the impact of this financial information on business decisions. Mentors should introduce successors to bankers and other trusted advisors and should explain that developing a relationship with these key people will help establish successors' credibility.

To move from being passive recipients of a gift to active owners of stock, successors must be willing to take their own financial risk. For example, in one family business that acquired a competitor, the bank asked all family members to personally guarantee the loans. Some family managers were unwilling to co-sign such a document, thereby demonstrating their lack of commitment to taking financial risk. The willingness to take on personal financial liability demarcates the difference between management and ownership roles.

Liquidity strategies and corresponding financial issues are rarely addressed in family-owned businesses. Most mentoring activities focus on the first five habits. Patience is a virtue. These seven habits of successful successors can't be developed all at once; they represent a gradual process, with each habit building on the previous one, over a time span of about two decades. As family members, successors must first take the initiative in developing adult independence and reshaping family communication patterns. In their roles as managers, they must develop technical competency and demonstrate leadership; they must also help to shape the business's strategic plan and must clarify the boundaries that distinguish operational, strategic, and financial roles. As owners, successors must be proactive in designing liquidity strategies and then be willing to assume financial risk to consolidate ownership for their generation.

Successors must be patient as they navigate their way through these seven steps. Mentors must demonstrate patience themselves by embodying this virtue in their interactions with their protégés. Mastery of these seven habits is a challenging process. The senior generation and other family members must be willing to accept and encourage the transition of the business from generation to generation.

Use the following exercise to rate the chances of your family enterprise based on the success factors reviewed above and make changes to your strategy as necessary.

Family Enterprise for Succession Success Assessment (1 = Poor, 5 = Excellent)

____ Habit One: Establish adult independence.

(Reflection question: Have family members achieved their own psychological and financial independence separate from the extended family?)

____ Habit Two: Reshape family communication.

(Reflection question: Has the family developed effective patterns of communication based on trust and respect?)

____ Habit Three: Develop competency.

(Reflection question: Do family members have the necessary competency to be effective in their current roles in the family business, and is there a career-development plan to develop additional competencies for advancement in the organization?)

____ Habit Four: Design strategy.

(Reflection question: Is there alignment within the family concerning corporate strategy, and do members of the rising generation participate in designing the strategy for the future?)

____ Habit Five: Clarify boundaries.

(Reflection question: Between the generations as well as among siblings and cousins are the boundaries, roles, and responsibilities clearly defined?)

____ Habit Six: Coordinate liquidity strategies.

(Reflection question: In addition to the estate plan for the transition of ownership at death, is there a plan to transfer ownership and control from the senior to the successor generation during the lifetime of the senior generation?)

____ Habit Seven: Take financial risks.

(Reflection question: Is the next generation willing to take on the financial risks of ownership?)

TOTAL
31–35, Excellent. 24–30, More Work Needed. Below 24, Danger Zone.

Additional Resources

Dean Fowler and Peg Masterson Edquist, *Love, Power and Money: Family Business Between Generations* (Brookfield, WI: Glengrove Publishing, 2002).

Dean Fowler and Peg Masterson Edquist, *Family Business Matters* (Brookfield, WI: Glengrove Publishing, 2017).

Dean Fowler, *Proactive Family Business Successors* (Brookfield, WI: Glengrove Publishing, 2011).

Biography

Dean R. Fowler, Ph.D., is recognized as one of the world's leading family business advisors. For more than 30 years, he has facilitated Forums for Family Business™—peer advisory boards—that specialize in personal and professional development through diversified experiences and accountability, while focusing on successful intergenerational transitions. Forum members are committed to living an amazing life and growing their family legacies with confidence.

With his team of consultants, Dean Fowler Consulting, LLC also serves families-in-business and families of wealth as they transition from one generation to the next. Through our research and years of experience we have identified 12 critical competencies that all families must master for success.

CHAPTER 42

The Intergenerational Dialogue

Susan Massenzio

Effective family communication is core to the flourishing of any family, and regular family meetings are a key practice for advancing family communication.

In using the rare and precious time together at a family meeting, it's common to want to talk about what matters most to the members of the family. What is it that's really on their minds? What concerns do they have? Where could they use each other's help? What would they truly like to say to each other?

As deep as this desire is, it can be hard to make it a reality. Most family members shy away from meaningful conversations. We fall into past patterns of communication or behavior. The business of the everyday fills the space.

That's why my Wise Counsel Research colleague, Dr. Keith Whitaker, and I developed what we call the Intergenerational Dialogue. A simple process, it gives structure to these meaningful conversations, and it helps family members use their time together as productively as possible.

Dr. Whitaker and I believe the two paramount goals of family meetings are, first, that family members leave the meeting feeling that the time together was very well spent, and second, they leave the meeting looking forward to the next one. The Intergenerational Dialogue is a great way to achieve both these goals, and while it can benefit from expert facilitation, some families can organize it on their own.

Goal

The goal of the Intergenerational Dialogue is enhanced communication and learning. It is a tool to help family members communicate effectively and learn what is most important to each other.

The Intergenerational Dialogue is structured around two main questions posed to each member of the family:

1. What messages would I like to share with or tell members of the other generation (or generations) of my family?
2. What questions would I like to ask or learn about from members of the other generation (or generations) of my family?

The Intergenerational Dialogue opens space in family members' heads and gets those important messages or questions on the table for other family members to receive or reflect upon.

The Intergenerational Dialogue is not about critiquing one another's messages. Nor is it primarily about answering all the questions. We have held many Intergenerational Dialogues that resulted in the family composing a list of questions that each generation then set out to research or think about and then come back at a future family meeting to answer. But this research or thinking couldn't take place when the questions remained in family members' heads, unspoken.

The Intergenerational Dialogue is set up as one between generations rather than individuals. For example, if a family has two adult generations present at a family meeting (parents and adult children), then the Dialogue is between these two generations. Parents will share their messages and questions with their adult children, and adult children will share their messages and questions with their parents. Sometimes larger families will have three adult generations present at a family meeting: grandparents, parents, and adult children. In that case, each generation will address its messages and questions to two different generations. The elder generation will share messages and questions for the middle generation and for the rising generation; the middle generation will share messages and questions for the elder generation, on the one hand, and the rising generation, on the other; and the rising generation will share separate messages and questions for the middle generation and for the elder generation.

The reason for setting up this Dialogue as between generations rather than individuals is twofold. First, it can be challenging, especially in a family meeting setting, for an individual to share deep, heartfelt messages or pressing questions with his or her family members. By speaking as a generation, no one individual is in the spotlight. Second, this process requires that the individuals in each generation work with each other, as a generation, to come up with messages and questions. Members of each generation get practice in communicating and making decisions together. This is a valuable additional benefit for any family that is managing finances or a business together.

Process

To prepare for the Intergenerational Dialogue, family members should know beforehand that the family meeting will include this exercise. They should understand how it will work and what its goals are. This step also gives each family member a chance to start thinking about the messages or questions he or she would like to share before the meeting takes place.

In designing the agenda for the family meeting, we recommend that the family set aside one hour for the Intergenerational Dialogue. A larger family, with three generations and many members, we recommend setting aside 90 minutes.

Within the meeting, the Intergenerational Dialogue session begins with each generation breaking off into its own separate space for 20 minutes. During this time, members of each generation will discuss those two questions: "What messages do I want to share with or tell members of the other generation(s)?" and "What questions do I want to ask or learn about from members of the other generation(s)?" Depending on the size of each generational group, each member can share his or her thoughts, or it can be a general discussion.

After the time for reflection as a generation, the generations rejoin as a whole family and begin to share their messages and questions in the ways that each group has decided. (Before rejoining the main group, we advise that each generation decide who will share that generation's messages and questions with the main group. Sometimes multiple members from each generation do the sharing.) As each generation shares its messages and questions, the other generation(s) should listen respectfully without asking follow-up questions or making comments. Someone—either a nonfamily facilitator or a family member—should keep track of the questions posed by each generation for the other(s).

When each generation has had a chance to share its messages and questions, the family may want to set aside 10–15 minutes for reactions or responses. The goal of this time is not to try to answer all the questions that have been posed, though if some of the questions can be answered, that is fine. Generally, families use this time to reflect their gratitude for the messages that have been shared and the questions that have been raised.

Follow-Up

Many families make the Intergenerational Dialogue a regular part of their annual or biannual family meetings. After the first Intergenerational Dialogue, it makes sense to use future meetings as a chance to respond to questions that were raised and deepen the messages that were shared.

Sometimes the Intergenerational Dialogue will surface questions that prompt extra reflection. For example, it's not uncommon to see rising generation family members ask their parents, "What are your expectations for us, regarding the money that you have given us or that you're planning to give us? Do you have specific wishes for how we should spend, save, or give the money that you are transitioning to us?" These are questions that the parents may want to think about and respond to at the next family meeting. The parents may even want to write up responses to such questions in the form of a Letter of Wishes or Statement of Intent.

Sometimes questions arise that require further research. For example, rising generation family members may ask how the trusts already established for them will "work." Often parents are not able to explain the distribution standards or fiduciary arrangements of trusts they've created, so these questions open the door for a future meeting, perhaps at which members of the family's estate planning team or trustees join to walk through those details.

Conclusion

Direct, honest communication is the lifeblood of a family. But it's not easy. Direct, honest communication is a challenge for many people in their interpersonal relations. When we try to communicate directly and honestly with family members, it is even more of a challenge. Then, if we add topics such as money, estate planning, family business succession, and the like to family conversations, we further intensify the challenge. The Intergenerational Dialogue is a proven and simple process for effectively enhancing communication within families. Dr. Whitaker and I believe the Intergenerational Dialogue can provide the structure that will encourage family conversations about what truly matters most to you and your loved ones.

Additional Resources

James E. Hughes, Jr., Susan E. Massenzio, and Keith Whitaker, *Cycle of the Gift* (New York: Wiley, 2012).

James E. Hughes, Jr., Susan E. Massenzio, and Keith Whitaker, *Voice of the Rising Generation* (New York: Wiley, 2014).

Hartley Goldstone, James E. Hughes, and Keith Whitaker, *Family Trusts* (New York: Wiley, 2015).

Biography

Susan Massenzio is a psychologist with extensive experience consulting to senior executives and leadership teams of Fortune 500 financial services firms and family businesses. She helps leaders make a positive impact through enhanced communication, effective decision-making, and cultivation of rising generation leadership. Susan is co-author of *The Cycle of the Gift*, *The Voice of the Rising Generation*, and *Complete Family Wealth.* Susan served as the senior psychologist for John Hancock Financial Services, senior vice president for Wells Fargo Bank, and professor and program director at Northeastern University. Susan holds a Ph.D. in psychology from Northwestern University and a BA in sociology and education from Simmons College.

SECTION 7

NAVIGATING FAMILY DYNAMICS

Readers will no doubt notice that many chapters of this book would be at home in multiple sections. For example, the same exercise may touch upon What Matters Most, Planning Thoughtfully, and Making Shared Decisions.

This is especially the case with tools and practices devoted to enhancing a family's dynamic, that is, its members' ability to communicate, collaborate, and treat each other with respect, fairness, and trust. The chapters that we have collected in this section represent just a few of those that can help readers in this area.

To begin, Keith Whitaker offers a summary of a very powerful exercise first developed by Charles Collier, senior philanthropic advisor at Harvard University, and described by Charlie in the first *Wealth of Wisdom* volume. This "Three-Step Process" involves individual reflection, sharing those reflections with the other family members (and hearing their thoughts), and then identifying common ground for next steps. It can be used in its simplest form by couples, but it can also be applied to siblings, parents, and children, or even conversations among cousins or more distant relations.

Most families don't recognize all the factors that keep them together; they observe these factors only in their absence, when conflict threatens to erupt. In the next chapter, Blair Trippe and Doug Baumoel give readers a construct by which to evaluate their "family factor"—the combination of shared history, shared vision, and trust—that allows a family to work together effectively. Based upon this evaluation, they also offer specific steps for building that family factor.

The family factor is one way to understand what ties families together. Another is through the genogram, a tool that Guillermo Salazar describes, which provides a graphical representation of family relationships, past and present. Family members can use this tool to better understand the source of certain beliefs or habits in their family history and, then, to identify ways to adapt current behaviors to enhance relationships and to redress old hurts.

Often these historical hurts or beliefs keep families from effectively discussing important choices, even in the midst of crisis. In the next chapter, Michelle Osry describes a process for communication—the Generative Dialogue Framework—that gives families structure for talking about emotionally difficult topics. This framework helps family members recognize when they are mired in "politeness" or stuck in "breakdown" and how to move the conversation to "inquiry" and ultimately "flow."

The next chapter, by Ian McDermott, is not specific to family dynamics, but the practice it describes fits so well with the other tools and practices described here, that this section seemed its natural home. In it, McDermott describes the difference between two sorts of questions: "Problem-Frame" and "Outcome-Frame." Neither is good or bad by itself, but McDermott shows how a problem-frame can often leave us feeling stuck, while switching to questions with an outcome-frame can make us and the people we're talking with feel empowered.

One of the most common dynamics felt within families with significant wealth is the burden of poorly communicated expectations. Many family members feel (accurately) that benefits come with "strings attached," which makes no one feel good. In the next chapter, Mimi Ramsey and Stephanie Hardwick offer readers a simple framework for evaluating how they are feeling in response to expectations, what unfulfilled expectations are causing these feelings, how they could request to clarify the expectations, and what agreements they could forge among family members to make all parties feel understood. This is a true journey from "problem" to "outcome."

When it comes to family dynamics, parent-child relations probably receive the most attention, especially in the context of the transition of finances or power from one generation to the next. However, sibling relationships often generate the greatest heat, and in families where the founding generation has passed away, siblings are the ones who have to find ways to work together. That is why in this next chapter Christian Stewart gives readers a worksheet to evaluate their sibling relationships on measures related to shared values, trust, honesty, collaborative skills, and much more. The results of the worksheet provide direction for specific efforts to improve these crucial relationships.

Another way to describe family dynamics is the "game" that each family plays. Family games have very specific (though unwritten) rules, and participants know their parts. The family game can help the family through many tough spots, though inevitably there come times when the game no longer works so well. It's at moments like this when Matt Wesley's contribution on "Gamechanging" can prove most powerful. Gamechanging involves carefully observing the family game and then deciding what one change to the game could serve as a "pivot" to change the family's behavior. It takes time and honest communication, but the model of gamechanging allows for fundamental reorientation rather than trying to change one practice or policy after another—only to see the "game" stymy these partial efforts.

CHAPTER 43

A Three-Step Process for Enhanced Communication

Keith Whitaker

Whether the topic is estate planning, philanthropy, or raising children with sound values, advisors often ask clients to step back and clarify what their goals are. But how does the typical set of parents—Mom and Dad—do that? It's easier said than done.

The closer we are to someone else, the more likely we assume we know what he or she is thinking. These assumptions can easily take the place of listening and understanding what's actually going on. Jumping to conclusions can nip communication in the bud before it's even taken place.

Alternatively, many couples know, from their partners' choices and behaviors, that they are in different places about important topics. Rather than confront those differences, it may seem easier to avoid talking about them altogether. As a result, planning or important decisions can be delayed, deferred, and ultimately abandoned.

But perhaps the greatest difficulty facing couples with regard to communication is not between the two partners but within each of them. Often each of us is so busy thinking about what the other person may be thinking or feeling, or what (we think) he or she is going to say, that we do not face, and clarify, what it is that we think or want. But how can we effectively communicate with our nearest and dearest if we don't even know what's in our own hearts?

Charles Collier

In the face of these challenges, our long-time colleague Charles "Charlie" Collier developed what he called the "three-step process" of communication for couples. For many years Charlie was the senior philanthropic advisor for Harvard College. He often spoke with couples who were contemplating major gifts to the school. Yet he made a point of talking little about Harvard. Instead, he would ask these givers what their dreams were, what their hopes and concerns were, what they wanted for their children and grandchildren and the world around them.

As a result of asking these and many more questions, Charlie often had occasion to observe that members of a couple came to these important topics with different perspectives and sometimes different values. He also observed how challenging it could be even for the closest couples to share and talk through these differences. From working through these challenges with his donors, Charlie developed the three-step process.

The Three-Step Process

As with most good things, the three-step process is simple—once someone like Charlie points it out.

1. First step: each member of the couple reflects on his or her own and through that reflection clarifies his or her own individual view of the topic.
2. Second step: each member of the couple shares his or her view with the other. The other member listens and does not ask questions or interrupt the speaker. Once the first member of the couple is done, the second partner has a chance to share his or her view, again without interruption.
3. Third step: the couple then has a conversation that identifies their common ground, their differences, clarifies each if need be, and on the basis of the common ground they decide what else they need to do, learn, or decide.

My partners and I have used this three-step process many times with couples with significant wealth. For example, one couple in their 60s who had amassed a considerable fortune through the husband's work as a senior executive were struggling with the execution of a trust that would make a large portion of that wealth available to their two children who were in their 30s. After hearing the couple go around a bit with their concerns and indecision, we asked them to take the first step right then and there: Each of them sat for about 10 minutes with a pen and paper and jotted down his or her thoughts about making this gift.

This step could be expanded, depending on the circumstances. If you have more time, each member of a couple could take a day or two to reflect and gather thoughts. The key to this step is not to "self-edit" based on what you think that your partner may say or think.

After those 10 minutes, we asked the husband and wife to share their thoughts, each one listening quietly to the other. The husband shared that he was primarily afraid of depriving his son and daughter of the opportunity to "make it on their own." At the same time, he struggled because he knew that his children were responsible and that access to these funds could help them each pursue experiences of personal growth. The wife, on the other hand, shared that she was concerned that she and her husband might not have enough for their own future, especially since she had a strong desire to give more philanthropically.

The key to this second step, of course, is *listening*. It is a hard skill to learn. After this husband and wife spoke, we gave each of them a chance to ask clarifying questions, which they found extremely helpful. Neither was completely surprised at the other's position. But each of them expressed relief at "getting on the table" what they knew was bothering the other without it being spoken out loud.

Don't worry if you need to repeat step two several times. Sometimes what each partner shares will lead to a desire for further reflection. If that's the case, make time for that reflection and then reconvene to share, listen, and decide whether to proceed.

In the third step, this husband and wife began to problem-solve and focus forward on what they could do. They decided to get further input from their wealth management team on the effect of making this gift on their financial future. In particular, they asked for input on what kind of philanthropic resources they'd have available if they set up the trust for their children.

They also had a follow-up conversation with us about the husband's ambivalence regarding the effect of the trust on his children. He himself came up with the formulation that he could support the trust if he saw it as an "investment" in his children's growth. This insight led him to further work on a letter of intent that would inform the beneficiaries and trustees about future distributions.

The main outcome of the three-step process in this case, however, had nothing to do with the trust or the couple's financial plan, but in their sense of truly understanding each other, empathizing with each other, and coming together in a course of action that reflects that true understanding.

Conclusion

Once you begin to get the hang of the three-step process, you can use it in everyday exchanges as well as more serious discussions. It applies not only to couples but to siblings, parents and children, friends, and coworkers. As with any simple tool, it is remarkably powerful.

The three-step process may lead to a direction that neither member of the couple would have predicted. It may mean delaying a choice or moving ahead more quickly than anticipated. It may mean sharing information with your children or other family members or deciding to stay quiet and revisiting the topic at a future date. But whatever the choice of action or communication is, you will have come to it in a truly shared way.

Charlie's three-step process takes time and patience to master. But if you stick with it, it can greatly strengthen your relationship as a couple and your relationships with other family members, too.

Adapted from *Complete Family Wealth*, 2nd Ed., New York: Wiley, 2022.

Additional Resources

James E. Hughes, Susan E. Massenzio, and Keith Whitaker, *Complete Family Wealth*, 2nd ed. (New York: Wiley, 2022).

Charles Collier, *Wealth in Families*, 3rd ed. (Cambridge, MA: Harvard College, 2012).

Biography

Dr. Keith Whitaker is an educator who consults with leaders and rising generation members of enterprising families. Family Wealth Report named Keith the 2015 "outstanding contributor to wealth management thought-leadership." Keith's writings and commentary have appeared in the *Wall Street Journal, New York Times,* and *Financial Times.* He is the co-author of *Wealth and the Will of God, The Cycle of the Gift, The Voice of the Rising Generation, Family Trusts, Complete Family Wealth,* and *Wealth of Wisdom: The Top 50 Questions Wealthy Families Ask.* Keith has served as a managing director at Wells Fargo Family Wealth, an adjunct professor of management at Vanderbilt University, and an adjunct assistant professor of philosophy at Boston College. Keith holds a Ph.D. in social thought from the University of Chicago and a BA and MA in classics and philosophy from Boston University.

CHAPTER 44

Strengthening Your "Family Factor" to Deconstruct Conflict

Blair Trippe and Doug Baumoel

At the beginning of *Anna Karenina*, Leo Tolstoy wrote that "Happy families are all alike; every unhappy family is unhappy in its own way." But what characterizes the proverbial happy family? A "happy family" is connected and resilient over time—able to capitalize on opportunities and weather the inevitable challenges that life throws their way. "Happy" families have what we call a strong Family Factor.

Understanding the concept of Family Factor gives you a framework for making your family stronger and more resilient. The stronger your family factor, the more likely you are to succeed in addressing current and future challenges. This takes time and commitment, but the benefits are real. There are no prerequisites beyond having a family and a desire to build family strength over time.

What Is the Family Factor?

The family factor is the answer to the question: *Is your family bond strong enough to leverage compromise, forgiveness, and commitment to change?* It is the glue that keeps all the parts of families together or fixes them when they are broken. It is a combination of three elements: shared history, shared vision of being family in the future, and trust. Through understanding these components, you will quickly understand the process of how you can build and/or strengthen your family factor.

Step 1: Understand the Components

Shared history forms the foundation of most relationships. Think about how you and your family members got to know each other, how you spent time together, what shared experiences you had, and what important memories you have. Not all these experiences and memories need to be positive—often challenging histories and difficult relationships are as important, if not more so, than the happy ones. If you have a rich shared history, you have something to lose if you don't keep your family bond strong.

Shared vision of being family in the future speaks to whether or not your family members want to, or believe they will, remain connected over time. When "being family" is important, family members have something to gain by investing time and effort in furthering that vision.

Trust is the linchpin that joins the past to the future for families. It is what bridges your family's history to its future vision. Beyond affection, alignment, affinity, or being able to feel safe while vulnerable, think of trust simply as a measure of predictability—do you know your siblings and/or cousins well enough to predict how they will act in a given situation? That knowledge is a necessary condition for trust.

Step 2: Evaluate Your Family Factor

To evaluate your family factor, consider each of the three components separately.

Evaluating Shared History: How do you evaluate your history growing up? Did you and your siblings/cousins live in the same town? Go to the same schools or camps? Did you spend vacation time together? How close in age are you? When there is a wide age disparity, shared experiences may be elusive—you may have grown up in the same house or in the same extended family but if, for example, your sister is 10 years older than you, she likely went away to college when you still were in grade school, resulting in few shared meaningful experiences growing up. Conversely, if you and your cousins grew up in the same neighborhood, went to the same schools, and played on the same sports teams, you likely had mutual friends and lots of opportunities to build on shared experiences. If you spent time at a shared vacation home, that too would have served to build a shared history. A strong shared history will make it easier for you to envision a future together.

Many families have a fraught history together. Arguments and disagreements might have cropped up frequently during get-togethers. Happiness is not a necessary condition for a meaningful shared history. What matters is connection with and knowledge of each other.

Evaluating Shared Vision: To evaluate your vision for continuing your connectedness in the future, you and your family members must determine if you expect to continue going to that family vacation home or to spend holidays together. How likely do you believe it is that you will continue your family traditions? If you anticipate that when the senior generation passes on you will stop having family events or reunions or that holidays will cease to be big family affairs, you have a vision of a limited future. Having a limited future vision makes it less likely that you personally will expend energy to organize or attend family events. If, on the other hand, you have a clear intention to continue spending time with family members and doing things together in the future, that points to a strong vision for remaining an intact family in the future.

If you share a vision for continuing to spend time together, that will in turn create opportunities for family members to get to know each other well. If you define trust as predictability, you can see how spending time together where you learn about how each of you handle situations, view relationships, or choose your lifestyles will result in an ability for you to trust one another. The more you and your family members spend time together the better you will get to know each other and, in turn, the more you'll be able to trust one another.

Evaluating Trust: Knowing your family members well and committing to the importance of the future of those relationships (shared vision) is crucial in building trust (predictability). However, building trust also requires an understanding of the systems at play—how the family governance system works—how decisions are made, how communication happens, and how things get done in the family. If a family has a well-articulated governance structure—regular meetings, written policies, transparency regarding shared enterprise, maybe even a constitution, then it is likely that trust, in the form of predictability, will be high.

Qualitative Scoring: A strong shared history, vision for remaining connected, and growing to trust each other creates a high family factor. The lower you "score" on those components, the lower your family factor. Knowing the strength of your family bond will provide insight into what might be lacking and what needs, in turn, you want to develop to help you and your family members work or make decisions together productively.

Step 3: Build Your Family Factor

Over time, as families grow and evolve, and especially if neither wealth nor a family enterprise holds you together, seeing fellow family members regularly may no longer be important. In addition, you may lose your vision of being family in the future. If that vision is lost, and if due to geographic dispersion, age disparity or other reasons, you and other next-gens didn't grow up knowing your aunts, uncles and cousins, your opportunity to develop a shared history or trust may be limited. This will make it challenging to remain connected let alone to make decisions together. But building your family factor is possible. It takes time, but its benefits are immeasurable. Obviously, if your family factor is low, there is more work to do than if it already is moderate to high. To build your family factor, think about each of the identified components individually. There are ways to build and/or strengthen each component.

Building Shared History: Think about people or places that had an impact on you or other family members. Pose questions such as the following:

> *Who were our family leaders a generation or two ago and how did we know or interact with them?*
>
> *How do we, in the current generation, connect with or benefit from what our grandparents did?*
>
> *How are our lives impacted by actions in the past?*

Telling the story of the family can be done in many ways. Time can be set aside at family gatherings for elders to recount their stories. Younger family members might be given tasks to interview older members. These stories can be memorialized in written narratives or recorded on video.

What should happen when shared history is fraught? Should only happy families be able to build family factor? When family history is difficult, it is still important for the next gen to inherit that history—albeit in a productive and forward-looking form. This is where a third-party advisor might be helpful. Spending time to work through a difficult past, to create a shared narrative that honors the truths and perspectives of family history, and to do so with a focus on lessons learned, forgiveness and healing can be transformative for families. When families can agree on the story they want to define them for succeeding generations, they can move past historical impasses and be stronger for their differences.

Building a Shared Vision: Just like businesses create (or should create) succession plans, strategic plan, corporate vision and mission statements, so too will families benefit from this same proactive type of work. To build your family vision, ask yourselves the following questions:

In 10 or 20 years, how will we connect with each other?

What shared properties or assets will we continue to share in the next generation and how can we ensure that they contribute to our well-being?

Who will host important holidays or celebrations?

Will I be going to weddings/funerals/celebrations of my relatives? How will I feel?

What stories do we want to be sure our next generation hears and then recounts to their children?

What traditions do we want to continue?

Building Trust: Building the third component, Trust, takes time and effort. There are two components—you need to build predictability in the individuals/relationships and also in the system.

Set times to get together as a family—this can be annually or more frequently. These events should provide opportunities for individual generations to have time together as well as other subgroups such as those with particular interests such as philanthropy, business, outdoor activities, or topical educational programming. Getting to know each other in ways that combine shared interests with regular contact will form the basis of trust for years to come.

Beyond getting to know each other well, you and your family members need to get to know and understand the systems in which you participate. You should get to know and understand your company (if you own an operating company) or the nature of the assets you own, including your shareholder agreements and trust documents. You also should understand the role of a trustee as well as a beneficiary and what policies and procedures exist within your family enterprise. Knowing these things will make it easier for you to function as an engaged participant, knowing what degrees of freedom you and others have in making decisions together.

Step 4: Putting It Together

Once you have clarity on the relative strength of each of the components of your family factor, how robust they are, and how you can make or have made them more durable, you can develop structures to preserve and further strengthen your family factor.

Many families choose to develop family governance (how families make decisions together) as a way to create that structure. Strengthening the family factor typically is a core mission of a family council. Through working together on committees, organizing family communication vehicles (newsletters, website), or participating in family philanthropy, family members begin to get to know each other better. Many families develop a family constitution that describes how decisions are made, how things get done, and expectations of behavior. These activities offer opportunities for cousins to get together, learn about each other and participate in projects together. Through this you will develop your own shared histories and likely will begin developing your vision of how you will be family in the future. As more and more family members participate and rising generation members do activities together, you will create bonds that will help you make important decisions over the years.

Families who strengthen and maintain their bond will reap benefits from their resulting connectedness. They will find it easier to make decisions and have difficult conversations because they know they have something to lose if they don't and they also know that they have something to gain if they do. With time and a desire to be connected, you can ensure that your family remains resilient and is able to make the most of your lives together.

Additional Resources

Doug Baumoel and Blair Trippe, *Deconstructing Conflict: Understanding Family Business, Shared Wealth and Power* (Beverly, MA: Continuity Media, 2016).

Bette Roth, Randall Wulff, and Charles Cooper, eds., Chapter 42:8 in *The Alternative Dispute Resolution Practice Guide* (St. Paul, MN: Thompson-West Publishers, 2021).

Biography

Blair Trippe is managing partner of Continuity Family Business Consulting where she works with families who own and manage operating companies and/or share assets together on issues related to succession planning, next-generation education, corporate and family governance development, and conflict management. She brings a highly specialized approach to the understanding of family systems and the relationship challenges encountered when families work and own together. In addition to her consulting work, Blair serves on the faculty of Family Enterprise Canada (formerly FEX) and is a nationally recognized speaker.

Blair earned an MBA from the Kellogg School of Management, a BA in psychology from Connecticut College, and certificates from the Program on Negotiation at Harvard Law School. She is a fellow of the Family Firm Institute and on the board of the Boston Symphony Orchestra.

Doug Baumoel is the founding partner of Continuity Family Business Consulting. As an executive in his own family business for many years, he brings a unique understanding of the stakeholder experience to his work with enterprising families. He is co-author, with Blair Trippe, of *Deconstructing Conflict: Understanding Family Business, Shared Wealth and Power* and has authored several articles on family business governance, conflict, and planning. He is a practitioner scholar and mentor for Cornell

University's Smith Family Business initiative and is a fellow of the Family Firm Institute and National Association of Corporate Directors.

Doug earned his MBA from the Wharton School and a BS in engineering from Cornell University. He also earned his certificate in mediation from MCLE and director professionalism from NACD. He serves on the board of One Family in Massachusetts, a nonprofit providing support for families facing homelessness, as well as on private company boards.

CHAPTER 45

Using Genograms to Understand Family Patterns

Guillermo Salazar

"Take a blank piece of paper and a pencil, give me 45 minutes. . .and I can help you discover and understand the important patterns that affect your family."

—Guillermo Salazar

The genogram is one of the most valuable tools available for understanding a family and a family enterprise. It helps families and advisors to become acquainted with the lives of the people in the family "system," how they interact, and what it might mean for the future.

It is like a family tree, with additional symbols representing the dynamics of the interactions among family members: It's a curious composition of circles, boxes, lines, and zigzags which tells the story of the family.

According to Family System Theory[1] your family of origin is the most significant influence you experience from birth. Usually, the genogram (also known in some contexts as a "family diagram") is drawn up at the diagnostic stage or during the *chemistry meeting* between a client and an advisor.

Family diagrams were initially developed over five decades ago by therapists and family doctors[2] as diagnostic and analytical instruments. In the 1980s, a group of prominent experts (among them Murray Bowen, Jack Froom, and Jack Medalie) standardized the graphic elements and language and organized them in a concise, efficient manner.

---

[1]Theoretically, a systemic epistemology implies looking at the family as a big picture, where the individual is part of a whole and the observer is introduced into the observed field. Family Systems Theory (Kerr and Bowen 1988) is a theory of human behavior that defines the family unit as a complex social system, in which members interact to influence each other's behavior.

[2]Murray Bowen is credited as the father of the family diagram. He developed it in the early 1970s to support his theory of family systems.

Later work, such as the study by Monica McGoldrick, Randy Gerson, and Sylvia Shellenberger (1999) illustrated the histories of world-famous families, bringing the genogram out of the clinical environment and improving its general accessibility and comprehension.

The most important benefit of the genogram is its capacity to simplify and clarify the complexities of family relationships. It can help both the external professional and the client family identify the strengths of the family system and the areas that need to be improved.

If well interpreted, it can even predict the reactions and behaviors of family members when faced with stress due to change and can offer valuable clues as to potential solutions.

The genogram has also become an important connecting element between professionals in different disciplines, weaving a typical story and organizing the various components that describe the complexity of each case.

How to Create a Genogram

There are various ways to create a genogram,[3] using PowerPoint or similar application, using one of many specialized software licenses available like Genopro, or even painting portraits of the protagonists of the family history on a canvas, as Frida Kahlo did.[4]

I prefer the classic paper-and-pencil drawing of the standard elements of all the different expression techniques.

The first step is drawing a family tree of at least three generations, identifying people by name, birth year, age, and gender, and adding family events such as births, deaths, engagements, marriages, separations, etc., using standard symbols.

You may also include family firms and nonfamily members who have impacted the family history, as well as notes regarding complex or toxic relationships, close ties, communication triangulation, diseases, addictions, scapegoats, and important events. You must be cautious regarding with whom you share this last level of information.

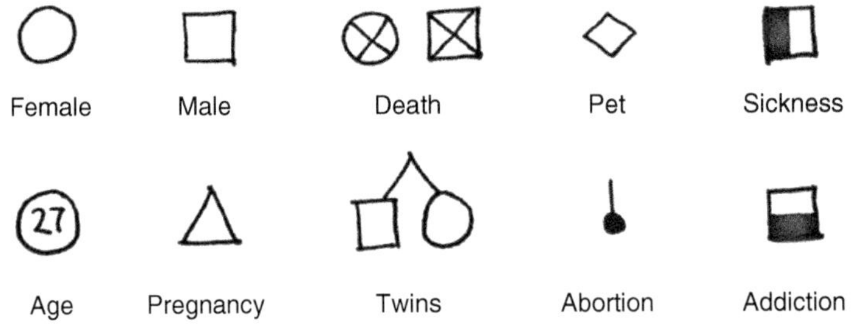

Some of the most important genogram symbols

[3]For a better comprehension of standardized techniques for representation in a genogram, I recommend the book by Monica McGoldrick, Randy Gerson, and Sueli Petry, *Genograms: Assessment and Intervention*, 3rd ed. (New York, NY: Norton, 2008).

[4]One of the best examples of this is found at MoMA, New York, the piece: "My Grandparents, My Parents, and I (Family Tree)," 1936.

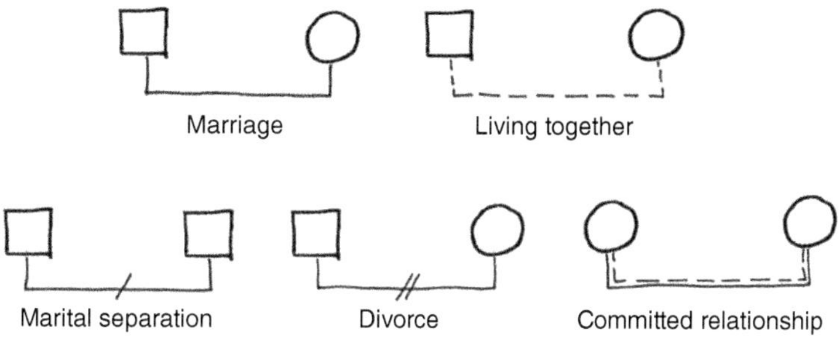

Relationship symbology

The ability to understand and generate these family stories depends directly on the ability to listen. When working with genograms, advisors will often feel compassion and empathy about a painful past. They must also be attentive to the subjective perspectives of those who narrate their stories through their genograms.

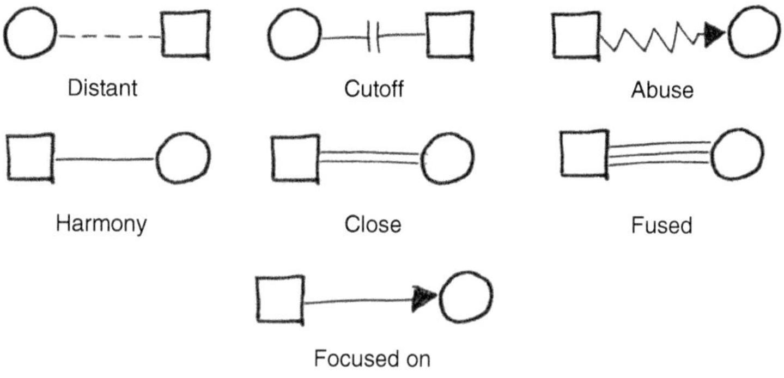

Emotional relationships

If an advisor is creating a genogram for a family, he or she must be humble and respectful, ask appropriate questions, and avoid value judgments. It is sensitive and confidential work.

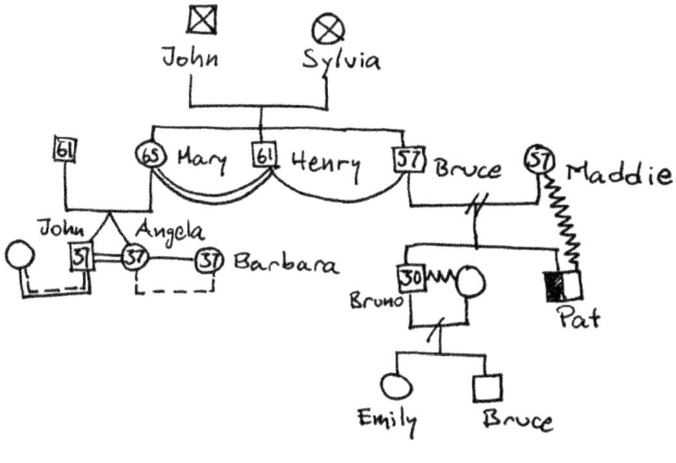

An example of a four generation genogram

Patterns

Once the genogram is drawn, many families will begin to see patterns emerge. These can include certain health concerns, relational patterns, tension, favoritism, community leadership, divorce and marriage, entrepreneurialism, etc.

You can also see how a family reacts to these situations, its capacity to adapt in new scenarios, how it handles crises in relationships, agreed-upon solutions, and notions of winners and losers. All of it creates patterns of behavior that remain in the family's legacy and culture. These patterns are transmitted from generation to generation, repeating (for good or ill) the same responses to similar stimuli over and over, often allowing some predictability of the family's reactions to future events.

As agents of change, advisors or key family leaders can help families detect those negative patterns that prevent them from evolving by facing situations in a courageous, original way, not beholden to the past, freeing them from what many call *family karma.*

After building their genogram with an advisor, one family identified a previously unnoticed pattern of favoritism of the eldest child and resultant family discord. They were surprised that this pattern showed up in every one of the last five generations. The current generation wanted to make sure they prevented this harmful pattern from continuing and decided to discuss it openly, practice full disclosure, and actively work toward fairness and equality among all siblings, including in estate planning.

Many other questions can be addressed through this process, such as "Who are most alike personality-wise in each generation?" "Which names repeat within the family?" "What was the historical, economic, and social context surrounding a given event?" "Who are the entrepreneurs in the family?" "What do they know about their grandparents' lives?" "What role have women played in their family's history?" These inquiries can help us find the keys to untangling the origins of behaviors that still show up in the family today and that need to be overcome or reinforced.

Genograms provide a standardized method of graphic representation, but of course no one genogram is exactly like another (and it may even change over time for the same family!).

One of the most interesting cases I have come across when analyzing genograms was the Smith family, owner of a major supermarket chain. As we created the genogram, we discovered a pattern in the family going back three generations: Husbands left their wives and started a second family, and miscarriages occurred in couples who remained together.

These events had marked all the women with a deep feeling of abandonment, unconsciously relegating them from active participation in "men's" affairs (the family business). It also generated a sense of sadness that floated throughout the family.

Once we detected the presence of the pattern in the genogram and found the same story repeatedly in each generation and each family branch, Craig, the eldest son of the founder, said that he did not want to continue living in that sadness and

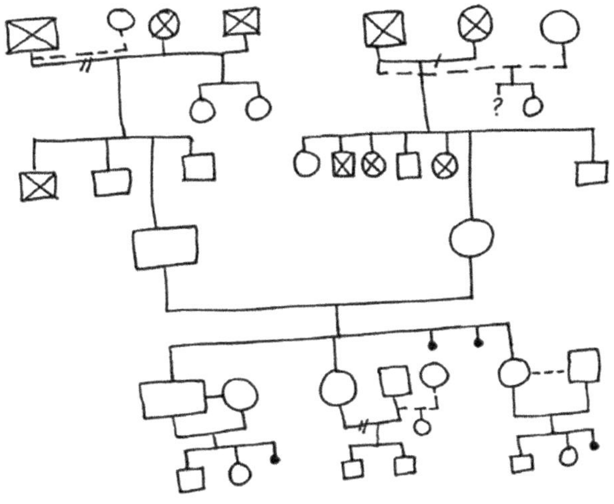

Smith family genogram

that he refused to be complicit in a family tradition that was denying his sisters and mother the right to participate in the family decisions.

From there, we were able to open the channels to discuss the role of women freely and their skills and abilities as essential assets to eventually become part of the governing bodies of the supermarkets.

Making Conscious the Unconscious

Developing and interpreting genograms effectively takes time and practice, but it can be worth the effort.

A focus on identifying the patterns and detecting those behaviors that don't add value to the individual's life may open a broad spectrum of decisions. One of the goals is often to empower family members of each generation with the motivation to commit to their long-term health and success and overcome their obstacles. Carl Jung's quote comes to mind: "Until you make the unconscious conscious, it will direct your life, and you will call it fate."

Conclusion

For more than two decades, I have been drawing genograms as support tools for therapeutic and consultancy interventions. Everyone is a story, each story is a genogram, and each genogram is a collection of experiences, feelings, dreams, and hopes that each family member has generously shared.

I have been a witness to understanding family members' points of most significant pain and happiness, and events of incredible pride and shame, but always from a place of professional respect and a therapeutic perspective. My goal is to help them find, within their self-drawn story, the keys to answer their important questions and discover the paths they must walk in search of their growth as individuals and as a family.

Additional Resources

Books

Ivan Boszormenyi-Nagy and Geraldine M. Spark, *Invisible Loyalties: Reciprocity in Intergenerational Family Therapy* (New York: Routledge,1984).

Victoria Harrison, *The Family Diagram and Family Research* (Houston, TX: Center for the Study of Natural Systems and the Family, 2018).

Monica McGoldrick, *Genograms: Assessment and Intervention*, 3rd ed. (New York: W.W. Norton, 2008).

Monical McGoldrick, *The Genogram Journey: Reconnecting with Your Family* (New York: W.W. Norton, 2011).

Anne Ancelin Schutzenberger and Anne Trager, *The Ancestor Syndrome: Transgenerational Psychotherapy and the Hidden Links in the Family Tree* (New York: Routledge, 1998).

Anne Ancelin Schutzenberger, *Aïe, mes aïeux!* 16th ed. (Paris, France: Desclée de Bouwer/La Méridienne, 2015).

Robert C. Solomon and Fernando Flores, *Building Trust* (New York: Oxford University Press, 2001).

Websites

The Family Firm Institute: The Practitioner, https://ffipractitioner.org.

The Murray Bowen Archives Project, http://murraybowenarchives.org.

Biography

Guillermo Salazar is a family business member and an expert on corporate governance and family legacy succession. He is the founder of Exaudi Family Business Consulting. He has served as an advisor for numerous business families on their protocols, generational transition, family vision and values for decision-making, and conflict resolution. He is the author of several books, including *A Road to Triumph in Family Business* and *Genograms in Family Business* (available late 2022). He is a lecturer and educator in the field of the family business in Latin America and a fellow of the Family Firm Institute (FFI) in Boston, USA. He has degrees in architecture, a master's in family business management, and a diploma in systemic family therapy. He is the recipient of the 2015 International Achievement Award of the Family Firm Institute.

CHAPTER 46

Achieving New Insights and Possibilities through Generative Dialogue

Michelle Osry

The day before I was due to facilitate a retreat with a business family which had self-declared themselves to be "stuck," I was given Kate's Sutherland's treasure-trove of a book *We Can Do This! 10 Tools to Unleash Our Collective Genius.* The family had tried numerous times, over the span of a decade, to launch a family governance process but had failed to make any meaningful progress. Knowing that the family was discouraged and fatigued, I had planned a series of activities that I hoped might encourage a fresh start.

By our first morning break, it became clear to me that the family desperately wanted a deeper, more honest conversation that would allow each member of the family to be seen and heard without triggering their familiar and unproductive communication patterns. Rather than return to the planned agenda, I sketched on a flipchart what I recalled of the Generative Dialogue framework I'd seen while skimming *We Can Do This!* the day before:

It produced a breakthrough! The framework helped the family to see that their conversational process was predictable—and fixable. The framework provided a roadmap for taking their conversational process deeper: from where they were and how they got stuck, to how they could get unstuck and where they could go. Over the span of a weekend, the family learned to talk and listen in new ways. At the close, each family member took time to express their gratitude to the family group for the opportunity to be heard. Finally, the work could begin.

Since this meeting several years ago, I've used the Generative Dialogue framework countless times in my work with families, and I continue to discover new sources of research backing its deceptively simple framing.

The Framework's Four Fields of Conversation

Originally developed by Otto Scharmer, a senior lecturer at the Massachusetts Institute of Technology who is dedicated to social innovation and systems change, the

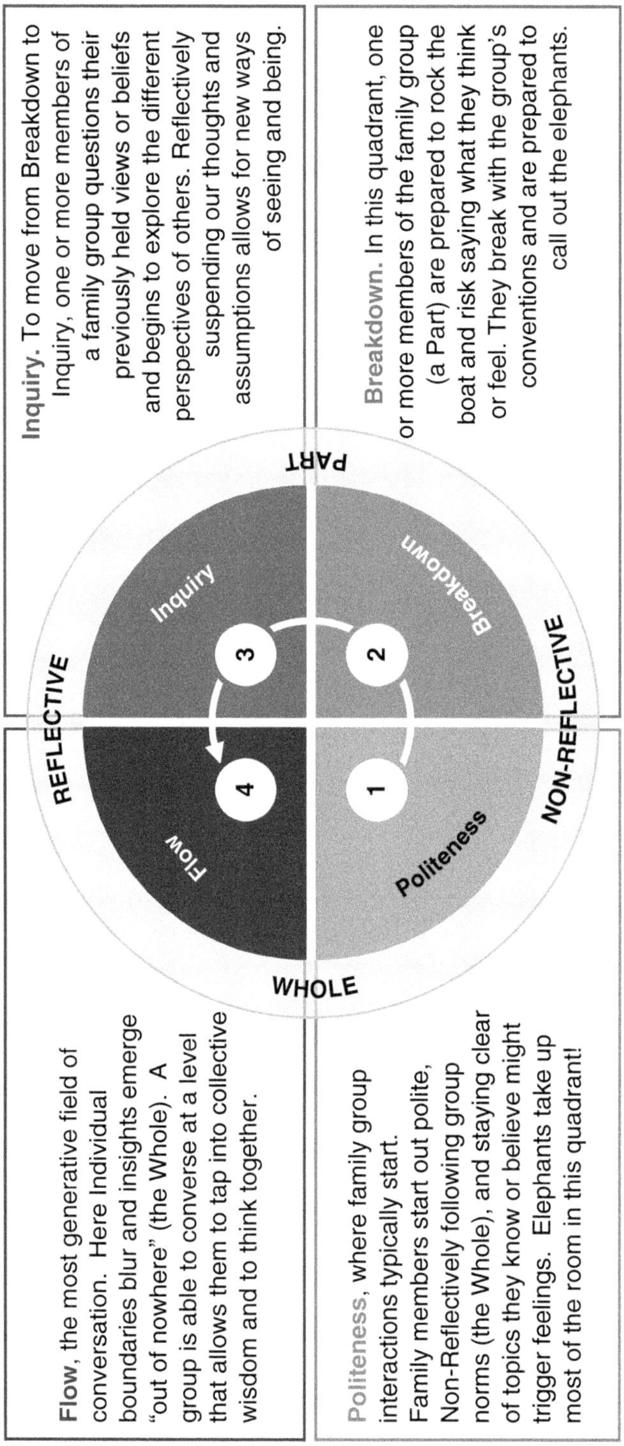
Inquiry. To move from Breakdown to Inquiry, one or more members of a family group questions their previously held views or beliefs and begins to explore the different perspectives of others. Reflectively suspending our thoughts and assumptions allows for new ways of seeing and being.
Flow, the most generative field of conversation. Here Individual boundaries blur and insights emerge "out of nowhere" (the Whole). A group is able to converse at a level that allows them to tap into collective wisdom and to think together.
Breakdown. In this quadrant, one or more members of the family group (a Part) are prepared to rock the boat and risk saying what they think or feel. They break with the group's conventions and are prepared to call out the elephants.
Politeness, where family group interactions typically start. Family members start out polite, Non-Reflectively following group norms (the Whole), and staying clear of topics they know or believe might trigger feelings. Elephants take up most of the room in this quadrant!
REFLECTIVE
NON-REFLECTIVE
PART
WHOLE
Inquiry
Flow
Breakdown
Politeness
1
2
3
4

FIGURE 46.1

framework is a simple and powerful way for groups to see their dynamics and identify ways to create deeper shared meaning.

The term "Generative Dialogue" refers to a group's ability to generate new insights and new possibilities through conversation together. The Generative Dialogue framework has four quadrants, created by two intersecting axes representing two polarities: Whole/Part and Reflective/Non-Reflective. Each of the four quadrants denotes what Scharmer called a conversational "field" (see Figure 46.1).

Practical Application

Let's look at each of the quadrants in the context of a family meeting:

1. **Politeness**
    - In this conversation field, family members assume from prior experience what is expected, what will happen, and how matters will conclude. Their listening and speaking are restricted to confirming what has gone before. The family group shies away from conversations on expectations, tensions, or differences.
    - Family groups tend to stay in the Politeness field if members perceive it unsafe to venture into real talk. They likely recall previous meetings where they felt blamed, criticized, humiliated, or where the people they care about were upset. Family status quo is more important than family openness.
    - Some versions of the Politeness field can be cruel and bad-mannered too. Politeness refers to the field, not how polite people are with each other.

While Politeness may impede change, it is also necessary. Without going through this field, the family cannot move on to deeper fields of conversation.

2. **Breakdown**
    - For family groups to move to the Breakdown field, they must perceive stability or safety in the meeting dynamic to allow more heat.
    - One or more family members will risk asserting themselves by challenging the group's conversational norms. Typically, the dissenter (or family "troublemaker") will seek to convince or persuade others of their non-norm position, often going to great lengths to defend their views and assumptions.
    - Self-interest reigns in this quadrant, and people may withdraw from the conversation.

Uncomfortable as it may be, Breakdown can be a good sign. It means the family group is prepared to risk discomfort in order to have a deeper conversation. On the other hand, it is not unusual for the group to retreat to Politeness if the conversation becomes too heated and unpleasant.

3. **Inquiry**
    - In this field, one or more members of the family group suspend their judgment to understand the perspectives of others.

- Instead of immediately reacting to what others say, this field unfolds when family members respond with "Please tell me more," or "I don't think I understand yet what you are saying."
- When family members recognize that their assumptions might be limiting, they begin to see through new eyes.
- Conversations become richer as different perspectives begin to emerge and the group engages with greater openness and vulnerability.

The field of Inquiry feels different, more reflective and thoughtful. The family group begins to slow things down and accept pauses in the conversation, and silence is to be encouraged to create an opportunity to reflect on what others are saying.

4. **Flow**
   - Achieving the Flow level of the conversational fields is rare, especially in the early stages of an engagement, and can be difficult to describe even after it occurs. In this conversational field, the group experiences a seemingly effortless creativity that allows for new thoughts and ideas to flow.
   - Old narratives are relinquished, and family members hold a space for something new to emerge. At this stage, the best intervention is often no intervention. Individual boundaries blur, and the group begins to explore and co-create new possibilities together.

It is important to know that this fourth field can be elusive. Reaching it requires suspending habitual thinking and perceptions and letting go of old identities, past hurts, and the urge to control outcomes. These achievements don't always occur, especially early in a family process.

Given the complexity inherent in family enterprise systems, most families will find themselves stuck at some point. But using Scharmer's Generative Dialogue framework, I regularly witness clients taking the leap of faith needed to achieve Flow, to sense and realize new possibilities and achieve their potential.

Practice Tips

1. Avoid using the framework for time sensitive, operational matters. It is more suited for conversations on complex, emotive, long-term matters where there are no obvious or quick fixes.
2. Ensure there is ample time on the family meeting agenda. Achieving Flow is almost impossible under the pressure of hard stops.
3. Consider adding questions to your family meeting agenda or even making each item on the agenda a question. This will help to send the message that the meeting is intended for dialog and not declarations!
4. Establish a clear purpose or goal for the conversation that will take place. Framing the conversation might take as much time as the conversation itself.
5. Pay attention to the meeting's location and surroundings. Use a quiet room in a neutral location that's spacious and has natural light.
6. While it's not always necessary to formally introduce the framework, it may be helpful to sketch and name the quadrants to bring awareness to where the family is and where they might want to go.

7. Establish a code of conduct or a set of ground rules to remind family members that their behavior matters. Examples might include: listen with a desire to understand others' points of view; speak your truth without blaming or criticizing others; don't be attached to outcomes; be open to challenge.
8. Signal that the meeting is important by starting with a short meditation or any other grounding exercise that helps to separate the family time from other everyday meetings (e.g., Start the meeting with a one-word check-in from everyone).
9. Pose questions for family members to ask themselves:
   - What field of conversation are we in? (Are we stuck in the Polite quadrant?)
   - How open am I to hearing new things?
   - Am I prepared to suspend assumptions and judgment(s)?
   - What story am I telling myself right now? What is triggering me?
   - How can I be more present?
10. Take frequent stretch breaks or even walks.
11. Don't expect too much too soon. Achieving the Inquiry and Flow phases takes courage, time, and inner shifts. Expecting Flow to happen on demand can end in frustration and disappointment.

Working together as a family in business requires courage to go into the unknown, patience to listen deeply to each other, and willingness to experiment together. As an advisor and facilitator for families, I too must venture into the unknown! I am deeply thankful to my family enterprise clients for showing me time and again what is possible when one engages in a Generative Dialogue. I hope that you can use the Generative Dialogue framework within your own family enterprise!

Additional Resources

Kate Sutherland, *We Can Do This* (Incite Press, 2017).
William Isaacs, *Dialogue and the Art of Thinking* (New York: Currency Book, 1999).
Adam Kahane, *Collaborating with the Enemy* (Oakland, CA: Berrett-Koehler, 2017).
C. Otto Scharmer, *The Essentials of Theory U* (Oakland, CA: Berrett-Koehler, 2018).
Edgar Schein, *Humble Enquiry* (Oakland, CA: Berrett-Koehler, 2021).
Peter Senge, C. Otto Scharmer, Joseph Jaworski, and Betty Sue Flowers, *Presence: Human Purpose and the Field of the Future* (New York: Currency Book, 2004).

Biography

Michelle Osry works with business families and family offices worldwide as an advisor and facilitator, helping families to address the complex issues of generational transition, family engagement and family governance. Committing to the family as a whole, Michelle brings 30 years in academia, corporate finance and consulting, wide-ranging travel and cross-discipline study, combined with innovative approaches and systems thinking practices.

Michelle today leads Deloitte Canada's Family Enterprise Consulting practice. She is a member of the boards of Family Enterprise Canada and SeeChange Initiative, and of Perimeter Institute's Emmy Noether Council, championing women in theoretical physics.

CHAPTER 47

How Powerful Are Your Questions?

Ian McDermott

Questions are one of the fundamental thinking tools we have at our disposal as human beings. Yet most people have little understanding of how they work or what they can do when properly honed.

Every time you ask a question, you frame people's thinking. Suppose you tell me there's something you'd like to talk through, and I respond with, "So what's the problem?" I'm presupposing that what you're dealing with is just that—a problem. This may well color the conversation that follows. But suppose you'd said exactly the same thing and I'd responded with "Oh, so what do you want?" Now I'm asking you about an outcome you desire and that's going to be a different conversation.

It's not that one of these questions is better. It just depends on what you're trying to achieve. Frame things as problems, and you'll probably start going into aspects of the past—for example, when, how, and with whom did this problem begin? Frame things as outcomes, and you'll probably learn more about what kind of future someone really wants going forward.

Every time you ask a question, you trigger an internal search in the brain and you send the listener on a journey. Both families and their advisors need to know this. There's a world of difference between asking "How do we stop the beneficiary from wasting trust assets?" (Problem Frame) versus "How do we help the beneficiary use trust assets more effectively to get where s/he wants to go?" (Outcome Frame). I'd like to show you how to ask more powerful questions by giving you a tool that you can put to use right away. The more you use it, the more proficient you will become.

+++++

Think of something that's an issue right now for you. I'm going to start by asking you just six questions. These all have something in common; they frame the issue as a problem. Have a pen and paper to hand if you want to get the most out of this tool. Just write your answers to each question and keep going until till you've answered all six. (Alternatively, you could do this with a partner and ask each other the questions.)

Problem Frame Questions

1. What is your problem?
2. How long have you had it?
3. Why did it start?
4. Who is to blame?
5. What is your worst experience with this problem?
6. Why haven't you solved it yet?

People often say these Problem Frame questions have an impact on how they feel as well as on what they think. Sometimes they find them useful for clarifying where they are and how they got here. Other times they report feeling stuck or just repeating what they already know but with no insight regarding what to do now. So, there's no one guaranteed response. What these questions *will* do is send a person into the past in search of causal explanations.

By contrast, the following six Outcome Frame questions will trigger very different responses. Again, just work your way through these six questions while thinking of the same issue you began with.

Outcome Frame Questions

1. What do you want?
2. How will you know when you've got it?
3. What else in your life will improve when you've got it?
4. What resources do you already have that can help you achieve your outcome?
5. What is something similar that you did succeed in doing?
6. What is the next step?

These questions make your brain work in a different way. I want to unpack them so you can see what I mean.

Q1 What do you want?

This question asks you to specify what you want—which is not the same as saying what you don't want! Saying you just want someone to stop doing something is not enough. We need to understand if they stopped doing it, what would that do for you? So what do you really want? Ultimately, we need something that is stated in the positive.

This is not about trying to be positive for the sake of being positive—it has to do with how our brains work. If I tell you don't think of a blue elephant, your brain has to conjure this image up to cancel it. Every time you say what you don't want, you invoke it one more time. This makes it hard to move on to what will replace it. So, what do you want?

Q2 How will you know when you've got it?

This question is designed to ensure your brain knows what success looks, sounds, and feels like. So often people have fluffy goals: "I just want to be happy or the family/the business to flourish." But until we can specify what we will see, hear, and feel when we achieve our goal, our brain has no clear representation of what we're aiming for. And this makes it hard to achieve.

Contrast this with what happens when we decide on what our next car will be. Suddenly we find the roads littered with that model. Why? Because our brain is now engaged in an easy, active search for something we have specifically flagged as significant. We can put this natural process to work for us with any issue we want to move forward on. We just need to be sensorily specific. So, how will you know when you've achieved your outcome? What will you see, hear, and feel that will let you know? And, if relevant, what will others see, hear, and feel that lets them know you've achieved your goal?

Q3 What else in your life will improve when you get it?

This question enlarges the scope of the search the brain is engaged in. It is easy for us to want something so badly that we don't see it in the larger context of our life. However, it's frequently the case that achieving an outcome may create additional beneficial ripple effects either for us or others.

This is the beginning of putting the desired outcome in a larger context and seeing a bigger picture; it is something that the next two questions will expand on.

Understanding what else in your life will improve can be a powerful motivator to do what it takes to make the change. As one family member put it, "I hadn't realized I would get so much from making this a priority."

Q4 What resources do you already have that can help you achieve this outcome?

Many times I've worked with people who are so fixated on the goal that they fail to take into account—and so fail to call upon—what else might assist them in achieving it. Stepping back to see more of the terrain and consider what else might help us can be incredibly helpful. Resources can range from material assets through contacts and well-wishers to the right state of mind—yours and others—and a sense of humor. Invariably people realize they have more resources to draw on than they imagined. People find this both encouraging and motivating.

Q5 What is something similar that you did succeed in doing?

When we're learning something that's new to us it's not uncommon to try and make sense of it by asking if this is like something we're already familiar with. If it is, we may be able to give ourselves a head-start by drawing on our previous trial-and-error learning. So much of our learning occurs through this process, which is called associative thinking.

This question encourages the brain to search out anything that is in some way like what we're currently endeavoring to deal with. Many, many times I've witnessed "Aha!" moments when people have suddenly joined up the dots and realized that what they're dealing with is not so unfamiliar after all. With this comes a newfound confidence and strengthened resolve to see the challenge through.

Q6 What is the next step?

This can be anything from "make that phone call" to "meet with the whole family and get clear about what really matters to each of us." As long as we end with an executable action, we've avoided the trap of setting some impossibly ambitious goal—it's a step, just a step.

+++++

I've used this format with boards, teams, families, and individuals. You may well develop your own additional questions, but always remember you will be most effective if you start where people are at. So, if they're talking in terms of problems, begin there. As you clarify what's happening for them, there'll come a time when you can move from the problem frame to the outcome frame. It only takes a sentence to join the two up: "Okay, so that's what you *don't* want. Now tell me, what do you *really* want?"

If they're already telling you about what they want, begin there and use the Outcome Frame questions to amplify and elucidate why this outcome really matters and what it will do for them. As long as your tone of voice is curious and respectful, people don't feel criticized and so don't become defensive. Many times, I've seen the various parties come to a deeper and fuller understanding of what the issues really are they're dealing with and why they matter. This is particularly valuable when someone's behavior is considered problematic.

Human behavior is always a means to an end. Once we understand what's driving the behavior, we have a much better chance of engaging effectively with it and coming up with new solutions. These questions can help us do this.

Problem Frame Questions	Outcome Frame Questions
What is your problem?	What do you want?
How long have you had it?	How will you know when you have got it?
Why did it start?	What else in your life will improve when you get it?
Who is to blame?	What resources do you already have which can help you achieve this outcome?
What is your worst experience with this problem?	What is something similar which you did succeed in doing?
Why haven't you solved it yet?	What is the next step?

Further Reading

Ian McDermott and Wendy Jago, *The Coaching Bible* (London: Piatkus, 2005).

Ian McDermott and Wendy Jago, *The NLP Coach* (London: Piatkus, 2001).

Ian McDermott and Ian Shircore, *Manage Yourself, Manage Your Life* (London: Piatkus, 1999).

Biography

Based in the United States and the United Kingdom, **Ian McDermott** has trained a generation of advisors, coaches, and consultants worldwide. An acknowledged thought leader, he has pioneered the application of practical techniques that are grounded in sound neuroscience for individuals, families, teams, and organizations. A widely published authority, he has written 15 books that have been translated into over 20 languages. In the United States, he is dean of innovation and learning for the Purposeful Planning Institute. In the United Kingdom, he is professor of practice at SOAS University of London. His primary focus is delivering practical "how-to's" to ensure that learning in leadership, change, and innovation really happens for individuals, families, and teams.

https://www.linkedin.com/in/ianemcdermott/

CHAPTER 48

Expectations versus Agreements

Mimi Ramsey and Stephanie Hardwick

Money is a very difficult subject for most families to discuss. It is quite common for individual members to have firm ideas about what their financial future looks like without ever having a money conversation with other family members. This lack of clear communication leads to what we have identified as one of the major causes of turbulence in affluent families. Families that are able to transform unshared *expectations* into co-created *agreements* strengthen relationships and thrive together.

An expectation is a belief that something will or should happen. When real life doesn't match that, it can lead to feelings like disappointment, frustration, and resentment. Left unaddressed, unmet expectations can become toxic to family relationships. We facilitate families in creating agreements to replace problematic expectations.

Expectations are formed in the mind of an individual based on their own perspective, opinions, and assumptions. Often, they are created with little to no input from those impacted by the expectation. The other person's view of what is "supposed to happen" will look very different. This is a recipe for misunderstandings and resentment and, in many situations, leads to blaming and shaming in families.

The ideal family culture reduces unspoken expectations and builds more harmonious relationships by embracing co-created agreements.

Description/Process

This exercise introduces a process for creating agreements where all sides have a chance to weigh in and agree or disagree. Family members learn to identify unmet expectations causing upset feelings, make clear requests, and co-create a new understanding, fostering greater family harmony.

The following diagram presents each step in the process and is to be used in conjunction with the related worksheet (see following example).

1	2	3	4
Upset/Complaints ⇒ *Disappointment ⇒* *Frustrations* *Resentment* *Jealousy*	**Unfulfilled ⇒** **Expectations ⇒**	**Requests ⇒** ⇒	**New Agreements**

Steps 1–3 are to be completed individually before coming together with other family members in Step 4.

Step 1. Upset/Complaints: Whenever we feel one of the unwanted emotions above, it is a signal that we may be holding an unmet expectation. The quickest way to identify unfulfilled expectations is to make a list of current upsets/complaints/frustrations, etc.

In Column 1, list the resentments, frustrations, complaints, or upsets concerning the family or family members that you are feeling.

Step 2. Underlying Expectation: Looking over the list in Column 1, what idea(s) or belief(s) is contributing to the upsets listed? Consider this critical question: What do I believe should have happened for me to feel better? This is where unmet expectations are identified.

In Column 2, list the expectations.

Step 3. Requests: This step is to convert the one-sided expectations listed in Column 2 into requests that will invite others to respond. The request helps to identify what is behind difficult feelings or family turbulence and suggests to others what is needed going forward.

There is a big difference between making a request and issuing a demand. A request is open for the other person to respond in any of the following ways: (1) agree as is, (2) suggest an alternative, or (3) decline. A demand is typically made with pressure for full agreement (e.g., I want you to do this). Each request is to be shared with the understanding that others can freely respond.

In Column 3, list the requests to be shared in Step 4.

Step 4. Co-Created Agreements: In this step, family members come together and share their requests. This stage of the process requires listening carefully, getting curious about each other's perspectives, and ultimately forming new agreements with input from those involved.

Sharing these requests can lead to difficult conversations because each person will have their own unique perspective about what should or should not happen and what is reasonable. An initial reaction to hearing a request might be to defend ourselves or find flaws with the other person's reasoning. Remember, the key goal at this stage is to understand each other rather than to debate or get stuck in disagreement.

Many families experience power dynamics that keep dissent silent, thereby causing requests to feel more like demands. For example, the younger generation may have difficulty disagreeing with their elders. The agreements formed in this step are more likely to succeed if family members can respond authentically without fear or pressure to respond in an affirmative manner.

Questions to facilitate greater understanding of another's perspective:

- Help me understand. . .
- How did you come to that decision, conclusion, or expectation?
- Tell me more about. . .
- What is behind your request or expectation?
- What would you like to see happen?

This is the most time-consuming part of the process and might take place over several conversations and meetings. Be patient with this stage and be willing to allow the conversation to take the time it needs for beneficial agreements to emerge.

Here are some helpful tips to consider in formulating effective agreements:

1. Is our agreement thoughtful, kind, compassionate, and does it involve compromise?
2. Identify how each party can support one another in keeping this agreement.
3. Invite each person to describe the agreement as they see it to make sure everyone has a shared understanding.
4. Test the Yes. Some people are naturally inclined to avoid conflict, so it is important to make sure each agreement is not just an attempt to please. (This is especially important in families with skewed power dynamics that tend to quiet any dissents.)
5. Solicit any concerns family members may have about keeping the agreement. Identify how individual family members can support one another.

The following columns include several examples of how this process facilitates transforming an upset into an agreement.

Column 1	Column 2	Column 3	Column 4
Upset/Complaint	Expectation	Request	New Agreement
Frustrated that we are paying for all of our 25-year-old son's living expenses	Children should be financially independent after finishing college.	"We would like you to be financially independent by age 27."	Son will work to cover 75% of his living expenses by age 27 and achieve financial independence by age 28.
Angry that son isn't showing up to work on time at the family business	Son's work should be measured on the same standard as other workers and demonstrate to us that he has "earned" his role at the company.	"We would like you to arrive at work on time and let someone at the office know when you are going to be absent or running late." "We would like you to spend 6 months in the company training program prior to taking on independent business responsibilities."	Son will keep regular business hours and will notify his direct supervisor if he will be late or absent. Son will participate in the training program and will have a senior mentor (of son's choice) to support his growth and development. Son will be subject to the normal company performance guidelines and assessment process as well as standard consequences for underperformance (performance improvement plan and/or termination of employment).

Column 1	Column 2	Column 3	Column 4
Resentful that daughter only wants to spend time with the family on expensive vacations, and that she runs credit card balance up to the limit	Parents shouldn't have to purchase their daughter's time and attention. Debt is irresponsible, and she should know how to manage it.	"We would like to have time together with you without spending money." "We would like you to create a budget, including a plan for paying down your credit card debt."	Parents will continue covering their daughter's expenses for family vacations. And they will plan to have a Sunday afternoon and dinner together at least monthly. Daughter will meet with a financial planner to create a budget. The details of that will remain confidential. Daughter will not ask parents to pay down her credit card debt.
Angry that my parents are creating trusts for my children without including me and my husband in their decisions	A parent should be in charge of any financial decisions that impact their own children.	"I would like my husband and me to be included in conversations with your attorneys drafting trusts for our kids."	Family will hire a wealth coach to facilitate conversations of wealth transfer before finalizing future transfers.

Outcomes

Families that have a culture of moving from upset into new agreements have a deeper level of connection and understanding among one another. They experience a reduction of negative feelings such as shame and blame. If the co-created agreements fail, it becomes an opportunity to formulate a new, stronger agreement rather than getting stuck in complaints and resentment. With a ready process to address any disappointment, individual family members take relationship difficulties less personally.

Next Steps

Moving forward, feelings of frustration, upset, and complaints do not need to cause family turbulence. This process is a way to continue to move through difficult family interactions. Emotions and frustrations occur naturally in any relationship. These feelings can become a cue to initiate this process. Expectations run rampant in our culture, and we can easily forget that agreements are far more useful. Rather than getting stuck in frustration, making this process a foundation for navigating challenges will support healthy relationships that thrive across generations.

Additional Resources

Steve Chandler, *Crazy Good* (Anna Maria, FL: Basset Publishing, 2015).

Marshall B. Rosenberg, *Nonviolent Communication,* 3rd ed. (Encinitas, CA: Puddledancer Press, 2015).

Richard Carlson and Joseph Bailey, *Slowing Down to the Speed of Life* (New York: Harper One, 2009).

For more information on Mimi and Stephanie visit www.thrivewithwealth.com.

Biography

Mimi Ramsey, ACC, is a professional leadership coach with more than 20 years of experience as a trusted advisor to high-net-worth clients. Her extensive work with entrepreneurs and inheritors gave her a unique view into the unexpected challenges that significant wealth can bring to families. This expertise, coupled with professional coach training, enables her to support her clients to foster individual and family wellbeing. Mimi is deeply committed to helping her clients to widen their perspective on what is possible, tackle the concerns that have them stuck, and reach easier decisions.

Stephanie Hardwick, MA, has counseled and coached families, individuals, and leaders with wealth since 2007. She has a deep passion for helping clients navigate the unique challenges of high net worth. Her work centers around 1:1 coaching, couples coaching, and facilitation of family engagements. Stephanie graduated with her master's degree in systems counseling from the Leadership Institute of Seattle at Bastyr University. Her years of doing therapy and leadership coaching brings a unique depth and breadth to her work. She has an excellent track record of helping clients move beyond their psychology, tap into their potential, and create positive outcomes.

CHAPTER 49

Enhancing Sibling Relationships

Christian Stewart

When financial capital or an enterprise is co-owned by siblings, it is critical that this group knows how to collaborate while respecting the various roles they each may have in the enterprise. A foundation of effective governance at this stage is a group of siblings who have positive relationships and can collaborate at the ownership level. But how do you intentionally strengthen relationships and collaborative skills? How do you go beyond vague commitments? And how do you ensure that each sibling does his or her fair share in working on a positive change?

A Sibling Relationship Self-Assessment Worksheet

Appendix A contains a Sibling Relationship Self-Assessment Worksheet ("worksheet").[1] The purpose of the worksheet is to allow readers who jointly own an enterprise or investments to prioritize specific steps they can take to enhance their relationships. Each sibling would complete it by him or herself, either together in a family meeting (each having own quiet reflection time to complete it) or as homework before the family meeting.

The results are shared in the group. Each sibling takes a turn to explain his/her results. If meeting virtually, then ideally each worksheet will be completed before the meeting, then scanned and sent to the meeting facilitator. The goal is to obtain a public commitment of the areas that each sibling agrees to work on to improve relationships, and to allow group feedback on these commitments.

The philosophy behind the worksheet is that rather than asking others to change, ask instead what it is that you are going to do to change. What are your individual goals to improve the sibling relationship? It is also designed to encourage focusing on taking one small step at a time.

By doing it as a group the exercise sends the message that every one of the siblings is being asked to contribute to the collective improvement. Completing it as a group exercise puts all siblings on a level playing field.

---

[1]The author gratefully acknowledges the help of Dennis T. Jaffe in reviewing the original version of this worksheet.

It is a self-assessment, therefore subjective. It can happen that one sibling says (in effect), "Everything is fine," while others say, "That is not true." Discussing each sibling's results in a meeting where there is a safe environment helps to reduce the chances of unrealistic self-assessment. At the same time, the worksheet allows each sibling to self-select the areas he or she believes important to work on, and with that choice there arises greater intrinsic motivation.

Process

1. Each sibling completes the worksheet prior to the meeting or has time in the meeting to complete the worksheet.
2. Siblings should pair off and compare their worksheet results with each other.
3. Each sibling shares his or her results with the whole group and shares what he or she is going to commit to focusing on.

The individual and collective results should be confidential to the sibling group and the facilitator. The facilitator should emphasize that individual results are not to be used to attack or blame a person; each sibling needs to keep the focus on him or herself and what are the small steps he or she is going to focus on improving.

Completing the Worksheet

The worksheet asks you to scale your response to each question, evaluating your relationships both 12 months ago and currently. It also asks you to check the areas you see as a priority for you to work on—keep this to no more than three areas.

The purpose for the scaling is to help give a sense of what is the trend or trajectory in the relationship.

1. Ask yourself about why one number was given in the past and a different number given currently—that leads to the question of what has changed.
2. You can ask questions about the implications if the current trajectory continues into the next 12 months, etc.

The scaling can help to highlight what could be priority issues to work on; and the scaling lends itself to a solution-focused coaching approach[2]—either (1) through questions asked by the facilitator in the family meeting with the siblings or (2) as a follow up in one-to-one coaching.

After the Meeting

1. Use each person's worksheet as the basis for one-to-one coaching and for providing that individual with additional topic-specific reference materials. For example, if forgiveness is identified as a priority area, then additional materials and tools can be provided on the topic of forgiveness. The collective answers might also point to areas for training for the sibling team.

---

[2]For example see Insoo Kim Berg and Peter Szabo, *Brief Coaching for Lasting Solutions* (New York: W.W. Norton, 2005).

2. Produce a shorter consolidated summary of the areas each sibling committed to focus on.
3. Use the summary to follow up in subsequent meetings to ask each sibling to report on what effort they have been putting into it since the last meeting.

Comparing Progress over Time

One sibling group working with a coach and an advisor first completed the worksheet five years ago. The coach kept copies of the old worksheets. They hold quarterly multiday family meetings, and this last year they revisited the worksheet exercise. They were able to contrast their old results with the current—by reviewing the old worksheets before completing the new ones—to give a big picture of the positive trend in the sibling relationships. They committed to reviewing their individual commitments in each of their quarterly meetings for the coming year and to each continue their own one-to-one work with the coach. One of the siblings decided to do some deeper work on his relationships with a somatic healer.

Appendix A

Sibling Relationships Self-Assessment Worksheet[i]

Your Name:	Date:

Instructions: For each item below, please rate yourself on the scale from 1 to 5, with 1 being the lowest (or worst) and 5 being the highest possible (or perfect) score. When rating yourself, think about your relationships with all of your "sibs" (i.e., siblings) "as a whole." If you think a question is not relevant to you (e.g., because it assumes a role you are not involved in), then just write "NA" for not applicable.

Explanation: The purpose of this worksheet is to encourage self-reflection on the role that you play in relation to your sibs, to get an idea of "what direction" you are going in, and to ask questions about what *you* can do to take one small step to invest in building a positive family culture. You could use this score card as a tool to help you set specific goals for your own personal development.

	Lowest score 1 2 3 4 5 Perfect score	The Past: How would you rate yourself 12 months ago?	The Present: How do you rate yourself today?	Check 1–3 areas you want to work on
1.	**VALUES AND SHARED FAMILY DREAM**			
1.1	My Values: I know what is important to me as an individual, what my personal values are.			
1.2	The Values of my siblings: I also know the values of each of my sibs. I know what is important to each of them.			
1.3	My Dream: I know what my own dream is.			

[i]This worksheet was developed by Christian G.G. Stewart. The feedback from Dennis T. Jaffe on the original version of this worksheet is gratefully acknowledged.

1.4	The Dreams of my siblings: I have asked each of my sibs about their own personal dreams.			
1.5	Shared Dream: I work to integrate my own dream with the dreams of each of my sibs.			
1.6	We > I: I am willing to give up some of my personal freedom for the good of the family because I believe that as a family, we are stronger together.			
2.	**SELF-AWARENESS AND PERSONAL RESPONSIBILITY**			
2.1	Self-Awareness: I am aware of how I am perceived by others within my family.			
2.2	Self-Awareness: I often ask for feedback and I have practices that help me develop my own self-awareness.			
2.3	Personal Responsibility: I am able to reflect on my own role in the family dynamics and how I contribute to the family dynamics.			
2.4	Hierarchy: When I deal with sibs who are younger than me, I treat them as an adult who is on the same level as me.			
3.	**TRUST—HOW TRUSTWORTHY AM I IN THE EYES OF MY SIBLINGS?**[ii]			
3.1	My behavior toward my sibs is PREDICTABLE.			
3.2	My behavior toward my sibs is RESPONSIBLE.			
3.3	I am a resource that my sibs can RELY on.			
3.4	My sibs find me to be CONSIDERATE toward them.			
3.5	I am COMPETENT at my roles.			
4.	**FORGIVENESS**			
4.1	Motivation: With my sibs, I am willing to forgive and let go of what has happened in the past.			
4.2	Skill: I have tools and practices to help me forgive.[iii]			
5.	**CONFLICT AND COMMUNICATION**			
5.1	Honesty: My communication with my sibs is honest and direct, so that they know what is really on my mind.			
5.2	Willingness to Address Issues: When I have differences with my sibs, I raise these issues with them directly rather than try to avoid conflict or talking behind their back.			
5.3	Attitude toward Conflict: I am willing to work through and resolve any conflicts that we have because I prioritize the importance of our relationship.			
5.4	Reflective Listening: I can listen to others with empathy, including the ability to paraphrase and repeat back what I have heard.			

[ii] Kenneth Kaye, *The Dynamics of Family Business: Building Trust and Resolving Conflict* (iUniverse, 2005).
[iii] Fred Luskin, *Forgive for Good: A Proven Prescription for Health and Happiness* (New York: HarperOne, 2002).

5.5	Curiosity: I am truly curious about the perspective and point of view of each of my sibs.			
5.6	Difficult Conversations: I have the necessary skills to have difficult conversations.[iv]			
5.7	Adult-Adult Conversations: I have "adult–adult" conversations with my sibs. This means that I consider them as an adult, and I behave as an adult.			
6.	**MY GENERAL ATTITUDE TOWARD MY SIBLINGS**			
6.1	Optimism: When I think about the ownership of our shared wealth/enterprise, I am optimistic that we can develop an effective sibling partnership together.			
6.2	Respect: I treat all of my sibs with respect.			
6.3	Empathy and Compassion: I demonstrate empathy and compassion toward each of my sibs.			
6.4	Acceptance: I understand that I cannot change my sibs. I accept them just as they are. I understand the only thing I can change is how I perceive my sibs.			
6.5	Invest in the Relationships: I consistently invest time and energy in the relationship. I meet with each of my sibs on a regular basis with no agenda other than to maintain the relationship.			
6.6	Strengths: From time to time I reflect on the individual strengths of each of my sibs.			
6.6	Gratitude: From time to time I reflect on the ways in which I am grateful for each of my sibs.[v]			
7.	**PRESENCE AND ATTUNEMENT**			
7.1	Presence: When I am with my sibs, I am able to be present with them, including I feel present in my own body.			
7.2	Attunement: When I am present with my sibs, I am able to have a felt-sense of them. I can attune to their emotional state and have some awareness of their internal state.			
7.3	Attunement: When we are present with each other, I can feel that my sibs are attuned to my own internal state; I can feel that they have a felt sense of me.			
7.4	Managing Anxiety: I take responsibility for managing my own stress and anxiety, and I have practices that help me do this.			

[iv]Douglas Stone, Bruce Patton, and Sheila Heen, *Difficult Conversations: How to Discuss What Matters Most* (New York: Penguin Books, 1999).
[v]Dr. Kerry Howells, *Untangling You: How Can I Be Grateful When I Feel so Resentful?* (Australia: Major Street Publishing, 2021).

8.	**COLLABORATIVE SKILLS**			
8.1	Collaborative Skills: I have the skills necessary to work collaboratively with my sibs.			
8.2	Helping: I know how to offer help; and I know how to receive help; and I can help as a part of a team.			
8.3	Giving Feedback: I know how to give constructive feedback.			
8.4	Accepting Feedback: I know how to receive feedback from my sibs.			
8.5	Facilitating: I have group facilitation skills, and I make sure I don't dominate.			
8.6	Consensus: I also know how to build consensus with my sibs.			
8.7	Professionalism: I am professional in approach, and I take our work together seriously, including I am prepared for meetings, actively participate, take my own notes etc.			
9.	**GOVERNANCE AND RESPECT FOR BOUNDARIES**			
9.1	Family and Management: I am careful to make a distinction between family matters and business matters. I don't confuse family issues with business issues.			
9.2	Ownership and Management: I am careful to make a distinction between the ownership role and the management role. I know that owners should not interfere in management issues.			
9.3	Organization Chart: I have respect for and follow the corporate organization chart and business roles.			
9.4	Proper Forums: I raise issues in the appropriate forum, i.e., family issues in family meetings, ownership issues in owners meetings, management issues in management meetings.			
9.5	Vote versus Voice: I understand the difference between when I have a voice (I can input on a matter, but it is not for me to decide) and when I have a vote (I have decision-making authority) on a matter.[vi]			
9.6	Accountability: If applicable, as a manager or executive, I hold myself accountable toward the collective owners of our enterprise.			
10.	**INDIVIDUAL OWNERSHIP PHILOSOPHY—AM I A STEWARD OR AN INHERITOR?[vii]**			
10.1	My Personal Ownership Philosophy: I am clear in my own mind on how I see my ownership interest, e.g., whether I see myself as a steward, or whether I look at my ownership as being just the same as any other financial investment (an "inheritor" mindset).			
10.2	Acceptance of Different Philosophies: I can accept the ownership philosophy of each of my sibs even where it may be different from my ownership philosophy.			

[vi]The distinction between vote and voice is made by Dennis T. Jaffe, Ph.D.

[vii]The distinction between the ownership philosophy of being a steward or being an inheritor is made by James E. Hughes, Jr.

Additional Resources

Andrew Bernstein, *The Myth of Stress: Where Stress Really Comes From and How to Live a Happier and Healthier Life* (New York: Simon & Schuster, 2015). His ActivInsight worksheet is a valuable relationship tool.

Roberta M. Gilbert, *Extraordinary Relationships: A New Way of Thinking about Human Interactions,* 2nd ed. (Leading Systems Press, 2021).

Kerry Howells, *Untangling You: How Can I Be Grateful When I Feel so Resentful?* (Australia: Major Street Publishing, 2021).

Fred Luskin, *Forgive for Good: A Proven Prescription for Health and Happiness* (New York: HarperOne, 2002). This offers both practices and processes to build the forgiveness muscle.

Ian A. Marsh, *If It Is So Good to Talk, Why Is It So Hard? Rediscovering the Power of Communication* (Leicester, UK: Troubador Publishing, 2018).

Douglas Stone, Bruce Patton, and Sheila Heen, *Difficult Conversations: How to Discuss What Matters Most* (New York: Penguin Books, 1999). This includes worksheets for preparing for difficult conversations.

Arbinger Institute, *The Anatomy of Peace: Resolving the Heart of Conflict,* 4th ed. (San Francisco, CA: Berrett-Koehler, 2022).

Biography

Christian Stewart is an independent family advisor based in Hong Kong and the founder of Family Legacy Asia. He assists family enterprises with family governance, succession, learning, and development. Christian is a fellow of the Family Firm Institute (FFI) and the recipient of the FFI's 2021 Interdisciplinary Practice Award. He has also received the Wealth Briefing Asia 2017 award for Leading Individual Advisor.

CHAPTER 50

Gamechanging

Matt Wesley

Gamechanging is a way to disentangle stubborn family dynamics. It focuses first on understanding the critical aspects of the family through a process of close observation. Once the dynamics are fully mapped, Gamechanging addresses the keystone habits that lock the problematic patterns in place.[1]

The goal is to foster positive change in one or two keystone habits that will cascade through the family system.

The Werner family was having difficulty with their family business. Some family members worked in the business and some did not. They had countless arguments about dividends, strategy, and management decisions. The generational transition was not going smoothly, and leaders of both the family and the business were not working well together. It looked like a mess.

Over a full day, we engaged the family in a deep dive using a Gamechanging approach. Within a year of that event, by changing just one keystone habit most of the major problems were resolved. The remaining issues were moving in a much better direction. Because they were focused on changing only one thing, the adjustment was relatively easy to make.

The Setup

The heart of Gamechanging, and the key to its success, lies in deeply observing the "game" itself. The facilitator sets up the conversation by identifying the game that the couple or family is playing. In the example above, the game was called "Family Business." The facilitator noted that while running the family business was truly serious, it would be helpful to treat it as though it was a game. In light of that, the

[1]Charles Duhigg, *The Power of Habit: Why We Do What We Do in Life and Business* (New York: Random House, 2012).

core observational question was, "How exactly, is the family playing the game of Family Business?"[2]

The facilitator suggested that, to change the game, the family should uncover game's core patterns and processes. She stressed that this observation phase was not to lay blame or try to understand the game's history or analyze the game, but to simply observe how it worked. The facilitator noted that the system had evolved as it had for its own reasons but that the way the game was currently played had outlived its usefulness to the family. The objective in this phase was to be purely descriptive—to detail how the game was being played as though it was being explained to a complete stranger.

Step 1: Observe the Game

After the initial setup, the facilitator started to ask questions. Those began with general questions about the game such as: Who plays? What are their roles? Who watches? Who referees? Who is allowed to play the game? After an initial round of baseline questions, the inquiry became more granular: What are the boundaries? What real game is this most like? How are winners and losers decided? What are the explicit rules? What are the implicit rules? When is a "round" over? How do you keep score? How are people penalized? What is the point of the game? Who benefits? Who leaves the field of play? And so on. From there the questions got even more specific.

In asking these questions, the facilitator responds to what emerges and asks questions that organically arise from the observations made in real time. The best questions are short—often, the shorter, the better. Three-word questions are good. Two-word questions are better. The questions will always begin with *who, what,* and *how*—and *never* begin with *why.*[3] The questions are limited only by imagination, and the facilitator will encourage the family members to start asking their own questions.

During this time of exploration, the facilitator uses flipcharts or whiteboards (an even better practice is to bring in a graphic recorder[4]). The goal is to create a visual map or representation of every aspect of the game. It is important to leave nothing out. If it is part of the game, it is recorded on the map.

The couple or family should spend a long time looking at the game. In many families, this can be a two- or three-hour process. With couples, it usually takes about an hour. After an initial rush of observations, things will begin to slow. The facilitator has to ask people to dig deeper. If things begin to stall, the facilitator will ask family members to each write out five new questions that haven't been asked.

---

[2]We have used this approach with games such as "Foundation," "Financial Dependence," "Trusts," "Decision-Making," and "Disengagement." It is a tool that can be used pretty much anytime there are systemic problems.

[3]"Why questions" are to be avoided because it leads to analysis, not observation, and can also lead to blame and judgment. You want this step to be purely descriptive. You might occasionally ask a "when" question, but these can also easily lead to blame and judgment, so we suggest avoiding these until you are fluent with the facilitation of Gamechanging.

[4]Graphic recording involves the use of large-scale imagery to lead groups toward a goal. There is a wide array of examples and illustrations on the web.

Often the most critical aspects will be revealed as people break through the obvious observations to new ways of seeing their shared problem.

In facilitating, it is important to avoid blame and judgment. The exercise itself supports this because the complex dynamics are seen in the frame of a game and as an interlocking set of conditions. This objectifies the dynamics; people often feel that the game metaphor distances the system dynamics from personalities. Often couples and families will become fascinated by the game itself and how it is unfolding. They develop insights into themselves and the family that have previously gone unnoticed.

That said, people will sometimes cross the line into an adversarial perspective. It is important for the facilitator to step in quickly to suggest that (1) the game has a life of its own apart from the individuals (it is a system—no one person is at fault), (2) the game had evolved to help the family survive, but the game has outgrown its usefulness, (3) everyone is doing their best, and (4) the point is not to blame people for the history of the game but to look at how to change the game for the future of the family.

The focus must be on the game as an "object"—something that everyone is looking at and trying to understand. A facilitator can also refocus the blaming person on the way they play the game in light of what they are complaining about. This puts the person back into their prefrontal cortex, helps to short-circuit amygdala reactions, and generates some self-reflection on how they are actually participating to perpetuate the patterns.[5]

Step 2: The Pivot

At some point, the couple or the family will have nearly everything out on the table. The entire game has been dissected, and the family can see all of the complexity of the system laid out. No more observation is necessary or helpful. The facilitator will know this has occurred when the family goes quiet with a sense of self-recognition and reflection. They will be done, not because they have reached a limit to their ability to observe, but because they have reached a point of insight and understanding. In our experience, a kind of stillness often descends on the group, and the room becomes deeply reflective.

After this pause, the facilitator will have people study the map for a good 10–15 minutes and then ask the question: "If you could only do one thing to change the entire game, what would it be?"[6] As each person answers, that person's "one thing" is recorded. Then the family boils these down into two or three core insights. Once these insights are boiled down, the facilitator can help the family develop one to three principles that will "change the game."

After going through this process, the Werner family had several insights about their Family Business "game." They realized there were too many cooks in the kitchen, roles were unclear, communication was overly personal, decisions were

[5]Daniel Goleman, *Emotional Intelligence*, 25th anniversary ed. (New York: Bloomsbury, 2020).

[6]This is based on the Pareto principle. In any endeavor, about 80% of the results arise from about 20% of the inputs. If you push this principle to extremes, very big results can arise from very small changes (provided they are the right changes).

made based on short-term gain, some family members were disengaged, control was vested in too narrow of a group, and so on. They had identified close to 50 issues. If they had tried to solve each of these one by one, it would not have worked. However, through facilitation, they decided that large pieces of these dynamics could be addressed if they approached the business through one lens and adopted one keystone habit. If they committed to being more professional, many of these issues would be addressed. So the family formally adopted the principle, "We will professionalize."

After the meeting, things began to change. Because they had only one thing to do—professionalize—they could focus on it and take action. Because it was essential, they were committed to the principle, and because it resulted in some early progress, they referred to it frequently. When a new issue emerged, they would ask how they could handle it professionally. Soon it became second nature.

To professionalize, they brought outsiders into the board, formalized decision-making, created a compensation committee, created more meeting discipline, initiated processes that made sense, and so on. Over one year, the principle, "We will professionalize," created massive cascading change and changed the game for the Werners. They kept to their agreement to professionalize because it solved so many of their issues and simply felt significantly better to the family. We have seen similar results in other families facing very diverse challenges.

Adopting Gamechanging

If you are interested, we suggest that you adopt Gamechanging in safe environments before launching it into a large family system dealing with complex issues. If you are a family advisor, you might start with a client couple facing a question of adult financial dependence or even an issue within your own team as it deals with a challenging problem. As you do this, be sure to linger in the period of observation. That process will seem slow, but the quality of your results will depend on the depth of your observations. Finding the one thing that will change the system will go much more quickly than the first step, and the development of the principle typically takes only a few minutes.

As you adopt a Gamechaning mindset, you will begin to see applications in multiple areas of your own life, in your family, in the organizations you work with, and for the clients you serve. It is a tool with broad applicability.

Additional Resources

James Carse, *Finite and Infinite Games: A Vision of Life as Play and Possibility* (New York: Free Press, 2011).

Charles Duhigg, *The Power of Habit: Why We Do What We Do in Life and Business* (New York: Random House, 2012).

John Kay, *Obliquity: Why Our Goals Are Best Achieved Indirectly* (New York: Penguin Press, 2012).

Gary Keller, *The One Thing: The Surprisingly Simple Truth Behind Extraordinary Results* (Bard Press, 2013)

Matt Wesley, "When Wolves Change Families," www.thewesleygroup.com/blog.

Some Gamechanging Questions

- What is the name of the game?
- Who plays? Who watches? Who coaches? Who referees?
- What is the point of the game?
- What are the rules?
- How do you keep score?
- What is the field of play?
- Who owns the ball?
- How does the team communicate?
- How does the team train?
- Who does the work? Who stars?
- When does a round end?
- What is the point?
- What is the strategy?
- What are the tactical moves?
- Who wins? Who loses?
- Who has gone home or tuned out?
- What calls the plays?
- Who is the opponent?
- When is a round completed?
- What are the positions on the team?
- Who gets benched? What for?

Now make up 21 more questions of your own to add to this list.

Biography

Matthew Wesley is a managing director in the Merrill Center for Family Wealth. He is an internationally recognized practitioner and thought leader on the issues facing financially successful families. With a career that spans 25 years as an estate planning attorney and 10 years as a family advisor, facilitator, and consultant, he helps address the complex issues of generational transition, family culture, and ongoing governance. These issues often affect family enterprise succession, philanthropy, and wealth transfer. He holds a JD from Stanford University and M.Div. from Fuller Theological Seminary.

SECTION 8

MAKING SHARED DECISIONS

One of the most challenging aspects of managing financial wealth together as a family is making shared decisions. All families make decisions. But the ways they make decisions are often left unspoken and unexamined. Perhaps there is one "true" decision-maker, the wealth creator or the eldest family member. Maybe whoever "pushes" the most drives the decision.

For families to succeed over time, they need to make, on balance, more good decisions than bad ones; they also need to decide how to decide—that is, in a clear and intentional way, think through how to make various decisions, decide what works best for them in which circumstances, and then communicate those decisions clearly. This work is sometimes called family "governance."

The chapters in this section explore different aspects of governance. In the first chapter, Lee Hausner offers an exercise that helps families visualize their existing structure of decision-making. Through asking family members at a family gathering to don different hats based on their roles in the family—parent, child, trustee, beneficiary, business owner, manager, etc.—a family can quickly see where authority for different decisions resides. They can also begin to discuss what information and communication are needed to make effective decisions. To top it off, it's a very fun exercise too.

Jim Grubman then offers a framework (first published in the first *Wealth of Wisdom* volume) for making wise decisions about different practices in the family. He asks readers to reflect on what family traditions, habits, practices, or ideas family members find helpful and want to preserve; which seem vestiges from the past and are no longer contributing to the family's well-being; and what new practices or ideas the family could adopt that would help them adapt to the future. This backward-and-forward gaze honors the reality that every family is in the midst of a journey from the past into the future.

In the next chapter, Stacy Allred moves the focus from the big picture to more specific decisions, such as sharing information about wealth with an adult child or making a loan to a friend. She invites readers to analyze such decisions using, first, a "premortem"—in which one envisions all the things that could go wrong, and so identifies risks—and then, second, a "promortem"—in which one envisions what steps could be taken to ensure a successful outcome.

As mentioned, in many families, decisions are made by one or two family members, usually parents. This paternalistic approach can lead to problems as children mature and grow into adults themselves. In the next chapter, Barbara Hauser uses insights from the governance of nations to highlight three principles that are key also to family governance: transparency, accountability, and participation. If these three principles are honored in a family's decision-making, the results are often more understood, more effective, and more long-lasting.

An extension of these principles comes in the next chapter, in which Kathryn McCarthy offers the "RACI" (pronounced RAY-SEE) framework to apply to decision-making in a complex family enterprise. This framework works best in a system where there are multiple boards or entities governing different parts of the family's affairs (such as an operating company board, management, foundation board, trustees, etc.). RACI distinguishes among people who are Responsible, those who are Accountable, those who should be Consulted, and those who need to be Informed. McCarthy offers the example of a matrix in which a family enterprise can keep track of these different categories for different stakeholders. This is advanced decision-making, but for families with this level of complexity, it can be extremely useful.

One form of a family enterprise is a family office—whether a stand-alone "single family office" or a family office embedded within a family-owned operating company—which handles all the family's financial affairs. In the next chapter, Eugene Lipitz takes up the important subject of developing internal controls and transparent workflows for the critical tasks of the family office. Development of such controls may sometimes feel too "formal" for an entity which is, after all, about the family—yet doing so can save a great deal of family confusion or conflict but also can guard against fraud or poorly informed decision-making.

One of the most valuable practices for families who are managing significant financial wealth or other assets together is to hold regular family meetings. These meetings can be for the purpose of educating family members about the finances, connecting with each other and having fun, or making shared decisions. Whatever the specific purposes, developing the habit of holding effective family meetings is a clear success factor for enterprising families.

That's why we devote the last two chapters in this section to family meetings. In the first, Katherine Grady and Wendy Ulaszek lay out practical, step-by-step considerations for families who want to hold a productive family meeting. They move from the question of why meet, to who should be invited, to how to assemble the agenda in line with the meeting goals, to the crucial considerations of where to meet, for how long, with whose direction, etc. Even for families who have a tradition of meeting, this chapter will provide insights into enhancing meeting design and execution.

In the final chapter, Keith Whitaker focuses in on one aspect of family meeting management: the articulation of meeting ground rules. Ground rules may feel awkward for a family meeting: We're family, after all! But experience shows that agreeing upon such rules at the beginning of a family meeting process can be invaluable for giving participants a sense that the meeting will be a safe place to discuss important topics, topics that sometimes come with strong emotional content. Sometimes in the heat of discussion, family members will break the rules, but then the group will be able to refer back to the rules and reaffirm the family's norms. And over time the ground rules become just "the way we treat each other." Deciding on meeting ground rules is one of the most important shared decisions a family can make.

CHAPTER 51

Hats Off to You!

Lee Hausner

A newborn infant has a clear role in its family: It's the baby.

As the years progress, the infant fills a variety of additional roles: brother, sister, father, mother, uncle, aunt, etc.

Years ago I heard a member of a prominent family enterprise describe his career path in the following manner: Upon graduating from college, he immediately entered the family business and was given a division to run. By his own admission, he neglected his duties, and one day the controller of the company told him his dad wanted to see him. It was the custom in this company that a meeting with dad generally meant a promotion or a raise. So, with great anticipation, this man drove to dad's home. His dad welcomed him, and the young man noticed two baseball caps on the table. Dad put on a hat with the word BOSS. He said, "Son, it is difficult to be a boss in a family business, but you have not met any of your goals in the past two years, and so this is your termination notice. You're fired." As the young man was reeling, his dad quickly put on the other baseball hat with the inscription DAD, and added, "Son, I understand that you were fired from your job today. Mom and I will be as supportive as we can." As a result of this exchange, the young man left the family business and worked for the next five years outside the family enterprise, before returning to it with a renewed sense of responsibility and stewardship.

Thus was born the exercise "Hats Off to You!"

Wearing Many Hats

This exercise does not take a lot of preparation, but you'll want one thing beforehand: a lot of baseball caps. Ideally, try to find hats in a variety of colors, e.g., five red ones, five blue ones, and so on. If you have a large family, the number of hats needed is going to grow exponentially.

This exercise is best done in the context of a family meeting. As you sit around a table, invite anyone who is a father or mother to put on a hat. Then invite anyone who is a sister or brother to don another hat. Many of the adults in the room will now be wearing two hats. You can decide whether to add further family relationships (such as son, daughter, uncle, aunt, etc.).

Turn then to the various roles within the family enterprise. These might include executive roles such as chief executive officer (CEO) of the family business, member of the board of directors, or specific management roles within the family enterprise, family office executive, family council, etc.

Finally, save some hats for ownership roles. These could include shareholder, member of a family LLC, trustee, or beneficiary.

Pretty soon, many of the people around the table will be trying to balance five, six, or more hats on their heads. Some members may have a stack of hats piled up in front of them. It is a lot of fun, and one of the most amusing aspects of the exercise is that oftentimes the most elderly family members are trying to wear the most hats.

Talking about Hats

Each of the hats in this exercise carries with it rights and responsibilities. The real key to the exercise is to come to see how many of these rights and responsibilities various family members hold at the same time.

To begin to do that, talk as a group about the various types of hats. You might want to reverse the order with which you put the hats on; first talk about the owner hats, then the management-related hats, and finally the family hats.

For example, observe how many people around the table are wearing or holding the "shareholder" hat. What rights and responsibilities does being a shareholder bring? Then notice who's wearing the trustee hat or the beneficiary hat. How are they different and alike? You can also talk about how your perspectives of each other shift when you look at the other person in light of the hat he or she is wearing. How do beneficiaries feel about the people wearing the trustee hat and vice versa?

You can do something similar with the management-related hats. How many people around the table have hats such as CEO, managing member, investment advisor, foundation director, family council member, or the like? Is it a large number or a small minority? Invite the wearers of management hats to talk about how it feels to be in this group. Then ask the rest of the family how it feels to look at that group from the outside. Here the goal is to get different members of the family to understand what it's like to be in each other's shoes (to vary the clothing metaphor).

The same goes with the family hats. This is an opportunity to talk about values: In your family, what does it mean to be a mother, father, sister, brother, etc.? Do aunts and uncles have some special value that they bring to family relations, for example, with their nieces and nephews? How about grandparents? Does your family have a way of identifying, honoring, and making good use of those who wear that often-unseen hat of "elder"? This is also an opportunity to talk about the differences between these very powerful family hats and the other roles in the family, just as that young man's father did so many years ago, by taking off his BOSS hat and putting on his DAD one.

One more step you can take is to use a whiteboard or flipchart to start documenting in writing the rights and responsibilities of your family's various "hats." This documentation can prove extremely helpful as you face the decisions that come with stewarding and managing a family enterprise. It can also help educate and remind family members about their roles, so that you all can be more intentional and clearer in navigating your different responsibilities.

Conclusion

There is a reason that kings and queens wear crowns or that gentlemen and ladies (at least back before John F. Kennedy was president) wore hats. The head is the authoritative part of our bodies, the part to which we look in communicating with each other. A hat signals the status and authority of its bearer for all to see.

Unfortunately, in a family enterprise, almost all those hats are invisible. As a result, navigating the web of authority and permission, rights and responsibilities can be extremely tricky. It's made all the more so by the emotional power that many of these relationships hold.

The Hats Off to You! exercise aims to make those relationships more visible and to give family members a chance to explore their meaning with each other. It is educational and fun. Nor is it a "one and done" sort of effort. As the relationships within the family enterprise change, so do the "hats" people wear. I recommend that you consider redoing this exercise every year or two, to remain conscious of those changes. My hope is that over time you become as expert in putting on and putting off your various hats as was that wise CEO who inspired this exercise.

Additional Resources

Lee Hausner, *Children of Paradise* (Author, 2017).

Lee Hausner and Douglas K. Freeman, *The Legacy Family* (New York, NY: Palgrave Macmillan, 2010).

Ernest A. Doud, Jr. and Lee Hausner, Ph.D., "Hats Off to You," in *Finding Success in Family Business Succession* (Author, 2004).

Biography

Dr. Lee Hausner is an internationally recognized clinical psychologist and business consultant. As a former psychologist for the Beverly Hills School District, she is an acknowledged expert on psychological issues involving wealth and wealth transfer issues as well as family business succession. A highly regarded speaker and author, she is a top-rated resource for Young Presidents' Organization, was a presenter at Davos, and is a frequent guest on national radio and television, as well as a recurrent participant at private client conferences for major financial institutions. She was a founder, member of the board of directors, and senior dean of the Learning Center Foundation and assisted USC create a Family Business Center.

CHAPTER 52

How to Balance Family Stability with Resilience over Generations

James Grubman

Financially successful families face many challenges within and across generations. Navigating these with a resilient, adaptive attitude is one of the strongest contributors to long-term family harmony and prosperity. How do families maintain both stability and resilience in the face of a rapidly changing world?

Keep in mind that the transition to wealth by the first generation is the initial challenge to be navigated in the family. There are myriad choices about how to spend or give, how to parent, and how to communicate in the midst of wealth. How these choices are handled will influence whether the second and third generations will be ready for adulthood. If the founding generation has been willing to weave together elements of their past and their present in flexible ways, the family will be well-suited to prepare the next generation and for wise decision-making within the family. On the other hand, parents too strongly wedded to the past or too quick to chase the pleasures of affluence will set the family on a path undermining the family's future.

As the rising generations of the family enter adulthood, those family members raised with wealth (the "natives" of wealth, compared to first-generation "immigrants" to wealth) will in turn influence the blending of the family's heritage with a willingness to adapt to changing conditions. This is the second major challenge for the family. Hold too tightly to the past, and the family will harden and crumble. Dive too eagerly into each passing trend of materialism, and the family will find itself untethered from its valued roots.

In certain ways, families must operate like Janus, the Roman god of beginnings, transitions, and passages (from whose name we get the first month of the year, January). Janus is typically depicted with one face looking to the past and one face toward the future. Like Janus, families must look to the past for the values and skills the family's founders learned during their experience of scarcity or adversity. Turning ahead, these values and skills must then be adapted for changing conditions as the family takes in new members, encounters new financial or business stressors, and copes with unanticipated social pressures.

To accomplish this balance of stability and resilience, it can be helpful to focus on three central questions:

1. What should we maintain from our heritage that has served us well?
2. What should we let go of that no longer serves us?
3. What new practices or ideas should we learn that will help us adapt in the future?

For the first question, think about which traditions, rituals, values, and skills are fundamental to the family. These have likely helped steer the family (and possibly their business) through challenging times. Perhaps elements of faith, spirituality, or social commitment are integral to these values. Prudent financial management and avoidance of extravagance may be core skills. There may be family rituals around holidays, transitions, and anniversaries that bring people together to renew the bonds of relationship. These traditions, values, and skills should feel so embedded in what makes the family unique and prosperous that discarding these feels like risking the family's very identity.

It's worth asking yourself: What are the cherished traditions of your family? Have some of these started to drift away or be neglected? What would be required to reactivate them in a fresh way, relevant especially to younger family members?

Second, think honestly about which elements of the family's heritage may be nostalgic, sentimental, or tied to times or places that have gone by. These may feel emotionally important to some in the family who see them as impossible to let go. Yet, the lessons linked to those events may no longer be as relevant to the world of today or tomorrow. Many families tell cherished stories of almost extreme frugality during the early days, or how a founder handled major setbacks in the business using clever or risk-laden strategies. These are the legacy stories of the immigrant journey to success and wealth. However, times may have changed enough that those strategies no longer fully apply. Or they have been superseded by more sophisticated strategies available to the family now. Like parables, keep the lessons of those wonderful stories but be willing to place them in the context of the past.

Consider: How willing are you to adapt some of the early experiences of the family to fit the current perspectives of younger family members? Could you engage in a dialogue to discover what might recapture their energy and commitment?

Finally, talk in depth about the family *as it stands now*. Who is a part of the family now who might not have been anticipated in the past? Are you more diverse, dispersed, or multicultural than the family's origins ever would have predicted? Does modern family life encompass experiences far beyond its traditional roots? If so, you must make a place at the table for a broader range of viewpoints, experiences, adjustments, and opportunities than your heritage would have envisioned. Like Janus, look ahead. What resources or networks does the family now have that are likely to be utilized in hard times in the future? How will the family become a learning organization? How is the family adapting to the current world in ways that are the *new* life lessons, values, and skills? These are likely to contribute to the family's current and future resilience alongside the family's heritage and traditions.

Think about: Looking past the ever-changing forms of digital communication to find their underlying substance of connection. There may be stronger opportunities than you may think. Are there ways to advocate for traditional values while making room for new interests? How can you establish learning and adaptability as the centerpiece of the family values?

Think of the following examples as you imagine blending past, present, and future for your own family's adaptability:

- A southern European food products family with a tradition of autocratic male leadership gradually transitions to a family council headed by dynamic women, even as the family proudly upholds its ethnic heritage and identity.
- A North American family enterprise in the automotive field develops franchises on three continents and prepares for disruptive change in the industry. Within the family, they welcome in-laws from the cultures where the new factories and business units are being developed, gathering every two years in the Midwest for a three-day family assembly and barbecue.
- A family enterprise stretching back five generations struggles to communicate and collaborate about the issues they must handle in the modern era. A young family member with entrepreneurial skills develops a technology platform for communicating securely and easily, then discovers the application has commercial potential for similar family enterprises. A new venture is born alongside the family's traditional businesses.

Balancing stability with resilience is neither easy nor simple under the pressures of everyday life, particularly when wealth is at stake. If the family constantly retells familiar stories of the past but isn't adding to them with new examples of success and spirit, the present will wither in favor of cherishing the past. It may be time to reevaluate the family's willingness to take risk, to explore new ventures, and to support those who want to look ahead more than behind.

On the other hand, if the family chases so many trends that a sense of focus has been lost, it may be time to regroup, do strategic planning, and find your center again. It also may be time to create new rituals that celebrate the family and its connections. Time and distance may have weakened the connections needed to sustain the family. Reestablishing the core values and traditions of the family may help regain a sense of grounding and cohesion.

No one person in the family can accomplish this blending of past, present, and future. Although individual family members or leaders may have vision for what must be done, maintaining family resilience requires dialogue crossing generations and family branches. The three questions of adaptation must be debated, positions heard, and consensus found. Achieving a balance between heritage and innovation requires the family to share in a vision. Like Janus keeping watch over both tradition and adaptation, prosperous families can face the unique challenges that come with wealth—guided by cherished values yet responsive to a constantly changing world.

Additional Resources

Starting or renewing a family-meeting process is often the first step in working together on the blending of tradition and adaptation. For help with family-meeting planning and facilitation, see the following whitepaper:

Dennis Jaffe and Stacy Allred, "Talking It Through: A Guide to Conducting Effective Multi-generational Family Meetings about Business and Wealth," available from Bank of America/Merrill Lynch or at www.dennisjaffe.com, 2014.

For more discussion on the adjustments needed as families move from the wealth-creating generation to subsequent generations, see the following book:

James Grubman, *Strangers in Paradise: How Families Adapt to Wealth Across Generations* (Turners Falls, MA: Family Wealth Consulting, 2013).

Biography

Dr. Jim Grubman is a senior consultant to multigenerational families and their advisors about the issues often arising around wealth. He has more than 40 years' experience in healthcare and financial psychology as a practitioner, educator, author, researcher, and speaker. Jim has been recognized, along with his long-time collaborator Dr. Dennis Jaffe, with the Outstanding Contribution to Thought Leadership award by the 2021 Family Wealth Report awards. He has published widely and been quoted in various media including the *New York Times, Wall Street Journal,* and CNBC. His global consulting practice, Family Wealth Consulting, is based in the Boston, Massachusetts, area.

CHAPTER 53

Making Better Decisions by Telling Stories That Have "Already Happened"

Stacy Allred

Recall a hospital scene in the movies where the operation has gone awry and the patient has died. The medical team is gathered around to perform a ***postmortem***—to analyze the situation *after* action and see what they can learn. Family wealth[1] decisions, all too often, are similar to the postmortem—learning and analysis is done *after* the fact and frequently with suboptimal results.

Consider the story of a generous couple who made a large outright gift to each of their three adult children.[2] Simply put, the sibling who was a saver saved, the risk-taker made an outsized bet, and the spender ran through the money and came back asking for more. Lamenting the mixed results, the matriarch commented, "I should have known; these gifts magnified their long-standing relationship to money."

Yet, there is a simple decision tool with the power to

- increase ability to correctly identify risk factors,
- see new opportunities, and
- build intuition about and sensitivity to future problems.

---

[1]Wealth in this context refers to the holistic definition of wealth, including the five capitals: Human, Intellectual, Social, Legacy, and Financial. Based on the ideas of James E. Hughes Jr., who encourages all to return to the original definition of wealth as well-being. See *Complete Family Wealth*, James E. Hughes, Jr., Susan E. Massenzio and Keith Whitaker (Wiley 2018).

[2]Compilation to protect confidentiality.

How Does It Work?

It starts with the idea of **prospective hindsight**;[3] that is, leveraging our natural ability to tell stories but to tell them as if they have "already happened" *before* the big event as a method to tap into deeper insights[4] and combat common decision biases (e.g., overconfidence). Prospective hindsight seems to spur more insights because it offers a firmer cognitive foothold by forcing a family to fill in the blanks between today and a certain future event (as opposed to the slipperier process of speculating about an event that may or may not happen).[5]

Leveraging the power of prospective hindsight, cognitive psychologist Gary A. Klein developed the practice of the *premortem*—a tool to identify risks in advance.[6] Years later Klein added the *promortem*[7] as a tool to identify and optimize leverage points and opportunities for success.

I was introduced to this tool years back during a lecture by a professor and used it that same afternoon to explore a question a rising generation 20-something daughter asked: How do I respond to a loan request from my friend? This young woman had struggled with requests for loans from her friends over the past several years. With the significant financial resources her inherited wealth provided her, she often felt obligated to help and experienced mixed results. In my work as a thinking partner to families, I have found these tools so powerful that I routinely leverage them on a weekly basis. It turns out that it's not just one of *my* favorite methods for making better decisions, but many others, including famed Nobel Prize winner Daniel Kahneman.[8]

To explain how this tool works, let's go back to our generous couple. What if, *before* making the gifts, they pictured the future (say five years out), and engaging their natural ability to tell stories that had "already happened," developed two distinct stories:[9]

---

[3]Prospective Hindsight—imagining that an event has already occurred originated based on the work of decision researchers J. Edward Russo and Paul J.H. Schoemaker.

[4]Research by Deborah J. Mitchell (Wharton), Jay Russo (Cornell) and Nancy Pennington (University of Colorado) found that using Prospective Hindsight increases the ability to identify reasons for future outcomes by 30%.

[5]Chip Heath and Dan Heath, *Decisive: How to Make Better Choices in Life and Work* (New York: Random House, 2013).

[6]Gary A. Klein, "Performing a Project Premortem," *Harvard Business Review* (September 2007), https://hbr.org/2007/09/performing-a-project-premortem.

[7]Gary A. Klein, "The Pro-Mortem Method: Creating a Blueprint for Success," *Psychology Today* (October 21, 2015).

[8]Nobel Prize winner Daniel Kahneman describes the "premortem" to eliminate thinking biases. Vimeo.com/67596631, accessed July 5, 2021.

[9]While many organizations today focus on using only the premortem, my experience is that for individuals and families, it's most effective to engage in both, starting with the premortem (disaster scenario) and ending on a positive note with the promortem (brilliant scenario).

STEPS TO CONDUCT A PRE- AND PROMORTEM

Adapted from Process Developed by Decision Researcher Gary A. Klein

STORY ONE: PREMORTEM
A Spectacular Failure

STORY TWO: PROMORTEM
A Brilliant Outcome

STEP ONE:

Accept that the plan failed and imagine a big disaster

Ex: The large outright transfers undermined growth and development of all three adult children. Despite noble intentions, the gifts were a burden. Everything that could have gone wrong has gone wrong.

Select a term in the future that makes sense (e.g., typically 1-10 years out) and use your natural ability to tell a story that "already happened"
Ex: It's <u>five years</u> out and ...

Accept that the plan succeeded and imagine an excellent outcome

Ex: All three adult children effectively integrated the large outright gifts into their lives. The gifts enhanced their capacity to actively build a meaningful life with positive impact on self, family and community.

STEP TWO:

List of reasons for failure

Example:

- *Lump-sum gift proved to be too much, too soon; the responsibility felt overwhelming leading to decisions made in haste or avoided altogether.*
- *Use of money didn't align to unspoken expectations (e.g., spent quickly, in a flashy way), negatively impacting family relationships.*
- *Invested an outsized sum in a friend's start-up that went under.*
- *Complacency, no skin in the game.*
- *Spending inconsistent with family values.*

Create a list of all the plausible reasons that contributed to the outcome of this scenario, thinking of each family member.

(If doing this with others, write down reasons individually before sharing.)

These factors collectively create a blueprint of risks to manage and opportunities to strengthen.

List of reasons for success

Example:

- *Clear understanding of purpose and shared guidelines for how to use the funds customized to each individual life journey. (Moved from expectation to agreement.)*
- *Individual values-based financial plan developed with trusted advisor at onset.*
- *Funds used in balanced ways that grew the family capital (experiential learning, supplemented income to pursue a lower-paid, socially responsible job, down payment on a first home, personal trainer, etc.).*
- *Practiced gratitude through actions, giving back time, treasure and talent.*
- *Ongoing focus on developing relevant core competencies (e.g., financial literacy, perspective taking, responsibility and accountability).*

STEP THREE:

Protect Against Risk Factors

- *Give money in incremental amounts, leveraging experiential learning for insights.*
- *Dialogue on purpose of gift, family values (in general and on the earning, spending, saving and sharing of money) and develop shared guidelines.*

Step back. Actively adjust and strengthen your plan.
Address the most relevant items with the greatest potential impact first.

Bolster Success Factors

- *Ongoing Family Meetings to share how gifts were used, learn from each other and build competencies.*
- *Incorporate trusted advisors to build a personalized financial plan, life coaching, etc.*
- *Reasoned risk taking, coupled with viewpoint of "failures" as "first attempt in learning."*

STEP FOUR:

Monitor.
Periodically review your list and consider and respond to what may be emerging.

I suspect that using this tool would have resulted in a different outcome. Recognizing that making these gifts represented a "moment that mattered" with outsized impact on the family system, the parents might have adjusted their casual approach and structured the gifts differently, including thoughtful communication, timing, "right sizing" the gifts by gifting in tranches, a focus on building the competencies necessary for effectively integrating financial capital, bringing in a trusted advisor to support thoughtful risk-taking, and making informed decisions to increase the probability of the gifts having a positive impact on all three siblings.

The process of creating the two stories actively mines for insights that might otherwise remain dormant until it's after the fact. This will provide the option to take appropriate steps to mitigate or prevent the most likely avoidable causes of failure and bolster key success factors.

How Long Does the Process Take?

Of course, the amount of time required depends on the complexity of the decision and the number of people involved. Step One is pretty easy. Often, it's helpful to start with 20 minutes to get through Step Two (creating a list of all the plausible reasons for the failure and the success), and then leave an hour or two to work through Step Three (strengthening your plan by addressing the most relevant items with the greatest potential impact). (Don't let time be a hurdle. Taking 15-minutes to engage in a streamlined version of the exercise still provides value.)

Why Does the Process Work?

Why does the decision process of a premortem and promortem approach generate better decisions, predictions, and plans? The work of renowned scholars including Kahneman, Klein, and Weick suggests that this approach helps decision-makers:

- Overcome blind spots
- Bridge short-term and long-term thinking
- Dampen excessive optimism

For What Types of Wealth Decisions Is This Tool Useful?

The tool is widely applicable. I have used the tool as a part of a playbook[10] with families grappling with a vast range of topics, including the following:

- Determining how much money to give family, friends, charity
- Making a loan to a friend or family member

---

[10]Charlie Munger, partner of Warren Buffett, touts the idea that everyone needs to build and continually update a list of mental models relevant to their particular situation. Munger's idea to create a latticework by combining diverse mental models is a powerful one. (See Munger's *A Lesson on Elementary, Worldly Wisdom as It Relates to Investment Management and Business*, 1994 speech at University of Southern California Marshall Business School.) With the more complex topics listed above, the premortem and promortem is one framework in a larger playbook to adequately address the topic.

- Building an effective wealth communication plan—ultimately leading up to the "big reveal"
- Selling or transitioning a family-owned business
- Passing on a legacy property (e.g., shared family vacation home)
- Designing a vibrant next chapter
- Starting a family council

Additional Resources

Chip Heath and Dan Heath, *Decisive: How to Make Better Choices in Life and Work* (New York: Crown Business, 2013).

Gary A. Klein, "Performing a Project Premortem," *Harvard Business Review* (September 2007), https://hbr.org/2007/09/performing-a-project-premortem.

Gary A. Klein, "The Pro-Mortem Method: Creating a Blueprint for Success," *Psychology Today* (October 21, 2015).

Biography

Stacy Allred consults with families to explore the big questions that keep them up at night. She began her career in public accounting. Armed with analytical training and thinking (master's degree in taxation) she addressed the structural questions of financial capital.

Twenty years ago, this all changed; while designing financial and estate plans, she experienced the tremendous energy behind the qualitative questions at the intersection of family and finances. Thoughtfully exploring these big questions led to adapting a holistic approach and dedicating her career to walking alongside individuals and families to effectively navigate the complexity and promise of wealth.

Grounded in the facilitation of family meetings, her practice spans the practical application of family governance and decision-making to creating a learning family. A curious, lifelong learner, Stacy is currently experimenting with the tools of foresight to elevate seeing around corners and identifying, planning, and shaping possible futures.

CHAPTER 54

Democratizing Family Decision-Making

Barbara Hauser

How can families avoid bitter conflicts and disagreements? One answer is to deliberately adopt a system of decision-making that is seen as just and fair by all the family members.

A family is, after all, a group of people. Why not learn from the way larger groups manage themselves? We can look at countries.[1] We can also look at large companies, for whom extensive work has been done, and published, about successful decision-making, another term for governance.

Key factors in democratic decision-making. Looking at the corporate governance principles developed by the OECD (the Organisation for Economic Co-operation and Development), we find two key principles: **transparency** and **accountability**. Based on my 30 years of practice with families, I would add a third key principle: **participation**.

I will share a personal example of how these three principles worked in my own family many years ago. Like many families, we had issues and disagreements, and no great way of solving them, other than that unhelpful parental command "because I said so." I read a book that suggested having family meetings to discuss any such issues. So I called together our three sons, ages 5, 8, and 10, and my good-natured husband and explained that we were going to have a family meeting. I said we would discuss issues, then vote. I said we would each have one vote. The boys looked at each other, doing the math. The middle son agreed to take written minutes. My husband went first with his issue: In the Minnesota winter, our oldest son refused to wear his boots while waiting for the bus. My husband expected an obvious answer in his favor. Instead after a pleasant discussion, the first written minute in the book we keep in our safe was "Jason wears his boots when he wants to."

This event had **transparency**: Each person knew what the facts were. It had **accountability**: People would honor the decisions. It had **participation**: Each of the five members participated in the discussion.

[1] In my book *International Family Governance: A Guide for Families and their Advisors*, I compare the governance models of six countries: the United States, France, India, Japan, England and the Navajo Nation.

The principle of transparency is extremely important; the lack of transparency causes substantial mistrust and conflict. As stated by the OECD in its Principle V on Disclosure and Transparency:

> *The corporate governance framework should ensure that timely and accurate disclosure is made on all material matters regarding the corporation, including the financial situation, performance, ownership, and governance of the company.*[2]

In my experience sharing information has been an excellent way to overcome distrust and jealousy. Sometimes this is very difficult to overcome, especially when control over information is a manner of control itself.

The second key principle is that of accountability. In a simple sense, the basis of accountability is that people will keep their promises. One of the great writers on justice, John Rawls, has a profound emphasis on the importance of keeping promises. In his view, one should be honest, keep promises, and comply with contracts voluntarily made. Even young children have this sense of fairness and will cry out "but you promised." On a more sophisticated level, we find the legal theory of promissory estoppel, the principle that certain promises will be enforced if the one who made it knew the recipient was relying on it. My own advice years ago for a business journal[3] article about leadership had the title "Leaders, Keep Your Promises."

The third principle, participation, can make the difference at a country level as well as on a family level between a closed government and an open and free one. The heart of democracy is to be able to participate in making the rules that people will live by. Increasingly studies are being done on the "happiness" of people.[4] Those living in countries that are ranked high in happiness report that one factor is that they feel they are participating in the government. In the United States the rallying cry for freedom during the Boston Tea Party was "no taxation without representation." The current movements in the United States to restrict voting are understandably called attacks on democracy itself. It can be helpful to think of the origins of the social compact described by John Locke. The members of a group in effect make a promise to each other, and everyone participates in this process. I think back to that first meeting of my own small family of five: Each person was promised the right to participate.

Applying the three principles is an illustration of democracy. Many years later, after a career as a tax lawyer, I returned to this model of family decision-making. Now it was not my family of five. It involved wealthy family business owners with complex holdings and complex personal relationships. I learned that even the most patriarchal family could learn to change their decision-making process into a democratic process, and the positive results were wonderful to see.[5]

---

[2]OECD Principles of Corporate Governance, available at oecd.org/corporate/ca/corporate governanceprinciples/31557724.pdf

[3]*Industry Week*, interview by Tom Brown.

[4]See the World Happiness Project, www.worldhappiness.report. The report includes annual rankings of countries.

[5]I am sometimes asked how I persuade a patriarch to change. The answer is that it is their decision, and they are motivated either by family pressure or by an understanding that they will not always be in charge.

An example illustrates the value of applying a democratic process to family decision-making. Identifying features have been changed, but not the substance. The family owned one of the largest businesses in the country, but they were at an impasse. One founding father had died, and his oldest son did not get along well with the father's brother. One son in the next generation asked me to help. I found a lack of transparency, a lack of accountability, and a lack of participation. There was very little trust. There was no sense of the businesses being run in a manner that was fair to everyone. The owners reluctantly agreed to listen to the consultant but asked me to stay in a more distant hotel so the word would not spread that the company was in trouble.

The first step was to understand the family and their concerns. This was done by private confidential interviews. Next was a written report describing the issues that seemed to be causing difficulties. It was suggested to use those issues as the agenda items for group discussions. It was important that the family owners act in a democratic manner—one they were not accustomed to. It had been a very patriarchal family. The two equal brothers made all the major decisions.

Now, with the son involved, nothing was simple. The first emphasis was on **transparency**: Did everyone have all the correct information? The second hurdle was to get agreement that whatever they decided would be honored—**accountability**. Third was to encourage **participation**. For this important goal, it was decided that all the adult family members could participate and each person would have one vote.[6] This was democracy in action.

As a positive unintended consequence of the group meetings, one adult daughter with teenage children told me she had started the practice of family meetings in their own small family.

For the family as a whole, a new entity was formed, called an Owners' Council, which deliberately included the adult members of the next generation who were not yet themselves owners but would be after a succession occurred. The new Owners' Council was able to agree on key management directions. They hired a management consultant and were able to reorganize the entire company. They also hired a local lawyer to help with the new legal structures.

The senior family members applied their democratic learnings to company management and had the first company-wide retreat of all top management. The top management were hesitant and fearful of the new project. The owners were worried that once the management was gathered together, they would be intimidated and afraid to speak at all. Instead, as the retreat got underway and discussion tables were assigned, the managers began to speak and were pleased to be included. They responded with enthusiasm to the opportunity to learn first-hand (**transparency**), to rely on the owners (**accountability**), and to voice their own concerns (**participation**). Part of the feedback from the recipients was a request to continue with quarterly meetings in the future. The senior family owners agreed during the retreat, and

[6]A note about voting: Even when voting rights are negotiated in great detail, in my experience, no issue has actually been settled by a vote—they have all been agreed to by consensus. This does mean the discussions can take a long time, but as the Japanese taught, a slow decision built by consensus is a decision that will last. Families may need to learn a discussion process free of domination or coercion. Some advisors see voting as a way to break those patterns.

they thanked me, by name. When the retreat ended, the owners asked me to stay at the closest hotel in the future.

This experience, repeated many times during a 10-year period of working with families in different countries, convinced me that the democratic process works. It seems to work in every culture and is a foundational element of justice. Whether it was my small family of five or 200 company managers, I do think that this process is a wonderful tool, for all families, everywhere.

Someone asked what families can do right now to begin. I have clear answers for all three principles:

- Transparency—Tell the truth.
- Accountability—Keep your promises.
- Participation—Listen to each other.

Additional Resources

Barbara Hauser, *International Family Governance* (Mesatop Press, 2009).
Barbara R Hauser, *The Benefits of Applying the Rule of Law in Family Governance* (Helbing & Lichtenhahn, 2022).

Biography

Barbara Hauser began as a traditional private client lawyer, after graduating from Wellesley College and clerking at the U.S. Supreme Court. Working with wealthy families, she began to think that the answer was not tight legal documents but issues of control in the family. She left her law firm partnership to work with families as an entire group, to teach and learn ways in which they could deal with inevitable conflicts and make better decisions. She worked with families as diverse as Saudis to Chinese. She is the author of *International Family Governance.*

CHAPTER 55

Using RACI to Determine Roles and Responsibilities in a Complex Multigenerational Family Enterprise

Kathryn McCarthy

To say that families and family enterprises are complex systems with many interrelationships is quite the understatement.

We've all had experiences with the "many hats" that family members wear. One and the same family member can be a trustee, beneficiary, chief executive officer, foundation head, spouse, etc. The same holds true for the multitude of participants in the family enterprise structures. Have you ever been asked, "I don't know where in our family enterprise to bring this issue up?" or "Who is ultimately responsible for making the decision about XYZ?" or "Why don't I ever seem to know on a timely basis what decisions have been made?"

The family enterprise structure and system, which often includes the family office, family foundation, operating businesses, trusts, trust protectors, family council, close advisors, and other operating partners, can be fertile ground for confusion and duplication if not managed efficiently and with transparency. Even with a very detailed organization chart and robust governance practices, like a family council or a family office board, questions arise. For example, which entity in the family enterprise structure is responsible for developing a strategy that may impact other parts of the family enterprise? Likewise, who or what group needs to be informed of these decisions and activities? Which group(s) needs to be consulted with first is often questioned. Not only does this complexity add to confusion about roles and responsibilities, but it can result in a lack of trust or even conflict and competition among the various interested parties.

Often in complex situations, every entity in the enterprise not only stands on its own individually but also needs to be considered as part of the whole system to clarify decision-making and to define roles and responsibilities among all the stakeholders. Of course, then there is the issue of communication protocols throughout the enterprise. What are the appropriate communication channels? Who is consulted and in what sequence?

So how can families (and their advisors) sort out the practical side of managing these complex relationships among various entities/structures to become more transparent, efficient, and informed? One business process management tool that can be used effectively to organize family enterprise-wide governance is RACI.

What Is RACI?

RACI (pronounced RAY-SEE) is a responsibility assignment matrix used for project management. The origins of RACI are murky even though it is a common tool used in business. It describes the participation and responsibility among the interested parties in completing tasks or deliverables for a project or business process. RACI is an acronym derived from the four key roles and levels most typically identified in the RACI matrix: responsible, accountable, consulted, and informed.

In a business setting, the definitions of the RACI categories are as follows:

- **Responsible:** person who performs an activity or does the work
- **Accountable:** person who is ultimately accountable and has Yes/No/Veto
- **Consulted:** person who needs to feedback and contribute to the activity
- **Informed:** person who needs to know of the decision or action

The RACI matrix is used to align the human elements in the decision-making process. Usually many different people are involved in any process/entity, and they have differing responsibilities. A RACI matrix explicitly documents roles/activities and is a handy reference guide too.

RACI helps a team or a group of interested parties understand who is responsible for what tasks or processes. RACI charts also identify and eliminate duplicate efforts and confusion by assigning clear ownership for each task or decision. In addition, RACI can be adapted to define communication channels among the various stakeholders, which is an added benefit especially in a multigenerational family situation with many entities/structures.

Using RACI in a Family/Family Enterprise Setting to Enhance Governance and Communication

The RACI matrix can easily be adapted into a governance tool designed to establish and record principles and to guide decision-making in a complex family enterprise system. RACI is most effective in family enterprises with complex, long lasting relationships where there are numerous governing bodies with many stakeholders in common.

In a family enterprise setting, a RACI matrix provides guidance on the governance of decisions. It documents the roles and responsibilities of the various stakeholders in certain key areas. Each family entity (e.g., operating business) or board (e.g., family office board) then is responsible for its own execution and implementation according to its specific mandate or charter.

When considering a RACI matrix in a complex family enterprise, some adaptation is often required to make the analysis more compatible with managing the governance of decisions versus managing a business activity or project. Care also needs to be taken to recognize the legal/fiduciary responsibilities of certain stakeholders like trustees, boards of directors, etc. Consequently, in a family enterprise setting, "recommend" usually replaces the more business-oriented "responsible" function. "Approve" is used instead of "accountable" in a family enterprise RACI, often to recognize legal or contractual authority over decisions. Here recommenders do the work and often advise those who have the ultimate authority to approve an action/policy/plan.

The categories or topics to be addressed are also quite different in the family enterprise setting than in a traditional business environment. The number of areas and the nature of what is covered in the RACI depends on the family enterprise. However, some common categories usually addressed relate to constitutional matters, policy, strategy, people/human resources, planning, and budgets. Identifying subcategories under these broad headings is core to effectively using the tool. This is the most challenging and time-consuming part of the exercise. It helps to have input from leaders throughout the enterprise so nothing important is overlooked.

The operation and effectiveness of RACI is best illustrated by an example. Let's consider the X Family Group Enterprise.

The X Family has two living adult generations (G3 and G4) with a global footprint. Most of the family's assets are in trust with a corporate trustee plus two individuals who act as trust protectors. (A trust protector essentially oversees the trustee(s) and has certain powers, like the power to remove the trustee(s) in the event of trustee(s) misconduct.)

The X family believes in good governance and has spent many years refining its family mission and vision. Likewise, social responsibility and environmental sustainability are values of paramount importance to the family.

A fully staffed family office oversees investment portfolios and several operating businesses as well as provides services to the family foundation and family members. The family has established a family council with multigenerational representation. All family entities—operating businesses, foundation, and family office—have their own governing boards. More than 40 individuals have responsibility for the various family entities, with family members serving on many boards in differing capacities.

Several years ago, the family office, at the request of some family members, embarked on a project to define roles and responsibilities in conjunction with other leaders in the enterprise, the trustees, the family council, the protectors, and close advisors. After many robust conversations among the family and the enterprise leadership teams, this is a summary of the X Family Group's RACI.

X FAMILY GROUP RACI **STAKEHOLDERS: Protectors, Trustees, Family Council, Family Office, Family at Large, Family Members individually, Operating Business, Foundation**	R **RECOMMEND**	A **APPROVE**	C **CONSULT**	I **INFORM**
CONSTITUTIONAL				
Appointment and/or removal of trustees	PROTECTORS	**PROTECTORS**	FAMILY COUNCIL	FAMILY, TRUSTEES, FAMILY OFFICE
Amendment of trust documents	PROTECTORS, TRUSTEES	**PROTECTORS, TRUSTEES**	FAMILY COUNCIL, FAMILY OFFICE	FAMILY
Family Mission, Vision, Values Statements	FAMILY	**FAMILY COUNCIL**	FAMILY	ALL STAKEHOLDERS

X FAMILY GROUP RACI **STAKEHOLDERS: Protectors, Trustees, Family Council, Family Office, Family at Large, Family Members individually, Operating Business, Foundation**	R **RECOMMEND**	A **APPROVE**	C **CONSULT**	I **INFORM**
POLICIES				
Adoption or Amendment of RACI	FAMILY OFFICE	**TRUSTEES, PROTECTORS**	FAMILY COUNCIL	FAMILY
Investment Policy Statement	FAMILY OFFICE	**TRUSTEES**	FAMILY COUNCIL	FAMILY
Charters for Various Enterprise Boards	FAMILY OFFICE	**TRUSTEES**	FAMILY COUNCIL	PROTECTORS
Board Nomination Policy	FAMILY OFFICE	**TRUSTEES**	FAMILY COUNCIL	FAMILY
Family Employment/Compensation Policy	FAMILY OFFICE	**TRUSTEES, PROTECTORS**	TRUSTEES, FAM-ILY COUNCIL	FAMILY
Family Office Compensation Policy (non-family)	FAMILY OFFICE	**TRUSTEES**	PROTECTORS	FAMILY COUNCIL
Family Office Policies and Employee Handbook	FAMILY OFFICE	**FAMILY OFFICE BOARD**	FAMILY COUNCIL	FAMILY, TRUSTEES
Family Sustainable Investment Policy	FAMILY	**TRUSTEES**	FAMILY COUNCIL, FAMILY OFFICE	ALL STAKEHOLDERS
STRATEGY AND BUSINESS PLANNING				
Family Office Strategic Rolling 3-year Business Plan	FAMILY OFFICE	**TRUSTEES**	FAMILY COUNCIL	FAMILY, PROTECTOR
Operating Companies Strategic 3-year Business Plan	OPERATING COMPANY BOARD	**TRUSTEES**	FAMILY OFFICE	FAMILY
INVESTMENT AND DISTRIBUTION ACTIVITIES				
Appointment / Removal of Wealth Manager / Investment Advisor	FAMILY OFFICE	**TRUSTEES**	FAMILY COUNCIL	FAMILY, PROTECTORS
New Direct Investment in a Portfolio Company	FAMILY OFFICE	**TRUSTEES**	FAMILY OFFICE BOARD, TRUSTEES	FAMILY, PROTECTORS
Full or Partial Sale of an Operating Company	FAMILY OFFICE	**TRUSTEES**	FAMILY COUNCIL	FAMILY, PROTECTORS
Payment of a Family Dividend	TRUSTEES	**PROTECTORS**	FAMILY COUNCIL, FAMILY OFFICE	FAMILY
Payment of a Distribution to Family Foundation or Charity	FAMILY OFFICE	**TRUSTEES**	PROTECTOR, FAMILY COUNCIL, FOUNDATION	FAMILY
FUNDING/BUDGETS				
Annual Treasury Plan	FAMILY OFFICE	**TRUSTEES**	TRUSTEES, PROTECTORS	FAMILY OFFICE BOARD
Family Office Annual Budget	FAMILY OFFICE	**TRUSTEES**	PROTECTORS	FAMILY COUNCIL
Other Operating Company Budgets	OPERATING COMPANY BOARD	**TRUSTEES**	FAMILY OFFICE	PROTECTORS
Foundation Operating Budget	FOUNDATION BOARD	**TRUSTEES**	FAMILY OFFICE	FAMILY COUNCIL, FAMILY

X FAMILY GROUP RACI STAKEHOLDERS: Protectors, Trustees, Family Council, Family Office, Family at Large, Family Members individually, Operating Business, Foundation	R RECOMMEND	A APPROVE	C CONSULT	I INFORM
PEOPLE/HUMAN RESOURCES				
Family Roles and Responsibilities	FAMILY COUNCIL	**TRUSTEES**	FAMILY OFFICE	FAMILY, PROTECTORS
Family Annual Compensation	FAMILY COUNCIL	**TRUSTEES**	PROTECTORS	FAMILY OFFICE
Family Office Chairman Appointment / Removal / Compensation	FAMILY COUNCIL	**TRUSTEES, PROTECTORS**	FAMILY COUNCIL	FAMILY, FAMILY OFFICE
Family Director Appointments	FAMILY COUNCIL	**TRUSTEES**	PROTECTORS, FAMILY OFFICE	FAMILY
Family Office Senior Executive Appointment	FAMILY OFFICE	**FAMILY OFFICE BOARD**	TRUSTEES, FAMILY COUNCIL	FAMILY, PROTECTORS
Family Office Director and Senior Executive Compensation	FAMILY OFFICE	**FAMILY OFFICE BOARD**	TRUSTEES	PROTECTORS
Protector Appointment/Removal/Compensation	FAMILY COUNCIL	**TRUSTEES**	FAMILY OFFICE	FAMILY
Operating Company Chair/Director/CEO Appointment/Removal/Comp.	OPERATING COMPANY BOARD	**TRUSTEES**	PROTECTORS, FAMILY OFFICE, FAMILY COUNCIL	FAMILY

Of course, this RACI matrix only applies to the X Family Group. Some general principles and practices can, however, be applied to other family enterprise situations. Essential to developing a family enterprise–based RACI are the following five steps:

1. Identify all stakeholders, entities, and governance structures within the family enterprise.
2. Consider all decision-makers, boards, and fiduciaries in the family system and in the family enterprise.
3. Determine the key areas to consider—governance, people, funding, policy, planning, and other key activities that apply to most or all of the family enterprise.
4. Once the major categories are defined, include a list of matters/activities as subcategories. For example, a conflict-of-interest policy is a subcategory under policies.
5. Use the RACI terminology—recommend, approve, consult, inform—to define lines of authority, influencers, interested parties, possible overlaps, joint activities.

Don't forget to carefully consider who is included to "inform" and to "consult" so that communication is enhanced throughout the family and the family enterprise. You might also appoint an owner of the RACI matrix since it will need to be updated from time to time. In a family enterprise setting, the family council or the family office generally assumes this role.

Adopting the RACI methodology offers many benefits to the family enterprise:

- Ensures that major decisions are approved by the right governing bodies
- Ensures that recommendations are made to the appropriate governing bodies
- Provides that information is communicated to all the relevant stakeholders
- Reinforces the practice of consulting with other parts of the organization for counsel, background information, and to enhance consensus
- Identifies which part of the enterprise is responsible for initiating and doing the work in the role of recommender
- Simplifies the understanding of complex enterprises especially for the next generation and those new to the family enterprise
- Builds working relationships, transparency and trust among the enterprise leaders and the family

Remember that RACI is a governance tool and not a solution. It works best when the family and its enterprises are aligned and each has at least some knowledge of the mandates and activities of the other parts of the enterprise. It is not a substitute for the actual communication required for healthy relationships within the family/ family enterprise. RACI works best when one recommender or responsible party can be clearly identified and agreed on. In the X Family Group's case, the family office was the driver of many activities. Its effectiveness was enhanced by having family members on the family office board.

RACI helps clarify, but does not eliminate, the "many hats" scenario. Hopefully, RACI will identify the correct hat for the issue at hand. There are also situations where the recommender may also be the approver. This occurred in the X Family Group where the trustees and protectors assumed both roles when amending trust documents because of legal considerations. In general, care should be taken to keep these roles distinct. One way to do this is to prioritize which entity has final approval or veto rights and to institute robust consultation protocols with the other interested parties.

A powerful benefit of RACI in the family enterprise is explicitly defining who is consulted in the decision-making process and who is informed as (or after) a decision is made. Sequencing consultations especially with family members can be tricky. In many families, privacy and confidentiality are of the utmost importance. Individual family members may be sensitive to consultations with others, particularly other family members, on issues that involve them or their families. One classic situation is when a family member wants to join a family or operating company board. Using the X Family as an example, a family member may not want to approach the family council (recommend) for privacy reasons but prefer to consult with the family office (inform) or even the trustees (approve) first. In this instance, taking an iterative approach, rather than a linear one, is the better course. There needs to be some flexibility built into RACI when it comes to sensitive family matters. In the end, however, all parties should be included appropriately.

Conclusion

Developing a RACI matrix for a family enterprise can have an important impact on the family itself as well as on others in the enterprise. The exercise will bring more clarity about the system and about the interaction among the various family entities. Just developing the matrix can help all stakeholders understand the family's structures better. This can lead to the enhanced governance of each individual entity as well as to improvements to governance enterprise-wide. Another ancillary benefit of RACI is its use as a teaching tool for on-boarding the next generation (or anyone new to the enterprise) because it shows how the pieces of the puzzle fit together. Finally, more collaboration and trust in the family's mission and its structures is often a by-product of using the RACI methodology. In the end, the well-being of the family enterprise is enhanced by using RACI.

Additional Resources

Dennis T. Jaffe, *Governing the Family Enterprise: The Evolution of Family Councils, Assemblies and Constitutions* (Milton, MA: Wise Counsel Research, 2017).

Gretchen Anderson, *Mastering Collaboration: Making Working Together Less Painful and More Productive* (Sebastopol, CA: O'Reilly Media, 2019).

Jose Maria Delos Santos, "Understanding Responsibility Assignment Matrix (RACI Matrix)," Project-Management.com, posted April 15, 2021, updated September 28, 2021, https://project-management.com/understanding-responsibility-assignment-matrix-raci-matrix/.

Biography

Kathryn McCarthy has more than 30 years of experience worldwide managing the financial affairs of wealthy families and their family offices. She advises families and family offices on a variety of issues, including strategic planning, transitions, family office design and assessment, and private trust companies. Kathryn serves on family office boards, private trust company boards, and investment committees of global families. She is a director of the Rockefeller Trust Company, N.A., and is a member of the board of directors of SEI. Kathryn holds an MBA in finance from NYU's Graduate School of Business Administration, and a JD from New York Law School. She earned her BA from Rosemont College.

CHAPTER 56

Creating Internal Controls and Policy and Procedures for a Family Office

Eugene Lipitz

Successful family offices establish procedures that protect the clients of the office, ensure focus on goals that have been agreed upon, and enforce the decision-making agreements that reinforce confidence in the family office by its members.

Each office will need to choose the frameworks appropriate for them depending on the services they deliver, the complexity of their operations, and the resources available to their offices. This framework may include a procedure manual, a set of internal controls, governance, fraud deterrence, and integrated risk management systems. Some single-family offices (SFOs) may find that, given their aspirations, some resources may need to be added to their operations in order to achieve a reasonable degree of standards.

The Committee of Sponsoring Organizations of the Treadway Commission (COSO) has developed an excellent set of frameworks and tools that are worth considering (www.coso.org).

Copedia (www.copedia.com) is also a good source of road-tested policy and procedure templates that can be customized to an SFO's needs. It is helpful to create workflow templates rather than a large book of text-only procedures because they are clearer and can be easily adapted eventually to a dynamic online system of workflows. If you already have a procedure handbook, you can start creating these workflows based on that material, updating as you go to conform with your current practices, and incorporate best practices from the organizations mentioned previously. And these standards, while not fully universal, apply to many family office operations. There is no need to create them from scratch as other family offices have already thought about and documented the necessary procedures. Collaboration among the community is key to better protection and productivity for the members of the community. Following is an example of one such procedure, expressed as a workflow, intended to manage the potentially risky activity of responding to capital calls:

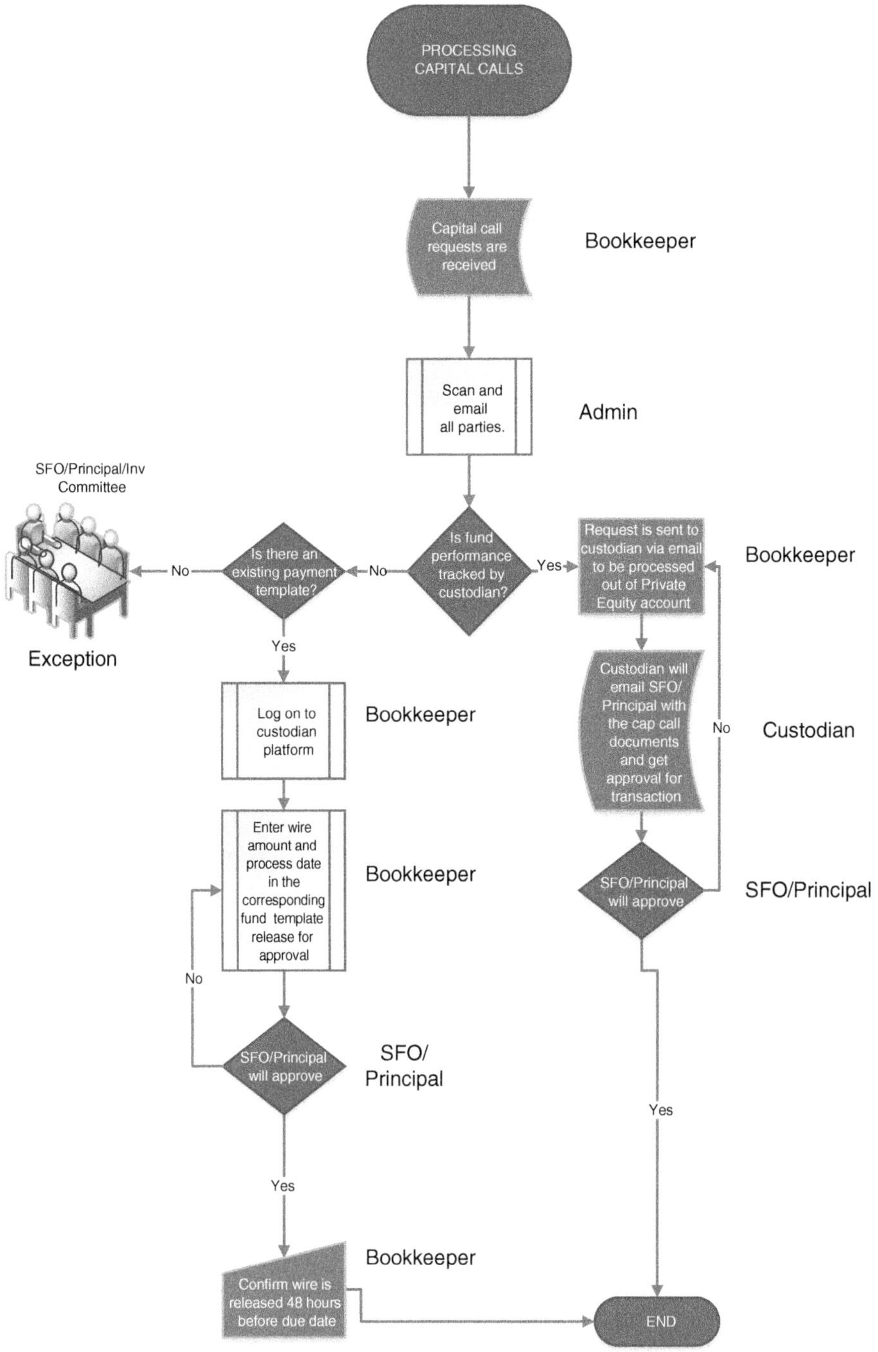

This workflow cites who is responsible for each step as well as the action that is to be taken. When an activity carries a higher level of risk, increasing management scrutiny is required. Also note that the published standard which justifies the activity should be documented (e.g., *COSO, Ch. 6, p. 73 "Segregation of Duties"*). Do not create unnecessary work for your staff. If they are like mine, they are already overtaxed!

Such online workflows, typically part of customer relationship management (CRM) systems, are the future of procedure implementation compliance. Procedures that only exist in a manual are seldom referenced and rarely updated to current standards, and they are difficult to enforce without an online regime. Such online systems (sometimes called process automation) have existed for many years and are used by many businesses, including registered investment advisors (RIAs). Redtail and Wealthbox are two examples of CRM/workflow management systems targeted at RIAs. Keep in mind that RIA procedures must take regulatory requirements into account, only a minority of which are applicable to an SFO.

I believe that these or other software vendors will begin to fill the more specialized needs of SFOs. Eton Systems, for instance, has developed a general ledger and performance system that is workflow-based. These are not yet customizable in a way that is useful for global procedures, but it would be theoretically desirable to have such procedures well integrated into a general ledger and bill payment system such as Eton's.

Family offices that have developed comprehensive procedures that are explicitly documented workflows will be well prepared to exploit these new technologies as they are deployed. Such systems ultimately will mean that a family office's processes can be automated, dynamically updated, audited, and managed in real time by office leaders. Such an advance would do much to standardize and de-risk the family office industry.

Additional Resources

Rose Hightower, *Internal Controls: Policies and Procedures* (Hoboken, NJ: Wiley, 2009).

Lynford Graham, *Internal Control Audit and Compliance* (Hoboken, NJ: Wiley, 2015).

Todd D. Mayo, ed., *Private Trust Companies, Part 1: Design and Operation of Private Trust Companies* (Surry, UK: Global Law and Business, 2020).

Biography

Eugene Lipitz is currently chief financial officer and wealth strategist of Commodore Management LLC, a private family wealth manager. Prior to this, he was a strategic consultant with Price Waterhouse and founded the strategic consultancy Document Concepts. He is the author of *Daddy, Are We Rich?* which critically reviews advice given to wealthy parents over the last two decades and "Blissfully Unaware: Family Offices Living in Operational La-La Land" in *The International Family Offices Journal*. He has also been a guest lecturer at the Berkeley-Haas School of Business on the subject of entrepreneurship within a family office. Among several professional organizations, Gene is a member of the Center for Families Flourishing, an international group of 100 of the professionals within the Wealth Management Community dedicated to service to families and the IPI investor network, where he has been a student, faculty advisor, and a speaker on the subjects of "Choosing a Trusted Advisor" and "The Use of Behavioral Finance in a Family Office." Gene holds the CPWA® designation, administered in cooperation with the University of Chicago and the Investment Management Consultant Association® and is a Global Fiduciary Strategist®.

CHAPTER 57

Leading Successful Family Meetings

Katherine Grady and Wendy Ulaszek

As your family business (or family office) moves into its second and third generations, leaders are likely to have new questions about the boundary between the enterprise and the family: What should we tell family and owners about the business? Is our business strategy or investment strategy aligned with the family's vision and values? Will family dynamics keep us from passing the company or the wealth to the next generation?

Advisors typically suggest answering these questions by holding regular family meetings and forming a family council to help separate family and ownership matters from the operating company's ongoing business.[1] Family meetings provide governance forums for family owners to define common values and a family mission and vision for the future.

But many owners will remember failed attempts to engage the family, such as jealousies around leadership succession or arguments related to financial distributions. So it is no surprise family leaders may hesitate to organize family meetings. They may be unsure of whom to include, what topics to cover, how to include people in decision-making, and how to handle inevitable emotional "elephants" in the room, along with how to find the time to organize and run meetings.

Part of the challenge is that while family business leaders may excel in launching and growing one or more businesses, those are not the same skills required to lead in the ownership and family circles, especially in a growing, geographically dispersed family. Our experience shows, in fact, that leaders in this complex context have the best outcomes when they practice what we define as "ambidextrous leadership,"[2] or tending to both family and enterprise needs with agility.

Ambidextrous leaders compartmentalize family, ownership, and business issues in their respective governance forums (e.g., family council, board), but also

[1] See Katherine Grady and Ivan Lansberg, "What Is the Point of Family Governance?" in *Wealth of Wisdom*, ed. Tom McCullough and Keith Whitaker (Hoboken, NJ: John Wiley & Sons, 2019).
[2] Ivan Lansberg and Wendy Ulaszek, "The Art of Ambidextrous Family Enterprise Leadership," *Financial Times* (Fall 2017).

integrate issues *across* forums, managing dilemmas and tensions between family and business. Further, they work to develop a rising generation of leaders with similar ambidexterity.

Such ambidextrous leaders, who often do not work in the business, are needed to develop and lead family meetings, where the family can work together to address and resolve family concerns, update family owners regarding the business, organize family gatherings that foster unity and shared understanding, and take on other important tasks at the intersection of family and business.

Following, we provide a checklist of 10 questions to ask in planning and leading your family meetings, to further develop ambidextrous leadership skills and make the most of this important governance forum.

1. Why meet? The first question should be about the "why": What is the purpose of the family meeting? Family meetings fall into three different categories based on whether they are focused primarily on business, ownership, or family. Business meetings serve to update everyone on business issues and performance—primarily to inform but also to seek family input on key topics. Ownership meetings also have an informing component, but more likely enable owners to discuss issues, consider options, and make decisions. Family meetings feature sharing of viewpoints and tackling of specific family matters, often with more emphasis on discussion than decision-making.
2. Who should be included? This depends on the meeting's purpose. Adult owners (or trust beneficiary owners) would be included in all ownership and family meetings. Nonowner spouses might be included, given their supporting role to spouses and parenting role to next-generation shareholders, but some families choose to include spouses only in family events, to avoid complications. For some family or ownership meetings, it is beneficial to include children over a certain age (18 or 21, typically) so they can begin learning about the family businesses and their role as future owners. If your family is too large to include everyone in family meetings, we recommend forming a family council. Family council members—selected by each branch, the entire family, or a nominating committee—act on behalf of the larger set of family members. While the family council might meet quarterly or more often, the entire family typically will continue to meet annually and receive updates from its family council during this reunion or assembly gathering.
3. What are the meeting goals? Before setting the meeting agenda, ask what you hope to accomplish. Be realistic. If this is a first or early meeting, set modest goals such as updates from the business or family, one or two easier topics, and identification of topics for future meetings. Agendas for more regular meetings will evolve over time, but be reasonable about how much to cover. Aim for substantive topics for each meeting, to engage participants well, but not so many that it preempts thoughtful discussion or leads to poor decision-making.
4. What agenda is best? Agendas should align with meeting goals. Select the order strategically, such as starting with easier topics before moving into more difficult ones. Keep in mind that you would like your family members to leave the meeting feeling like they have made a contribution to decision-making

for the family enterprise system. Send agenda topics ahead of time, along with any reading or reference materials. Before the meeting, encourage participants to respond with additional topics to discuss, and include an open agenda item at the meeting's end for thoughts and concerns.

5. How long to meet and where? Once the purpose, goals, and agenda are determined, it will be relatively easy to determine specific meeting parameters. Early on, a meeting duration of two to three hours will enable you to introduce topics and establish how to work together over time. Some families opt for a one- or two-day retreat covering a full topic range. This can be a good way to jumpstart the new governance structure, but it requires more preparation. The agenda also guides location choice. More business-focused meetings can be held in the business office, and ownership meetings can be held in a private corporate office or a neutral setting (e.g., hotel conference room). Family meetings might fare better in family homes or an outside setting. Food is always helpful; a meal for all before or after the meeting can help people connect and "break bread" together. The 2020 pandemic pushed families to consider virtual family meetings. Now, many enterprising families take a hybrid approach, including both in-person and virtual meetings, which helps engage family members who may not be able to attend in-person meetings due to distance or mobility challenges.
6. Who will lead? Selection of a qualified family meeting or family council leader is of paramount importance. This leader sets the agenda, facilitates discussion, guides decision-making, and moderates family members' use of "air time." The business leader may be a reasonable choice, but it is usually better to find a more family-oriented leader, given the time and energy required. Business leaders almost always contribute significantly to the meeting agenda, provide updates, and participate in discussion. Skills required for family meeting leaders or council chairs include high emotional intelligence, excellent communication, and interest in diverse opinions. These ambidextrous leaders take the needs of the family, owners, and business into account in a balanced way. The advantages of using an outside facilitator include having an experienced professional manage meeting time, ensure all voices are heard, and bring an objective perspective. The primary disadvantage is overdependence on the facilitator to do the work, which precludes the family experience of collaborating toward important ends. Thus many families benefit from having an advisor in early stages of the process and then handling later meetings more on their own.
7. How to start? Personal updates make a good start to the meeting, along with major business or family updates. If the group is less than 15 to 20 people in size, everyone can take a couple of minutes to update, then have the business leader present the business update. If there are more people or the meeting is virtual, consider using breakout rooms to connect smaller groups with an icebreaker or brief update before beginning. The leader may also start by helping the family formulate meeting rules (e.g., come prepared to share your opinion, no cellphone use until breaks, respect everyone's viewpoint), subject to later revision.

8. How to balance task and process elements? For every agenda item, there will be task elements (e.g., what to cover, what should be decided, what happens next) and process elements (e.g., are people working together, is conflict impeding progress, is everyone being heard). The leader must seek to balance these two components appropriately for the specific group. Good leaders recognize some groups need significant structure and task focus and can tolerate conflict; others need more process discussion and collaborative working relationships. Leaders must also be mindful of their own preferences and sometimes deprioritize these (such as diminishing their preferred focus on emotional connection for a more task-oriented group).
9. How to end? Just as you considered the right opening for the meeting, you want to consider the right ending. At the most basic level, the leader should briefly summarize the main topics discussed and their outcomes, followed by a list of the next steps and "owners" of each. The leader can then offer a note of gratitude to the family members. If there has been some emotional discussion or disagreement, it helps for the leader to provide some related perspective. Time permitting, the group can engage in a "go-around" where each member makes a final comment or provides a mini-review of what worked and didn't in the meeting. A useful frame here is one-minute "plus-deltas" of the two or three things that each person found valuable (plusses) and one or two items that should be changed (deltas) for the next meeting.
10. What follow-up? Meetings should be followed by a succinct summary of topics discussed, decisions made, and next action steps and their owners. It is valuable for leaders to summarize these key points and action steps in writing for distribution to members. Usually, the action items become the next meeting's agenda and can be accompanied by additional resources or information the family needs to move forward with decisions. It is best for subsequent family meetings to be scheduled well in advance so members can hold the time.

We started this chapter with questions that enterprising families face as they transition beyond the first generation. Now review those queries and ask yourself: Who in your family business system should answer these questions? Who are the ambidextrous leaders who can help lead these family meeting discussions and steward your family enterprise into the future? What holds you back from implementing family or owner meetings?

Family meetings provide critical forums to hear family and owner voices. When properly structured, these meetings connect, inform, educate, and engage your family and the owners, for everyone's benefit.

Additional Resources

Katherine Grady and Ivan Lansberg, "What Is the Point of Family Governance?" in *Wealth of Wisdom,* ed. Tom McCullough and Keith Whitaker (Hoboken, NJ: John Wiley & Sons, 2019).

Ivan Lansberg and Wendy Ulaszek, "The Art of Ambidextrous Family Enterprise Leadership," *Financial Times* (Fall 2017).

Biography

Katherine Grady, Ph.D., is a partner with Lansberg Gersick Advisors in New Haven, Connecticut. Formerly on the faculty at Yale University and the Center for Creative Leadership, she has been a family business consultant for more than 25 years. A licensed psychologist, Katherine's expertise as both a family business advisor and an executive coach has allowed her to focus on individual and organizational development within different family and organizational contexts. She also lectures and publishes on continuity planning, leadership, career development, personality differences, team building, and family dynamics.

Wendy Ulaszek, Ph.D., is a partner with Lansberg Gersick Advisors. She holds a Ph.D. in clinical psychology and has a special focus on leadership coaching and the education and development of rising generations. Wendy is an FFI fellow and enjoys coaching at the Kellogg School of Management program and teaching at the University of Connecticut School of Business. She is currently co-leading a research project examining the coordination of collaborative multigenerational family philanthropic work. Wendy's consulting focuses on leadership and the implementation and sustainability of sound family governance structures and policies, which will serve the family and the family enterprise for generations to come.

CHAPTER 58

Establishing Ground Rules for Family Meetings

Keith Whitaker

Regular family meetings are a key practice to ensure family flourishing over generations. To better understand the process for planning an effective family meeting, readers should check out Grady and Ulaszek, "Leading Successful Family Meetings" in this volume. This chapter will focus more narrowly on the task of establishing ground rules for those meetings.

Why Ground Rules?

That's a natural question. Most family gatherings don't require explicit rules. That said, every gathering of human beings includes many implicit or unspoken rules. Each family also has its unspoken rules or norms that it carries with itself into work, vacation, and formal and informal get-togethers.

Family meetings can be stressful events, even if well prepared and attended by family members who love and trust each other. A family meeting may involve discussions of money, investments, spending, giving, not to mention family members' mortality. Because these are family meetings, not just business meetings, they may also be overlaid with emotions and dynamics that reach far back into family history.

For these reasons, it can be very helpful to make explicit the "rules of the road." Clarity about the ground rules helps to ensure that the meeting process will feel safe and productive for all participants.

Process

The process of establishing family meeting ground rules is as important as the rules themselves. If you haven't had family meetings before, then use a portion of your first meeting to establish the rules. If you have had family meetings but haven't talked about ground rules, make it the first order of business for the next meeting.

All the participants in the meeting should have a say in establishing the rules. You may want to start with some sample rules, like the ones offered in the next section. But feel free as a family to come up with your own rules. These rules can reflect the particular vocabulary and needs of your family. One family I worked with had a habit of saying things to one another that they instantly regretted; in response, they came up with the rules, "No barbs," and "Care and repair."

You'll also want to make sure that the rules you choose suit your family's style. For example, if your family culture is that everyone talks at once, don't expect to feel comfortable with a rule that tries to enforce complete silence when others are speaking. Be realistic when deciding on your rules, and have some fun with it.

Once you've come up with an initial list, I recommend revisiting those rules at the next family meeting to see if, based on experience, the family would like to make any changes. Also, it can be a powerful practice to begin each subsequent family meeting by having each family member read one of the rules aloud, going around the table in order. This ritual may seem a little formal, but it helps impress everyone with the importance of the rules to your family.

Once adopted, ground rules must be upheld. In the heat of a discussion, members will inevitably start to break the rules. What's crucial is how the family responds. Having to stick to the rules just like everyone else offsets any sense of entitlement. The rules are living testimony that, although wealthy, the family acts responsibly and respectfully to all people.

Sample Ground Rules

Be Present

Demonstrate your respect and commitment by setting aside potential distractions. Turn off phones, tablets, and computers. If you need to be reached in case of emergency for your children or business, designate a contact person. Be present at the scheduled start time so the meeting can get the job done. Devote room in your life and your heart to this meeting.

Be Respectful in Words and Deeds

Speak respectfully, pay attention when someone else is talking, and avoid jumping in to finish sentences. Avoid negative body language such as eye-rolling, shaking heads, or other indications of emotional reaction unless you follow up by talking directly about your reaction. Keep profanity to a minimum. If you have a question or point to make, wait for an opening or raise a hand to indicate you have something to bring up. You will appreciate it when others do that while you are talking.

Listen

Listening is a skill that must be practiced, but it pays off tremendously. Be willing to demonstrate you understand what the other person is saying before making your own point. You may find you are reacting to what you *believe* someone said, not what was really said. When someone else is saying something that you disagree with, make sure you are listening to what is being said.

Be Patient

Recognize and accept that, with limited time overall, not all comments or questions must be dealt with right away. Be willing to let some things go. Pick the issues you think are most important. Over time, it is likely that the important things will get dealt with.

Own Your Views

Make "I" statements rather than broad, global statements that imply you know the truth or that something "is obvious." Saying, "Everyone knows that is ridiculous," is unhelpful. Saying, "I really disagree with what you just said," is more honest and may be more accurate. If others do share your views, it will be clear there is a shared perspective on an issue. If it turns out your view is not shared by others, you may then open yourself to new viewpoints or solutions.

Be Willing to Edit What You Say

Saying anything and everything you feel under the guise of honesty can simply be a license to attack. Deliver your points with tact and respect. Appropriate editing of your message will make you more likely to be heard. It will also reduce the chances that other people will get defensive.

Conclusion

If there is any one practice that I have found essential to long-term family flourishing, it is holding regular, effective family meetings. And if there is one practice essential to effective family meetings, it is establishing and upholding agreed-upon ground rules. What those rules command or prohibit should reflect your family culture and goals. The key is to have them, and to use the process of establishing them to strengthen your shared sense of purpose.

Additional Resources

James E. Hughes, Jr., *Family Wealth* (New York: Wiley, 2004).

James E. Hughes, Susan E. Massenzio, and Keith Whitaker, *Cycle of the Gift* (New York: Wiley, 2012).

James E. Hughes, Susan E. Massenzio, and Keith Whitaker, *Complete Family Wealth* (New York: Wiley, 2022).

Biography

Dr. Keith Whitaker is an educator who consults with leaders and rising generation members of enterprising families. *Family Wealth Report* named Keith the 2015 "outstanding contributor to wealth management thought-leadership." Keith's writings and commentary have appeared in the *Wall Street Journal, New York Times,* and *Financial Times.* He is the co-author of *Wealth and the Will of God, The Cycle of the Gift, The Voice of the Rising Generation, Family Trusts, Complete Family Wealth,* and *Wealth of Wisdom: The Top 50 Questions Wealthy Families Ask.* Keith has served as a managing director at Wells Fargo Family Wealth, an adjunct professor of management at Vanderbilt University, and an adjunct assistant professor of philosophy at Boston College. Keith holds a Ph.D. in social thought from the University of Chicago and a BA and MA in classics and philosophy from Boston University.

SECTION 9

GIVING TOGETHER

One of the main findings in Wise Counsel Research's "100-Year Family Study" (a study of over 100 families that had succeeded in transitioning a major family enterprise through at least three generations of leadership) is that "connection to communities beyond the family" is a key factor in each family's success.

It is no surprise that many families intuitively turn to philanthropy as a way for individual members to make a positive difference in the world and for the family as a whole to feel connected through giving. As with any activity to do with families, self-understanding, communication, and empathy are crucial for this pursuit to go well.

In the first chapter of this section, Etienne Eichenberger, Małgorzata Smulowitz, and Peter Vogel offer a comprehensive approach for evaluating and enhancing giving together as a family. This process moves from understanding the family's current focus and possible trade-offs it involves (e.g., between depth and breadth of impact), then to reformulating that focus based on input from family members. The authors also include a number of tips and insights for engaging rising generation family members in shaping the family's philanthropic focus.

The rising generation is very much the focus for the second chapter, James "Jay" Hughes' reflections on grandparent-grandchild philanthropy. Jay guides readers in a simple way to structure shared giving between these two generations (key step: parents stay out!). He also points out the numerous benefits beyond the charitable from grandparent-grandchild philanthropy, in the form of sharing stories, giving grandchildren a chance to explain their choices, and fostering true understanding across the generations. It is a fine gift for families to give to themselves.

As the example of grandchild-grandparent philanthropy suggests, giving as a family is never a static activity: it changes as the family members themselves grow and change. Families can also intentionally change their style of philanthropy. That is the insight offered by Leslie Pine in the third chapter in this section, in which she describes a "philanthropic curve"—from becoming a donor to becoming more strategic to, ultimately, achieving high impact. This curve is a useful tool for evaluating where a family is now in its giving, where it wants to be, and what steps are needed to get there.

If charity begins at home, then, by the same principle, one could say that giving starts with the giver. In the final chapter in this section, Susan Winer asks the individual philanthropist to step back and reflect on the reasons or motivations for his or her giving. This checklist of motivations then can flow into defining the scope of one's giving and even a statement describing its principles. This process of individual reflection is fundamental to giving well.

CHAPTER 59

Finding a Philanthropic Focus and Integrating the Rising Generation Perspective

Etienne Eichenberger, Małgorzata Smulowitz, and Peter Vogel

Philanthropy is an important and highly rewarding way for individuals and families to make a difference in a rapidly changing world. Like the world around us, philanthropy is changing and transforming, and philanthropic families are seeking out new ways to ensure that their giving is meaningful and impactful. For this reason, we developed the Family Philanthropy Navigator as an easy-to-use, step-by-step inspirational guide for new and existing philanthropic families to initiate or enhance their journey in giving. This hands-on guide enables families to get together to answer the core questions at the heart of any voyage in giving: Why, What, Who, and How?

The "Focus" stage in the Navigator provides a platform to make choices about the causes, scope, and final port of call for your giving. It helps to define what could interest you and be your focus. For the novice, this is a voyage of discovery; for the established philanthropist, it's an opportunity to conduct a check on the current focus of activities and, if necessary, consider a change of direction. Depending on what drives you to be philanthropically active, you might already have identified a specific problem or cause. For example, if someone in your family has suffered from a disease and your motivation is to help others who suffer from, or to prevent, that disease, your focus is pretty clear. In other cases, you might approach philanthropy more broadly and work through a list of different possibilities before choosing which causes to focus on.

Deciding where to focus takes time, research, and careful consideration. It could require the involvement and agreement of family members, who may have different views and interests. It may help to discuss these early on and seek solutions that will promote engagement. Perhaps it may require adopting different avenues to achieve different aims amongst the family, or perhaps you can align your interests and efforts behind one core focus for giving.

In this chapter, we discuss how to explore your philanthropic focus, guiding you and your family to selecting the most appropriate cause for you and your family's history, context, and ambition.

Activity 1—Review Trade-Offs and Set Your Compass!

When it comes to a philanthropic focus, there is an almost infinite number of needs for philanthropists to address. Many philanthropists face challenges when reconciling their own interest in philanthropy with that of their family members. In our work, we have identified a number of important trade-offs linked to focus that you ought to consider when exploring the reach possibilities and causes in which you and your family can contribute. By reflecting on the following trade-offs and dilemmas, you will be able to explore and define the focus of your giving.

Step 1

Review the following various trade-offs and, individually, answer the following questions. Use different colors to highlight where you stand in relation to the two questions in each of the trade-offs. You can position yourself anywhere along the spectrum, from one end to the other of the trade-off.

1. Where is our philanthropy today?
2. Where would I like our philanthropy to be in the future?

Step 2

As a family, compare and discuss where each one of you positioned the dots for "Where are we today?" and "Where would we like to be?" What are similarities and differences? Where are you aligned or not? How can this further shape your journey?

Step 3

If there are any differences in your perspectives, discuss how you wish to address these.

Supporting a specific cause or project in one area

Considering the relationship between the depth and breadth of your giving helps to ensure your aims, partners, resources and structures are aligned. If you are driven toward depth of impact, you might focus all of your giving on a specific cause, such as helping unemployed women in their local community transfer to the labor market. If it's all about breadth, you might want to share efforts across a number of organizations working in diverse fields. This could be influenced by differing or common interests within the family.

Spreading your support across diverse causes and projects across a multitude of areas

→ What are your **interests** and **passions** as a family?
→ Do you want to **support** only one specific cause as a family?
→ Are you more interested in spreading your giving across a range of **different causes** and activities, such as education, healthcare, arts?
→ Are there **differing interests** between family members that might require a **blended approach**?

NOTES

____

____

____

____

**Note to aspiring philanthropists: If you are not yet philanthropically active, you can simply focus on question 2 in Step 1.*

LOCAL — **GLOBAL**

Giving to causes and projects on a local level only

You might have a specific connection to a certain community, due to personal, family or business reasons, and want to align your giving accordingly, such as supporting schools close to your business operations. You may be more interested in giving on a wider scale to, for example, alleviate poverty or tackle climate change. In practice, families might give across a range of geographies for different reasons. The regionality of your giving could also include multiple levels, such as your community, your city, your state, your country, your continent and globally. It could also be a combination of different local areas such as providing access to clean sanitation in villages in India.

→ Is your giving **focused on a specific geographic region**?
→ Are you focusing on **global issues**?
→ Are there **several areas** that are of **particular interest** to you?

Supporting more general and globally relevant causes

ROOT CAUSE /SYSTEM CHANGE — **EFFECT /SYMPTOMS**

Directly addressing the root cause or trigger point of an issue or problem

There are many ways to tackle the focus areas of your giving—from seeking to address the root causes to reducing the symptoms of an issue. Sometimes it makes sense to focus on the symptoms, for example, backing an emergency appeal during a pandemic to provide critical support when it is most needed. On the other hand, many philanthropists are keen to focus their giving on solutions that lead to lasting change. Take a family who wants to make a difference for dementia patients, perhaps inspired by personal experience. They could tackle the root causes and fund medical research, they could support initiatives that make life easier for dementia patients and their families, or they could blend both approaches.

→ Do you want to **focus** on the cause or **effect** of a certain issue?
→ Are there **compelling reasons** for addressing the symptoms?
→ Does it make more sense to tackle the **root causes**?
→ Could you take a **twin approach**?

Focusing on ways to treat or reduce the symptoms of an issue or problem

NOTES

Activity 2—Formulate Your Focus

After you have reviewed the trade-offs, we recommend that you actively engage your family in the next steps, formulating your joined focus.

Step 1

Respond to the following questions: What causes are you passionate about, in which regions do you give/want to give, and who or what ultimately benefits from your giving?

Step 2

Describe why you feel that these causes are important and that you and your family should address them. Why are you passionate about them?

Step 3

As a family, discuss all your selected causes and create a shortlist of your family's top three causes.

Step 4

Formulate your philanthropic mission statement. The more specific your focus of giving is, the easier it gets to write this statement. A mission statement is important when you are engaging others in your philanthropic activities. A good statement should be short, simple, specific, ambitious, and easy to remember or to associate with you.

Including the Rising Generation

If philanthropy ought to be a family endeavor, it will be important to consider having an inclusive approach to allow the rising generation to become an integral part of your journey. Our experience is that when the philanthropic focus (what) differs among multiple generations, based on their varied interests or expectations, it is important to also consider one's motivation (why) for giving.

There is no "correct" reason to give. In fact, we often observe that families have lots of different motivations. In this context, it's important to know what these are and how to balance them. Why do you and your family want to give? Are you driven by conviction or events?

For more experienced philanthropists, has something changed within your family or outside? Is it time to reevaluate or put your existing reasons to the test?

Different motivations are not mutually exclusive. You and your family may regard multiple motivations as relevant and important. Irrespective of what your motivations are, it is crucial that you and your family are aware of the full spectrum of points of view so that you can plan accordingly.

The following figure presents the feedback from 25 global rising generations that we have been working with to deepen our understanding of their needs and expectations. The core question was: What do the rising generations have to say or would like to say about family philanthropy?

Communicating within families is a challenge in the context of philanthropy. The following testimonials share the experiences of a group of next-generation family members who are part of a peer group discussion that we regularly facilitate in their dealings with senior generations:

→ **What do we want to learn from our family philanthropy?**
Best practices, diplomacy, learning perspectives, experience, diversity of opinions, entrepreneurship, patience, respect, credibility, networks, legacy, greater sense of purpose, values, professional connections, family bonding.

→ **What do we want to bring to our family philanthropy?**
Innovation, creativity, change, education, perspectives, vision, passion, uniting the family, structure for the NextGen, Millennial ideas, focus and growth.

→ **What do we want to hear from our parents?**
Acceptance, openness, trust, encouragement, autonomy, support, values, be the change, communication.

→ **What do we want to say to our parents?**
Show interest in current projects, be involved, tell us your stories to inspire us, collaboration, trust, include us, empower us but please do not hinder, have faith in us, authority vs autonomy, try to understand the world we live in.

Engaging the Next Generation Early

Philanthropy lies at the crossroads of family dynamics and wealth. It is not always easy to get an initial, straightforward impetus or connection between donors and their rising generation members. Here are some practical tips on the many ways to engage the next generation effectively:

Young children

→ Start discussing the causes you care about with your children when they are young, as well as the service you do for society and your favorite way of giving.

→ Pocket money should initially be a way to "experience" money. The Rockefeller family developed the notion of the three-part allowance, the "3 S's" for pocket money with an equal weight between spending, saving, and sharing.

→ Children are inspired by behavior: Tell them about your family rituals, and volunteer.

Adolescents

- → Talk about the meaning of money.
- → Encourage peer activities at school, or during summer camps.
- → Involve them in Site visits to meet with giving partners or to see what you support.
- → Explore creating a grandchildren's fund to add a conversation beyond your own generation.
- → If you have a family fund/foundation, involve them informally in the board or conversations to make these activities feel tangible and "real."

College age and young adults

- → Create funds matching their own gifts to support their nascent endeavors.
- → Develop with your family foundation discretionary grant making (that is, give your family members a portion of funds to donate as individuals) so that they can explore their own responsibilities in giving.
- → Encourage and support apprenticeships during vacations or free time as well as training.
- → Reflect on including them via an adjunct/next-generation foundation board so that they can explore philanthropy among themselves.

Adult "children"

- → Be transparent about the process and requirements for becoming full trustees.
- → Share with them official foundation documents such as donor intent and bylaws.

Concluding Comment: Getting Your Focus Right

Giving is choosing. It is worth thinking about how to align your motivation for giving with the interests and topics you and your family are passionate about, not just the needs that you see or hear about in the world.

Including the rising generation, as demanding as it may sound, is even more relevant today as traditional governance models are being challenged by increasing diversity. In that sense, philanthropy does offer a unique opportunity for enterprising families to build an integrated approach that includes the generational diversity. If you can align your motivations, interests, and the causes you want to support, it can help to sustain engagement and deliver better outcomes. Global challenges certainly need the impetus, the ambition, and the resources of engaged philanthropists. And your family philanthropy is likely to be a journey rather than a one-time process.

This chapter is an abstract from the Family Philanthropy Navigator published by The Institute for Management Development (IMD), Lausanne, Switzerland.

Additional Resources

Tom McCullough and Keith Whitaker, eds., *Wealth of Wisdom: The Top 50 Questions Wealthy Families Ask* (New York: Wiley, 2017).

Paul Schervish and Keith Whitaker, *Wealth and the Will of God* (Bloomington, IN: Indiana University Press, 2005).

Biography

Etienne Eichenberger co-founded WISE-philanthropy advisors, the first company in Europe to provide philanthropy advisory services to entrepreneurs and their families, helping them define and implement charitable projects. He previously worked for Foundation Avina for social entrepreneurship and the World Economic Forum.

A graduate of the University of St Gallen, Etienne is also a chairman of the Swiss Philanthropy Foundation, a co-founder of Sustainable Finance Geneva, co-founder of Foundation Board Academy in Switzerland, and board member of the Debiopharm Chair on Family Philanthropy at IMD. He has also co-authored the *Family Philanthropy Navigator* in 2020. Finally, he is married and father of three children.

Małgorzata Smulowitz is a research fellow at the Debiopharm Chair for Family Philanthropy at IMD Business School. She conducts research on family firm governance and management practices that allow family owners and managers to translate their larger vision into workable strategies and explore their relation to philanthropy, performance, and innovation. She is experienced in using data to expose and narrow the range of plausible explanations to provide managers with data-driven answers to practical managerial challenges. Małgorzata earned her Ph.D. in economics, management, and organization from Universitat Autònoma de Barcelona (UAB) in Spain.

Peter Vogel is professor of family business and entrepreneurship and holder of the Debiopharm Chair for Family Philanthropy at IMD Business School. He is also the director of the Global Family Business Center and the Global Family Business Award. Peter works with families, owners, boards, and executives of family enterprises and family offices around the world, focusing on transformations, governance, ownership and leadership succession, entrepreneurship, wealth management, and on establishing professional boards and leadership teams. Peter has published academic articles and books, such as the award-winning Family Philanthropy Navigator. He is frequently referenced by leading media outlets around the world, and he is a sought-after keynote speaker. Peter is the founder and chairman of Delta Venture Partners, an associate partner of the Cambridge Family Enterprise Group, and features among the "Top 100 Family Influencers" by Family Capital.

CHAPTER 60

Facilitating Grandchild-Grandparent Philanthropy

James E. Hughes, Jr.

To introduce this practice I think it's useful to reinterpret the Chinese proverb, "Grandparents and grandchildren are the natural enemies of the parents." I would reinterpret that wisdom as, "Grandparents and grandchildren are natural allies."

History and literature, as well as my own personal experience, all indicate that a grandparent's relationship with his or her grandchildren is filled with pure love. Grandparenting offers the chance to teach the family positive virtues, stories, and myths without the parental obligation of being concerned with discipline and passing on by admonition the family's negative experiences.

Often in my work with families, the grandparents ask me what role they can play in family governance. Frequently they feel unsure of their relationships with their adult children and are all too aware of the missteps that they made in parenting. They seek with their children a mature *modus vivendi,* while recognizing that past difficulties in their relationship cannot be expunged. Necessarily with this history, the roles in family governance of older parents and their adult children are those of equals seeking to preserve the family. Also, given their respective ages, the adult children will normally be taking on the active governance responsibilities in investing and administering the family's financial wealth. The senior generation will be moving to the roles of observers and, most importantly, to acting as elders when a need for dispute resolution arises. While the latter role is critical to successful family governance, it is by its nature rarely called upon. Given the longevity of individuals today, limiting 65 or 70 year olds and older to passive roles in family governance simply wastes the vitality of significant family human capital. At the same time, not to permit the rising generation of adult children to assume the active roles in family governance will lead to its frustration, and a different waste of family human capital will occur.

Recognizing the desirability of using the complete family wealth fully, I believe that within the special relationship between grandparents and grandchildren, families can better employ the vitality and wisdom of their elders. I suggest that families employ philanthropy as the means to accomplish this end.

The Practice

Philanthropy, in and of itself, can serve as a practical teaching tool for learning virtues through the process of giving to others. As a vehicle for grandparents to take an active role in family governance, philanthropy offers a means for them to teach their grandchildren the family's values and particularly the values of gratitude and stewardship.

How does this shared philanthropy work? First, start young—beginning with six-year-olds—and think small in terms of dollar amounts. Scale donations to the children's ages. Even gifts of $50–$100 will seem very large to young children, whereas gifts of $500 or $1,000 feel meaningful to teens.

Second, use the simplest structure possible. If the family already has a significant private philanthropy, set aside a small portion of its capital for this purpose. If such a philanthropy does not already exist, a Donor-Advised Fund can be arranged with most community foundations or financial services firms for amounts of $10,000 or more.

Third, be inclusive: Include all the grandchildren ages six and over. In some families there can be an age spread among the grandchildren of more than 20 years. Despite this age difference, I find that there is a commonality of relationships between the grandchildren in their love and admiration for their grandparents that creates a bond that overcomes the age gap. In addition, in families which have trusts, the grandchildren frequently form a class of beneficiaries in which there is no discrimination regarding age. As a class, all the grandchildren share the same financial interests in the trust. This similarity of financial position can lead to a need for the older grandchildren to mentor and lead the younger as they learn about their common situation. This similarity of situation forms another bridge of commonality within the group.

Fourth, invite grandchildren ages 12 and older to form an investment and administrative committee for the grandchild-grandparent philanthropy. While it's easy to see the benefits that come from philanthropy in learning to give, we often fail to appreciate that a philanthropy is a business and can provide an educational setting for acquiring needed investment and administrative skills that are immediately transferable to the for-profit section of a family's enterprise. I strongly urge that the grandparents give the investment and administrative responsibilities to the older grandchildren as soon as possible. The grandparents can act as mentors and advisors to their grandchildren in this function. And the grandparents would retain ultimate decision-making authority until they are confident of their grandchildren's capabilities.

Fifth, include both the grandchildren and the grandparents in the grants committee. It is important that each grandchild make a grant each year. The process of how the grant is requested and voted on is critical to the learning experience of the grandchild and to the grandparents' ability to mentor the process. In my experience, almost all children ages six or older are capable of proposing and advocating for grant requests. The older the grandchild, the more written material regarding the grant recipient should be required by the grants committee. When grandchildren are age 10 or older, I also strongly suggest that, as a part of their requests, they indicate that they have made site visits to the location of the proposed grantee or, if this is impossible, that they have interviewed the director of the proposed recipient.

While the written material and site visits are important, the truly important part of the grant request process is the oral presentation by the requesting grandchild at the annual meeting of the grandchild-grandparent philanthropy. At this meeting, each grant recipient should present her or his grant request. Following the presentation, the grandparents and the other grandchildren should, with great care and affection, discuss the request, asking any appropriate follow-up questions, and then vote on the application. As the grandchildren get older (at 10 and over), the questions, suggestions, and possible additional homework requirements to ensure that the grant will be used wisely should increase. For the oldest grandchildren, the grants committee may also require that the grandchildren "put their skin in the game" by progressing to some form of active participation in the organization to which their requested grant will be made.

From the grandparents' perspective, what could be more fun than to sit with one's grandchildren and discuss their passions and to discover who they are? From the grandchildren's perspective, to get to know their grandparents through their wisdom and the stories of their own giving will deepen their knowledge of and respect for their grandparents. The grandchildren will, with great fun, be initiated into the family's wisdom and rituals.

Sixth, it is very important that the parents of the grandchildren be excluded from this process to as large an extent as possible. The exclusion is not an unfriendly act. To the contrary, for this process of intergenerational giving and sharing to work, the parents will want to promote the direct collaboration of the two generations and will quickly understand that their intervention can only inhibit that process. I do recognize that some individuals whose relationship with their parents is unsatisfactory or sadly broken may see no benefit in this practice. They may feel they are putting their children in "harm's way," as they see it. I fully sympathize with such feelings and suggest that in those cases this practice may not be appropriate until the relationship between the grandparent and the adult child is restored.

Seventh, hidden in my description of the grant-making process (the fifth point above) is a critical life skill. When each grandchild comes forward and makes his or her request, he or she is learning the life skills of public speaking and leadership, in addition to learning to passionately advocate and ask for something from others, for others. I cannot begin to count the number of times adult clients of mine have said how much they wish as young people they had learned how to overcome their anxieties about public speaking. They wish they had lost their fears of coming into a room of people and asking for something, their inability to prepare an agenda or a proposal, and their inability to successfully advocate a position in which they passionately believed. Think about how much more successful in life we would each be had we learned these skills at an early age!

Conclusion

The secret behind grandchild-grandparent philanthropy is that in making and advocating a grant request, all of these skills are brought into play in an atmosphere of love and caring and with an outcome that benefits, not just oneself, but also others. Many of the families I work with have created this form of philanthropy and are actively using it as a device for the teaching and practicing of these skills. These families understand that if their young are to be ready to take on leadership roles in or outside of the family, then these are critical skills necessary to successfully carry out such roles and ultimately to the successful practice and leadership of family governance.

To combine learning about one's own passions through giving to others and the learning of these life skills makes the grandchild-grandparent philanthropy an excellent tool in a family enterprise. For grandparents, it offers an active role in family governance at a level where their wisdom plus their love and affection for their grandchildren can be fully engaged. For both grandparents and grandchildren it offers a shared experience of learning about one another while also discovering the world and its needs.

Adapted from James E. Hughes, Jr., *Family Wealth* (New York: Wiley, 2004).

Additional Resources

James E. Hughes, Jr., *Family Wealth,* 2nd ed. (New York: Wiley, 2004).

James E. Hughes, Jr., Susan E. Massenzio, and Keith Whitaker, *Voice of the Rising Generation* (New York: Wiley, 2015).

James E. Hughes, Jr., Susan E. Massenzio, and Keith Whitaker, *Complete Family Wealth,* 2nd. ed., (New York: Wiley, 2022).

Biography

Widely considered the father of the field of family wealth, **James E. Hughes, Jr.** (Jay) is a retired attorney and author of *Family Wealth: Keeping It in the Family* and *Family: The Compact Among Generations.* Jay is co-author of *The Cycle of the Gift, The Voice of the Rising Generation,* and *Family Trusts: A Guide for Beneficiaries, Trustees, Trust Protectors, and Trust Creators.* Jay was the founder of a law partnership in New York City. He is a member of various philanthropic boards and a member of the editorial boards of various professional journals. Jay is a graduate of the Far Brook School, which teaches through the arts, the Pingry School, Princeton University, and the Columbia School of Law.

CHAPTER 61

Helping Families Move Up the Philanthropic Curve

Leslie Pine

Philanthropy takes many unique forms—and that is certainly the case with family philanthropy. The Philanthropic Initiative (TPI) opened its doors in 1989 to help individual donors, families, companies, and other funders increase the impact of their philanthropy. While every family and approach to family philanthropy is unique, we know that the philanthropic journey often follows certain patterns and pathways.

To reflect these patterns in a useful way, TPI developed the TPI Philanthropic Curve, which we offer as a tool to help families and other funders assess where they are, where they want to go, and what will help them to progress.

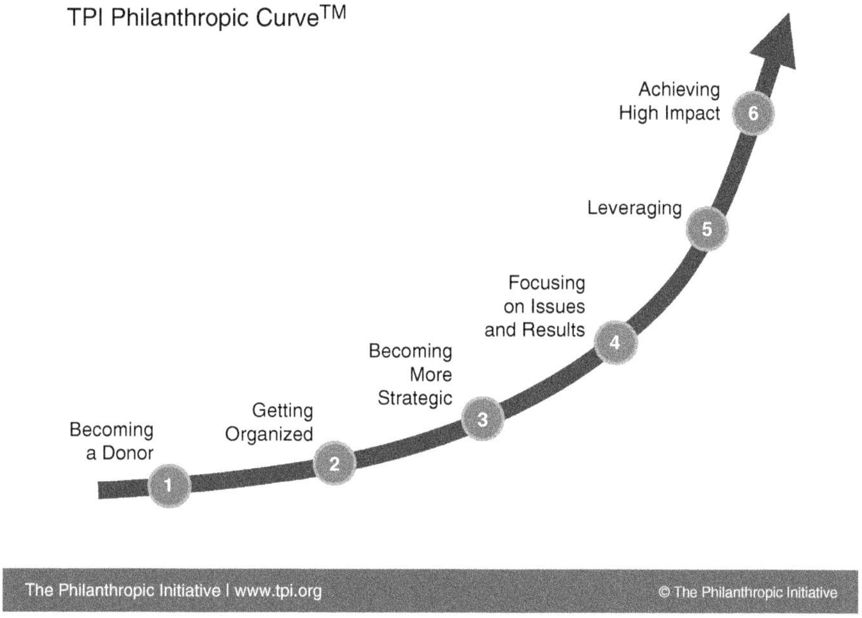

Source: The Philanthropic Initiative (TPI)

What Is the TPI Philanthropic Curve?

The TPI Philanthropic Curve has six levels.

Level One: Becoming a Donor

If you sit at level one, you regularly or sporadically receive requests from nonprofit organizations and fundraising events. Requests come from your college, friends, neighbors, and business associates, or the schools, activities, and programs in which your children participate. From time to time, you make a gift because you are moved by an experience or a need in the community. For some people, charitable giving is familiar ground—it's something that is expected by your place of worship, for example, or something your parents did. For others, it is a new experience. Giving has become part of your life, part of who you are, and one of the roles you play in the community in which you live.

Level Two: Getting Organized

Moving into level two, your capacity to give has increased and that fact is now known by others. The number of requests you receive and gifts you make has increased, and it is a challenge to manage the process. You decide to get organized, perhaps for tax reasons as well. You establish a donor-advised fund, or if warranted, you create a private foundation. These mechanisms help somewhat, but they do not solve the problem of receiving constant requests that require a response. You begin to try to prioritize your giving, learning better how to say yes or no. But at the end of the year there may still be a struggle to deal with the numerous requests for gifts.

Level Three: Becoming More Strategic

In level three, you conclude that your giving is not satisfying. It is "an inch deep and a mile wide", and has more to do with being asked to give than reflecting your own values and passions. You take a step back, become more proactive, more purposeful, and strategic. You sort out which organizations, programs, and issues really interest you and focus more of your time and money on them. You make a distinction between those gifts that reflect personal and community responsibilities and those that you care very deeply about. Your philanthropy now has goals and objectives, and it has taken on a different role in your life.

Level Four: Focusing on Issues and Results

Shifting into the top half of the curve, you still do not know as much as you would like about the complex issues that you wish to address. So, you set out to learn about best practices and discover who is at the leading edge of the work. You go deeper, gaining greater clarity in the process, and you may work with organizations to establish goals, metrics, and indicators of success. You may explore ways to increase the capacity of organizations to do the work better or to go to scale. Your goal is to achieve impact and results, so you begin to use measurement and evaluation as tools to determine if you have made a difference.

Level Five: Leveraging

In level five, you realize even more than ever that you cannot do important social change work alone and that collaboration with others is essential. You build or join a community of interest around the issues you care about, find or create networks of other donors, and, where appropriate, advocate for government and business investment or structural changes that can lead to much greater impact in the future. You have become a knowledge center for others.

Level Six: Achieving High Impact

Landing in level six, you have become a donor-leader. Philanthropy is among the most satisfying aspects of your life, and you have learned to use your wealth, your passions, and your skills to make the world a better place.

Family Self-Assessment

For many families, simply engaging in a discussion about where they are along the Curve and how they might move to the next level can be illuminating. To encourage and support these conversations, we offer a series of discussion questions that focus on three overarching questions: Where are we? Where are we going? How do we get there?

Assessing Where We Are

Where are we on the curve? How long have we been here? Is it time to move forward?

- Why should we give more or in a different way? What's wrong with how we are giving now?
- How do we know if we're achieving any impact with our philanthropy?
- How much of our family's giving is relationship-based and responsive to inquiries and requests, and how much is going toward the issues we care most about? Should we rethink this allocation?
- How does our family work together? Should we revisit our values, philanthropic passions and strategies, governance and decision-making, and timing and process of family philanthropy meetings? What else might enable our family to work better together?
- Is it time to involve the next generation of the family or other family members? If so, what approaches will work best?

Determining Where We Want to Go

What is next for us? What level should we aspire to move to next?

- How do we find our focus, agree on goals for our philanthropy, reflect and revisit our strategies, and achieve greater impact?
- How do we balance individual interests with collective philanthropic goals and strategies?

- How do we find the time to learn more, create a strategy, find funding opportunities that fit our interests, structure grants, and understand results?
- What does it mean to leverage greater long-term impact? How can we work with other sectors (e.g., government, business, nonprofit)?
- How can we become more strategic and focused without abandoning the institutions where we have a long history of giving?

Exploring How to Get There

If we want to progress, what are our next steps? What support do we need?

- How much work will it take to move to the next level on the curve?
- How do we identify the issue or entry point where we can really make our mark?
- How can we learn more about issues, needs, best practices, and models? How do we become wiser and bolder in our philanthropic approaches and decisions?
- What resources, in addition to money, can we use to achieve more impact? Do we have connections, knowledge, skills, and other resources?
- What unconventional tools and approaches should we explore (e.g., impact investing, communications, advocacy, support for social movements)? How do we find other funders and organizations to partner with?

Potential Outcomes and Next Steps

The exercise of locating your family on the TPI Philanthropic Curve can be simple and enlightening. Engaging in the discussion itself can inspire family members to lift their sights and aspire to accomplish more with their philanthropic resources.

Some 15 years ago, several family members found themselves named as trustees of a foundation created by a beloved aunt (they found themselves at level one on the curve). In their first year of grantmaking, they began to get organized (level two), and each trustee suggested giving grants to one or two nonprofit organizations where they had some connection. The result was a mix of grants with little in common. Though the trustees did not know about the Curve at that time, a trusted advisor helped them quickly realize they could achieve much more impact if they could become more purposeful and focused (moving to level three).

They engaged TPI to lead them through a planning process, which resulted in a clear focus and strategy built around the compelling legacy of their aunt, who had some extraordinary qualities. Over time, they have refined their philanthropic goals and strategies, become increasingly results-oriented, and employed a variety of leveraging strategies to increase the impact of their grants (graduating to levels four and five). They have created strong partnerships with their grantee partners and continue to evolve and seek greater impact (aspiring to reach level six).

Regardless of whether your family has started down the path toward greater philanthropic impact or how far it has evolved on its own philanthropic journey, we encourage you to take a few minutes at your next family gathering or family foundation meeting to talk about where you are on the TPI Philanthropic Curve and open a dialogue about how you might go further. You may be pleasantly surprised by where this conversation leads you and your family.

Additional Resources

Strategic Philanthropy: A Primer on Roles and Strategies (Boston, MA: The Philanthropic Initiative, n.d.).

Exponent Philanthropy, *The Trustee Handbook* (Washington, DC: Author), https://www.exponentphilanthropy.org/publication/the-trustee-handbook-the-essentials-for-an-effective-board-member/.

National Center for Family Philanthropy, *The Family Governance Pyramid: Enhancing and Guiding Your Family Philanthropy* (Angus, 2021), https://www.ncfp.org/wp-content/uploads/2021/07/The-Family-Governance-Pyramid-Angus-NCFP-2021-1.pdf.

GrantCraft, *Mapping Change Using a Theory of Change to Guide Planning and Evaluation,* Candid. Learning, https://grantcraft.org/content/guides/mapping-change/.

Biography

Leslie Pine, managing partner of The Philanthropic Initiative (TPI), started with TPI at its founding by Peter Karoff, who also developed the TPI Philanthropic Curve. Leslie has been the principal architect of TPI's creative approach to program design and strategy, overseeing research, design, implementation, and evaluation of philanthropic strategies. This work has transformed the concept of strategic philanthropy into high-impact philanthropic action, helping funders develop effective approaches to the issues that concern them.

Prior to joining TPI when it opened its doors in 1989, Leslie worked in the academic and government sectors. She is a graduate of St. Lawrence University and received a Master of Science degree in Health Policy and Management from the Harvard School of Public Health.

CHAPTER 62

A Roadmap to Successful Philanthropy

Susan Winer

Whether you are just starting out on your philanthropic journey or are considering retooling an existing philanthropic strategy and charitable portfolio, you need to have the building blocks of effective/impactful charitable giving in place to both *guide* your charitable activities and provide *a baseline* for measuring the impact of your philanthropic gifts.

A staggering amount of money is dedicated to charitable gifts each year: In 2020 in the United States, individuals, bequests, foundations, and corporations, in aggregate, gave an estimated $471 billion to U.S. charities, the large bulk of which came from individuals or families.[1] But despite the numbers, only a percentage of these funds actually account for measurable change and impact. There are real, and in some cases very good, reasons for this: funds dedicated to general operating expenses that keep organizations in business; small amounts contributed that cannot be measured; and disaster-directed funds that become part of a larger gift. In great part, however, the reason that impact and change may not be demonstrated is because many philanthropic dollars are not distributed based on a clearly defined strategy and impact action plan.

The first step toward ensuring that your philanthropic resources are deployed effectively and are aligned with your intent and interests is to have a clear understanding of what that intent is and to quantify and qualify your interests or passions. In this chapter we will explore the building blocks of successful and meaningful philanthropy, and you will find exercises that you and your family can do to help focus your efforts and create a meaningful philanthropic plan. The exercises and commentary are drawn, in large part, from the workbook *Developing Your Philanthropic Framework* developed by Strategic Philanthropy, Ltd.

While interpreting and building on your responses to the exercises may require professional assistance, you can certainly deepen your understanding by completing the exercises on your own.

---

[1]Giving USA 2021, *The Annual Report on Philanthropy for the Year 2020*, https://www.givinginstitute.org/page/GivingUSA.

The starting point is to take a look at what is motivating you. Why are you engaging in philanthropy? Aside from any tax benefits that may be derived, what is important to you? What do you seek to accomplish? Following are reasons and motivations for being philanthropic. Check off what is most important to you.

____ Share good fortune by giving back to society
____ Help those who have less and meet critical needs in society
____ Address (or move the needle on) a specific problem, issue, cause, or population
____ Religious and/or ethical beliefs
____ Redistribute my wealth
____ Set an example for my family
____ Set an example for peers and others
____ Social reciprocity—asked by friends and colleagues
____ Leave a legacy
____ Honor someone
____ For the experience and joy
____ Avoid or reduce taxes
____ A means of keeping the family together
____ Teach the next generation
____ Advance the family reputation and recognition
____ Respond to disasters and emergencies
____ Other ________________________________

After you have reviewed your selections, prioritize them. Put a mark next to the ones that are truly ***most*** important to you. You can have several reasons for being philanthropic, but it is important to figure out what drives your philanthropy. This is an important step in creating a framework for making philanthropic decisions.

There are **other considerations** that will shape your philanthropy. For example, how would you answer the following questions?

What does success in your philanthropy look like? Complete the sentence: I will consider my philanthropy to be successful if. . .

What are your immediate philanthropic goals? Identify the top three or four.

What are your long-term philanthropic goals? Identify the top two.

How much do you intend to give away each year?

How much time and how much involvement do you want to have in your philanthropy?

What is the time horizon for your philanthropy?

What expertise, skills, and special talents do you bring to the table?

Defining Focus

The next step in building out your philanthropic strategy is to ***define your focus***. The needs are infinite, and it can be hard to choose from the myriad worthy causes. Concentrating your giving on specific issue areas, populations, and/or geography provides critical boundaries for your giving, enabling you to deepen your knowledge and communicate to external stakeholders about what you do or don't support. Narrowing your focus areas for proactive giving helps prioritize your resources and increase the effectiveness and impact of your available resources.

Start by answering the following questions. Write the answers down and you will see that there is likely a clear path for you to follow with your charitable activities.

What are you passionate about?

What do you want to change in the world? How would you address this?

In what issue areas do you feel there is an opportunity to make a difference?

Do you want to give back to specific communities e.g., where you live, where you grew up, or where your wealth was created?

How important is it to you to be able to visit the organizations you are supporting and be close to their work?

Do the issues you want to focus on lend themselves to a particular geography?

Are there specific populations you feel have the most need? Has your family been impacted by a particular issue?

Are there specific issues or causes that are particularly important to your family?

A number of factors influence a giving strategy: your mission and values, budget, interests and capacities, and the needs in the field. Of the preceding, the mission driving your philanthropy is critically important. It sets the tone and provides the parameters for your gifts and serves as the "steering wheel" of whatever charitable vehicle you may have in place: foundation, Donor Advised Fund, or checkbook.

The most useful mission statements address the following questions:

- What do you believe? What sort of world are you trying to create?
- What are you seeking to achieve?
- Who will benefit from your philanthropy?
- How will you achieve your goals?
- Where will you seek to have an impact?

If you don't have a mission statement, here's a start toward creating one. Just fill in the blanks.

We believe that (vision and values) ________________________________. We seek to (promote/provide/create/assist) ________________________ for (who) ____________________ by funding and supporting (what) ____________________ ________________________________ in (geographic parameters) ______________ ____.

If you do have a mission statement, take a step back and review it. Does it truly represent you and your philanthropic goals and focus? Is it clear and easily understood? Mission statements can change over time just as your interests and intentions change. With that in mind, they should be reviewed at minimum every three years.

In Closing

Philanthropy is not just a "good" thing to engage in; it also provides a platform for establishing common ground in a family or society and is a means for perpetuating values. It is both a landscape that tolerates and encourages different perspectives and a context for deepening financial and business skills for younger people. If you are considering involving the next generations in your family's philanthropy, encourage them to complete these same exercises. Then get together and compare notes. Where are the similarities? Where are the differences? Is there room in your family's philanthropic strategy and plan for different perspectives? This conversation and these exercises can be empowering, meaningful and fun for everyone.

Biography

Susan Winer is co-founder and chief operating officer of Strategic Philanthropy, Ltd., a philanthropic advisory firm providing customized support to high-net-worth individuals, families, and closely held companies to help them effectively maximize the impact of their charitable gifts. Prior to launching Strategic Philanthropy Ltd., Susan was president of Stratenomics, Inc., which helped closely held and family-owned businesses find solutions to market and operating challenges and ensure stable and manageable growth. She is on the board of directors and serves as chair of the Social Impact and Philanthropy Domain for the Ultra High Net Worth Institute.

Conclusion

We hope you have enjoyed *Wealth of Wisdom: Top Practices for Wealthy Families and Their Advisors* and can put some of the practices, exercises, and tools to use in your own family or the families you work with.

As mentioned in the Introduction, this book was not meant to be read in one sitting or even necessarily straight through from beginning to end. We suspect that you will have gravitated to the chapters that resonate most for your family based on your particular needs, makeup, and stage of life. And it is likely that the practices you value most today may be different tomorrow as your circumstances change and as the family develops. We hope you will keep this book handy and come back to it from time to time.

As you will have noticed, this book follows the same format as our first volume, *Wealth of Wisdom: The Top 50 Questions Wealthy Families Ask*, and is a sort of community project where people pool ideas and share resources. The *Wealth of Wisdom* books are based on the following principles:

- No single family or advisor has all the best ideas.
- No one has yet faced all the issues that are to be faced.
- We have a lot to learn from each other—from our mistakes as well as our successes.
- Together we can find answers to key questions that challenge us all and share practices that will help us progress and flourish.

In that vein, we invite you to share practices, exercises, and tools that have been helpful in your family or community. We expect to publish more books in the *Wealth of Wisdom* series and will also post ideas on our website (wealthofwisdombook.com). We also host a podcast series where we interview each of the contributors to allow readers to delve deeper into the practices and hear stories of how they have worked in many families.

Finally, we want to express our gratitude to all the contributing authors who are living examples of the benefits of community. They have generously shared practices that they have found most valuable over the years and in so doing have been active builders of what has truly become a "wealth of wisdom" for families all over the world. We are also grateful to the many families who have had the courage to work together and try these practices, exercises, and tools. Our experience tells us that, depending on the topic, it can take some time to "get the hang" of it and so we encourage you to be brave, have fun, and persevere. We think you will find that it is worth the investment.

Bios

Tom McCullough

Tom McCullough is the chairman, CEO, and co-founder of Northwood Family Office. Northwood was established in 2003 to provide integrated and holistic family office services to Canadian and global families of wealth. It is regularly ranked as the #1 Multi-Family Office in Canada in the Euromoney Private Banking and Wealth Survey. Tom is the co-author of *Wealth of Wisdom: The Top 50 Questions Wealthy Families Ask* (Wiley, 2018) and *Family Wealth Management* (Wiley, 2013). He is an adjunct professor and executive-in-residence at the University of Toronto's Rotman School of Management MBA program where he teaches the management of private wealth and is a faculty member in Rotman's Family Wealth Management program for families. Tom also serves on the board of directors for the Ultra High Net Worth Institute and was recently awarded Best Individual Contribution to Thought Leadership in the Wealth Management Industry (North America) by the *2020 Family Wealth Report Awards.*

Keith Whitaker

Keith is president of Wise Counsel Research, a leading think-tank and consultancy in the field of family wealth. Keith is an educator who consults with leaders and rising generation members of enterprising families. *Family Wealth Report* named Keith the 2015 "outstanding contributor to wealth management thought-leadership." Keith's writings and commentary have appeared in the *Wall Street Journal, New York Times,* and *Financial Times.* He is the co-author of *Wealth and the Will of God, The Cycle of the Gift, The Voice of the Rising Generation, Family Trusts, Complete Family Wealth,* and *Wealth of Wisdom: The Top 50 Questions Wealthy Families Ask.* Keith has served as a managing director at Wells Fargo Family Wealth, an adjunct professor of management at Vanderbilt University, and an adjunct assistant professor of philosophy at Boston College. Keith holds a Ph.D. in social thought from the University of Chicago and a BA and MA in classics and philosophy from Boston University.

Index

Page numbers followed by *f* and *t* refer to figures and tables, respectively.